Controlling Global Warming

NEW HORIZONS IN ENVIRONMENTAL ECONOMICS

Series Editors: Wallace E. Oates, *Professor of Economics, University of Maryland, USA* and Henk Folmer, *Professor of General Economics, Wageningen University and Professor of Environmental Economics, Tilburg University, The Netherlands*

This important series is designed to make a significant contribution to the development of the principles and practices of environmental economics. It includes both theoretical and empirical work. International in scope, it addresses issues of current and future concern in both East and West and in developed and developing countries.

The main purpose of the series is to create a forum for the publication of high quality work and to show how economic analysis can make a contribution to understanding and resolving the environmental problems confronting the world in the twenty-first century.

Recent titles in the series include:

Environmental Co-operation and Institutional Change
Theories and Policies for European Agriculture
Edited by Konrad Hagedorn

Valuing Environmental and Natural Resources
The Econometrics of Non-Market Valuation
Timothy C. Haab and Kenneth E. McConnell

Controlling Global Warming
Perspectives from Economics, Game Theory and Public Choice
Edited by Christoph Böhringer, Michael Finus and Carsten Vogt

Environmental Regulation in a Federal System
Framing Environmental Policy in the European Union
Tim Jeppesen

The International Yearbook of Environmental and Resource Economics 2002/2003
A Survey of Current Issues
Edited by Tom Tietenberg and Henk Folmer

International Climate Policy to Combat Global Warming
An Analysis of the Ancillary Benefits of Reducing Carbon Emissions
Dirk T.G. Rübbelke

Pollution, Property and Prices
An Essay in Policy-making & Economics
J.H. Dales

The Contingent Valuation of Natural Parks
Assessing the Warmglow Propensity Factor
Paulo A.L.D. Nunes

Environmental Policy Making in Economics
with Prior Tax Distortions
Edited by Lawrence H. Goulder

Recent Advances in Environmental Economics
Edited by Aart de Zeeuw and John A. List

Sustainability and Endogenous Growth
Karen Pittel

Controlling Global Warming

Perspectives from Economics, Game Theory and Public Choice

Edited by

Christoph Böhringer
Centre for European Economic Research, Mannheim, Germany

Michael Finus
University of Hagen, Germany

Carsten Vogt
Centre for European Economic Research, Mannheim, Germany

NEW HORIZONS IN ENVIRONMENTAL ECONOMICS

Edward Elgar
Cheltenham, UK • Northampton, MA, USA

Published by
Edward Elgar Publishing Limited
Glensanda House
Montpellier Parade
Cheltenham
Glos GL50 1UA
UK

Edward Elgar Publishing, Inc.
136 West Street
Suite 202
Northampton
Massachusetts 01060
USA

A catalogue record for this book is available from the British Library

Library of Congress Cataloging in Publication Data

Controlling global warming: perspectives from economics, game theory, and public choice / edited by Christoph Böhringer, Michael Finus, and Carsten Vogt.
    p. cm.–(New horizons in environmental economics)
  Includes index.
    1. Global warming–Prevention. I. Böhringer, Christoph, 1965–
  II. Finus, Michael, 1965– III. Vogt, Carsten, 1965– IV. Series.

QC981.8.G56 C66 2002
363.738'746–dc21   2002018835

ISBN 1 84064 821 X

Printed and bound in Great Britain by Bookcraft, Bath

Contents

Figures and tables

Contributors

Christoph Böhringer
Centre for European Economic Research
Mannheim
Germany

Jan-Tjeerd Boom
The Royal Veterinary and Agricultural University
Frederiksberg
Denmark

Michael Finus
University of Hagen
Germany

Andreas Löschel
Mannheim University and
Centre for European Economic Research
Mannheim
Germany

Carsten Vogt
Centre for European Economic Research
Mannheim
Germany

Acknowledgements

In writing this book, the various authors have benefited from intellectual and financial support in many ways, which they would like to acknowledge.

Michael Finus would like to point out that his chapter is the culmination of research carried out during the last years with Alfred Endres. Michael benefited immensely from many discussions with him, which substantially improved upon the selection and presentation of topics treated in Chapter 2. He would also like to acknowledge that the idea of critically reviewing game theory and its application is also due to Alfred Endres and Volker Arnold, both from the University of Hagen. Chapter 2 has also benefited from numerous discussions with Pierre van Mouche, and from comments by participants of seminars and lectures at the University of Wageningen, The Netherlands. Michael was lucky to enjoy research assistance by Frank Brockmeier and Frank Lobigs which was very helpful for the completion of Chapter 2. Finally, he gratefully acknowledges financial support from The Volkswagen Foundation, Germany, under grant number II 69 982.

Christoph Böhringer and Andreas Löschel would like to acknowledge financial support from the European Commission (DG XII) under the projects 'Climate Change Policy and Global Trade (CCGT)', 'The Role of Innovation and Policy Design in Energy and Environment for a Sustainable Growth in Europe' (TCH-GEM-E3) and 'Greenhouse Gases Emission Control Strategies'(GECS). They owe a major note of thanks to Thomas F. Rutherford for stimulating research cooperation during the last years that provided an essential input to their chapter.

Carsten Vogt gratefully acknowledges funding from the research group 'Institutionalization of International Negotiation Systems' by the Deutsche Forschungsgemeinschaft (German Science Foundation). He benefited much from discussions with Michael Finus and Roger D. Congleton at a workshop held by the research group at the Centre for European Economic Research, Mannheim, Germany, May, 2001. Inspiring discussions with many research group members including Christoph Böhringer, Bernhard Boockmann,

Andreas Lange and Roland Vaubel also helped to shape his thoughts on the topic.

Jan Tjeerd Boom would like to thank Andries Nentjes, Bouwe Dijkstra and Gert Tinggaard Svendsen for their very useful comments on previous versions of his papers. Furthermore, he would like to thank the Institute of Economics, University of Copenhagen, for its hospitality and the facilities offered during a stay as visiting scholar. Financial support by The Netherlands Organization for Scientific Research (NWO) was also very helpful in the completion of his chapters.

When putting this book together Christoph, Carsten and Michael received great assistance by Andreas Pfeiff. He showed a lot of patience, enthusiasm and great skill when processing the manuscripts. Special thanks to Noelle Crist-See for cross-reading all chapters.

They also would like to thank the editors of this series, Henk Folmer and Wallace E. Oates, for helpful comments on structuring this book. In particular, they would like to thank people at Edward Elgar, Dymphna Evans (Senior Commissioning Editor), Matthew Pitman (Commissioning Editor), Julie Leppard (Managing Editor) and Melanie Waller (Desk Editor), for their extremely professional work, which made the production of this book at each stage a straightforward and very enjoyable exercise.

Christoph Böhringer, Michael Finus and Carsten Vogt
Hagen and Mannheim, March 2002

1. Introduction

Michael Finus

Global warming is believed to be one of the most serious environmental problems for current and future generations. This shared belief led more than 180 countries to sign the Framework Convention on Climate Change in Rio de Janeiro in 1992, which declares that serious action should be taken to reduce man-made greenhouse gas emissions. To this end, the Kyoto Protocol was signed in 1997 by 38 countries which agreed to reduce their greenhouse gas emissions by an average of 5.2 per cent compared to 1990 emission levels by the target period 2008–2012. The 38 countries comprise mainly industrialized countries, including the US, all countries of the European Union and some other European countries like Norway and Switzerland, Australia, New Zealand, Canada and Japan; and a few countries in transition to a market economy such as Russia and Ukraine. Since its signature, the Protocol has been widely celebrated as a major step towards mitigating global warming. In particular, economists were in favor of the Protocol, since it constitutes the first international environmental agreement which seeks to achieve environmental targets using market-based instruments. However, four years after the signature of the Kyoto Protocol, euphoria has turned into great disappointment. Despite many negotiation rounds, the parties still could not agree on the final details of the design of the Kyoto Protocol, and hence it has not been ratified by any of those countries which committed themselves to binding abatement targets and it is therefore not yet in force. Even worse, most countries' emissions have increased over the last few years and after taking office, President Bush declared that the US would withdraw from the Protocol.

Not surprisingly, this ecologically important and highly debated political issue has also initiated a great amount of research on the problem of 'Controlling Global Warming'. In this book, three perspectives of economic research on this topic are presented: game theory (Chapter 2), cost-effectiveness analysis (Chapter 3) and public choice (Chapters 4, 5 and 6).

GAME THEORY

Global emissions exhibit a negative externality not only in the country of origin but also in other countries. Hence, there is a high interdependence between countries, and strategic considerations are important. Game theory analyzes the interaction between agents, formulates hypotheses about their behavior and predicts the final outcome of the interaction. Therefore, this method has been widely used to analyze global environmental problems. Important questions which have been analyzed with game theory are for instance: Under which conditions will an agreement be signed and ratified? On which reduction targets will the signatories agree? How many and which countries will participate in an agreement? Will the treaty be stable? Which measures are suitable for stabilizing an agreement?

The game theoretical literature has provided many insights into these questions in recent years. Many results have been obtained which help to explain the difficulties of establishing effective and efficient cooperation. However, game-theoretical approaches have also been criticized for ignoring too many practical problems and for being based on very specific assumptions. It has been argued that important aspects of international pollution problems have been neglected and that results were not general and were therefore ill-suited for policy analyses and recommendations. Chapter 2 tries to qualify this critique by laying out fundamental assumptions and important results and by pointing out those aspects which have to be considered in future research. It proceeds in four steps: (1) The fundamental assumptions underlying the analysis of global pollution problems are laid out. The need for cooperation and the problems of cooperation are defined (Section 2). (2) Two frameworks which have been used frequently to analyze global environmental problems, are described (Section 3). (3) Important findings, which help to explain the difficulties of cooperation, and measures to establish cooperation are discussed. Section 4 looks at measures for avoiding asymmetric welfare distributions and for enforcing an international environmental agreement (IEA). Section 5 discusses the properties of different policy instruments and their implications for the success of an environmental treaty, and Section 6 summarizes the results on the formation of coalitions. (4) The model frameworks outlined in Section 3 and the results and conclusions of Sections 4, 5 and 6 are critically reviewed. On the one hand, open theoretical questions are described. On the other hand, practical problems which are not captured by theory are mentioned and evaluated as to their effect on influencing policy recommendations. The theoretical results and the derived conclusions of Sections 4 to 6 are applied to the analysis of the Kyoto Protocol (Section 7). It is shown that the theoretical results are helpful in explaining and evaluating this IEA. Section 8 briefly describes open issues for future research.

COST-EFFECTIVENESS-ANALYSIS

Successful climate protection policies require a reconciliation of two fundamental issues: efficiency in terms of overall abatement costs, and equity in terms of the distribution of these costs across countries. Though these issues are also relevant in other fields of international environmental policy, given the magnitude of abatement costs at stake, their importance in the context of greenhouse gases is unique. Considering that the benefits of mitigating global warming are uncertain and will accrue only in the long run, abatement policies aiming at achieving climate protection will be more acceptable to current society the cheaper, i.e., the more cost-efficient, they are. A high participation in an environmental agreement with ambitious abatement targets is only possible if the parties perceive the burden sharing rule to be fair. Whereas economics has little to say on equity *per se*, the description of economic effects across different agents due to policy interference is a prerequisite for any equity debate.

For rational policy making, both issues – the magnitude as well as the distribution of costs – require quantitative assessment. The main challenge of economic modeling is to capture the key factors and their impact on the agents involved. Since modeling of larger socio-economic systems is a very complex undertaking, simplifying assumptions on system boundaries and system relationships are needed. However, these assumptions crucially determine the sign and magnitude of quantitative results and therefore drive policy conclusions to a large extent. Therefore, it is not surprising that when studying the large amount of empirical literature on the economic impacts of various greenhouse abatement strategies, one may get the impression that results and conclusions are not very reliable. In particular, due to the high complexity of most empirical models and the limited amount of space in scientific journals, the underlying assumptions of different models are sometimes not very transparent to the reader and are difficult to evaluate. In fact, some critiques argue that basically any policy recommendations can be derived if the assumptions are chosen accordingly.

This contribution tries to qualify this critique by laying out the fundamental factors and the crucial assumptions of empirical models and by conducting various sensitivity analyses. It is shown that empirical models can be a very powerful tool for policy recommendations if assumptions and results are carefully related to each other. The chapter proceeds in four steps: (1) After a short introduction to the topic, Section 2 describes methodological issues in the modeling of climate change policies. Important results of the literature are critically reviewed and evaluated as to their impact on the results. The objective is to create an understanding of key determinants which drive results. Topics which are covered include baseline scenarios (projections and market imperfections), system boundaries (bottom-up versus top-down approaches, international spillovers), technological change and burden sharing rules. (2) In Section 3 a generic computable general equilibrium model is outlined. All components of this model are described, comprising production, households, foreign trade, carbon emissions and market clearing conditions as well as the data and calibration procedure. (3) Based on the model and calibration of Section 3, an assessment of greenhouse gases abatement is conducted in Section 4. For the abatement targets of the Kyoto Protocol, several policy scenarios and sensitivity analyses are computed and evaluated. Policy scenarios include (a) no trading of emission permits, (b) only trading among Annex B countries of the Protocol, (c) globally unrestricted trading and (d) no trading assuming that the US follows a business-as-usual emission path. The last scenario takes into account the decision of President Bush (March 2001) to withdraw from the Kyoto Protocol. Sensitivity analyses include the impact of (a) transaction costs from trading, (b) higher baseline emissions resulting from higher economic growth, (c) different substitution elasticities between imports and exports, (d) different supply elasticities for oil supply and (e) different ways of revenue recycling of the receipts from implementing environmental policies. (4) Results are summarized and a final evaluation and interpretation is presented.

PUBLIC CHOICE

The bulk of the politico-economic literature of environmental policy has mainly focused on national environmental problems, though some of the most recent literature has also made an attempt to analyze global environmental problems. In contrast to classical environmental economics, which assumes that politicians (should) pursue the goal of increasing the welfare of its citizens, the politico-economic literature assumes that politicians strive to enhance their prestige, increasing their chance of being re-elected and maximizing their available budget. Thus, public choice approaches are particularly useful in explaining the divergence between policy recommendations and their implementation (*ex-post*), and anticipating the political acceptability of policy recommendations (*ex-ante*). Important questions which have been addressed by the public choice literature are for instance: Why is the level of environmental protections frequently lower than would be advisable from a cost-benefit perspective? Why are command and control instruments the predominant instrument in environmental policy though economists favor market-based instruments on efficiency grounds?

Whereas Chapter 4 determines the level of global emission reductions in a politico-economic framework, Chapters 5 and 6 derive the equilibrium choice of the policy instrument.

Chapter 4 proceeds in three steps: (1) It starts out with a theoretical analysis. It compares the cooperative and non-cooperative equilibrium if governments behave as welfare maximizers in climate negotiations – which is the underlying assumption of the game-theoretical analysis – with the political equilibrium in a median voter model. It is shown that the commonly-held conjecture is wrong that capturing the political dimension of global environmental policy would lead to more positive predictions with respect to the prospects of a cooperative abatement policy compared to the standard game-theoretical analysis. In fact, whether the level of environmental protection will be higher or lower in a public choice setting than in a game-theoretical setting depends on the 'green preferences' of the pivotal voter. (2) Subsequently, studies estimating the public demand for mitigating greenhouse gases emissions are discussed. A distinction is made between contingent valuation studies and public opinion polls. Both approaches are evaluated with respect to their conceptual properties. It is argued that results very much depend on the design of the study and that current studies allow only for cautious conclusions since they suffer from many shortcomings. Given this qualification, there seems to be evidence that there is a gap between people's concern that action should be taken to combat global warming and their willingness to pay. The more the questions are specifically related to actual payment and sacrifices of economic wealth by people in order to reduce greenhouse gases, the lower is their stated willingness to pay for ambitious abatement policies. People are much in favor of their governments taking serious action to control global warming, but their average willingness to pay for this is very low. (3) Results of empirical studies are used to interpret the position of different countries in negotiations on various international environmental agreements and the outcome of these negotiations. It is shown that the empirical results are helpful in explaining the different stakes and roles of various countries within the negotiations of the Montreal Protocol, the Framework Convention of Climate Change and the Kyoto Protocol. However, it is also argued that much more empirical research is needed to draw sound policy conclusions.

Chapter 5 discusses the choice of environmental policy instruments on the basis of an interest group approach. It surveys a large amount of literature on this topic, which also serves as a basis for Chapter 6, where the public choice approach is used to analyze the design of a permit regime under the Kyoto Protocol. Chapter 5 proceeds in five steps: (1) After a short introduction to the problem, different policy instruments are systematically described in Section 2. (2) In Section 3 the main actors in the political arena are identified, including politicians, the environmental bureaucracy, industry (owners, managers, labor unions), environmental organizations and consumers. (3) For these actors, different hypotheses about possible arguments in their objective functions are presented in Section 4. It appears that there are many and very different hypotheses around what guides the behavior of agents. (4) In Section 5, preferences of different interest groups are derived for different policy instruments based on the hypotheses of Section 4. Moreover, empirical evidence is presented to test the theoretical conclusions. It is shown that a public choice approach helps to explain why the recommendations of economists to use market-based instead of command and control instruments in environmental policy have not fallen on very fertile ground. (5) A final assessment of assumptions and conclusions is provided in Section 6.

Chapter 6 analyzes the controversy among the signatories of the Kyoto Protocol about how a permit trading system should be designed. For three different permit trading schemes, a welfare economic as well as a politico-economic evaluation is conducted. The aim of this chapter is to predict what kind of permit trading system will finally emerge within the political system (given that permit trading systems are implemented and that the Kyoto Protocol is ratified) and whether this differs from the best choice from an economist's point of view. The first scheme considered only allows for the trade of permits between governments. Governments must implement some national policy in order to match their country's emissions and the number of permits they hold. The second scheme allows permit trading among private entities at the national and international level. The third scheme differs only slightly from the second in that not permits but credits are traded. Thus, private entities are not regulated via permits but via other instruments. Emissions reduction must be certified by some agency and can then be sold to other domestic and foreign private entities. Thus, under the first and the third scheme, governments have some leeway for choosing some instrument at the national level. Consequently, the permit trading schemes may be seen as a two-level game at the national and an international level. For the national level, instrumental preferences of different interest groups as derived in Chapter 5 are used.

The chapter proceeds in four steps: (1) After a short description of the problem, the three trading schemes are laid out in Section 2. This section provides a first judgment on the three schemes according to economic and political criteria. Specific points related to the politico-economic analysis are treated in Section 3. (2) In Section 4, the preferences of various interest groups are derived from a theoretical perspective, considering the national and international level of implementation. It turns out from the theoretical analysis that most interest groups prefer a combination of credit trading and government trading and some form of direct regulation of the command and control type at the national level, though for very different reasons. In contrast, from a welfare economic perspective, the trading scheme among private entities would be first choice. (3) In Section 5, interest group preferences are investigated empirically based on a survey of press releases on the Internet. Given the lack of empirical data, this procedure must be judged as an important first step in order to test the theoretical conclusions of Section 4. The survey covers a large number of different organizations across different countries and basically confirms the theoretical conclusion.

SUMMARY AND CONCLUDING REMARKS

In the last chapter of this book, the most import results of the previous chapters are summarized. Each method is evaluated with respect to its weaknesses and strengths. Particular emphasis is given to outlining a research agenda for the future on how the three methods can be combined, in order to have a powerful tool for the analysis of global pollution problems.

AIM AND SCOPE OF THE BOOK

This book provides the newest insights into the economic research on global
warming from three perspectives: game theory, cost-effectiveness analysis
and public choice. The aim is to provide the reader with an overview of each
method, demonstrating the advantages and disadvantages of each method in a
rigorous though easily accessible manner. The chapters survey a large amount
of literature and provide many applications.

All chapters stress very much the thinking behind all arguments and
results, though Chapters 2, 3 and 4 use some mathematics. However, this
should pose no problem for those readers who are less technically oriented. In
Chapter 2 on game theory and its application, all important findings and
conclusions are compactly summarized in each section and therefore the line
of arguments can easily be followed by skipping over the technical details. In
Chapter 3 on cost-effectiveness analysis, only Section 3 uses some
mathematics when laying out the technical details of the general computable
equilibrium model used in the subsequent sections for the simulations. Again,
the technically less interested reader may either just skip Section 3 and
proceed directly to subsequent sections or just follow the arguments in
Section 3 and ignore the formulae. In Chapter 4 on the politico-economic
analysis of the level of abatement in global pollution control, only in Section
2, in which the political equilibrium is compared to the welfare economic
equilibrium, is some mathematics used, though the basic line of argument can
easily be followed by ignoring the mathematics. In any case, subsequent
sections in Chapter 4 are more or less self-contained and can also be
understood without Section 2.

Overall, this book should be accessible and interesting to anybody working
and studying in the field of global environmental problems with an economics
or political science background, ranging from undergraduate and graduate
students to scholars working in international organizations, the public sector
or academia. For anybody interested in a compact and up-to-date survey on
the economic, game-theoretical and politico-economic analysis of global
warming, this is the book.

2. Game Theory and International Environmental Cooperation: Any Practical Application?

Michael Finus

---

1. INTRODUCTION

The game-theoretical analysis of international environmental problems has received increasing attention in recent years. This is not surprising. Game theory analyzes the interaction between agents, formulates hypotheses about their behavior and predicts the final outcome. Therefore, game theory is particularly suited to analysing the incentive structure of international environmental problems. Central questions which can be investigated with this method are: Under which conditions will an international environmental agreement (IEA) be signed and ratified? On which reduction targets will the negotiators agree? How many and which countries will sign an IEA? Will the agreement be stable? Which measures may be used to stabilize an IEA?

The game-theoretical literature has provided many insights into these questions in recent years. Many results have been obtained which help to explain the difficulties of establishing effective and efficient cooperation. However, game-theoretical approaches have also been criticized for ignoring too many practical problems and for being based on very specific assumptions. It has been argued that important aspects of international pollution problems have been neglected and results were not general and therefore ill-suited for policy analyses and recommendations. This chapter tries to qualify this criticism by laying out fundamental assumptions and important results and by pointing out those aspects which have to be treated in future research. We will proceed in five steps. In a first step we explicitly lay out the fundamental assumptions underlying the analysis of international environmental problems (Section 2). The need for cooperation and the problems of cooperation are defined. For simplicity the analysis will be restricted to global environmental problems. In a second step we introduce two frameworks which have been frequently used to analyze international environmental problems (Section 3). In a third step the chapter summarizes important findings and adds some new insights which help to explain the difficulties of cooperation and discusses measures to establish cooperation. Section 4 looks at measures for avoiding asymmetric welfare distributions and enforcing an IEA. Section 5 discusses the properties of different policy instruments in global pollution control and Section 6 summarizes the results on the formation of coalitions. In a fourth step, the model frameworks outlined in Section 3 and the results of Sections 4, 5 and 6 are critically re-viewed. On the one hand, open theoretical questions are described. On the other hand, practical problems which are not captured by theory are mentioned and evaluated as to their effect om influencing policy recommendations. In a fifth step, the theoretical results and the derived conclusions of Sections 4 to 6 are applied to the analysis of the Kyoto Protocol (Section 7). It is shown that the theoretical results are helpful in ex-plaining and evaluating this IEA. Section 8 briefly proposes open issues for future research.

Two things should be pointed out right at the beginning. First, this chapter is not a classical survey which tries to cover a large amount of literature. In contrast, the selection of topics reflects the importance of issues in actual international environmental policy as perceived by the author. Moreover, some space is devoted to outlining and evaluating the two frameworks used in the game-theoretical literature to study international environmental problems. Second, this chapter emphasizes intuition but also uses some theory to present some points. Therefore, statements can never be as precise as in a mathematical text. Moreover, the style of presentation is a compromise between the technical treatment of those issues where this can be done relatively easily and a survey of results where a technical treatment would require too much space.

2.   THE BENEFITS AND PROBLEMS OF COOPERATION

2.1   Fundamental Assumptions, Results and Conclusions

Let there be N countries, $i \in I = \{1, ..., N\}$, and welfare of country i, π_i, comprising benefits from emissions, $\beta_i(e_i)$, and damages caused by global emissions, $\phi_i(\Sigma e_j)$.

$$\pi_i = \beta_i(e_i) - \phi_i(\sum_{j=1}^{N} e_j) \qquad [2.1]$$

On the one hand, emissions generate benefits as an input in the production and consumption of goods. On the other hand, emissions released by country i, e_i, cause environmental damages in country i but also in the other countries. Equation [2.1] assumes a global pollutant, that is, emissions disperse uniformly in the atmosphere (as is the case for instance for greenhouse gases) and therefore damages depend only on aggregate emissions, Σe_j.

We assume country i's strategy space to be given by $e_i := [0, e_i^{max}]$ with $e_i^{max} > 0$ the upper bound of emissions sufficiently large. The benefit and damage cost functions are assumed to be continuous and twice differentiable. The benefit functions are assumed to be strictly increasing and strictly concave and the damage cost functions to be strictly increasing and convex. That is, we assume

$$\beta_i' > 0 \ (\ e_i \in (0, e_i^{max})), \ \beta_i'' < 0 \ (\ e_i \in (0, e_i^{max}]), \ \phi_i' > 0$$
$$(\Sigma e_i \in (0, \Sigma e_i^{max}]) \text{ and } \phi_i'' \geq 0 \qquad [2.2]$$

to hold.[1] One way to interpret e_i^{max} in economic terms is to assume $\beta_i' = 0$ if $e_i = e_i^{max}$ and $\beta_i' < 0$ if $e_i > e_i^{max}$. A country chooses its highest emission level if it does not recognize damages at all. That is, e_i^{max} is the (unique) solution to $\arg\max \beta_i(e_i) \Leftrightarrow \beta_i'(e_i^{max}) = 0$. We make this assumption in the following to provide a straightforward interpretation of e_i^{max}.[2]

If a government behaves non-cooperatively, it maximizes [2.1] with respect to its own emissions, e_i, considering only damages in its own country but not those in other countries:[3]

$$\max_{e_i} \pi_i \Rightarrow \max_{e_i} \beta_i(e_i) - \phi_i(\sum_{i=1}^{N} e_i) \Rightarrow \beta_i'(e_i) = \phi_i'(\sum_{i=1}^{N} e_i) \qquad [2.3]$$

The term on the right–hand side of the second arrow in [2.3] states the optimality condition of a government: marginal benefits from emissions in country i are equal to marginal damages in this country. This condition implicitly defines the reaction or best reply function of country i, $R_i := e_i = e_i(e_{-i})$. This function contains information about the optimal choice of e_i for a given level of foreign emissions e_{-i}. This choice is unique due to the assumptions in [2.2]. The best reply emission level of country i, $e_i(e_{-i})$, is a (strictly) decreasing function of emissions in all other countries, e_{-i}, i.e., $\partial e_i(e_{-i})/\partial e_{-i} \leq (<)0$ (if the damage cost function is strictly convex). The slope of the reaction function, R_i', is given by

$$R_i' = \frac{\partial e_i(e_{-i})}{\partial e_{-i}} = \frac{\phi_i''}{\beta_i'' - \phi_i''} \; ; -1 < R_i' \leq 0; \; e_{-i} = \sum_{j \neq i}^{N} e_j \qquad [2.4]$$

which follows from totally differentiating the first order conditions of country i in [2.3], noting that $\partial e_{-i}/\partial e_j = 1$ in a pure global emission game, and rearranging terms.

In the non-cooperative equilibrium (Nash equilibrium) the first order condition in [2.3] holds simultaneously for all countries. We denote the Nash equilibrium emission vector by $e^N = (e_1^N, ..., e_N^N)$. The equilibrium is unique due to the assumptions in [2.2].[4]

The interdependence between countries via the release of emissions and the Nash equilibrium are visualized in Figure 2.1.[5] The Nash equilibrium is the point where both reaction functions intersect and therefore the first order conditions hold simultaneously. It is plausible (though not necessary) to assume that this equilibrium reflects the status quo before an IEA is signed (*status sine pacta*). We follow this assumption in the remainder.

From our assumptions and interpretation of e_i^{max} it follows that $e_i^{max} > e_i^N > 0$. That is, in the Nash equilibrium, though governments behave non-cooperatively, they reduce some emissions compared to a 'no-abatement policy' where country 1 would emit e_1^{max} and country 2 e_2^{max}.

If a government behaves fully cooperatively, it contributes to maximizing aggregate welfare. That is, a government should not only consider damages caused by its emissions in its own country but also those caused abroad (note 3 applies):

$$\max_{e_1,..,e_N} \sum_{i=1}^{N} \pi_i \Rightarrow \max_{e_1,..,e_N} \sum_{i=1}^{N} \beta_i(e_i) - \sum_{i=1}^{N} \phi_i(\sum_{i=1}^{N} e_i) \Rightarrow \beta_i'(e_i) = \sum_{i=1}^{N} \phi_i'(\sum_{i=1}^{N} e_i). \qquad [2.5]$$

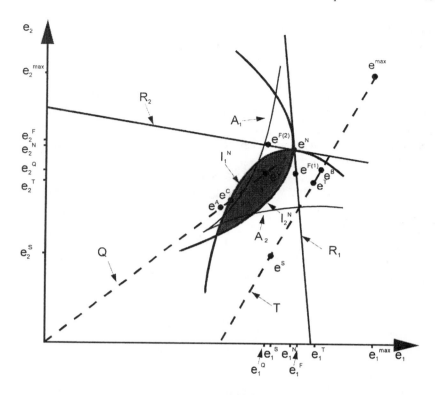

Figure 2.1 Non, partial and full cooperative abatement policies

The optimality condition of country i requires that marginal benefits equal the sum of marginal damages in all countries. In the fully cooperative equilibrium (sometimes also called global or social optimum) the first order condition in [2.5] holds for each country. Consequently, marginal benefits from emissions are equal across countries in the fully cooperative equilibrium, i.e., $\beta_i'(e_i) = \beta_j'(e_j) \ \forall \ i{\neq}j$. The socially optimal emission vector $e^S = (e_1^S, ..., e_N^S)$ is unique due to the assumptions in [2.2].[i] This vector has the following properties.

Fundamental result 1

A fully cooperative emission vector generates the highest global welfare and is therefore group rational. Global emissions in the fully cooperative equilibrium are lower than in the Nash equilibrium.

Proof: The first statement follows immediately from the definition of a fully cooperative equilibrium. The second statement is proved for instance in Finus (2001), ch. 9.

Of course, between the 'non-cooperative' (Nash equilibrium) and the 'fully cooperative' outcome, other more pragmatic solutions are conceivable. Such 'partially cooperative' solutions may call for modest emission reductions (compared to the status quo). They lead only to a partial internalization of global externalities. Aggregate emissions are generally higher than in the social optimum but lower than in the Nash equilibrium. Global welfare is lower than in the social optimum but higher than in the Nash equilibrium. Such pragmatic solutions will be discussed in detail in Sections 5 and 6. At this stage we will only briefly discuss two options.

The first option we call a 'moderately efficient emission reduction'. Efficiency implies that global benefits from emissions are maximized, given some constraint on global emissions.

$$\max_{e_1,..,e_N} \sum_{i=1}^{N} \beta_i(e_i) \ \text{s.t.} \ \sum_{i=1}^{N} e_i^N > \overline{\sum_{i=1}^{N} e_i} \geq \sum_{i=1}^{N} e_i^S \ \Rightarrow \ \beta_i'(e_i) = \beta_j'(e_j) \ \forall \ i{\neq}j. \qquad [2.6]$$

Optimality requires that marginal benefits from emissions are equal across all countries (see note 3). In Figure 2.1, line T represents all efficient emission allocations. Moderately implies that global emissions are reduced compared to the Nash equilibrium but that aggregate emissions are higher than in the social optimum, i.e., $\Sigma e_i^N > \Sigma e_i \geq \Sigma e_i^S$. In Figure 2.1 all emission combinations lying between point e^B and e^S on line T satisfy this constraint, as for instance point e^T.

The second option we call a 'uniform proportional emission reduction'. It implies that each country reduces emission by the same percentage compared to the status quo, i.e., $e_i = (1-r) \cdot e_i^N$, $0 < r \leq 1$, where $r \cdot 100$ expresses the percentage of emission reduction.[7] In Figure 2.1 line Q represents all uniform proportional emission reductions, of which those lying between point e^N and e^A are moderate. Moderate implies $\Sigma e_i^N > \Sigma e_i^N(1-r) \geq \Sigma e_i^N(1-r^*)$ where r^* follows from maximizing global net benefits given uniform proportional emission reductions. Note that, generally, uniform proportional emission reductions imply an inefficient allocation of emissions, i.e., $\beta_i'(e_i) \neq \beta_j'(e_j)$.

Only by coincidence or if countries are symmetric will marginal benefits equalize across countries.

Fundamental result 2

A moderate efficient emission reduction as well as a uniform proportional emission reduction generates a higher global welfare than in the Nash equilibrium.

Proof: See Appendix 3 for a sketch of the proof.

According to the Fundamental Results 1 and 2 there is an incentive for countries to cooperate on global pollution control. Consequently, the question arises:

Fundamental question: why is cooperation so difficult?

The difficulty arises because there is no supranational institution at the global level which can enforce cooperation. At least from a game-theoretical perspective it is argued that international law – though it might provide a guidance of 'good conduct' – is not binding. A party may accuse another party of some wrongdoing and might appeal to the International Court of Justice. However, the Court can only deal with the matter if the accused party agrees to a trial. Thus, in fact, the Court has no enforcement power.

Fundamental assumption

There is no third party which can enforce cooperation at the global level. This leads to the following conclusions:

Fundamental conclusions

(1) IEAs have to be signed voluntarily, (2) the parties must agree on the design of an IEA by consensus and (3) the enforcement of the treaty must be conducted by the parties themselves.[8]

In the light of the Fundamental Conclusions and based on our simple static framework, we may make an initial analysis of the problem of cooperation. A more detailed analysis will follow in subsequent sections after we have laid out the two model frameworks which have been frequently used in the analysis of IEAs and which also consider dynamic aspects.

2.2   A First Draft of the Problems of Cooperation

Individual rationality[9]

Suppose countries cooperate and decide that they will reduce emissions compared to the non-cooperative equilibrium. Intuitively, we expect that a minimum requirement for a country to cooperate is that it receives a higher welfare than in the status quo. That is, cooperation must be individually rational. In Figure 2.1 this implies that a cooperative emission vector must lie in the ellipse formed by the indifference curves I_1^N and I_2^N (gray area) provided there are no transfers.[10] However, if countries have different welfare functions (heterogeneous countries), individual countries may well receive a lower welfare from cooperation than in the status quo (though global welfare increases through cooperation). This is true for a fully cooperative solution but may also hold for a partially cooperative solution, as for instance a moderately efficient emission reduction. For instance, a country may be worse off in the social optimum compared to the status quo if it has relatively low marginal benefits from emissions and puts a low value on environmental damages compared to other countries. Such a country has to contribute a relatively large amount to a fully cooperative (or any other efficient) abatement program but benefits only little in the form of reduced damages. Such a case is shown in Figure 2.1 where e^S (and also any other efficient emission combination on line T) lies outside the ellipse formed by the indifference curves I_1^N and I_2^N.

Result 1

If countries have heterogeneous welfare functions, full or partial cooperation may imply that some countries receive a lower welfare than in the status quo.

Proof: Follows by example. See for instance Finus (2001) Chapters 9, 11.

It turns out to be a crude rule of thumb that abatement programs which imply a relatively asymmetric distribution of abatement targets also imply a relatively asymmetric welfare distribution, which may violate individual rationality in some countries. Thus, it might sometimes be necessary to implement an inefficient abatement policy which leads to a more symmetric welfare distribution than an efficient one (see Sections 5 and 6). This is exemplified in Figure 2.1 where there is no efficient (not even a moderately efficient) emission vector guaranteeing each country a higher payoff than in the Nash equilibrium. In contrast, an IEA calling for uniform proportional emission reductions does meet this requirement for not 'too' high reduction targets.[11] In the example in Figure 2.1 these are emission combinations lying between e^N and e^C.

Another obvious candidate to balance an asymmetric welfare distribution resulting from some abatement programs are compensation mechanisms. Unfortunately, however, it turns out that many instruments which are ideally suited for efficiently balancing asymmetric welfare distributions may suffer from instability. Therefore, compensation mechanisms which have to be judged as second-best on efficiency grounds may have to be used in the context of global pollution control (see Section 4).

Free-rider incentive

In reality, IEAs face two types of free-rider incentives. The first type of free riding implies that a country is a non-signatory or, at a more general level, a member of a coalition carrying a lower abatement burden than other countries. The second type of free riding implies that a country is a member of an agreement but does not fulfill the obligations of the treaty. Conceptually, these two types of free riding are difficult to separate.

The first type of free-rider incentive may be captured as follows in Figure 2.1. Assume that if countries 1 and 2 form a coalition, they maximize aggregate payoffs. That is, they choose emissions e_1^S and e_2^S. If one country leaves the agreement, the remaining country in the coalition and the deviator will maximize their own payoffs. That is, countries chose e_1^N and e_2^N. Since $\pi_2^S < \pi_2^N$, country 2 has an incentive to remain a non-signatory and the agreement formed by the two countries is not stable. In contrast, suppose that countries 1 and 2 agree on emissions e_1^Q and e_2^Q. Then $\pi_1^Q > \pi_1^N$ and $\pi_2^Q > \pi_2^N$. This type of agreement faces no free-rider incentive of the first type. However, suppose country 1 leaves the agreement and country 2 sticks to emissions e_2^Q, then $\pi_1^Q(e_1^Q, e_2^Q) < \pi_1^Q(e_1(e_2^Q), e_2^Q)$ where $e_1^F := e_1(e_2^Q)$ is country 1's best reply to e_2^Q. In this case, country 1 faces a free-rider incentive of the first type.

More generally, the first type of free riding is checked for by comparing the payoff each country receives in a particular coalition structure with the payoff it receives in alternative coalition structures. For the alternative coalition structure it is assumed that countries change their strategies. Hence, some kind of dynamic story is required on which this comparison is based.

The simple example already allows the following conclusion to be drawn.

Conclusion 1 (based on example)
The first type of free-rider incentive depends on what (a) coalition(s) agree(s), that is, the design of an agreement, and how countries react if a country or group of countries changes its membership. In a dynamic framework, it might be possible to overcome the first type of free-rider incentive through implicit threats.

In a setting with more than two countries, the first type of free-rider incentive also depends on the coalition structure. For example as long as a certain number of countries have not acceded to an IEA, a non-signatory may have an incentive to join the coalition; above a certain threshold a country may have an incentive to remain a non-signatory. The details will be discussed in Section 3.

The second type of free riding is captured in Figure 2.1 by assuming for instance that countries 1 and 2 sign an IEA in which country 1 has to reduce emissions to e_1^Q and country 2 to e_2^Q. Then country 1 has an incentive to increase its emissions from e_1^Q to e_1^F and country 2 from e_2^Q to e_2^F. That is, the second type of free-rider incentive implies that a signatory is better off by violating an agreement than by complying with its terms provided all other signatories comply. By taking a free ride, a country can reduce its abatement burden substantially, though environmental quality will only be affected marginally. More generally, we have:[12]

Result 2
Suppose all countries agree on an emission vector $e^* = (e_1^*, ..., e_N^*)$ where $e_i^* < e_i^N \ \forall \ i \in I$, and define the second type of free-rider incentive as the distance between cooperative emissions, e_i^*, and its best reply, $e_i(e_{-i}^*)$, then (1) each country faces a free-rider incentive, (2) then each country faces a free-rider incentive which is higher, the lower are emissions in the home and the neighboring country.

Proof: 1) follows from $e_i^* < e_i^N \ \forall \ i$ which implies $e_i(e_{-i}^*) - e_i^* > 0 \ \forall \ i$ by the slopes of the reaction functions (see [2.4]). Moreover, $\partial(e_i(e_{-i}^*) - e_i^*)/\partial e_i^* < 0$, which is trivially satisfied since $\partial(e_i(e_{-i}^*))/\partial e_i^* = 0$ and $\partial e_i^*/\partial e_i^* = -1$. Finally $\partial(e_i(e_{-i}^*) - e_i^*)/\partial e_{-i}^* < 0$, which is trivially satisfied since $\partial(e_i(e_{-i}^*))/\partial e_{-i}^* = R_i'$ and $\partial e_i^*/\partial e_{-i}^* = 0$ for any joint abatement program as defined above.

From Result 2 we conclude:

Conclusion 2 (based on Result 2)

The second type of free-rider incentive depends on the design of an agreement. Any emission vector different from the Nash equilibrium cannot be stable if the global emission game is played only once (one-shot game). However, in a dynamic framework, it might be possible to overcome the second type of free-rider incentive through threats to establish sanctions in the event of the violation of a treaty.

Conclusions 1 and 2 will be discussed in more detail in Section 3. From the discussion, two points will become apparent: (1) The two types of free-rider incentives are captured quite differently in the two model frameworks. (2) The main problem of establishing cooperation arises from the fact that it is not enough to threat to punish free riding; sanctions have to be credible. However, already at this stage the conceptual difficulty of separating both types of free rider is apparent. If a country leaves a coalition, that is, if it changes its membership, it will also change its strategy with respect to emissions (and possible other strategies). If a member of a coalition violates the terms of an agreement, that is, if it changes its strategy with respect to emissions (and possible other strategies), it becomes *de facto* a non-signatory or, at a more general level, changes its membership.

Consensus

Even if countries agree that something should be done to tackle global pollution, they usually disagree about (1) the extent of emission reduction, (2) the allocation of the abatement burden among signatories, (3) the amount of possible compensation payments, as well as (4) the net donors and net recipients of such transfer payments. An agreement on issues 1 and 2 defines the (global) gain from cooperation. An agreement on issues 3 and 4 determines (given that issues 1 and 2 have been settled) the distribution of the global welfare gain. Of course, in the negotiation process leading to an IEA, all issues are linked and are subject to strategic considerations by governments.

Conclusion 3 (based on discussion and assumptions)

Since accession to an IEA is voluntary, the design of a treaty has to be agreed on by consensus.

Obviously, the design of a treaty has an immediate implication for an individual country's welfare and the free-rider incentives. Consequently, one would expect that the design of an IEA would have attracted much attention in the game-theoretical literature on international pollution control. Surprisingly, however, this is not the case. Only a few articles have studied the effect of exogenously given designs and bargaining rules on the stability of treaties, on aggregate welfare and global emissions and on the membership of treaties (see Sections 3, 5 and 6).[13] A first attempt at an endogenous treatment of the bargaining process in the coalition formation process may be found in Ray and Vohra (1999).

2.3 Empirical Evidence

The Fundamental Results 1 and 2 as well as Results 1 and 2 are theoretical findings and therefore do not require empirical backing. Only the issue of consensus, where there is no general result available, requires support by some empirical evidence. Nevertheless, it would be interesting to review the extent of the gains from cooperation, the asymmetries resulting from some cooperative abatement strategy and the two types of free-rider incentives. Due to lack of space, however, we only discuss the problem of free-riding and possible countermeasures as well as the issue of consensus in this section. For the other two issues, the interested reader is referred to Chapter 3 in this book and the literature cited there.

Free-rider incentive

Empirical evidence for the first type of free-rider incentive is clear-cut. For instance, the Kyoto Protocol on the reduction of greenhouse gases has been signed by 38 states, though all countries should have an interest in curbing greenhouse gases. Similarly, the Montreal Protocol on the reduction of substances which deplete the ozone layer had been signed by 23 (90) states in 1987 (1993) despite the fact that it is a problem of global dimensions. An investigation of other IEAs would confirm this finding. For most environmental problems, the number of signatories falls short of the number of countries which are involved in the problem. This is particularly true for those agreements which are not only declarations of goodwill (e.g., the Rio Declaration 1992) but which require some efforts from signatories to curb an environmental problem (e.g, the Kyoto Protocol).

With respect to the second type of free-rider incentive, there are four points which have to be clarified: (1) Does the free-rider incentive only exist in a (game-) theoretical framework (Result 1) or does it also exist in reality? (2) If the free-rider incentive exists in reality and therefore there is a need for sanctions to establish cooperation (Conclusion 2), can sanctions be generally derived from international law or do they have to be specified within an IEA? (3) What are the possibilities for imposing sanctions for non-compliance within an IEA and which are effective? (4) What does the empirical evidence tell us about the implementation and conduct of sanctions within IEAs in the past?

Does the free-rider incentive exist in reality?　Looking at the compliance record of past IEAs, it is evident that non-compliance is not an exception but rather the rule. As Keohane (1995, p. 217) puts it: '[...] compliance is not very adequate. I believe that every study that has looked hard to compliance has concluded [...] that compliance is spotty'. In their prominent empirical study on compliance of IEAs, Brown Weiss and Jacobson (1997, pp. 87ff) find serious instances of non-compliance for all IEAs covered by their study. Sand (1997, p. 25) reports that over 300 infractions of the CITES treaty have been revealed per year. Also, the whaling convention was frequently breached by all important parties to the treaty (Heister 1997, p. 68).[14] Thus, we clearly reject the assumption of Chayes and Chayes (1993, p. 187) that states comply with treaties because of their 'sense of obligation to conform their conduct to governing norms'. We conclude: there is a free-rider incentive and therefore a need to sanction non-compliance.

Sanctions　There are basically two alternatives for dealing with non-compliance. The first option is to settle the case by calling upon the International Court of Justice and thereby referring to international law. This option is not very promising for two reasons. First, as pointed out above, any party which is accused of some wrongdoing must agree to a trial. Thus, formally, the Court has no enforcement power. Second, leading scholars of international law hold the view that there are no legal options for parties to punish the breach of multilateral treaties (see the literature cited in Heister 1997, pp. 91ff and 135). Therefore, we conclude: since most IEAs comprise more than two countries, in particular those which deal with global environmental problems, such as global warming, only the second option of dealing with the violation of a treaty within the institutions of an IEA is feasible.

Effective sanctions　Within the institutions of an IEA, again, two basic measures to enforce compliance are conceivable. The first measure, which we may call the 'soft option', is to include a provision in a treaty which calls for the establishment of an arbitration and dispute settlement committee once a party accuses another of violating the spirit of an agreement. The second measure, which we may call the 'tough option', is to specify punishment rules explicitly in a multilateral environmental treaty (Sand 1992, pp. 14ff). That is, the severeness of the punishment in relation to the misconduct is laid out as well as who is to conduct the punishment. Again, we believe that only the second option is likely to have an impact on the enforcement of a contract at all. First, the arbitration and dispute settlement schemes as laid out in some modern IEAs work on a purely optional but not on a compulsory basis. (All parties including the accused party have to agree that a committee is set up to handle the case.)

Second, as long as sanctions are not specified, their deterrence potential is basically nil. We conclude: sanctions should be laid down explicitly in an IEA to be effective.

Implementation and conduct of sanctions   Empirical evidence suggests that the tough option is not part of any IEA signed in the past.[15] Those few IEAs (e.g. the Montreal Protocol and the CITES agreement) which contain sanctions, refer to trade sanctions. However, those treaties only call upon the signatories to impose sanctions on non-signatories for not acceding to their treaty, but those sanctions are not used as a tool to penalize the non-compliance of signatories (Jenkins 1996, pp. 221ff). In contrast, the soft option is part of most IEAs (Barratt-Brown 1991, pp. 519ff, Ladenburger 1996, pp. 44ff, Marauhn 1996, pp. 696ff, Széll 1995, pp. 97ff and Werksman 1997, pp. 85ff).[16] Due to the voluntary character of the arbitration scheme, it is not surprising that there are no reported instances where the soft option has been applied (Sands 1996, p. 777).

The observations reported under the last point are puzzling since, by now, it should not only be academic but also public wisdom (though not to the extent that has been laid out above) that there are gains from cooperation. However, these gains can only be realized if the second type of free-rider incentive can be controlled.

Three explanations for the lack of sanctions come to mind: (1) Governments hesitate to endow an IEA secretariat with much enforcement power since this would restrict their sovereignty. (2) A less friendly interpretation would be that signatories intend to violate the treaty by the time they deposit their signature. This strategy could be rational if the political gain from signing the agreement today is higher than the loss from violating the agreement tomorrow.[17] (3) Tough punishment provisions face technical problems and difficulties in designing 'credible sanctions' in a 'second-best world'. Soft punishment provisions allow at least small gains from modest emission reductions. Which of the three explanations is (are) correct is an open question.

The subsequent sections, however, lend support to the third explanation without denying the relevance of the other aspects.

Consensus

The conclusion that the design of IEAs has to be agreed by consensus may be supported by three observations:

1. Sovereign states cannot be forced to sign an agreement. Clearly, a government has the right to veto any issue with which it does not agree. Thus, agreements are frequently based on the unanimity decision rule, which is sometimes also called the smallest common denominator decision rule (SCD-decision rule).
2. The unanimity decision rule is laid down in many IEAs (e.g. The Kyoto Protocol, Article 20). Amendments of a protocol have to be agreed by consensus. If no consensus can be reached, the amendments are only binding for those signatories which have signed the amendment protocol. Moreover, we observe that many important decisions within the EU and the United Nations are made by consensus.
3. The struggle for consensus is evident by considering how long it takes from the recognition of an environmental problem, the commencement of negotiations leading to an IEA and the signature of an IEA. For instance, the negotiations on the CITES agreement (Kyoto Protocol) have already lasted five years (six years). In the case of the Kyoto Protocol it is noteworthy that this agreement has not been ratified yet, since important details of the treaty could not be agreed upon.

3. TWO FRAMEWORKS OF MODELING INTERNATIONAL ENVIRONMENTAL AGREEMENTS

In the analysis of IEAs, two approaches can be distinguished: reduced stage game models (RSG models) and dynamic game models (DG models).

3.1   RSG Models

3.1.1 Outline

The RSG models comprise three stages. In the first stage, countries (governments) decided on their membership. That is, countries decide whether and with whom they want to form a coalition. In the second stage, countries decide on the level of emissions. A typical – though not necessary – assumption is that within a coalition, emissions are chosen cooperatively so as to maximize the aggregate welfare of the coalition. Towards outsiders, coalitions behave non-cooperatively. In the third stage, coalition members decide how the aggregate welfare gain to the coalition is distributed. In this stage, possible asymmetries between the coalition members may be balanced via transfers.

Until now, all models have made some assumptions with respect to the strategies in the second and third stages which are, in fact, exogenous to the coalition formation process. Due to these assumptions and since the time structure of the three stages is not explicitly modeled,[18] the three stages can be reduced to one stage (by backward induction). That is, all relevant information for a country to decide on its membership can be compactly summarized in the payoff it receives in a particular coalition and under a particular coalition structure. The equilibrium is determined by assuming that countries immediately adjust to any change of the coalition structure. How countries react depends on the equilibrium concept. We restrict attention to two equilibrium concepts which have been frequently used in the past: internal and external stability and the core.[19]

The concept of internal and external stability exogenously assumes that there is only one coalition. The members of this coalition are called signatories and all other countries which remain singletons are called non-signatories. An equilibrium is defined as follows.

Definition 1: Internal and external stability   Let the superscript J denote signatories and NJ non-signatories, I^J the set of signatories and I^{NJ} the set of non-signatories, e^* emissions and t^* transfers in the coalition equilibrium comprising N^* signatories and $N - N^*$ non-signatories and $e^{*'}$ and $t^{*'}$ optimal strategies for a coalition structure different from the equilibrium coalition.

A coalition is internally stable if there is no incentive for a signatory to leave the coalition. That is,

$$A_1 := \pi_i^J(N^*, e^*, t^*) - \pi_i^{NJ}(N^* - 1, e^{*'}, t^{*'}) \geq 0 \ \forall \ i \in I^J.$$

A coalition is externally stable if there is no incentive for a non-signatory to join the coalition. That is,

$$A_2 := \pi_j^J(N^* + 1, e^{*'}, t^{*'}) - \pi_j^{NJ}(N^*, e^*, t^*) \leq 0 \ \forall \ j \in I^{NJ}.$$

In Definition 1, N^*, e^*, t^* may be interpreted as 'state variables' and $N^* - 1$, $N^* + 1$, $e^{*'}$ and $t^{*'}$ indicate a deviation from this state which, according to the definition, should not be beneficial to any country in equilibrium. If a player accedes or leaves the equilibrium coalition, $e^{*'}$ and $t^{*'}$ are the reoptimization strategies. As mentioned above, these strategies may be dropped in Definition 1 and attention can be restricted to the number of signatories, since the strategies emissions and transfers follow from the assumptions.

As pointed out above, a typical assumption of all models in the literature is that signatories choose emissions so as to maximize the aggregate welfare of the coalition. Two versions can be distinguished. The first version assumes that signatories and non-signatories simultaneously choose their emission levels as in a Nash equilibrium. This is called the Nash-Cournot version. The second version assumes that the non-signatories choose their emission levels first and then the signatories. Thus, as in a Stackelberg oligopoly, signatories can observe non-signatories' strategies before choosing their optimal strategies. This is called the Stackelberg version. The Stackelberg assumption implies that signatories have an informational advantage over non-signatories. They can take the reaction of non-signatories into consideration when choosing their optimal emission strategy. Hence, they can deal better with leakage effects, that is, the expansion of emissions by non-signatories if signatories reduce emissions (see Section 6).[20]

With respect to transfers, three typical assumptions have been made in the literature: (1) no transfers (Barrett 1994b and Bauer 1992), (2) transfers according to the Nash-bargaining solution (Botteon and Carraro 1997 and 1998) and (3) transfers according to the Shapley value (Barrett 1997b and Botteon and Carraro 1997 and 1998).[21] If countries are assumed to be *ex-ante* symmetric,[22] all signatories receive the same payoff and a redistribution via transfers is obviously not necessary.[23] In the case of asymmetric countries, assumptions (2) and (3) are popular allocation rules, though other rules are also conceivable.

Generally, irrespective of whether countries are symmetric or heterogeneous and irrespective of which transfer scheme is applied among the signatories, the equilibrium number of signatories may range from zero to all countries depending on the specification of the payoff function and the sequence of the choice of emissions. The equilibrium can be related to the cost and benefit parameters of the payoff function and can therefore be interpreted in economic terms. The details are discussed in Section 6.

The concept of the 'core' does not restrict attention to a single coalition and basically allows for all possible coalition structures. A coalition structure is an equilibrium (lies in the core) if there is no alternative coalition structure in which a country or group of countries receives a higher payoff. For a given coalition structure, an alternative coalition implies a deviation and an alternative state in the game. It is assumed that deviation triggers a break-up of the coalition to which the deviator(s) belong(s). The weakest reaction of the remaining countries is to choose (as singletons) emissions in a Nash equilibrium fashion (γ-core).

The literature on the core stability of IEAs has focused on the check for stability of the grand coalition (a coalition comprising all countries). Consequently, a country must receive a higher payoff than if it forms a singleton coalition and all others play as singletons, if it forms a coalition with one other country and all others play as singletons, if it forms a coalition with two other countries and all other countries play as singletons and so forth. This literature has always assumed the possibility of transfers, though generally, there are also definitions of the core in non-transferable utility games. Chander and Tulkens (1995, 1997) have shown for quite general conditions that the grand coalition establishing a socially optimal emission vector lies in the core if a transfer scheme is applied which resembles that of Kaneko's ratio equilibrium.

3.1.2 Evaluation

Design of an agreement   The assumption that cooperating countries act as a single entity when choosing their emission levels implies that difficulties in agreeing on an important detail of an agreement are not captured by these models.[24] In order to structure this problem, two cases may be distinguished: (1) transfers can be used to balance asymmetries resulting from some abatement program; or (2) transfers are not available. In the first case, it seems obvious to assume that a coalition chooses that emission vector which maximizes aggregate payoffs to the coalition. Consequently, the analysis can focus on how the transfer scheme affects the equilibrium coalition structure. Unfortunately, only little is known so far about this issue. It is only evident that in the case of heterogeneous countries, the transfer scheme will affect the equilibrium number of signatories and the membership if the internal and external stability concept is applied (Botteon and Carraro 1997, 1998). However, no general results are available about the exact relationship. In the case of the core, it is only known that a particular transfer scheme implies that the socially optimal emission vector lies in the core. Whether other transfer schemes or a particular class of transfer schemes also possess this property is not known.

In the second case, the equilibrium number of signatories depends on the choice of emission levels of the coalition. It may well be the case if countries are heterogeneous, that the emission vector which maximizes aggregate payoffs to the coalition leads to a smaller number of signatories than if some other emission vector had been chosen. In fact, it cannot be ruled out that some other emission vector may be more beneficial to potential signatories and may lead to a higher global welfare and lower global emissions. In future research, it would be interesting to investigate this issue in detail, since in reality transfers have hardly been used in past IEAs (see Section 4.4).

Conclusion 4 (based on discussion)
The design of an agreement has an effect on the membership in RSG models. However, the literature has paid little attention to how countries agree on the design of an agreement and how the design affects membership and the overall success of an IEA.

Individual rationality   Individual rationality, which we identified in Section 2.2 as one condition of signing an IEA, is not explicitly captured in RSGs. At a most general level, in an equilibrium in an RSG, a country is a member of some coalition since it is better off belonging to this coalition rather than belonging to some other one or remaining a singleton. However, this does not automatically imply that a country is better off than it would be in the status quo in which countries chose their Nash equilibrium emissions as singleton players. Some countries may form coalitions which create a situation for a country which does not allow it to obtain its initial welfare level. Thus, in RSGs, the fact that individual rationality is not explicitly accounted for is a logical and correct consequence of these approaches.

Implicitly, however, the condition of individual rationality as defined in Section 2.2 is mostly met. By the definition of the γ-core, each member of the grand coalition must receive a higher payoff than if it plays as a singleton and other countries choose their Nash equilibrium emission levels. Also in an internal and external equilibrium, individual rationality will be met for most specifications of the payoff function. By the definition of an equilibrium, no signatory has an incentive to leave the coalition to become a singleton and the incentive to form a coalition derives from the fact that the loss of benefits from emission reductions is lower than the gains from reduced damages. Moreover, non-signatories benefit as free riders from the abatement efforts of signatories. However, there is no general proof of the conditions under which individual rationality as defined in Section 2.2 is satisfied in an internal and external equilibrium.

Free-rider incentive From the definition of the internal and external equilibrium and the core, it is evident that the focus of the analysis in RSGs is on the first type of free-rider incentive. Only in an equilibrium, is it true that no country has an incentive to change its membership. Also, however the second type of free-rider incentive does not vanish in an RSG. For any non-trivial coalition (i.e. any coalition comprising at least two countries), which chooses an emission vector different from that in the Nash equilibrium, this type of free-rider incentive is present (see Result 2 and note 12). This incentive is controlled in an RSG by the implicit threat to impose sanctions on free riding via a change of the strategies of the non-deviating countries. In equilibrium, this threat is sufficient to deter deviations. However, in RSGs, sanctions are immediately carried out.

Thus RSGs do not allow for the possibility that some time may pass between free riding, discovering the violation and taking action. Hence, there are no temporary gains from cheating, which is a typical source of the second free-rider incentive.

Taken together, we conclude:

Conclusion 5 (based on discussion)
RSGs capture the first type of free-rider incentive very well but the second type only partially. The focus of the analysis is on the membership of agreements. Therefore, RSGs are suited for analysing accessions to and withdrawals from agreements but are less suited to analysing whether a particular design of an agreement can be enforced by its members.

For this reason, we use an RG and not an RSG framework to analyze measures to enforce an IEA and to balance possible asymmetric payoffs in an IEA. However, we report on the results of the formation of IEAs obtained in an RSG framework in Chapter 6.

Sanctions and credibility In RSGs, the direction and exact nature of sanctions cannot be determined at a general level. However, it is evident that in equilibrium, the deviator must lose through the reaction of the remaining countries. Generally, there are two channels of sanctions: emissions and transfers, which may be used unilaterally or simultaneously: a) after the deviation, the remaining countries increase their emissions so that global emissions increase and the deviator(s) suffer(s) higher environmental damages; b) a country which is a net recipient of transfers may be excluded from transfers, may receive a lower transfer or even become a net donor after the deviation. A country which is a net donor of transfers may have higher transfer obligations after the deviation. In equilibrium, the effect of these sanctions of type (a) and/or (b) are stronger than the possible gain from reduced abatement efforts through the deviation.

In an internally and externally stable equilibrium, the threat of sanctions implies that all countries would make the best response if a deviation occurred which could be regarded as a credible threat. This assumption is in line with two facts. First, accession to an IEA is voluntary. Thus, the best signatories can do is to revise their strategies if a country withdraws. Second, the empirical evidence on which we reported in Section 2.3 tells us that there is no IEA which has a provision for sanctions in case of violation of a treaty. Thus, the reoptimization strategy nicely reflects the limited punishment options available to countries in international politics. However, in some other respects, this implicit strategy of sanctions may not be credible: (1) if a signatory leaves the coalition, it is assumed that the remaining countries do not revise their decision about membership. However, it may well be the case that after a deviation, it is in the interest of some of the remaining signatories to leave the agreement too. Thus, internal and external stability takes a short-sighted view of stability (Carraro and Moriconi 1997).[25] (2) The reoptimization strategy may well imply that the signatories are worse off after the deviation and therefore the treaty is not renegotiation-proof. The details will be discussed in Sections 4.1 and 4.2. (3) Under the Stackelberg assumption, a signatory behaves as a clever Stackelberg leader as long as it is a member of the coalition, but loses this strategic informational advantage once it leaves the coalition. This assumption is hard to defend by any means.

In the γ-core, the threat of sanctions also implies that strategies are revised in a best-reply fashion.[26] However, after a deviation, it is assumed that the remaining countries of the coalition to which the deviator(s) belonged split up into singletons. This may not be in their own interests, and is very harsh, and we think that it is not a credible threat. This implies that the grand coalition lies in the core if a particular transfer scheme is administered. In reality, however, we neither observe full participation in an IEA, nor socially optimal emission levels, let alone substantial amount of transfers. Thus, models based on the concept of the core do not contribute much to the understanding of actual IEAs. Therefore, they are not considered further here.[27]

3.2 Dynamic Game Models

3.2.1 Outline
The DG models depict the relations between countries as a 'true' dynamic game. Two basic features are helpful in structuring these models. The first feature is whether a game is modeled as a finite or infinite game. It is important to note that for an infinite game, it is not necessary that the game actually lasts until perpetuity; it suffices if the end of the game is not known with certainty. In other words, at each point in time there is a probability – though this might be very small – that the game will continue. The second feature is whether structural time dependency is captured. Differential and difference games capture this dependency (Basar and Olsder 1982 and de Zeeuw and van der Ploeg 1991), whereas repeated games do not (Sabourian 1989). Structural time dependency implies that payoffs derived at some point in time depend on payoffs received and actions taken in the past. Whereas *differential games* assume continuous time, *difference games* assume discrete time intervals as in repeated games. The disadvantage of differential games is that – as in RSG models – free-riding of the second type, namely joining an agreement but not complying with its terms, cannot be captured adequately since there is no time lag between free riding and sanctions. The disadvantage of difference games is that they are difficult to solve and that not as many general results are available as they are for repeated games or differential games. In contrast, *repeated games* (RG), assume discrete time in the same way as difference games but are much simpler. Payoffs in each stage depend only on actions taken at that time. Thus, despite the fact that many pollutants are stock rather than flow pollutants, so it would be adequate to capture

structural time dependency, we will restrict attention to repeated games in the following.[28] Moreover, we will not treat finitely repeated games, but only look at infinitely repeated games (IRGs); this may be justified as follows.[29]

IEAs are generally in force for a long period of time without specifying the termination of the contract. Though some of them are replaced (e.g. the Oslo Protocol in 1994 on sulfur reduction in Europe has replaced the older Helsinki Protocol signed in 1985) or modified at a later stage (e.g. the various amendments of the Montreal Protocol), by the time they are signed, negotiators face an apparently infinite game (Finus and Tjøtta 1998, chapter 1). That is, governments agree on an emission target (which may not be socially optimal) and some transfer scheme where each country has to meet its obligation in the following years after the year of ratification. If a violation is detected, this will be punished via sanctions. An IEA is stable if the threat to impose sanctions on non-compliance deters a country from free riding. That is, in equilibrium, sanctions are not carried out.

For the subsequent discussion, it will be helpful to formalize this idea with the help of a simple trigger strategy. Aspects which are not captured by this simple strategy will be considered separately in Section 4. Moreover, we do not consider transfer at this stage for reasons of simplicity. In a repeated game, we distinguish between a stage game strategy and a dynamic strategy of the entire game. A stage game strategy is an action (e.g. emissions) played in a particular round of the repeated game. A dynamic strategy is a collection of instructions on what to do at each point in time (which stage game strategy should be played) for each situation which might arise in the game (for each stage game strategy which is played by other players, see Eichberger 1993, pp. 220ff).

Let $e^* = (e_1^*, ..., e_N^*)$ denote the emission level agreed upon in an IEA, e_i^F the best stage game reply of a free rider, i.e., $e_i^F = e_i(e_{-i}^*)$ and $e^N = (e_1^N, ..., e_N^N)$ emissions in the Nash equilibrium of the stage game. The (dynamic) trigger strategy we consider calls upon the suspension of the contract once non-compliance is detected. The punishers revert to the status quo emission levels, e_{-i}^N, to which the best reply of the punished country is e_i^N by the definition of a stage game Nash equilibrium. The emission vector e^* can be sustained as a subgame-perfect equilibrium[30] provided the average discounted payoff from complying exceeds the average payoff from free riding and subsequently being punished.[31] That is,

$$\pi_i^*(e^*) \geq (1-\delta_i)\pi_i^F(e_i^F, e_{-i}^*) + \delta_i \pi_i^N(e^N) \Leftrightarrow \delta_i \geq \frac{\pi_i^F - \pi_i^*}{\pi_i^F - \pi_i^N} = \delta_i^{min} \ \forall \ i \quad [2.7]$$

holds. Hence, provided countries discount time by a discount factor greater than δ_i^{min}, cooperation can be sustained. We call δ_i^{min} the 'minimum discount factor requirement'. The discount factor is defined by $\delta_i = p_i/(1 + r_i)$, $0 \leq \delta_i < 1$, where p_i is the (subjective) estimation of country i about the probability that the game continues and r_i is the discount rate (see Gibbons 1992, p. 90 and Osborne and Rubinstein 1994, p. 135).[32] We say in the following that the higher δ_i^{min}, the lower the likelihood that an IEA is stable.

Definition 2: Stability in an infinitely repeated game An agreement is stable in an infinitely repeated game if for every signatory the discounted welfare stream from compliance exceeds the welfare stream from free riding in one period and subsequently being punished for some time.

3.2.2 Evaluation

Design of an agreement Whether condition [2.7] holds depends on (a) the actual discount factors by which countries discount payoffs accruing at different times, (b) the membership in an agreement, (c) the cooperative emission vector, (d) the punishment, and in an extended setting also on (e) transfers. It is very likely that there is not just one combination of these factors which satisfies [2.7] but many. That is, the number of equilibria may be very large in an infinitely repeated game. Consequently, the details of the coalition formation process as well as the procedure on how countries agree on the design of an IEA have to be specified in order to make progress in drawing policy conclusions. As in the RSG models, assumptions with respect to the choice of the transfer scheme and the emission vector of the coalition will be exogenous to the RG. Assumptions with respect to discount factors are also necessary to test for the stability of an IEA. Moreover, and in contrast to RSG models, the equilibrium membership does not follow directly from the equilibrium concept and requires some additional modeling effort.

The fact that in an IRG there are so many factors which determine the success of an IEA has two implications. First, the effect of only some factors has yet been studied in the literature. Second, the subsequent discussion can only highlight some interesting aspects and will have to be incomplete.

Conclusion 6 (based on discussion)

In IRG models, the design of an agreement has an effect on the membership and the stability of an IEA. Though the literature has captured some aspects of how the agreement procedure of countries forming an IEA can be modeled and how the design affects membership and the overall success of an IEA, there remain many open questions.

Individual rationality Individual rationality is captured in an infinitely repeated game as the minimum requirement that an IEA is stable. If an agreement is stable, a participant receives an average payoff π_i^*. Thus, the minimum requirement may be expressed as $\pi_i^* \geq \pi_i^B$ where π_i^B is some lower bound. This bound is determined by noting that the likelihood of a stable agreement is higher, the higher the discount factor by which payoffs are discounted, the longer the punishment time and the harder the punishment in case of non-compliance. The highest discount factor is $\delta_i = 1$. The longest punishment duration is the trigger strategy used in [2.7], assuming a punishment for the rest of the game once deviation takes place. The harshest punishment for country i is if all other countries $-i$ choose their highest emission level, $e_{-i}^{\max}$, since $\partial \pi_i / \partial e_{-i} < 0$. The best reply of the punishment player is $e_i(e_{-i}^{\max})$, which leads to the minimax payoff $\pi_i^{\min\max}(e_i(e_{-i}^{\max}), e_{-i}^{\max})$. Inserting $\delta_i = 1$ and replacing π_i^N by $\pi_i^{\min\max}$ in [2.7], we derive the condition $\pi_i^* \geq \pi_i^{\min\max}$. All payoff vectors which satisfy $\pi_i^* \geq \pi_i^{\min\max}$ for all participants are called individual rational payoff vectors.

There are four things to note about the minimax payoff. First, the higher the upper bound of emissions $e_i^{\max}$, the lower will be the minimax payoff. Second, as long as $e_j^{\max} > e_j^N \ \forall \ j$ as we assumed, it is evident that $\pi_i^{\min\max} < \pi_i^N \ \forall \ i$. Third, as outlined in Section 2.2, economic intuition suggests that the lower bound of participation in an IEA is the payoff in the status which we identified with the payoff in the Nash equilibrium (of the stage game). One way to reconcile economic intuition with game theory is to restrict punishment of a country j in order to punish country i, e_j^i, to $e_j^i \leq e_j^N$. Then $\pi_i^{\min\max} = \pi_i^N$. We may argue that the harshest possible punishment is to suspend an agreement. Any emissions above e_j^N could be judged as an artificial and not very credible expansion of emissions above the status quo emission levels. Fourth, whatever assumption we make and on whatever arguments they are based, our decision may be criticized as arbitrary.[33] Despite the above qualifications, we assume $e_j^i \leq e_j^N \ \forall \ j$ in the following, implying that an agreement is individually rational if and only if $\pi_i^*(e^*) \geq \pi_i^N(e^N) \ \forall \ i$.

Free-rider incentive It is apparent that the second type of free-rider incentive of signing an agreement but not complying with its terms is very well captured in repeated games. The possibility of gaining a temporary free-rider advantage from violating an agreement is explicitly taken account of. The first type of free-rider incentive to remain a non-signatory and to benefit from the abatement efforts of signatories is only partially captured. It is captured in so far as for any number of signatories smaller than the grand coalition, non-signatories may choose a non-cooperative emission level and thereby benefit from the higher abatement efforts of signatories. Moreover, if [2.7] does not hold for a signatory, this country will chose its best stage game deviation and become *de facto* a non-signatory. However, whether non-signatories have an incentive to belong to the coalition is not modeled. This incentive is only captured in so far that a minimum requirement for a country to accede to an IEA is that it receives an individual rational payoff under the agreement. Therefore, we conclude:

Conclusion 7 (based on discussion)
Repeated games capture the second type of free-rider incentive very well but the first type only partially. The focus of the analysis is on the stability of a particular agreement but not on the membership of IEAs. Thus, repeated games are suited to analysing measures to enforce an IEA and to balancing asymmetric payoffs resulting from some abatement strategy. They are less suited to analysing which countries will accede and withdraw from an IEA.

For this reason, we use an IRG framework for studying the factors which influence the stability of an IEA and measures of enforcement (Sections 4 and 5). Despite the shortcoming of capturing the first type of free-rider incentive only incompletely, we nevertheless discuss coalition formation in an IRG in Section 6, but will point out the limitations of the models.

Sanctions and credibility In IRGs, threats to impose sanctions on free riding are explicitly modeled. This has two advantages. First, the importance of sanctions for the stability of an IEA can be studied. Second, such a framework allows us to study the reasons which help to explain the empirical finding in Section 2.3 that sanctions have played a minor role in past IEAs. We deal with these issues in Section 4.

The threat to impose sanctions on non-compliance by returning to the stage game Nash equilibrium is credible in the sense of subgame-perfection: countries play their best reply after a deviation. This strategy is not credible in the sense of a renegotiation-proof contract, as will be explained in Section 4.1.

3.3 Factors Influencing the Success of an IEA in an IRG Model

Recalling that the focus of the analysis in an IRG framework is on the second type of free-rider incentive, we can identify seven factors which are important for the success of an IEA:

1. As discussed previously, the harsher the expected punishment in case of non-compliance (low value of π_i^N in the example) and the longer the punishment time, the more likely it is that an agreement can be stabilized. However, it is not sufficient to put up severe threats to deter a country from free riding. Threats must also be credible. Credibility has a strategic and a technical dimension. The strategic dimension refers to the extent to which the punisher(s) and the punished player(s) are affected by punishments. This aspect of credibility will be outlined in Section 4.1 and applied subsequently. The technical dimension refers to the technical limitations of various sanctions and will be stressed throughout Section 4.

2. The more a country can gain by violating a treaty (that is, the larger $\pi_i^F - \pi_i^*$), the more difficult it is to stabilize an agreement. As demonstrated already in Section 2.2 (Result 2), the more ambitious the abatement targets envisaged in an IEA, the higher will be (*ceteris paribus*) the free-rider incentive. Moreover, an asymmetric welfare distribution (where some countries receive a low π_i^*) may also jeopardize the stability of an agreement. Though transfer payments can generally help to reduce the free-rider incentive, they face a bundle of problems, as will be laid out in Section 4.3. Alternative measures to balance asymmetries are issue linkage (Section 4.4) and the choice of appropriate policy instruments to achieve a particular abatement target (Chapter 5).

3. The more frequently compliance is monitored, the higher the chances for cooperation (see Section 4.5 for a formal exposition). On the one hand, the transitory gains from free riding are limited through frequent checks. On the other hand, punishment becomes a higher threat potential since the time between discovery of non-compliance and punishment is shortened.

4. The lower the rate of detecting non-compliance, the less deterrent are threats of punishment and the more likely it is that a country will take a free ride (see Section 4.5 for a formal exposition).
   Points 3 and 4 are analyzed in Section 4.5 under the heading of 'Monitoring'.

5. The more governments discount time (high value of r_i), that is, the more they value short-term success (gains from free riding) against the long-term gain from cooperation, the more difficult it is to enforce an IEA. In a public choice context, one should expect that short-term success is particularly important prior to elections (Hahn 1989). Hence, long-term commitments may be particularly jeopardized during election campaigns.[34]

6. Discounting will also depend on the estimation of agents about the uncertainty of future events, the general risk attitude of politicians, the evaluation of political stability in neighboring countries and so forth. Thus for instance civil war, social unrest or any kind of political instability has a negative effect on the stability of a treaty (via a low value of p_i).
   The factors mentioned under points 5 and 6 have an impact on the discount factor. Measures to influence the discount factor will be discussed in Section 4.6.

7. Inequality [2.7] may hold for some countries but not for all. Thus, it may only be possible that a sub-group of countries forms a stable IEA. Moreover, whether and for which countries [2.7] holds depends on the design of an IEA. Additionally, which countries accede to an IEA will depend on how membership is decided. The coalition formation process in an IRG framework will be studied in Section 6.

4.　MEASURES TO AVOID ASYMMETRIC PAYOFFS AND TO ENFORCE AN AGREEMENT

In this section, we study measures which help to avoid asymmetric payoffs and to enforce an IEA in an IRG framework. Since there are so many factors which affect the success of an IEA in IRGs, we propose to concentrate on only one factor at a time and make some assumptions about other factors. In order to simplify the following exposition, we discard transfers, as long as they are not the issue of investigation. Similarly, if the nature of punishment is not analyzed, we assume that countries use emissions and choose the harshest, though credible punishment strategy which guarantees the lowest minimum discount factor requirement. Since the choice of emissions within an IEA and the membership will be treated in Sections 5 and 6 respectively, we assume in the following that all countries participate in an IEA and that the countries are already agreed on some cooperative emission vector leading to a particular cooperative payoff vector. Except for Section 4.6, where we study the effect of external factors on the actual discount rate, we treat discount factors as parameters.

Whenever this is appropriate, we express the effect of a factor on the stability of an IEA as the effect of this factor on the minimum discount factor requirement, though it is certainly possible also to capture this effect in other ways.

4.1 Credible Sanctions and Incentive-Compatible Compensation Measures

Sanctions

Though the basic idea of sanctions has been outlined, it remains to clarify what credible sanctions mean in the context of IRGs. This question is closely related to the definition of an equilibrium. A convincing concept developed in recent years which captures the gist of the problems governments face in international pollution control is Farrell and Maskin's (1989a, 1989b) renegotiation-proof equilibrium. To allow for a direct comparison with the trigger strategy in Section 3.2, we illustrate the concept by restricting the choice variable to emissions (though modifications to include other variables are straightforward). Let e'_{-i} denote the punishment emission vector of the punishers $-i$ to punish country i, $e_i(e'_{-i})$ the best reply of the punished country i if it shows *no* repentance, e^i_i the emission level of country i if it goes along with the punishment, t^P_i the punishment time to punish country i and j a particular punisher. Then the following four conditions for a stable agreement must be satisfied:[35]

$$\pi_i^*(e_i^*, e_{-i}^*) \geq (1 - \delta_i)\pi_i^F(e_i(e_{-i}^*), e_{-i}^*) + \delta_i(\pi_i^{P_1}(e_i(e'_{-i}), e'_{-i}) \tag{C_1}$$

$$\pi_i^{P_2}(e_i^i, e_{-i}^i, e_i^*, e_{-i}^*) \geq \pi_i^{P_1}(e_i(e'_{-i}), e'_{-i}) \tag{C_2}$$

$$\pi_i^*(e_i^*, e_{-i}^*) \geq (1 - \delta_i)\pi_i^F(e_i(e_{-i}^*), e_{-i}^*) + \delta_i\pi_i^{P_2}(e_i^i, e_{-i}^i, e_i^*, e_{-i}^*) \tag{C_3}$$

$$\pi_j^*(e_i^*, e_{-i}^*) \leq \pi_j^{P_2}(e_i^i, e_{-i}^i, e_i^*, e_{-i}^*) \Leftrightarrow \pi_j^*(e_i^*, e_{-i}^*) \leq \pi_j^R(e_i^i, e'_{-i}) \tag{C_4}$$

$\forall$ i and j where

$$\pi_i^{P_2} = (1 - \delta_i^{t_i^P})\pi_i^R(e_i^i, e_{-i}^i) + \delta_i^{t_i^P}\pi_i^*(e_i^*, e_{-i}^*).$$ (C$_A$)

C_1 There must be a punishment harsh enough to deter free riding when a country continuously violates the spirit of an agreement (retaliation). That is, the discounted average payoff from cheating, π_i^F (best deviation payoff), and subsequently receiving the 'retaliation phase payoff', $\pi_i^{P_1}$, must be lower than the average payoff in the cooperative phase, π_i^*. This deters deviation in the first place.

C_2 However, the punishment should not be too harsh to provide the treaty violator with an incentive to go along with the punishment (repentance) so that all parties can return to 'normal terms' as quickly as possible. Consequently, the punisher must find it more attractive to 'cooperate' during his punishment instead of being punished for a long time as mentioned under C_1. Therefore, the average payoff if a player complies with his punishment, $\pi_i^{P_2}$, must be at least as high as when punishment is continued, $\pi_i^{P_1}$.

C_3 However, the punishment should also not be too weak since otherwise it would pay for a government to violate the agreement and to subsequently demonstrate repentance with 'great regret'. That is, the discounted average payoff from cheating, π_i^F, and subsequently receiving the 'repentance payoff', $\pi_i^{P_2}$, must be lower than the average payoff in the cooperative phase, π_i^*.

C_4 Governments conducting the punishment in the case of a violation of a treaty should suffer no disadvantage. That is, there should be no room for a treaty violator to offer his potential punishers a deal to treat bygones as bygones, promising to resume cooperation. Such a renegotiation would imply that the threat of punishment would lose its credibility in the first place and the stability of an IEA would suffer. For this, the average payoff when conducting the punishment, π_j^R, must be at least as high as in the cooperative phase, π_j^*.[36] This last condition especially represents the central idea of the concept of renegotiation-proofness and distinguishes it from that of subgame-perfection.

C_A The continuation punishment payoff of country i at the beginning of its repentance phase, $\pi_i^{P_2}$, is a linear combination of the repentance payoff, π_i^R, and the cooperative continuation payoff, π_i^*. Thus, the continuation punishment payoff rises as the punishment proceeds (providing an incentive to the punished player to accept the punishment).

Conditions C_1 and C_3 are the typical conditions which deter free riding via the threat of punishment. Conditions C_2 and C_4 restrict possible sanctions. In the light of the possibility that a signatory can leave an IEA (which is possible under most contracts after a government has given notice some time in advance of its decision), only moderate punishments are feasible. Though violations must be punished (otherwise violations pay and stability is jeopardized; see C_1 and C_3), the violator should have an incentive to remain in the IEA despite the (necessary) punishment (C_2). Thus, generally, a trigger strategy which calls upon the suspension of a treaty for ever is not renegotiation-proof. Because of C_2, C_3 is a stronger requirement than C_1. Hence, C_1 can be dropped. Condition C_4 is particularly important in an international context and ensures that a threat is credible. It represents the central idea of a renegotiation-proof treaty.

Of course, it is not difficult to satisfy each condition by itself. However, designing a punishment code which satisfies all conditions *simultaneously* is a difficult task. For instance, by choosing a weak punishment it will not be difficult to convince a violator to remain in the IEA (C_2 is satisfied). Then, however, non-compliance may be encouraged in the future (C_1 and C_3 are violated). The above-mentioned mediation procedure within most IEAs (soft option) is a punishment with such properties. In contrast, the threat to suspend an agreement or – in a wider context – to impose trade sanctions, may deter free riding (C_1 and C_3 are satisfied) but may also negatively affect the punishers (C_4 is violated). This is one of the main reasons why, for instance, trade embargoes have hardly been successful in the past.[37]

Solving C_2, using (C_A), we derive

$$(1-\delta_i^{t_i^P})\pi_i^R + \delta_i^{t_i^P}\pi_i^* \ge \pi_i^{P_1} \iff \delta_i^{t_i^P} \ge \frac{\pi_i^{P_1} - \pi_i^R}{\pi_i^* - \pi_i^R}. \qquad [2.8]$$

If we choose t_i^P such that [2.8] becomes binding, then from C_2 and C_A we have $\pi_i^{P_2} = \pi_i^{P_1}$. Substituting this into C_3, we derive

$$(1-\delta_i)\pi_i^F + \delta_i\pi_i^{P_1} < \pi_i^* \iff \delta_i \ge \frac{\pi_i^F - \pi_i^*}{\pi_i^F - \pi_i^{P_1}}. \qquad [2.9]$$

Taken together, the discount factor minimum requirement of country i is given (Finus and Rundshagen 1998b) by

$$\delta_i \geq \delta_i^{\min} = \min\left[\max\left(\frac{\pi_i^{P_1} - \pi_i^R}{\pi_i^* - \pi_i^R}, \frac{\pi_i^F - \pi_i^*}{\pi_i^F - \pi_i^{P_1}} \right) \right] \text{ s.t. } \pi_j^* \leq \pi_j^R \ \forall \ j \neq i. \qquad [2.10]$$

If we compare [2.10] with [2.7] it is evident that the discount factor minimum requirement for a renegotiation-proof contract is generally higher than for a subgame-perfect contract. That is, $\delta_i^{\min, RPE} \geq \delta_i^{\min, SPE}$. This is for three reasons. First, restriction $\pi_j^* \leq \pi_j^R$ (see C$_4$) must be additionally satisfied. Second, note that generally $\pi_i^{P_1} > \pi_i^N$ as long as $e_{-i}^i \neq e_{-i}^N$. Thus, the second term in brackets in [2.10] will usually be higher than $\delta_i^{\min}$ in [2.7]. Third, the first term in brackets constitutes an additional restriction compared to [2.7]. (The first term may be bigger than the second term in brackets.) Again, trivially, from $e_{-i}^i \leq e_{-i}^N$ $\pi_i^* \geq \pi_i^N$ follows as minimum participation requirement in a renegotiation-proof IEA.

Of course, the fact that $\delta_i^{\min, RPE} \geq \delta_i^{\min, SPE}$ holds can be concluded even quicker by noting that renegotiation-proof condition C$_1$ corresponds to the subgame-perfect condition [2.7], except that $\pi_i^{P_1} > \pi_i^N$, implying that condition C$_1$ is more restrictive than condition [2.7], and that C$_2$ to C$_4$ constitute additional restrictions in a renegotiation-proof equilibrium compared to a subgame-perfect equilibrium.

In [2.10], we derived $\delta_i^{\min}$ for a given e^* (implying a given π^*) without making particular assumptions about the discount factors, assuming an 'optimal' punishment code. This code reflects an optimal mix of punishment strategies (e^i) and punishment time (t_i^p). As argued above, the optimal punishment time makes [2.8] binding. The optimal punishment profile allocates the punishment duties such that [2.10] is minimized. As long as countries have different payoff functions, this requires a complex allocation rule. Though from a theoretical point of view, it is straightforward to construct such optimal punishment profiles (see Finus and Rundshagen 1998b), in reality, several restrictions may cause the actual $\delta_i^{\min}$ to be higher than in [2.10]. Though some of these difficulties apply to sanctions in general, we will discuss them in the next Section (4.2) under the heading of 'emissions'.

An alternative way of demonstrating that renegotiation-proofness imposes additional restrictions on an IEA compared to subgame-perfection is to solve conditions C_1 to C_4 for equilibrium cooperative emissions or average payoffs. Denoting the set of all equilibrium cooperative emissions vectors by $E^{*,\delta}$ and average payoffs by $\Pi^{*,\delta}$ which satisfy renegotiation-proof condition C_1 to C_4 for a given set of discount factors, then $E^{*,\delta,RPE} \subseteq E^{*,\delta,SPE}$ and $\Pi^{*,\delta,RPE} \subseteq \Pi^{*,\delta,SPE}$.

Result 3

For a given cooperative emission vector, the minimum discount factor requirement for renegotiation-proof strategies is at least as high as for subgame-perfect strategies i.e., $\delta_i^{min,\,RPE} \geq \delta_i^{min,\,SPE}$. For any given set of discount factors, the set of equilibrium emission and payoff vectors is smaller (or equal) for renegotiation-proof than for subgame-perfect IEAs, i.e., $E^{*,\delta,RPE} \subseteq E^{*,\delta,SPE}$ and $\Pi^{*,\delta,RPE} \subseteq \Pi^{*,\delta,SPE}$.

Proof: The first statement has been proved in the text. The second statement follows from the fact that conditions C_1 to C_4 are more restrictive than condition [2.7].

Conclusion 8 (based on Result 3)

If threats have to be credible to deter the violation of the terms of an IEA, cooperation is more difficult to establish.

It is easily checked that all factors which determine the stability of an IEA as discussed in Section 4.1 in the context of a subgame-perfect trigger strategy apply to renegotiation-proof strategies as well.

Compensation measures Those compensation measures which are directly targeted at their aim to balance asymmetric welfare distributions and which involve only small transaction costs should be given preference. However, compensation measures must be self-enforcing. That is, it must be ensured that donors and recipients fulfill their obligations. That this is a difficult task will be described in Section 4.3.

4.2 Emissions

If the abatement duties are chosen cleverly, asymmetric welfare implications can be avoided. Since the allocation of abatement burdens is immediately related to the choice of environmental policy instrument and the bargaining outcome of negotiations, the 'asymmetry issue' is discussed under the heading of 'Instruments in Global Pollution Control' in Chapter 5. In this section, we therefore restrict attention to the role of emissions as a means of enforcing an IEA.

The use of emissions as a means of imposing sanctions on treaty violators implies that the punishers reduce their abatement efforts compared to their treaty obligations for some time. Since for global pollutants, such a strategy also implies higher environmental damages in those countries which conduct the punishment, a renegotiation-proof contract requires that the violator increases his abatement efforts above cooperative levels during the repentance phase as compensation. This finding allows us to draw three conclusions:

1. The trigger strategy outlined in Section 3.2 in the context of an IRG where $e_i^i = e_i^N$ and $e_{-i}^i = e_{-i}^N$ is not renegotiation-proof, since this implies that C_4 is violated, i.e., $\pi_j^* > \pi_j^R = \pi_j^N$.
2. Punishment strategies which call for the suspension of an IEA without the offer to return to normal terms after some time (infinite punishment) are not renegotiation-proof since they violate C_3.
3. Though from a theoretical point of view one cannot rule out the possibility that the simple strategy of *temporarily* suspending an agreement is renegotiation-proof, it is most likely that condition C_4 will be violated for at least some punishers.[38] Renegotiation-proof punishment will tend only to involve a moderate increase in emissions with the aim of returning to initial cooperative levels soon.

In reality, some additional limitations apply to sanctions via emissions which have a negative effect on the stability of an IEA:
1. Punishers actually have less flexibility regarding an increase in their emission releases as a means of sanctioning a violator. Once abatement measures have been implemented, it might not be technically feasible to increase emissions substantially. Particularly, most abatement measures involve some set-up cost which would be 'sunk' if signatories changed

their environmental policy. Also such a change may take time, rendering the threat potential rather low.[39]

In this context, note the following dilemma: On the one hand, the more ambitious emission targets are realized over time, the higher the second type of free-rider incentive becomes. On the other hand, the lower emissions are, the less credible is the threat to increase emissions temporarily as a reaction to a breach of an IEA (Finus 2001, ch. 12).

2. In reality, the treaty violator has less flexibility regarding a reduction in emissions to show repentance. For technical reasons, this may either not be possible or at least it may require some time. Again, there is a dilemma: the more a country has already reduced emissions, the more difficult it is to show repentance (Finus 2001, ch. 12). This dilemma could be solved if a free rider shows repentance by paying a fine instead of reducing additional emissions. However, in this case, secondary punishments must be available to ensure that the fines are actually paid.

3. In practice one should expect that instead of complex and differentiated punishment obligations, simple punishments would be employed (Finus and Rundshagen 1998a). The reason is that differentiation makes coordination of sanctions difficult, involves transaction costs, causes delay and might not be transparent to the parties.

4. Even though international law does not allow the enforcement of an IEA, it may nevertheless be regarded as a 'code of conduct'. According to international law, punishments should be subject to the *principle of proportionality* (Kelsen and Tucker 1967, pp. 20ff). This principle implies that violations can only be punished in proportion to the severity of the misconduct. This imposes a restriction on the flexibility of punishments.

Obviously, the last two restrictions apply to sanctions in general but are mentioned in this section since this allows a compact discussion. All four restrictions imply either that for a given emission target, e^*, the minimum discount factor requirements increase or that the set of equilibrium emission vectors or average payoff vectors for a given set of discount factors shrinks compared to a situation without restrictions. The second implication is illustrated in Figure 2.1. All emissions tuples lying to the right of A_1 and to the left of A_2 are renegotiation-proof in this example. The stronger the above restrictions, the smaller the corridor of feasible and stable emission targets will be (lines A_1 and A_2 move inward). Similarly, the lower the actual discount factors are, the smaller will be this corridor.[40] Of course, the actual nature of this corridor depends on the values of the parameters of the example. However, as a tendency, the following conclusion can be derived.[41] The lower the actual discount factors and the more severe punishment restrictions are, the lower and the more symmetric must emissions reductions be so that they can be enforced in an IEA.

Conclusion 9 (based on discussion)
Emissions are not a very flexible tool as sanctions for free riders and therefore have only limited suitability to be used as a strategic variable to enforce an IEA. If emissions are the only instrument to discipline free riders, only modest and relatively symmetric emissions reductions can be stabilized in an IEA.

Despite the qualifications mentioned above, emissions may play some role for disciplining free riders and have two distinctive advantages: First, increasing emissions is in accordance with the principle of reciprocity. Each government will recognize that if it does not meet its reduction duties, other governments have the right to follow suit. Moreover, this kind of punishment does not jeopardize cooperation in other policy fields as may be the case under issue linkage (see Section 4.4). Second, emissions can be used as sanctions for donor countries, which is not possible via monetary and in-kind transfers (see Section 4.3). On the one hand, recipient countries may punish donors (e.g. if they do not pay their promised transfers) and donors may punish each other (e.g. if they do not fulfill their obligations of contributing to a fund) using emissions. However, we have to be aware that punishment of countries with low environmental preferences is not very effective. These countries suffer less from an increase of emissions and are therefore less vulnerable to this kind of punishment. Thus, emissions tend not to be very useful in disciplining developing countries or countries in transition, which usually have lower environmental preferences than industrialized countries. These countries are better disciplined via transfers, as shown in Section 4.3.

Finally, we discuss briefly the idea of renegotiation-proof treaties in the context of RSGs, though we have to be aware that the concept has been defined for repeated games. In RSGs which apply the concept of internal and external stability, it is very likely that the reoptimization strategy is not renegotiation-proof. If it was beneficial to the signatories to include the violator in the treaty in the first place (though this is not a requirement of the concept!), exclusion $(N^* - 1)$ and reoptimization (e^{**}) after free riding would imply a welfare loss, i.e., $\pi_j^*(N^*, e^*) > \pi_j^*(N^* - 1, e^{**})$. Hence renegotiation-proof condition C_4 would be violated. In RSGs which apply the concept of the core, sanctions are never renegotiation-proof. For instance, under the γ-core concept a single deviation triggers the resolution of the grand coalition so that each country receives the Nash equilibrium payoff during punishment. By the definition of the γ-core, however, each country receives more in equilibrium than its Nash equilibrium payoff and therefore condition C_4 would be violated.

4.3   Transfers

Facts

Transfers have played a minor role in international environmental policy in the past. Only a few 'modern' IEAs have a provision for transfers, for instance the Montreal Protocol on the depletion of the ozone layer (DeSombre and Kauffman 1996, pp. 89ff), the Convention on Biological Diversity (Beyerlin 1996, p. 617) or the Kyoto Protocol. The most important fund is the Global Environmental Facility (GEF), which manages transfers under the three IEAs mentioned above. Industrialized countries are supposed to contribute to this fund. Developing countries may receive transfers, which usually cover only the incremental costs of environmental projects. Incremental costs are those costs which occur in excess of abatement activities in the status quo. Most of the transfers are paid as in-kind transfers (Jordan and Werksman 1996, pp. 247ff and Kummer 1994, p. 260). The subsequent discussion explains this phenomenon with incentive problems of the second type between donor and recipient countries and within the group of donor countries.

Measures to avoid asymmetric payoffs

The classical role of transfers is to balance asymmetric payoffs. Transfers may help to meet the individual rationality constraint and to increase the stability of an IEA by compensating 'critical' countries. Monetary transfers are an efficient instrument since they target the problem directly. Transfers can either be used directly between donors and recipients or they can be channeled via a fund. One main obstacle of transfers is the incentive problem between donor(s) and recipient(s). If the donor pays the transfers, the recipient may take the money but may not deliver the promised emission reduction. If the recipient implements an environmental project, the donor may not pay its promised transfers. Thus, in a static setting, both parties involved in transfers face a free-rider incentive of the second type. In the following, we investigate the effects of transfers in an IRG. Without loss of generality, we may assume a simultaneous move of donors and recipients.[42]

Consider first the effect of transfers on a recipient country i. Let the transfer a recipient receives be T_i, the contribution of a donor country to transfers T_i be T_j, the set of recipients be $i, k \in I^R$, $i \neq k$ and the set of donors be $j, l \in I^D$, $j \neq l$. Note that if a recipient takes a free ride, a best-reply deviation involves deviating with respect to transfers *and* emissions. Including transfers in renegotiation-proof conditions [2.8] and [2.9], we have:

$$(1 - \delta_i^{t_i^P})\pi_i^R + \delta_i^{t_i^P}(\pi_i^* + T_i) \geq \pi_i^{P_1} \iff \delta_i^{t_i^P} \geq \frac{\pi_i^{P_1} - \pi_i^R}{\pi_i^* - \pi_i^R + T_i} \qquad [2.11]$$

$$(1 - \delta_i)(\pi_i^F + T_i) + \delta_i \pi_i^{P_1} < \pi_i^* + T_i \iff \delta_i \geq \frac{\pi_i^F - \pi_i^*}{\pi_i^F - \pi_i^{P_1} + T_i} \qquad [2.12]$$

from which

a) $\qquad \delta_i \geq \delta_i^{\min} = \min\left[\max\left(\frac{\pi_i^{P_1} - \pi_i^R}{\pi_i^* - \pi_i^R + T_i}, \frac{\pi_i^F - \pi_i^*}{\pi_i^F - \pi_i^{P_1} + T_i}\right)\right]$ s.t.

b) $\qquad \pi_j^* - T_j \leq \pi_j^R$ and

c) $\qquad \pi_k^* + T_k \leq \pi_k^R \qquad\qquad\qquad\qquad\qquad\qquad\qquad\qquad [2.13]$

follows where j is a donor and k a recipient among the punishers. A comparison of [2.10] and [2.13] reveals that the minimum discount factor requirement for a recipient decreases through transfers ([2.13a]). In the case of free riding, the temporary suspension of transfer payments allows for a harsher punishment than if emissions are the only sanction available for free riding. The treaty violator can be provided with an incentive to go along with the punishment and to remain in the treaty by gradually increasing transfers to old levels during the punishment phase. The suspension of transfers also means that it is easier for donors (countries j) to punish a free rider in a way which is renegotiation-proof ([2.13b]). The suspension implies automatically that donors are compensated. Since it is now more difficult for other recipient countries (countries k which comply) to punish a free rider ([2.13c]), some of the transfers which have previously been paid to the free rider i should now be earmarked for these countries during the punishment phase of t_i^P periods.

What about the effect of transfers on the side of the donors? Proceeding in the same way as above, we derive

a) $$\delta_j \geq \delta_j^{\min} = \min\left[\max\left(\frac{\pi_j^{P_1} - \pi_j^R + T_j}{\pi_j^* - \pi_j^R}, \frac{\pi_j^F - \pi_j^* + T_j}{\pi_j^F - \pi_j^{P_1}}\right)\right] \quad \text{s.t.}$$

b) $$\pi_l^* \leq \pi_l^R \quad \text{and}$$

c) $$\pi_k^* \leq \pi_k^R \qquad\qquad\qquad\qquad\qquad\qquad [2.14]$$

where l is a donor and k a recipient among the punishers. A comparison of [2.10] and [2.14] reveals that the minimum discount factor requirement of donors (countries j) increases through transfers ([2.14a]). The conditions for the punishers do not change ([2.14b, c]). Consequently from [2.13] and [2.14] it follows that transfers can only stabilize an agreement if the actual discount factors of donor countries, δ_j, are well above the minimum discount factor $\delta_j^{\min}$, i.e. $\delta_j \gg \delta_j^{\min}$. In other words, monetary transfers are only sensible if there is a slack of enforcement power on the side of the donors, which is transferred to recipients which face a lack of enforcement power via compensation payments.

In-kind transfers are less efficient than monetary transfers since they only indirectly target balancing asymmetries. In-kind transfers comprise for instance, technological assistance of recipients through donors and the installation of scrubbers and of environmental friendly power plants in recipient countries through donors.[43] Since the donors usually possess less information than recipients about the most productive investment in abatement technology, in-kind transfers may entail efficiency losses. Therefore, it might be helpful to have a central authority, as for instance the Global Environmental Facility (GEF), which coordinates transfers. Experts in the GEF may decide together with local authorities in developing countries, which projects are expected to generate the highest input–output ratio. Moreover, coordination has the advantage that donors do not compete for the same recipients.

The advantage of in-kind transfers is that the second type of free-rider incentive on the side of the donors and on the side of the recipients is less of a problem. This may explain why most transfers have been paid in the form of in-kind transfers under the GEF. On the one hand, environmental projects, such as the construction of environmental power plants in developing countries by industrialized countries, cannot usually be used for other purposes. Thus, enforcement on the side of the recipients is *de facto* automatically ensured. Moreover, the GEF constitutes *de facto* a cartel of donor countries which are equipped with additional enforcement power, which eases monitoring of the implementation of projects. On the other hand, recipient countries can wait until the project has been finalized before they have to fulfill their part of the deal. For instance, a power plant can only start operation after the plant has been built. Of course, in-kind transfers are also only sensible if enforcement power on the side of the donors is slack, and recipients lack enforcement power.

Measures to enforce compliance
From the discussion above, it follows immediately that monetary transfers are only suitable as sanctions on recipient countries. Sanctions take the form of partial or complete suspension of transfers for some time. Though transfers are a flexible and efficient instrument to punish recipients in a renegotiation-proof way they are not suited to disciplining donor countries. On the contrary, transfers increase the free-rider incentive of donors. Apart from not complying with the agreed abatement duties, a donor country has an incentive to delay or not pay the promised transfers at all. Therefore, for donors, other forms of sanctions are necessary. However, transfers may be used as an auxiliary device. As mentioned above, since one of the main obstacles in the international context is to construct sanctions which do not harm the punishers as well (renegotiation-proof condition C_4), a global fund may be used as a 'fund for sanctions'. Similarly to union funds, which are used to back up strikes by reducing the negative effect of strikes on their members (suspension of payment, lay-off of workers and so forth), an environmental fund may mitigate the negative effects of sanctions for the punishers. Thereby, the credibility of sanctions can be improved.

In-kind transfers are less suited as a punishment for recipients. Since these investments cannot be withdrawn in the short-to mid-term, they do not constitute a flexible instrument for sanctions. For the same reason as monetary transfers, in-kind transfer cannot be used to discipline donors.

Treaty obligations

Despite the qualifications on the use of transfers mentioned in the previous paragraphs, we have to be aware that both kinds of transfer constitute an additional tool in an IEA to balance asymmetric payoffs and to enforce an IEA. Therefore, transfers can only improve the chances of cooperation or leave them unchanged. The main obstacle to the use of transfers derives from the fact that though donors may benefit from transfers, they are better off by taking a free ride.[44] The importance of this problem is evident when recalling the large backlog of payments of major contributors to the United Nations. The payment behavior of donors can only be influenced if sanctions are available to enforce payments beyond those already necessary to enforce abatement duties. Since no IEA has a provision to discipline the donor countries and since it is already difficult to enforce abatement duties, it is not surprising that transfers have not yet played an important role in international environmental protection. Of course, a global fund may temporarily alleviate this problem by ensuring regular payments to recipient countries. However, if the fund runs out of money, it has to suspend transfers in the long run.

Conclusion 10 (based on discussion and demonstration)

Monetary transfers are an efficient and flexible instrument to balance asymmetries and to stabilize an agreement if enforcement power on the side of the donors is slack and there is a lack of enforcement power on the side of recipient countries. However, donors cannot be disciplined via monetary transfers. In-kind transfers are less efficient than monetary transfers but suffer less from the incentive problem between donors and recipients. They are therefore better suited to balancing asymmetries. However, in-kind transfers cannot be used to enforce an IEA. Generally, monetary and in-kind transfers face the problem that they have to be stabilized within the coalition of donors.

We would like to finish this section with three remarks. First, we have demonstrated the effect of transfers assuming a given number of signatories and a given cooperative emission vector. However, it should be evident that transfers may also be used to increase participation in an agreement by providing non-signatories with an incentive to accede to an IEA. Moreover, transfers may also be used to enforce more ambitious abatement targets. Technically, this could be demonstrated by setting up a similar inequality system as above and solving it for the respective variable. However, in both cases, it would turn out that the basic problems of transfers mentioned above also apply. Second, the lack of transfers in historical IEAs has been explained with the free-rider incentive of the second type. Therefore, it is evident that this phenomenon could only partially be explained using an RSG.

Third, in the literature (e.g. Hoel 1992 and Mäler 1990) three more problems of transfers have been mentioned, though their theoretical foundations are rather weak and the arguments are tainted with an *ad hoc* flavor.[45] Nevertheless, we would like to mention them for completeness, being aware that these arguments have been the only explanations so far to rationalize the lack of transfer payments in international pollution control.

1. Transfers provide an incentive for governments to misrepresent strategically their preferences. Donors and recipients have an incentive to understate their environmental preferences and overstate their abatement costs. Donors try to convince other signatories that they should contribute only a small amount to an environmental fund if at all. Recipients try to convince other countries that they should be generously compensated if they are required to contribute to a joint abatement policy at all.
2. Any transfer scheme must be based on some criteria which requires that the welfare implications of an abatement policy are estimated and publicly disclosed. Such a transparency, however, may not be in the interest of all governments since it limits their strategic behavior in the future.
3. Governments may be skeptical of paying transfers since they fear that they may be judged as weak bargaining partners, which may weaken their bargaining power with respect to other issues in the future.

4.4 Issue Linkage

Issue linkage refers to the fact that, usually, relations between governments concern not only one policy issue but several issues. Governments may cooperate in the field of international pollution control, international defense and disarmament (e.g. being a member of NATO), in the field of free trade (e.g. being a member of GATT/WTO, the European Union or ASEAN) and in the field of global pollution control (e.g. being members of the CITES agreement or the Montreal Protocol). In the literature on infinitely repeated games, it has been suggested that issue linkage may help to balance asymmetries and to enforce an agreement. We proceed in three steps. First, we summarize the main findings. Second, we characterize open issues and critically review the results. Third, we mention practical problems of issue linkage. For illustrative purposes we restrict the number of issues to two.

Results

Typically, it is assumed that two public good agreements are linked to each other where the incentive structure in each game is that of a prisoners' dilemma (Cesar and de Zeeuw 1996, Folmer, van Mouche and Ragland 1993, Ragland, Bennett and Yolles 1996). The prisoners' dilemma is a simple matrix game with only two–stage game strategies (cooperation and no cooperation) frequently used to illustrate the problems of cooperation in international pollution control (see, e.g. Finus 2001, ch. 3). The incentive structure is that outlined in Section 2: there is a global welfare gain from cooperation but each country faces a free-rider incentive of the second type. Examples of issue linkage cited in the literature include the 1944 International Boundary Waters Treaty between the USA and Mexico (Kneese 1988 and Ragland, Bennett and Yolles 1996) or the Columbia River Treaty of 1961 between the USA and Canada (Kneese 1975). The basic idea of issue linkage in a repeated game framework is that if an agreement 1 leads to an asymmetric welfare distribution so that either the individual rationality constraint or the minimum discount factor requirement is not met for some countries, it may be linked to an agreement 2. This strategy works if agreement 2 also exhibits an asymmetry which is more-or-less the reverse of that in agreement 1. To see this immediately, we restrict attention here to the simple trigger strategy encountered in Section 3.2 (and as assumed in most papers on issue linkage; see, e.g. Folmer and van Mouche 1994 and 2000b) and the treatment of renegotiation-proof strategies in Appendix 2.[46] Whereas in the two isolated games

$$\pi_{ik}^*(s_k^*) - (1 - \delta_i)\pi_{ik}^F(s_{ik}^F, s_{-ik}^*) - \delta_i \pi_{ik}^N(s_k^N) \geq 0 \ \forall \ i \text{ and } k \in \{1, 2\} \quad [2.15]$$

must hold to sustain cooperation on both issues,

$$\sum_{k=1}^{2} \pi_{ik}^*(s_1^*, s_2^*) - (1 - \delta_i)\sum_{k=1}^{2} \pi_{ik}^F(s_{i1}^F, s_{i2}^F, s_{-i1}^*, s_{-i2}^*) - \delta_i \sum_{k=1}^{2} \pi_{ik}^N(s_1^N, s_2^N) \geq 0 \ \forall \ i$$

$$[2.16]$$

must hold in the interconnected game (also called hyper- meta- or tensor-game) where k refers to the game (issue), i to the country and s_{ik} to the stage game strategy of country i with respect to issue k. It is easy to see that [2.16] is implied by [2.15] and hence condition [2.16] is less restrictive than [2.15]. That is, strategies and payoffs which could not be sustained in the isolated game(s) may be sustained in the linked game. To allow for a direct comparison with our previous discussion, the above relations may also be expressed in terms of minimum discount factors. We have

$$\delta_i \geq \max\left[\delta_{i1}^{\min}, \delta_{i2}^{\min}\right] \geq \left[\delta_{i1+2}^{\min}\right] \ \forall \ i \tag{2.17}$$

where the term after the first inequality sign states the minimum discount factor requirements in the isolated games and the term after the second inequality sign that of the tensor game.

From [2.15], [2.16] and [2.17] it evident that it is not important whether the isolated games are prisoners' dilemmas. The result is more general and basically applies to any game (e.g. a global emission game) where there is a free-rider incentive of the second type and where cooperation generates a global welfare gain (non-constant sum games). Such a game may be called a social dilemma game.

Result 4[47]
In an infinitely repeated social dilemma game with additive payoffs, issue linkage either improves the chance that mutual cooperation can be sustained or leaves it unchanged.

From Result 4 and its derivation, the similarity between issue linkage and transfers is apparent. However, instead of exchanging money or technology, issues are exchanged. Consequently, like transfers, issue linkage may be used to balance slack enforcement and lack of enforcement power. However, whereas transfers are used to balance enforcement power between countries, issue linkage aims at balancing enforcement power between issues (Finus 1997 and 2001, ch. 8 and Spagnolo 1996).

Variations and extensions of Result 4 may be found in Folmer and van Mouche (1994) and van Mouche (2000). One interesting variation is the following: instead of studying the effect of issue linkage on the minimum discount factor requirements for a given s_1^*, s_2^*, one can also investigate the effect on average payoffs for a given set of discount factors. Not surprisingly, we find $\overline{\Pi}_1^{*,\delta} + \overline{\Pi}_2^{*,\delta} \subseteq \overline{\Pi}_{1+2}^{*,\delta}$. That is, the set of average equilibrium payoffs in the linked game is at least as large as in the isolated games. Some payoff vectors may only be sustainable in the linked game, but not if each game is played in isolation. In other words, global welfare may be increased through issue linkage.

An implicit assumption in deriving Result 4 was that utility functions of governments are separable. That is, though governments link and negotiate two issues together, they value the payoffs of each game independently. This is the standard assumption in the literature on issue linkage.[48] However, a more natural assumption seems to be that governments' evaluation of an issue depends also on other issues. In this case, the effect of issue linkage is less straightforward and relies on the shape of governments' objective functions. Results in Finus (2001), ch. 8 and Spagnolo (1996) indicate that issue linking is conducive to cooperation only if issues are substitutes in governments' objective function; this is not the case, however, if they are complements. This result has been established if two prisoners' dilemmas are linked to each other. The results of Spagnolo (1999 and forthcoming) in another economic context indicate that a more general proof for social dilemmas with continuous strategies is possible.

The issue of non-separable objectives has an interesting political implication. It suggests that if issues are complementary, governments should delegate decision power on one or both issues to separate independent agencies. In contrast, if issues are substitutes, decision power should remain with governments.

In the environmental context, one should expect for instance that all pollutants (e.g. SO_2 and NO_x) which are covered under the term long-range transboundary air pollutants (LRTAP) are complements in governments' objective function. A reduction strategy which aims at only one pollutant will not be successful in reducing the acidification of soil (Ierland and Schmieman 1999, Schieman and Ierland 1999). Accordingly, though a joint effort to reduce all LRTAP pollutants is necessary, negotiations should be conducted by independent national agencies. Therefore, in retrospect, one should expect that it was conducive to cooperation that LRTAP pollutants were dealt with in different protocols,[49] which may be regarded as a first step in separating issues. In contrast, within the Kyoto Protocol, not only CO_2 but also five other gases which contribute to global warming are regulated.[50] Though it is certainly true that such a regulation limits the possibility that countries reduce CO_2 at the expense of expanding other greenhouse gases, according to theory, it would have been better to set up different agreements for those other pollutants.

Evaluation

In Result 4 we have used the weak inequality sign (and in the variation of this result the '$\subseteq$' sign). Currently, it is not clear for which games and under which conditions the strong inequality sign (the '$\subset$' sign) holds (see Folmer and van Mouche 2000b and van Mouche 2000). Moreover, most papers on issue linkage demonstrate their results for simple matrix games, e.g. prisoners' dilemmas. Though we have demonstrated Result 4 for a broader class of games, which we called social dilemma games, a full characterization of such games awaits treatment in future research. The basic question is: What kind of asymmetry is needed so that issue linkage strictly improves upon the chances for cooperation?

Most papers on issue linkage motivate their research by pointing out that issue linkage is one possibility for balancing asymmetries instead of using transfers, which historically have hardly been used in international pollution control. Though this empirical observation is certainly true, it seems to us that theory does not provide an explanation of why countries may prefer issue linkage to transfers. It would certainly be wrong to claim that it is easier to sustain an agreement 1 because in case of free riding, agreement 2 may be used as an additional punishment. Of course, in the setting above, we assumed that punishment involves the suspension of both agreements. However, we also assumed that there is a free-rider incentive in both agreements. It also seems obvious that if issue linkage takes place in a larger group of countries, that each country is *de facto* a net donor with respect to one issue. Therefore, there is the same kind of free-rider incentive within the group of countries which offer compensation with respect to the same issue, as has been discussed in the context of transfers under the heading of 'Treaty Obligations'. For this group as a whole, it is rational to offer compensation; for a single country, however, it is rational to hold back its offer. It seems that the driving force of Result 4 is simply the fact that through issue linkage, the number of strategies increases. For instance, in a prisoners' dilemma game, each country has two strategies, implying in the two country case, four strategy combinations in each stage game. In contrast, in the linked game there are not $2 \cdot 4$ but 16 strategy combinations. However, this is the same reason why transfers may be useful in establishing cooperation. More policy options simply imply more options to establish cooperation. Either a policy option has a positive effect, is neutral or has a negative effect. In the last case, however, it is just not used if players are rational.

In the case of non-separable issues, it remains for future research to generalize the results and to clarify the following points: (1) Which issues are substitutes and which are complements in governments' objective function? (2) If issues are complementary, what role do national and international agencies play in delegating decision power? (3) How should such agencies be designed to ease cooperation? Though there are preliminary answers to the second and third questions, it will be of importance to provide practical guidelines for implementation and relate recommendations to existing international agencies.[51]

Practical problems

In the context of multilateral agreements, issue linkage faces a bundle of problems which have not been captured by the theoretical models yet. First, issue linkage is less efficient than monetary transfers since it only indirectly targets balancing asymmetries. This inefficiency may eat up some of the gains from cooperation. Second, in a multilateral context it will be difficult to design compensation deals. For many countries, it is very likely that several issues are needed to balance asymmetric payoffs. This renders negotiations rather complex. It should be expected that the transaction costs of issue linkage increase more than proportionally with the number of signatories to an IEA. Therefore, it is not surprising that most reported examples of issue linkage concern bilateral agreements.[52] Third, punishing a free rider using other issues may violate the principle of proportional punishment and therefore may be of limited use in reality. Fourth, negotiations leading to an IEA generally run over a long period of time and therefore involve high 'negotiation costs'. Therefore, it should be expected that governments are cautious about using some issues for punishment since they fear that cooperation may be jeopardized on other issues. Fifth, designing punishment renegotiation-proof is already complex with respect to one issue but will be even more complicated with respect to several issues (though Appendix 2 shows that from a theoretical point of view this is possible). Thus only simple punishments such as the temporary suspension of several agreements have a chance of being imposed in reality. However, because of the voluntary signature of a package deal it is expected that all signatories will benefit from the deal. Therefore, this kind of punishment may imply a welfare loss for at least some punishers, violating renegotiation-proof condition C_4.

Conclusion 11 (based on Result 4 and discussion)

From a theoretical point of view, linking several issues with each other can help to avoid asymmetric welfare implications and may help to enforce an IEA. Most results are not very general and have been established for specific assumptions. From a practical point of view, issue linkage is of only limited suitability for multilateral agreements comprising many countries.

Despite the practical qualifications raised above, issue linkage may be used as an auxiliary device to balance asymmetric payoffs if other instruments are not available for some reason. For instance, bilateral transactions under Joint Implementation (JI) and the Clean Development Mechanism (CDM) within the Kyoto Protocol may be conducted via issue linkage if governments prefer this to monetary transactions.

4.5 Monitoring

Stability

The quality of the monitoring system is crucial for the stability of an IEA (see Section 3.1). The higher the detection rate in the case of non-compliance, k, $0 \leq k \leq 1$, the higher will be the stability of an international environmental agreement. That is, the lower the minimum discount factor requirement will be. Similarly, the smaller the intervals, f, $f = \{1, ..., t\}$, in which monitoring checks are conducted, the lower the minimum discount factor requirement will be. Considering f and k in the inequality system C_1 to C_4 of a renegotiation-proof IEA gives (see Appendix 3)

$$\delta_i \geq \delta_i^{\min} = \min \left[\max \left(\frac{\pi_i^{P_1} - \pi_i^R}{\pi_i^* - \pi_i^R}, \frac{\pi_i^F - \pi_i^*}{\pi_i^F - \pi_i^{P_1} - (1-k)(\pi_i^* - \pi_i^{P_1})} \right)^{1/f} \right] \text{ s.t. } \pi_j^* \leq \pi_j^R$$

$$\forall j \neq i. \quad [2.18]$$

from which it is easy to see that $\delta_i^{\min}$ decreases in k and increases in f. A low detection rate implies that free riding may not be discovered and consequently may also not be punished. A low frequency of monitoring checks (high values of f) implies that free riding is discovered with a relatively large time-lag. Consequently, the violator can net a free rider gain for a longer period of time and punishment is delayed.

In reality, there are several reasons why k will be smaller than 1 and why f may be bigger than 1. First, though scientists may identify the total amount of pollutants released into the atmosphere, it might be difficult for technical reasons to assign these emissions to single countries. There may remain some uncertainty about the exact amount of emissions each country releases. The problem is aggravated by the fact that non-compliance can only be punished if the breach can unambiguously be attributed to a party. Second, monitoring of most IEAs relies on self-reporting by countries, which is usually rather patchy (GAO 1992, pp. 3ff, Sand 1996, p. 55 and Bothe 1996, pp. 22ff). In particular, developing countries and Eastern European countries often submit incomplete monitoring reports. Obviously, there is a general incentive problem to provide an IEA secretariat with 'true' information. An obvious countermeasure would be to establish an independent monitoring institution. However, it has to be expected that governments will be reluctant to accept such external monitoring since they fear that this interferes with their sovereignty. Third, even if almost complete and frequent monitoring were technically feasible, monitoring costs would probably exceed the gains from cooperation. Therefore, a monitoring system has to rely on unannounced occasional spot checks, reflecting a compromise between a high detection rate, frequent monitoring and low monitoring costs.

Treaty obligations

Most IEAs contain a provision for national monitoring.[53] Even though international and independent monitoring would be preferable, national monitoring is a first step in the right direction. In particular, the more national monitoring systems are linked to each other and the more effort is spent on formulating clear and transparent guidelines on how to prepare a monitoring report, the higher the quality of monitoring will be. However, the incentive structure of monitoring is that of a social dilemma. That is, from a global point of view, fostering the quality of the monitoring system increases the effectiveness of an IEA. From an individual perspective, however, each country faces a free-rider incentive, since monitoring is costly. In fact, ignoring other treaty obligations and considering monitoring only by itself, it seems most likely that the individual rationality constraint is violated. Every country has an interest in ensuring that other countries are monitored. However, monitoring of its own performance is only associated with negative effects. At best a country can only prove that it should not be punished because it has complied with the terms of the agreement. This may explain why it is so difficult to establish a well-functioning national monitoring system, let alone an internationally independent one.

Conclusion 12 (based on demonstration and discussion)
The quality of the monitoring system is important for the stability of an agreement. An independent monitoring authority, frequent checks and a high detection rate are conducive to cooperation but are costly and difficult to establish. The establishment of a well-functioning monitoring system is difficult since monitoring constitutes a social dilemma type of problem where the individual rationality constraint is most likely to be violated.

4.6   Discount Factors

Points 5 and 6 in Section 3.3, as well as the previous discussion, made it clear that the stability of an agreement crucially depends on the actual discount factors by which governments discount the stream of net benefits accruing from an IEA. Though in game theory the discount factor is treated as a parameter, from a policy point of view it is interesting to review briefly the factors influencing this parameter. As pointed out in point 5, Section 3.3, the stability of an IEA may be jeopardized if politicians are interested in short-term success (high value of the discount rate r_i). Therefore, one could think of transferring national enforcement from the government to the bureaucracy which, by nature, is less dependent on election cycles. A further measure could be to transform the (international) obligations of an IEA into national law.[54] Since interference by the judiciary involves high political costs in most democracies, opportunistic behavior of governments could be limited by such a measure.

Moreover, it is usually assumed that there is an inverse relationship between the wealth of nations and the discount rate. Following this assumption, fostering economic development in developing countries would lead these governments to discount time less and the prospects for cooperation would be brighter. Since, however, development projects are associated with high costs, one should expect that there would be more efficient measures to influence the discount rate.

According to point 6, Section 3.3, discounting also depends on the evaluation of political stability in neighboring countries and the estimation of politicians about future events. Consequently, transfers from industrialized countries to developing countries and countries in transition to a market economy could have a positive influence on the discounting of industrialized countries. However, as pointed out above, the question arises as to the efficiency of such a measure. In contrast, investment in research about the effect of global warming and the expected abatement costs may be a more efficient measure.[55] This may reduce the uncertainty of future events and thereby increase the discount factor by which governments discount time. However, research is costly and governments may hope that they can free-ride on other countries' research efforts. Thus, research is also plagued by a social dilemma type of problem. Less costly and simpler measures may be regular meetings of the signatories of an IEA and the exchange of information. These measures may help to build up confidence without facing a social dilemma type of problem.

Conclusion 13 (based on discussion)
Most measures to influence the actual discount factors by which governments discount the net benefits accruing from an IEA are costly and inefficient. Promising measures are regular meetings of politicians of different member states (to build up mutual confidence), the incorporation of international treaty obligations into national law and the delegation of enforcement responsibility to national environmental agencies which are less dependent on short-term success than politicians.

5.   INSTRUMENTS IN GLOBAL POLLUTION CONTROL

5.1   Introduction

Up to now, we have not looked at how countries agree on abatement targets and how this might be translated into policy. In this section, we suggest a possible bargaining process which reflects our discussion about consensus in Sections 2.2 and 2.3 and investigate how the choice of the policy instrument affects the individual rationality and stability of an IEA. As in Section 4, we assume that all countries participate in an agreement, and postpone the discussion about the relation between instrumental choice and membership until Section 6 on coalition formation. We shall keep the subsequent discussion at a general level and therefore it will suffice to recall that we identify individual rationality in an IRG with a payoff vector where each country receives more than in the Nash equilibrium of the stage game.

Historically, market-based instruments have played a minor role in international pollution control. Neither emissions charges nor emission permits are part of an IEA. In this respect the Kyoto Protocol is an exception and has to be judged as a major benchmark in international pollution control. In Article 17 it allows for the trade in emission quotas among Annex 1 countries. However, we have to be aware that the protocol is not in force yet and it is currently not at all clear whether this will eventually happen.

In contrast, command and control instruments have played a dominant role in environmental protection. Frequently, a uniform emission reduction quota is assigned to each signatory.[56] This is equal to the proportional emission reduction we discussed in Section 2.1. It requires each signatory to reduce emissions by the same percentage from some base year. Economists have criticized quotas as being inefficient and recommended permits or taxes instead. The following subsections will help explaining why economists' recommendations have not fallen on fertile soil. In the following, we distinguish between the general properties of an instrument and the properties of the bargaining process and equilibrium.

5.2   General Properties

Emission reduction quotas
As pointed out in Section 2.1, a uniform emission reduction quota is generally inefficient as long as quotas cannot be traded. However, it leads to a relatively symmetric distribution of welfare. For emission reductions which are not 'too large', individual rationality is satisfied. Since the quota is directly related to initial emissions in the status quo, the interests of all countries are more-or-less considered under a quota regime. Though countries contribute differently to a joint environmental policy, in relative terms they all contribute the same. We may recall that in Figure 2.1, Q represents the abatement path under a quota regime and that as long as r is not 'too' large (i.e. $(e_1^N + e_2^N)(1-r) \leq e_1^C + e_2^C$ in Figure 2.1) individual rationality is ensured. We denote this instrument fixed uniform quota in the following.

Emission charges
In the context of global pollutants, only a uniform emission tax is efficient. A country's industry performs max $\beta_i(e_i) - t \cdot e_i$, from which $\beta_i'(e_i) = t$ follows in equilibrium and therefore the efficiency condition $\beta_1'(e_1) = ... = \beta_N'(e_N)$ (see Section 2.1) is ensured in the tax equilibrium. The tax receipt may be used in different ways. For instance, an international tax implies that a supranational body imposes the tax and receives the receipts. However, this option will

hardly be realized since it is very unlikely that governments will hand over their tax sovereignty to an international body. A national tax may imply that the receipts are either passed on to an international institution or remain in the country of origin. The first possibility involves large transfer payments even though parts of the tax may eventually be redistributed. Due to the incentive problems of transfers mentioned in Section 4.3, the first option will have only a small chance of being realized. Therefore, we concentrate in the following on a national tax where the receipts remain in each country. This national tax leads to the efficient emission reduction mentioned in Section 2.1, which is represented by line T in Figure 2.1. Therefore, we may recall that in contrast to the quota, the welfare implications of a tax may be very uneven and may violate the individual rationality of some countries.

Emission permits
Permits may either be freely allocated or auctioned. Since auctioning implies large transfer payments to an international body, this option will be discarded in the following for the same reasons mentioned under emission charges. A free allocation can be conducted in many ways. Those allocation rules only differ with respect to their distributional effects, but lead to the same efficient allocation of emissions after trade has taken place. If permits are distributed to firms, a representative industry in country i performs $\max \beta_i(e_i) - p(e_i - \overline{e}_i)$, which implies $\beta_i'(e_i) = p$ in equilibrium, where p is the permit price and $\overline{e}_i$ is the amount of emissions implied by the permits allocated to industry i. (Thus, $\Sigma\overline{e}_j$ is the global emission target and $p(e_i - \overline{e}_i)$ is the outlay for the purchase of permits if $e_i > \overline{e}_i$ or the receipt from the sale of permits if $e_i < \overline{e}_i$.) Thus in equilibrium, $\beta_1'(e_1) = ... = \beta_N'(e_N) = p$ holds, which is the condition for efficiency (see Section 2.1). Alternatively, if permits are distributed to countries, a government performs $\max \beta_i(e_i) - \phi_i(\Sigma\overline{e}_j) - p(e_i - \overline{e}_i)$, which also leads to $\beta_i'(e_i) = p$ (since $\partial\phi_i(\Sigma\overline{e}_j)/\partial e_i = 0$ provided there is perfect competition!)

Theoretically, it is always possible to construct an allocation rule such that individual rationality is met for all participants. However, in reality things are less straightforward. First, in order to compute the direction of trade and the welfare implications, information on abatement costs and damage cost functions is needed. Though information on benefits may be available, damage cost estimates are difficult to come by. For strategic reasons, governments may 'hide' this information. Second, since there is not just one allocation rule which meets the individual rationality constraint, governments will have different opinions about the 'most adequate' allocation rule. For instance, industrialized countries will favor an allocation rule based on historical emission levels or GDP, while developing countries will prefer an allocation rule based on per capita.

An allocation rule which meets the individual rationality constraint for not 'too' high emission reductions and which implies a relatively symmetric welfare distribution, is implied by tradable uniform emission reduction quota, which we abbreviate to tradable uniform quota in the following (Endres and Finus 1999).[57] Each country receives permits in proportion to emissions in the status quo, devalued by the same uniform percentage (grandfathering). This allocation has two advantages. First, it does not require information about benefits and damage costs since the above-mentioned result is known. Second, even if trade does not take place and the tradable quota is *de facto* a fixed quota, individual rationality is met for not 'too' large emission reductions. This may explain why the main global players under the Kyoto Protocol have settled approximately for such an agreement (see Chapter 7).

In contrast to a fixed quota regime, there is an incentive problem under a tradable quota regime.

If a country buys permits, then it cannot be sure whether the seller reduces its emissions accordingly. By the same token, if a seller reduces its emission, it cannot be sure whether the potential buyer will transfer the money. Hence, permits face a similar incentive problem to monetary transfers. However, a permit transaction with a particular country does not happen repeatedly. Hence, the free-rider incentive cannot be neutralized that easily on the side of the recipient (seller of permits), as was possible for monetary transfer in an IRG framework. Consequently, setting up a permit system will be difficult in the global context.

5.3   Properties of the Bargaining Process and Equilibria

In this section we investigate the bargaining process if governments either negotiate on the level of a fixed uniform emission quota, a tradable uniform emission quota or a uniform tax where the tax receipts remain in each country as defined in Section 5.2. Since according to Conclusion 3, an agreement must be based on consensus, one plausible assumption is that countries put forward proposals during negotiations and finally settle for the smallest common denominator (SCD-decision rule; Endres 1993 and 1995). That is, governments agree on that proposal which implies the smallest emission reduction.

Information requirement

In order to make a proposal under a fixed uniform quota regime, it is sufficient if each country observes emissions in the status quo and of course knows its own net benefit function as given in [2.1]. Information about the benefit and damage cost functions of the other negotiators and potential participants is not necessary.[58] In contrast, under the permit and tax regime, governments have to know the benefit functions of the other participants to put forward a proposal. Under the tax regime this is necessary to estimate how the other countries adjust to a uniform tax. Under the permit regime this is necessary to compute the direction of permit trade and its welfare implications.[59] Thus, the information requirement under the fixed uniform quota is lower than under the two other regimes (Endres 1995).

Strategic behavior

Though the SCD-decision rule generally implies that global welfare in the bargaining outcome under all three regimes falls short of global optimality, it has the advantage that countries have no incentive to put forward biased proposals. Considering that strategic behavior would delay an agreement or render it impossible, the SCD-decision seems less inefficient on second thought.

Result 5

Let the payoff function of countries be a strictly convex function with respect to the policy levels under the fixed and tradable uniform quota and uniform tax regime, then countries have no incentive to put forward biased proposals under SCD-decision rule.

Proof: See Endres and Finus (1998b and 1999).

Result 5 is best explained by using a counter-example. Assume governments were to agree on the arithmetic mean of the proposals. Then under the fixed uniform quota regime, countries which would like to see a high quota would bias their proposals upward and those which would prefer a low emission reduction would bias their proposals downward. In contrast, under the SCD-decision rule there is no incentive to bias proposals. Each country makes a proposal which maximizes its payoff, which we denote r_1, r_2, ..., r_N (see note 58). Suppose that proposals can be ranked according to $r_1 \leq r_2 \leq ... \leq r_N$ and therefore countries agree on r_1. Since r_1 maximizes country 1's payoff, this country cannot do any better. Consider some other country $i \neq 1$. Any biased proposal r_i' for which $r_1 \leq r_i'$ is true has no effect on the outcome and any proposal for which $r_i' < r_1$ holds would reduce welfare by strict concavity.[60]

Individual rationality, global welfare and emissions

Under the tradable and non-tradable quota regime, the SCD-decision rule ensures that the individual rationality constraint is always met (Endres and Finus 1998b and 1999). In contrast, as has been discussed already, under a tax regime there may be no tax, regardless of how small it is, for which this condition can be met. In Figure 2.1, e^Q and e^T are the bargaining equilibria under the fixed quota and the tax regime, respectively. The permit regime cannot be visualized in Figure 2.1 since payoffs depend not only on emissions but also on transfers from permit trading. The bargaining equilibria of all three regimes imply higher global welfare than in the Nash equilibrium; however, due to the SCD-decision rule (and as long as countries are not totally symmetric) the globally optimal level is not achieved (Endres and Finus 1998b and 1999).

Since some of the discussion in this and previous paragraphs is based on some general findings, we summarize them in the following result.

Result 6

Let payoff functions be strictly concave at the policy level. For not 'too' large emission quotas and in particular if countries agree on the smallest quota proposed in the negotiation process, individual rationality is met under the fixed and tradable uniform quota regime. Under the uniform tax regime there may be no tax rate for which individual rationality can be met for all countries. If the bargaining outcome under the SCD-decision rule is individually rational, global welfare under all three regimes will be lower than in the global optimum as long as proposals differ. Global emissions will be lower than in Nash equilibrium.

Proof: See Appendix 3 for a sketch of the proof.

Free-rider incentive

Conclusions with respect to the second type of free-rider incentive are difficult at a general level. Nevertheless, we will outline some tendencies (Finus and Rundshagen 1998a, 1998b). We may distinguish two cases: countries with relatively symmetric welfare functions and countries with relatively asymmetric welfare functions. In the first case, proposals in the negotiations will not differ much and countries will agree on relatively ambitious emission reductions. Consequently, following Result 2 in Section 2.2, the second type of free-rider incentive will be relatively large for all countries under all three regimes. In other words, all minimum discount factor requirements will be relatively large, though they are more-or-less the same for all countries. Moreover, under the permit regime there will not be much trade, in particular if benefit functions are relatively similar. Therefore, the incentive problem resulting from the exchange of permits will play a minor role. In the second case, proposals in the negotiations will differ considerably and countries will agree on relatively low emission reductions. Consequently, the free-rider incentive will be relatively low in this respect. However, in this case the minimum discount factor requirements may be quite different. This is particularly true under the tax regime, which leads to an uneven welfare distribution. Under the uniform tax regime, the minimum discount factor will be particularly large for those countries which put forward low proposals, which may be called the bottleneck countries in the negotiations. In contrast, under a fixed uniform quota regime, the welfare distribution will be more even and therefore the minimum discount factor requirements will not differ that much among countries. Under the permit regime there will be some trade (in particular if benefit functions differ) and therefore the free-rider incentive resulting from the exchange of permits will be relatively large.

5.4 Summary

Summarizing the discussion we conclude:

Conclusion 14 (summarizing results and discussion)
Under the fixed uniform quota regime, emissions are reduced inefficiently. The amount of information needed to make a proposal in negotiations is small. The welfare distribution is relatively symmetric and individual rationality is met for not too large emissions reductions and those agreed on under the SCD-decision rule. The free-rider incentive is relatively symmetrically distributed among countries, putting no particular strain on bottleneck countries. Under the tradable uniform quota regime, emissions are reduced efficiently. The amount of information needed to make a proposal in negotiations is higher than under the fixed quota regime. The welfare distribution is relatively symmetric and individual rationality is met for not too large emissions reductions and those agreed on under the SCD-decision rule. The free-rider incentive stemming from permit trading is particularly

large if countries have asymmetric benefit functions and is difficult to control in a global context. Under the uniform tax regime, emissions are reduced efficiently. The amount of information needed to make a proposal in negotiations is higher than under the fixed uniform quota regime. The welfare distribution is relatively asymmetric and individual rationality may be violated if countries exhibit asymmetric welfare functions. The free-rider incentive may be very asymmetrically distributed among countries, putting a particular strain on bottleneck countries.

Conclusion 14 provides some indication why the fixed uniform quota regime has been so popular in past IEAs despite being an inefficient policy regime. Though this instrument is inferior in a first-best world (enforcement and individual rationality constitute no restrictions on implementation), in a second-best world a fixed quota may be superior. In future research it will be important to generalize the results. First, the nature of asymmetry under which the superiority of the fixed quota holds should be more clearly determined. Second, the analysis should be extended to other versions of the three policy regimes discussed above.

6.   COALITION FORMATION

In this section, we summarize the main findings which have been derived from RSG and IRG models (Finus 2001, ch. 13 and 14). The objective of these models is to investigate how many and which countries join an IEA, on which factors this depends and whether the coalition helps to mitigate the global externality. For the RSG models we first discuss the formation of an IEA and then look at whether participation in an IEA can be increased through issue linkage. For IRG models we only look at the formation of an IEA, since issue linkage has already been treated in Section 4.4.

6.1   RSG Models

6.1.1 Coalition formation in an IEA
Since the number of models is very large (see note 18) and models are very heterogeneous, we have to restrict attention to a small selection of models. As argued in Section 3.1, among the RSG models we restrict attention to those which apply the concept of internal and external stability and do not treat those which apply the concept of the core. This also implies that new stability

concepts which allow for multiple coalitions are not covered (see Bloch 1997, Finus 2001, ch. 15, Finus and Rundshagen 2001 and Yi 1997).

Symmetric countries Since the computation of a coalition equilibrium gets rather complex, some papers have assumed symmetric countries. Even for this restrictive assumption, it turns out that results have to be derived from specific welfare functions, of which we select two to demonstrate important results:[61]

$$\text{Type 1: } \pi_i = b(de_i - \frac{1}{2}e_i^2) - \frac{c}{2N}(\sum_{j=1}^{N} e_j)^2 \qquad [2.19]$$

$$\text{Type 2: } \pi_i = b(de_i - \frac{1}{2}e_i^2) - \frac{c}{N}(\sum_{j=1}^{N} e_j) \qquad [2.20]$$

We refer to these welfare functions as welfare functions of type 1 and 2 since there is some indication (Finus and Rundshagen 2001) that qualitative results do not depend on the exact specification of these functions but on their properties, though there is no general proof yet. The slope of the reaction functions of the welfare function of type 1 is greater than zero and smaller than 1 in absolute terms ($-1 < R_i' < 0$) and the slope of welfare functions of type 2 is zero ($R_i' = 0$; orthogonal reaction functions).

Welfare function of type 2 implies that countries have a dominant strategy and choose their emission level independently of the emission level in the other countries. This type of function has been used by some scholars because of its mathematical simplicity (e.g. Bauer 1992 and Carraro and Siniscalco 1991), though it does not capture a typical feature of global environmental problems, namely the interaction of countries.

It turns out that all subsequent results can be expressed in terms of two variables: the number of countries suffering from an environmental problem, N, and the benefit–cost ratio $\gamma=b/c$. With the help of these variables, some indicators can be computed which allow us to evaluate the coalition equilibrium.

Result 7

Define $I_1 := (\Sigma e_i^N - \Sigma e_i^S)/\Sigma e_i^S$, $I_2 := (\Sigma \pi_i^N - \Sigma \pi_i^S)/\Sigma \pi_i^S$ and $\gamma=b/c$, then for payoff functions in [2.19] and [2.20]: $\partial I_1/\partial N > 0$, $\partial I_1/\partial \gamma < 0$, $\partial I_2/\partial N > 0$, $\partial I_2/\partial \gamma < 0$. That is, the externality problem is particularly pronounced if the number of countries is large and if the benefit–cost ratio of emissions γ is small.

Proof: Follows from standard computations (Finus 2001, ch. 13).

The first part of Result 7 reflects a typical problem of public goods: a country's own contribution to a public good is perceived to have only a marginal effect if the number of countries is large. This causes the underprovision of the public good 'clean environment'. The second part of Result 6 reflects the fact that if the benefit–cost ratio is large, it is not sensible from a global point of view to reduce emissions much. Therefore, the relative difference between the Nash equilibrium and the global optimum is small.

Conclusion 15 (based on Result 7)
Cooperation is particularly attractive from a global point of view if environmental damages are high compared to the opportunity costs of abatement and if many countries are involved in the externality problem (critical parameter constellations).

We call the parameter constellations mentioned in Conclusion 15 the critical parameter constellations for reference reasons. For the two types of welfare functions, the equilibrium coalition sizes are displayed in Table 2.1.
From Table 2.1 it appears that welfare functions of type 1 and the assumption of sequential moves are best suited to explaining actual IEAs since the equilibrium number of signatories ranges from 2 to N, depending on the benefit–cost ratio. Table 2.1 implies the following results:

Result 8
The number of signatories and global welfare is at least as high if countries choose their emissions sequentially as if they choose their emissions simultaneously.

Result 9
A coalition, even though this may be small, increases individual and global welfare and reduces global pollution. The participation rate (number of coalition members in relation to the total number of countries, N^*/N) in the coalition decreases with the number of countries suffering from global pollution, N, and decreases with the benefit–cost ratio of emissions, $\gamma=b/c$. A

coalition mitigates the externality problem if the number of countries suffering from the externality is small and if the benefit–cost ratio is large. For the critical parameter values, a coalition achieves only little.

Table 2.1   *Equilibrium coalition size*

Welfare Function	Slope of the Reaction Function	Sequence of Moves in the Second Stage	
		Simultaneous (Nash-Cournot)	Sequential (Stackelberg)
Type 1	between −1 and 0	$N^*=2$	$N^* \in [2, N]$
Type 2	0	$N^*=3$	$N^*=3$

Source: Compiled from Finus (2001), ch. 13.

Proof: See Barrett (1997a) and Finus (2001), ch. 13.

Result 8 confirms the conjecture that a coalition is more successful in tackling global pollution if signatories take possible leakage effects into consideration.[62] In other words, it may not pay the coalition to be too enthusiastic about reducing emissions. It might be better to observe first the reaction of non-signatories and then choose an optimal strategy.

Result 9 confirms that it pays to seek partners in pollution control. However, whenever cooperation would be needed most from a global point of view, a coalition achieves only a little. Though for the critical parameter values, many countries join an IEA, they have only a marginal positive effect on mitigating the externality problem. This finding stresses that from the participation rate one cannot infer the success of an IEA. On the contrary: a small number of countries may achieve more than a large group. As a tendency, this conclusion is supported by the IRG model discussed in Section 6.3.

According to Barrett (1994b) the depletion of the ozone layer may serve approximately as an example of a small benefit–cost ratio. Many countries joined the Protocol, though from Result 9 one should expect that the impact of the protocol would only be small. An example of a higher benefit–cost ratio are greenhouse gases. Though only a relatively small number of countries signed the Kyoto Protocol (38 out of roughly 200 countries), Result 9 suggests that this may not be a disadvantage.

Heterogeneous countries   Heterogeneity can be modeled in many ways, and results crucially depend on the specific assumptions. The coalition size depends on the nature and the degree of heterogeneity and how the gains of the coalition are distributed among its members. Nevertheless, we would like to highlight four results.[63]

First, it appears for welfare functions of type 2 that the number of signatories is smaller for heterogeneous than for symmetric countries (Barrett 1997b, Bauer 1992 and Hoel 1992). This result conforms to intuition: it is more difficult to form stable coalitions if countries are heterogeneous. This result is confirmed by Finus and Rundshagen (1998a) in an IRG.

Second, Barrett (1997b) confirms via simulations that for welfare functions of type 1 and 2 and for the Stackelberg assumption, a coalition achieves only little whenever cooperation would be needed most. Thus Result 8 appears to carry over to heterogeneous countries as well, though one has to be cautious with respect to general conclusions.

Third, Bauer (1992) shows for welfare functions of type 2 that countries with similar welfare functions form a coalition. If these coalitions act as one country, then several smaller coalitions may form larger coalitions. Of course, it is a rather 'heroic' assumption that several countries can act as a single entity. Nevertheless, the result indicates that an expansion of an IEA is best achieved if countries with similar interests sequentially form larger coalitions as a first step. Similar to the design of the European Monetary Union, an expansion should wait until the economic and ecological fundamentals of potential signatories have converged to those of the core countries.

Fourth, Botteon and Carraro (1997) show that the coalition structure (membership) depends on the allocation rule of the gains of the coalition using estimates of five world regions for the parameters of welfare functions of type 2. For their data set the Shapley value leads to a coalition generating a higher global welfare than a coalition in which the Nash bargaining solution is applied. Though this result does not allow us to draw general conclusions, the finding supports Conclusion 4 in Section 3.1 that the design of an agreement has an impact on membership and on the success of an IEA.

Evaluation   We have already pointed out the limitations of RSGs in Section 3.1. One important point was that the process leading to the design of an agreement is not explicitly modeled in RSGs. Another point was that the exogenous assumption with respect to the choice of strategies in the second and third stage do not reflect Conclusion 3, namely that the design must be agreed by consensus. A third point was that there has not been enough research on how the design of an agreement affects membership in the coalition formation process. Now we would like to add a fourth point: results depend very much on the payoff functions. Since it can hardly be expected that results can be established for general payoff functions (like payoff functions in [2.1]), we suggest two routes for research: (1) Results are derived for a larger set of (specific) payoff functions. (2) Results are established by defining some general properties of payoff functions. This would provide a broader basis for more reliable conclusions (see Finus and Rundshagen 2001).

6.1.2 Issue linkage

RSG models have focused on package deals where the public good (non-excludable good) agreement IEA is linked to a club good (excludable good) agreement (Carraro and Siniscalco 1998 and Finus 2001, ch. 8 and 13) in order to increase participation in an IEA. Typical examples of club good agreements include the institutionalization of cooperation on R&D between firms through governments (Botteon and Carraro 1998, Carraro and Siniscalco 1997 and Katsoulacos 1997) and trade agreements (Barrett 1997c and Finus and Rundshagen 2000). The (possibly) higher participation in club good agreements is due to two forces: the gains of the club good agreement can be made *exclusive* to its members; and members of club good agreements often exhibit a negative externality on outsiders. Both forces provide an incentive to join a club good agreement. For instance, non-members of the European Union are not only denied the access to tariff-free intra-trade within the Union, they also face stiff external tariffs at the border of the Union. Thus, apart from paying tariffs, the terms of trade of outsiders worsen through the European Union.

Issue linkage in RSGs implies that signatories are required to hold a simultaneous membership of both agreements. Consequently, a government may accede to an IEA just for the sake of not being excluded from the benefits accruing from the club good agreement. Thus, issue linkage may increase the participation in an IEA. An example of this kind of issue linkage is the Montreal Protocol on the Depletion of the Ozone Layer. Trade with non-signatory countries which produce goods with substances that are controlled by the regime is suspended (Barratt-Brown 1991, Benedick 1991, and Blackhurst and Subramanian 1992). Thus, the Montreal Protocol may be thought of as an environmental agreement with an associated trade agreement. The trade agreement constitutes a free-trade area among the signatories. A similar link is established within the CITES agreement on the protection of endangered species.

From the RSG-literature on issue linkage, three central results can be identified:

Result 10

In a RSG framework one can show: 1) increasing the participation in an IEA via the linkage to a club good agreement may be a successful policy (e.g. Barrett 1997c). 2) There are limits to such a package deal. Issue linkage may only be a successful policy by increasing the participation rate of an IEA up to a certain threshold level, but full participation may not be possible (Carraro and Siniscalco 1997 and 1998). 3) There are cases where issue linkage reduces the participation in an IEA and global welfare (Carraro and Siniscalco 1997 and Finus and Rundshagen 2000).

Proof: See the papers cited in Result 10.

Result 10 has been established using quite sophisticated models involving a lot mathematics. However, all three parts of Result 10 are based on a simple relationship (Carraro 1997). To illustrate this, recall Definition 1 of an internally and externally stable equilibrium and the fact that strategies in the second and third stage are determined from exogenous assumptions and therefore may be dropped in the definition of an equilibrium. Let the IEA be agreement 1 and the club good agreement be agreement 2, then issue linkage implies:

A_1:
$$\pi_{i1}^{J}(N_1^*) - \pi_{i1}^{NJ}(N_1^* - 1) \geq 0 \; ; \; \pi_{i2}^{J}(N_2^*) - \pi_{i2}^{NJ}(N_2^* - 1) \geq 0$$

$\Rightarrow$
$$\pi_{i1}^{J}(N_{1+2}^*) + \pi_{i2}^{J}(N_{1+2}^*) - \pi_{i1}^{NJ}(N_{1+2}^* - 1) - \pi_{i2}^{NJ}(N_{1+2}^* - 1) \geq 0$$

$$[2.21]$$

A_2:
$$\pi_{j1}^{J}(N_1^* + 1) - \pi_{j1}^{NJ}(N_1^*) \leq 0 \; ; \; \pi_{j2}^{J}(N_2^* + 1) - \pi_{j2}^{NJ}(N_2^*) \leq 0$$

$\Rightarrow$
$$\pi_{j1}^{J}(N_{1+2}^* + 1) + \pi_{j2}^{J}(N_{1+2}^* + 1) - \pi_{j1}^{NJ}(N_{1+2}^*) - \pi_{j2}^{NJ}(N_{1+2}^*) \leq 0$$

From [2.21] it is evident that issue linkage implies that functions A_1 and A_2 of the isolated games are added. Now suppose that $N_1^* \leq N_2^*$, then $N_1^* \leq N_{1+2}^* \leq N_2^*$. That is, the participation in the linked agreement is at least as high as in the IEA since participation in the club good agreement is higher than (or equal to) participation in the IEA. This explains part 1 of Result 10.

Part 2 follows from the fact that if $N_2^* < N$, $N_{1+2}^* < N$ will be true. It is evident that Part 3 follows from a situation where $N_1^* > N_2^*$ holds and therefore $N_2^* \leq N_{1+2}^* < N_1^*$ or $N_2^* < N_{1+2}^* \leq N_1^*$ is true.

Three remarks are in order to appreciate the results and their explanations:

1. The explanations above simplify matters. Functions A_1 and A_2 depend on the exact specification of the payoff function in the isolated games. Though the explanations apply to most models cited above, they may not hold for all.

2. Part 2 of Result 10 relies on $N_2^* < N$. Full participation may not be obtained in the club good agreement since there are diminishing returns in holding a membership in the club good agreement which decrease with the number of participants. For instance, consider the case of cooperation on R&D. On the one hand, cooperation reduces production costs and thereby increases the profits of firms in signatory countries. These firms gain a competitive advantage over those firms located in non-signatory countries. On the other hand, the more countries sign the R&D agreement, the more competition will increase and profits shrink. At some participation rate, the latter effect dominates the former effect. This may happen at a participation rate below full participation.

3. Part 3 of Result 10 relies on $N_1^* > N_2^*$. If the returns of holding a membership in the club good agreement decrease very fast, this results in a low participation rate. A low participation in a club agreement is even more likely when removing the inconsistency in the definition of the stability of a club good agreement (Finus and Rundshagen 2000).

   The definition of external stability implies that a country which would like to accede to an agreement can do so. However, the very definition of a club good implies excludability. That is, signatories to an IEA should be able to reject an application for accession to their agreement if this implies a lower payoff for them. If this aspect is accounted for in the definition of external stability, participation may be lower in the club good agreement. That is, signatories to a club good agreement may restrict membership for strategic reasons, though an outsider may like to join.

Evaluation We would like to mention three shortcomings of the literature on issue linkage using RSG models. First, Result 10 has mostly been established via simulations. Though Finus and Rundshagen (2000) have derived all their results from general propositions, they do not provide a full general description of the public-club good package deal. So the question is: Under which general conditions can we expect part 1, 2 or 3 of Result 10 to hold? A first attempt to structure the problem may be found in Carraro and Marchiori (2001). Second, RSG models may overestimate the positive effects of linking a public to a club good agreement. On the one hand, stability of a club good agreement may be overestimated since the second type of free-rider incentive is captured only deficiently in RSGs. Though it is rational for the members of the club group agreement as a whole to cooperate on R&D, R&D involves costs. Hence, a country has an incentive to spend little on R&D and to hold back its own research results in order to benefit from the efforts of other members. On the other hand, one factor of the possible success of issue linkage is that there is an incentive for countries to join the IEA in order not to be excluded from the benefits of the club good agreement. Thus, through issue linkage the incentive to violate the terms of an IEA may in fact increase; this is only partially captured by RSGs. Third, the RSG literature on issue linkage has assumed the separable utility functions of the isolated games. From Section 4.4 we know that results may change if we give up this assumption.

Practical problems In reality, a package deal of a club and public good agreement faces a number of problems. First, it is hardly conceivable in reality that all countries belonging to an IEA are also accepted as members of a large trade agreement or a defense pact. Since each agreement has different member states, those states which hold a simultaneous membership may not be able to convince other states to accept a member just for the sake of issue linkage.[64] The Montreal Protocol and the CITES agreement do not face this problem since the 'associated trade agreement' did not exist before and was created in the course of the negotiations. Accordingly, the trade embargo extends only to those products which are directly related to CFCs. Second, the exclusion of a country from an agreement because it does not sign an IEA violates the principle of proportionality and reciprocity. Additionally, any measure which restricts trade (trade embargoes, fine tariffs, exclusion from a custom union) could violate the terms of GATT/WTO (e.g. Lang 1996, pp. 265ff). Third, the threat to exclude a country from the club good agreement if it does not sign an IEA will generally not be credible in the sense of a renegotiation-proof contract. If it was beneficial for the club good members to offer membership to a country, such an implicit punishment would also harm the punishers (see Sections 4.1 and 4.2).

6.2 IRG Models

Formation and stability of coalitions in IRG models have been analyzed by Barrett (1994a, b), Finus and Rundshagen (1998a) and Stähler (1996). Since Barrett assumes symmetric countries and only analyzes the stability of the grand coalition and Stähler considers only three countries, we report in the following only on the results of Finus and Rundshagen (1998a). As pointed out in Section 3.2, the focus of IRG models is on the second type of free-rider incentive. Moreover, membership of IRGs does not follow immediately from the equilibrium concept and requires some additional account of how coalitions form. As in RSGs, the analysis has to rely on specific assumptions with respect to the net benefit functions of countries. Finus and Rundshagen assume the following payoff function:

$$\pi_i = b\left(de_i - \frac{1}{2}e_i^2\right) - i \cdot \frac{c}{2N} \cdot \left(\sum_j^N e_j\right)^2 \quad i \text{ and } j \in \{1, ..., N\}. \qquad [2.22]$$

That is, benefits are assumed to be the same in all countries but damages differ and increase in the index i. For this function Result 7, on the relative importance of cooperation from a global point of view with respect to the parameters $\gamma = b/c$ and N, holds. Stability is defined in terms of a renegotiation-proof equilibrium. That is, conditions C_1 to C_4 in Section 4.1 must hold for all signatories. Thus, the only possibility for punishment is emissions. The analysis focuses on two of the instruments discussed in Section 5: a fixed uniform emission reduction quota and a uniform national emission tax where the tax receipts remain in the country of origin.

Grand coalition

Finus and Rundshagen consider stability of a coalition comprising all countries for five different designs of a treaty: (1) a uniform emission reduction quota where countries agree on the smallest quota proposal (SCD-decision rule), (2) a uniform emission reduction quota with an agreement on the median country's proposal, (3) a uniform tax where countries agree on the smallest tax proposal (SCD-decision rule), (4) a uniform tax with an agreement on the median country proposal and (5) socially optimal emission reductions.

Designs 1 to 4 are possibilities for capturing agreement by consensus (see Conclusion 3). For [2.22] it turns out that it is country 1 which puts forward the smallest quota and tax proposal since it is this country which suffers the lowest damages. An agreement on the median country's proposal implies a higher emissions reduction than under the SCD-decision rule. For [2.22] it turns out that the median proposal is equal to a globally optimal emission reduction under a particular regime. Since a uniform tax is an efficient instrument in the context of global emissions, the median proposal leads to the same emission reduction as in the social optimum. Taken together, the median proposals and the social optimum imply substantially lower emissions than if countries agree on the smallest common denominator under the tax and quota regime. The results of Finus and Rundshagen, which they derive from a large set of simulations, may be summarized as follows:

Result 11
Irrespective of the treaty design, stability of a grand coalition is particularly jeopardized whenever the gains from cooperation would be great (critical parameter values; see Result 7 and Conclusion 15). For global pollutants, where the number of countries affected by the externality is large, neither globally optimal emission reductions nor those implied by the median country's proposal are stable. The likelihood that the smallest tax or quota proposal is stable is higher, though for global pollutants also very low. The stability of a quota proposal is higher than that of a tax proposal.

Result 11 emphasizes that demanding abatement targets, though they may be advisable from a global point of view, can hardly be enforced in an IEA. That is, the minimum discount factor requirements are either very high or cannot be satisfied. Due to the heterogeneity of countries, only moderate abatement targets have a chance of being realized if at all. The Rio Declaration confirms this finding: it has been signed by almost all countries but is at best a declaration of good intentions with no binding abatement obligations. Thus, the finding derived in a RSG; that a coalition achieves only little whenever cooperation would be needed most from a global point of view, is confirmed in an IRG. The last statement in Result 11 confirms the findings in Section 5, namely the superiority of the quota over the tax regime in terms of stability due to a more even distribution of welfare. Particularly for the bottleneck countries, the discount factor requirements are higher under the tax than under the quota regime. For some parameter constellations, the minimum discount factor requirements cannot be satisfied under the tax regime, though this is possible under the quota regime.

Sub-coalition

Due to the pessimistic result obtained for a grand coalition, Finus and Rundshagen investigate the formation of a sub-coalition. The formation process may be viewed as a sequential process. In a preliminary step, we leave out the choice of the policy instrument. Countries with the highest environmental preferences are assumed to be the initiators which seek partners in order to form an IEA. 'New' countries are asked to submit a bargaining proposal with the understanding that the members of a sub-coalition will have to agree on the smallest common denominator. Since countries are asked in decreasing order (N, N-1, N-2, and so forth), it is always the new member who is the bottleneck. Based on this proposal, the initiators decide whether to offer the new country membership. This decision is taken either by unanimity or by majority rule. Three factors determine the equilibrium coalition size: first, additionally signatories imply less free-riders; second, an agreement is more effective if the abatement burden is shouldered by more countries; and third, additional signatories may imply a lower environmental standard due to the SCD-decision rule. As long as the first two effects dominate the third, a coalition is expanded. At the break-even point (coalition equilibrium), all three effects balance (beyond the break-even point the third effect is stronger than the first and second effects).

As a second step, the choice of the policy instrument may be added to the formation process, in which countries belonging to a sub-coalition are assumed to decide by majority vote. It turns out that countries with higher indexes prefer a tax whereas those with lower indexes prefer a quota. However, under a quota regime it may be possible to form a larger coalition. Hence, countries with high indexes may also eventually be better off under a quota agreement. Together with the first three effects, the fourth effect determines the coalition equilibrium with the equilibrium number of signatories, the policy instrument and the abatement target chosen by the coalition.

Result 12

A sub-coalition may achieve more (in terms of emission reduction and global welfare) than a grand coalition. This is particularly true for the critical parameter values. This result not only holds for the SCD-decision rule, but is also true if one assumes that the grand coalition implements the highest emission reduction which is stable. As long as the number of countries affected by the externality is not very small, the coalition will agree on a fixed uniform emission reduction quota.

The advantage of sub-coalitions is that relatively homogeneous countries form an IEA. Though sub-coalitions are assumed to agree on the smallest common denominator, they have to compromise less on ecological targets than the grand coalition and stability poses less of a problem. The reason is that members of the sub-coalition only offer membership if this is conducive to the overall success of the coalition. Result 12 suggests that it is not necessarily a good strategy to get all countries into the 'climate boat' (as has been tried under the Montreal Protocol and is demanded by the US under the Kyoto Protocol). A smaller coalition may achieve more. This conclusion is in line with the findings in RSG models (see Result 9). The agreement on a uniform quota is due to its relatively symmetric welfare distribution, which gives a higher priority to the interests of the bottleneck countries than the tax regime (see Chapter 5). Consequently, larger coalitions are stable under the quota regime than under the tax regime, implying a higher welfare for signatories (and non-signatories alike). Though the initiators may prefer a tax to a quota, the prospect of a larger and stable coalition also 'convinces' these countries to agree on a quota. This result provides an additional rationale to the arguments already presented in Section 5 on why a fixed uniform emission reduction quota has been so popular in the past.

Evaluation
The advantage of the Finus and Rundshagen model is that it pays more attention to modeling how countries agree on the design of an IEA and to providing some evidence which helps to explain the design of past IEAs. The shortcomings of this, but also of other IRG models, are the following: 1) Results rely on specific payoff functions and most results have to be derived from simulations. 2) The aspects of membership are only captured partially. Barrett (1994a, 1994b) only looks at the stability of the grand coalition. Though Finus and Rundshagen look at sub-coalitions, they capture only one dimension of the coalition formation process. Internal stability of the sub-coalition considers only whether compliance can be enforced (the second type of free-rider incentive). However, whether signatories have an incentive to leave the coalition is only captured via individual rationality. External stability is modeled in an extended and certainly interesting version: signatories decide whether outsiders are allowed to join their club. However,

whether non-signatories actually want to join is not considered. Taken together, there remains some work to be done in the future to generalize results and to capture this aspect of membership more convincingly in an IRG framework.

7. THE KYOTO PROTOCOL

In this section we use the results and conclusions of the previous sections to evaluate the Kyoto Protocol. Only those issues of the Protocol which can be related to the previous discussion will be treated.

7.1 Targets and Timetables

Facts

The protocol sets annual emission targets for 38 industrial countries (plus the EU as a whole entity) to be achieved by 2008–2012. Each country is required to demonstrate progress towards meeting this target by 2005 (Article 3). Developing countries have not been assigned any emission reduction targets. The targets amount to a global annual emission reduction of 5.2 per cent based on the emissions of the 38 countries in 1990. Among the main global players, the USA accepted a reduction of 7 per cent, Japan of 6 per cent and Canada of 6 per cent. The countries of the EU have either to reduce emissions as a 'bubble' by 8 per cent or each country has to meet this target. Among the smaller global players, New Zealand and Russia have committed themselves to a freeze on 1990 emissions. Australia is allowed to increase its emissions by 8 per cent. The Protocol has not been ratified by any participant yet.

Evaluation

For the four major global players (USA, Canada, Japan and the EU) the abatement targets imply roughly a uniform emission reduction quota based on status quo emissions in 1990. Thus, according to Conclusion 14, one should expect a fairly symmetric welfare distribution irrespective of whether parties eventually agree that quotas are tradable. Given that countries agreed on the smallest common denominator, the individual rationality constraint would be met for all signatories. Whether countries agreed on the quotas according to the SCD-decision rule is an open question. However, there are two facts supporting this possibility. First, Article 20 to the Protocol states that all amendments to the Protocol should be made by consensus. Second, the negotiations leading to the signature of the Kyoto Protocol took six years, stressing how difficult it was to find unanimous consensus (see Section 2.2).

The abatement targets for the global players seem quite demanding. This is evident when the effective emission reductions and those computed to be socially optimal are considered. Effective emission reduction means that reductions are not expressed in terms of some base year (e.g. 1990 as under the Kyoto Protocol) but compared to the 'business as usual' scenario (BAU-scenario).[65] According to Böhringer (2000), effective emission reductions are as follows: USA: 27.5 per cent, Canada: 27.5 per cent, EU: 13.7 per cent, Japan: 26 per cent, Australia/New Zealand: 15.8 per cent and the Former Soviet Union: −48.1 per cent. Cost–benefit studies indicate that socially optimal global emission reduction would be roughly 10–30 per cent compared to BAU.[66] Thus a high free-rider incentive has to be expected for most countries (except Russia). Consequently, an efficient system of sanctions appears to be a basic prerequisite if the stability of the Kyoto Protocol is to be ensured.

According to Section 6, the fact that developing countries did not accede to the Protocol may not be a disadvantage. First note that the result is in line with the results obtained in Section 6. If the benefit–cost ratio is 'not too small' (as may be assumed for the problem of global warming), only a few countries will accede to an agreement. Second, according to Result 9, the coalition, though small, will have an impact on reducing the externality. Also Result 12 confirms that smaller coalitions may achieve more than larger coalitions. Moreover, it can be concluded from Result 11 that a grand coalition would not be stable anyway. A 'not too small' benefit–cost ratio also implies that reaction functions are not very steep, implying that leakage effects will only be moderate. This is even more true given the low perception of environmental damages in developing countries, suggesting (for welfare functions for which the standard assumptions in [2.2] hold, e.g. for welfare functions [2.19] and [2.22]) the slopes of the reaction functions of non-signatories are close to zero. However, extrapolating the past economic progress of countries like China, their population growth and their high emission per GDP ratio, leakage effects may become larger in the future. Therefore, it may be sensible to observe and account for linkage effects in the future according to Result 8, and to include some developing countries in the Protocol at a later stage. Probably, the second option will prove to be a difficult task. On the one hand, without any direct or indirect transfer payments, developing countries can hardly be convinced to join the agreement. On the other hand, it is known from Section 4.3 that transfers are difficult to enforce.

7.2 Flexibility of Emission Targets and Implementation

Facts

1. The protocol allows Annex 1 countries to jointly hit their targets (Joint Implementation, abbreviated JI; Articles 3 and 4). However, the details of JI have not been settled yet. Moreover, a party may 'bank' its emissions rights if its emissions in some commitment periods are less than assigned under the Protocol (Article 3).
2. Under Article 17 the protocol allows for emission trading among Annex B countries (almost the same countries as Annex 1). However, the details of permit trading have not been agreed yet. Whereas the USA favors unrestricted trade, the EU accepts only limited trading.
3. Under Article 12 of the Protocol (Clean Development Mechanism, abbreviated CDM) Annex 1 countries are allowed some flexibility to finance 'project activities resulting in certified emission reductions' in developing countries, thereby reducing their abatement burdens. The purchased reductions must be additional to 'any that would occur in the absence of the certified project activity'. The developed country is expected to cover the 'incremental costs' of the project. The exact accounting procedures have to be specified in future amendments to the protocol.
4. The Protocol allows each country to figure out how it translates its target into domestic policy. That is, there is no article requiring specific technological standards or harmonized measures.

Evaluation
Since according to Böhringer (2000) marginal abatement costs (marginal benefits in our setting) for fixed quotas under the Kyoto Protocol vary substantially between countries (USA: 43.7, Canada: 62.8, EU: 29.2, Japan: 81.8, Australia and New Zealand: 20.7 and the Former Soviet Union: 0; unit: US/$ per ton of CO_2 reduction), global abatement costs can be reduced through JI and permit trading. Since marginal abatement costs in developing countries are generally lower than in industrialized countries, CDM also contributes to reducing abatement costs. Moreover, emission banking allows some flexibility in the abatement path, so that each country can choose its optimal

time path, which also reduces abatement costs. By the same token, it has to be judged positively that no harmonized measures are proposed by the Protocol.

However, the question arises what JI is good for if there is a functioning permit system. It has to be expected that the transparency and efficiency of emission trading may suffer from the coexistence of JI and the permit scheme. Obviously, the founders of JI did not believe in the permit system. According to the discussion in Section 4.3 on transfers and in particular on the permit system in Section 5, their suspicion may not be unwarranted. Permit trading will be subject to high free-rider incentives of the second type (between sellers and buyers). Probably the founders of JI had in mind that most bilateral transactions under JI would not be conducted in the form of monetary transfers but in the form of in-kind transfers or maybe issue linkage.

From Sections 4.3 it is known that in-kind transfers face a smaller incentive problem between donor (buyer) and recipient (seller). Though both instruments are less efficient than monetary transfers, JI may turn out to be an efficient second-best instrument.

The problem of CDM is how to measure 'additional measures'. Since they can only be determined via contra-factual reasoning, it may happen that measures are certified which would have been undertaken by developing countries anyway. This may cause a crowding out of domestic investment by foreign investment. The fact that details of CDM await elaboration in future meetings, stresses the conceptional difficulties facing CDM. From an incentive point of view, however, the advantage of CDM is that transfers take the form of in-kind transfers. Thus transfers under CDM are less jeopardized by the free-rider incentive of the second type compared to monetary transfers under a permit trading system (see Section 4.3 and Section 5).

The problem of banking is that this may imply some temporary hot spots in the future if some countries simultaneously make use of this option. Moreover, a government may postpone emission reductions, promising to clear its account later. If governments discount time much or are not re-elected, temporary deficits may become permanent. In the light of deficient monitoring (see Section 7.5), non-harmonized measures may be difficult to monitor. From a practical point of view, harmonized measures (e.g. technical standards), though inefficient, may be easier to monitor and to evaluate with respect to their effect in serving the aims of the Protocol.

7.3 Greenhouse Gases

Facts

The Protocol covers not only CO_2 but also five other greenhouse gases (see note 49). All greenhouse gases and emission targets are expressed in CO_2 equivalents, which measure the global warming potential of a greenhouse gas.

Evaluation

On the one hand, the inclusion of five other greenhouse gases apart from CO_2 has to be judged positively. First, this regulation takes into account the fact that other greenhouse gases are also important contributors to global warming. Second, this avoids the danger that countries might pursue an abatement strategy of reducing CO_2 at the expense of expanding emissions of other greenhouse gases. Third, this allows for some flexibility in meeting the targets, which reduces abatement costs. The conversion of greenhouse gases into CO_2 equivalents (global warming potential) implies that countries can reduce those greenhouse gases where they face the lowest abatement costs. Fourth, the conversion into CO_2 equivalents provides a good basis for monitoring.

On the other hand, according to Section 4.4 on issue linkage, if the various greenhouse gases are complements in a government's objective function treating these greenhouse gases within different IEAs would have been better. However, negotiating six separate agreements may imply high transaction costs, eating up all the gains from issue linkage. Therefore, a more promising strategy may be to delegate some responsibility for environmental policy from governments to independent national or international institutions to increase the stability of the treaty.

7.4 Carbon Sinks

Facts

The Protocol allows for carbon sinks (Article 3). That is, land and forestry practices which remove carbon emissions may be accounted for in a country's emission target. Carbon sinks may also be traded among Annex 1 states (Article 6). However, only the establishment of carbon sinks which are in addition to those 'that would otherwise occur' are considered as tradable. The accounting procedures of carbon sinks have not been settled yet.

Evaluation

Carbon sinks may provide a low cost option for some countries and therefore help to reduce abatement costs. So far, however, sinks are ambiguously defined and therefore will be a challenge to measure and to monitor. In particular, it is difficult to define what constitutes 'additional carbon sinks'. As long as The Conference of the Parties has not finally agreed on the guidelines for implementation, verification and reporting, this provision may be a major loophole in the treaty.

7.5   Monitoring of Emissions

Facts

Articles 5, 7 and 8 specify the monitoring procedures. Each party has to establish a national emission inventory system one year prior to the first commitment period (2005). This includes an inventory of carbon sinks. The methodologies to estimate emissions as well as the conversion factor into global warming potentials are those agreed by 'The Conference of the Parties'. The report has to be submitted annually and will be reviewed by a panel for compliance. The panel experts are nominated by the parties to the Protocol.

Evaluation

The clear and uniform guidelines on how to prepare inventories have to be judged positively. They do not leave room for different interpretations and make it easier to identify violations of the treaty. However, this statement has to be qualified, considering the composition of the expert panel. Independence of the panel would have been served better if no signatory were assigned a seat. The frequency of the reports ensures that violations are swiftly detected. A major shortcoming is the fact that the inventory is not conducted by an independent scientific auditing panel reporting directly to the secretariat. In particular, reliable reports can hardly be expected from countries which are undergoing a transition to a market economy. This problem may be a major obstacle for establishing an efficient emission trading scheme for which reliable certified emission reductions are a basic prerequisite. A similar problem faces CDM, where not even national inventories will be available to the 'review panel' of the Protocol. Taken together, monitoring is far from being perfect under the Kyoto Protocol. These deficiencies will be a potential source of instability in the treaty and will provide many loopholes for cheating.

Another issue (mentioned in Section 4.5) concerns the (technical) problem of detecting non-compliance unambiguously, which is a prerequisite for sanctions. This problem is less urgent in the context of global warming.[67] Presently, there are no technical options for reducing global warming gases. Hence from the different energy sources and energy consumption of a country, one can more-or-less accurately infer emission releases. Only the accounting of carbon sinks is difficult.

In the light of the above-mentioned problems and the unlikely event that the parties will agree on an international monitoring system, Nentjes and Zhang (1997) have proposed a two-step approach for implementing a permit system. They argue that in the first step only those countries which can provide a high-standard inventory should form a permit trading bubble. In the second step, those countries which prove that they can comply with the criteria of the forerunners are allowed to join the permit club. Their approach basically resembles that of the establishment of the European Monetary Union. (Each prospective member has to prove that the four important indicators of its economy converge to the economical fundamentals of the monetary union members.) However, this approach implies that Russia and many Eastern European countries, which are expected to be potential permit sellers, would not be members of the first step and therefore efficiency gains from trading would be lost.

Another open question related to monitoring is whether permit trade should be allowed between private and public entities across borders or only between governments (see also Chapters 5 and 6). The first option has the advantage that it allows for a higher flexibility and hence ensures a higher efficiency. Moreover, the second option bears the danger that inefficient policies are implemented within a country, undermining the performance of the tradable permit system. However, it is obvious that transactions at a country level are far easier to monitor than transactions under the first option. Thus, given the severe problems of monitoring, the second option appears preferable for the next couple of years.

7.6 Assisting Development

Facts

Article 11 states that developed countries should assist developing countries to pursue the goals of the Protocol by monetary and in-kind transfers and by providing technological assistance.

Evaluation
This provision is standard in all modern IEAs and is basically only a statement of good intentions since no targets are mentioned at all. Though these measures may be beneficial for the group of signatories, individual signatories face a strong free-rider incentive of the second type, which can hardly be controlled due to the lack of credible sanctions (see Section 4.4, Conclusion 10). Instead signatories have an incentive to spend their money on CDM, on buying permits or in other ways.

7.7   Enforcement

Facts
Article 18 states that at the first session, The Conference of the Parties shall 'approve appropriate and effective procedures and mechanism to determine and to address cases of non-compliance [...], including through the development of an indicative list of consequences, taking into account the cause, type, degree and frequency of non-compliance'. Any such measure 'shall be adopted by means of an amendment to this Protocol'. Article 20 states that amendments shall be reached by consensus and if this not possible, amendments become binding only for those parties which have ratified the them. Article 27 states that any party may withdraw 'from the agreement after three years from the date on which the Protocol has entered into force [....]. Any such withdrawal shall take effect upon expiry of one year from the date of receipt by the Depository of the notification [...]'.

Evaluation
The lack of any enforcement measure is an important drawback of the Kyoto Protocol. Given the demanding abatement targets agreed under the Protocol (see Section 7.1) and due to the inherent instability of any transfer scheme (JI, CDM and permit trading) as identified above, this shortcoming is particularly serious. Other factors associated with the problem of global warming make this shortcoming even more important. First, the effects of global warming as well as expected abatement costs are uncertain by their nature. Second, political stability in developing countries and some countries of the former Soviet Union is relatively low. Third, the problem of unemployment is on the top of the agenda of most governments in Europe, whereas environmental issues have become less important. All these factors imply that governments discount time, much of which is a source of instability (see Sections 3.3 and 4.6). Another source of instability is the low rate of detecting non-

compliance, which has to be expected as a result of the shortcomings of the monitoring system mentioned above. The only factor which may work in favor of the Protocol is the frequent monitoring through the expert panel based on the annual inventories submitted by the signatories.The fact that enforcement measures have to be established via amendments which have to be agreed upon by consensus does not leave room for much hope that such measures will be implemented in the future. Moreover, any party foreseeing that it might not be able to comply with its target always has the option not to ratify the amendment; the sanction procedures will not apply to the free rider.

A general problem which arises from Article 27 is that even if sanction measures are established in the future, any non-complying party can withdraw from the treaty within one year. This short interval basically leaves very little leeway to design renegotiation-proof sanction procedures. It implies that possible sanctions may not last longer than a few months and must be very soft so as not to induce a country to leave the agreement (see Section 4.1). It would be conducive to the stability of the Protocol to extend the opting-out clause to at least three years, as is common under most other IEAs.

8.   CONCLUSION

The previous chapters have shown that game theory is a useful tool for analyzing global pollution problems. The difficulties of cooperation and also the measures to establish cooperation have been discussed. Due to the many results and the concise summaries in conclusions in previous sections, we will not summarize the discussion here again. Instead, we will briefly discuss open issues and provide a guideline for future research.

First, there remain some empty spaces on the theoretical research agenda. Some important issues which have not been covered in this article are incomplete information and the risk preferences of agents.[68] Of those issues which have been covered here, further research is particularly important on issue linkage and coalition theory. Both issues should be investigated in a more general framework where both types of free-rider incentives are captured. In coalition theory, the effect of simultaneous coalitions, the choice of abatement target and the burden–sharing rule on the success of IEAs should be given a high priority on the agenda of future research. In the theory on issue linkage, the analysis of the effect of non-separable utility functions on the success of package deals is important.

Second, the game-theoretical research has so far almost exclusively focused on the analysis of international environmental problems. However, policy recommendations have played only a minor role in the literature. For example, it has been extensively explained why IEAs face a stability problem and why only moderate abatement targets will be agreed upon in a treaty. However, recommendations on how this problem may be mitigated are almost completely lacking.

Third, only a few attempts have been undertaken to relate the theoretical results to actual IEAs. For example, it has been concluded that threats to sanction non-compliance are necessary to stabilize an IEA. Moreover, it has been stressed that these threats must be credible. However, there needs to be much more work done on how credible sanctions can be designed for practical purposes.

Fourth, the link between game theory and empirical research is very loose. There are only a few articles in which cost–benefit analysis and game theory are linked.[69] Of those few papers, however, most have analyzed only hypothetical abatement targets and not those which have actually been agreed upon by the parties.[70]

Fifth, the game-theoretical analysis has assumed in the tradition of welfare economics, that governments maximize the welfare of their countries (benevolent dictators). It thereby removes this aspect from the decision process within a country (black box) and from other politico-economic aspects. For instance, a government is assumed to behave opportunistically and to take a free ride whenever the gains exceed the punishment. However, in a public choice context, reputation effects may also play some role in influencing a government's decision. This concerns the reputation of a government towards its voters but also towards other governments (see Chapter 4).[71]

Thus taken together, the game-theoretical analysis of international environmental problems, though it is a relatively young field of research, has generated many interesting insights. However, there still remains a large field for applied and empirical game theoretical research to be treated in the future.

NOTES

1. We ignore in this exposition at least two facts. First, there might be a time lag between the time when benefits and damage costs accrue to agents. Second, global warming gases are

stock pollutants (that is, damages depend on accumulated greenhouse gas emissions) rather than flow pollutants as assumed in [2.1]. Our framework allows us to concentrate on the incentive structure for countries to sign and comply with an IEA in the simplest way. For a similar assumption see Chander et al. (1999), Falkinger, Hackl and Pruckner (1996) and Fankhauser and Kverndokk (1996). A mathematically more rigorous analysis in a similar framework may be found in Folmer and van Mouche (2000a), van Mouche (2001) and Welsch (1993). The first two papers also cover the more general case of transboundary pollution.

2. From a mathematical point of view, this additional assumption is not necessary for the subsequent results.

3. For simplicity, we only consider games with interior solutions throughout this chapter. Corner solutions are considered for instance in Finus (2001, ch. 9).

4. Uniqueness follows from standard theorems (see, e.g. Finus 2001, ch. 9). An alternative and more sophisticated proof is provided in Folmer and van Mouche (2000a) and van Mouche (2001).

5. In the example, linear reaction functions have been assumed, though generally this need not be true. See Finus (2001, ch. 9).

6. See Folmer and van Mouche (2000a) and van Mouche (2001) for a proof.

7. Uniform proportional emission reductions have been analyzed and compared to the Nash equilibrium and to the global optimum in Endres (1993 and 1997b), Endres and Finus (1998a and 1999).

8. We define an IEA as a strategy set different from the Nash equilibrium. This comprises at least an emission vector different from the Nash equilibrium. However, an IEA may also specify obligations with respect to transfers, monitoring, punishment in case of non-compliance and so forth. Those other strategies are discarded for the moment and taken up later.

9. The definition of individual rationality we present here is confined to the static framework. It differs from the game-theoretical definition used in the context of repeated games and reduced stage games. Both definitions will be related to each other in Section 3.

10. The indifference curves I_1^N and I_2^N represent all emission vectors which give a country i the same net benefit as in the Nash equilibrium. Any emission vector south-east (north-west) of I_1^N (I_2^N) gives country 1 (country 2) a higher payoff than in the Nash equilibrium.

11. For details see Section 5.

12. It is straightforward to show that Result 2 also holds if a sub-group of countries choose a cooperative emission vector.

13. Three reasons can be identified for this shortcoming. First, modeling the whole bargaining process leading to the design of a particular IEA endogenously is an extremely complex undertaking (see Bloch 1997, Ray and Vohra 1999 and Yi 1997). Second, the pragmatic approach of testing the effect of a large number of different designs on the stability and equilibrium number of signatories and deducing general results by statistical inference hits natural boundaries even with computers. Third, bargaining theory has mainly been studied by scholars of cooperative game theory, whereas stability aspects of contracts have been investigated by scholars of non-cooperative game theory. This artificial barrier was not conducive to developing an integrated model to depict the entire formation of IEAs.

14. Moreover, many IEAs also have a very poor compliance record with respect to reporting requirements (Bothe 1996, pp. 22ff, GAO 1992, pp. 3 and Sand 1996, p. 55). Since official monitoring in almost all IEAs relies exclusively on self-reporting of states, some suspicion with respect to the good official compliance records of some IEAs seems also justified (Ausubel and Victor 1992, pp. 23ff).

15. None of the relevant surveys on the enforcement of international environmental treaties has found any provision for sanctions to penalize parties for non-compliance (Bergesen and Parmann 1997, pp. 80-205 and Sand 1992; see also the survey articles of Birnie and Boyle 1992, chapter 4, Bothe 1996, pp. 13, Boyle 1991, pp. 229ff, Kummer 1994, pp. 256ff, Lanchberry 1998, pp. 57ff, O'Connell 1992, pp. 293ff, 1995, pp. 47ff, Sand 1991, pp. 236ff, 1994, pp. 75ff, Sands 1996, pp. 48ff and Shihata 1996, pp. 37ff).

16. Examples include for instance the 'Convention to Combat Desertification' (Paris, 1994) and the 'Convention on the Protection of the Marine Environment of the Baltic Sea' (Helsinki, 1974).

17. This requires for instance that for an environmentally concerned voter it is more difficult to monitor compliance of an IEA than the accession to an IEA and that information is costly.

18. That is, payoffs are received only once after the third stage. Thus, time is not explicitly modeled as in repeated games. See the discussion in Section 3.2.

19. The concept of internal and external stability has been used for instance by Barrett (1994b), Bauer (1992), Botteon and Carraro (1997, 1998), Carraro and Siniscalco (1991, 1993) and Hoel (1992). The concept of the core has been applied for instance by Chander and Tulkens (1995, 1997). Other concepts which may be superior from a conceptual point of view as well as from the perspective of 'realistic modeling' may be found in Bloch (1997) and Yi (1997). First results and an evaluation of these concepts in the context of IEAs may be found in Finus (2001, ch. 15) and Finus and Rundshagen (2001).

20. Leakage effects have been studied by Bohm (1993), Felder and Rutherford (1993) and Golombek, Hagem and Hoel (1995) in the energy market. Energy conservation by 'green countries' leads to a reduction of demand for crude oil. Consequently, energy prices drop. This in turn triggers higher demand from less environmentally conscious countries, which renders the environmental policy of green countries less effective. See also Bohm and Larsen (1993) and Hoel (1994) on leakage effects and countervailing measures.

21. Simply speaking, the Nash-bargaining solution allocates the global gains to the coalition in proportion to the payoff in the Nash equilibrium. The Shapley value allocates the global gains according to the marginal contribution of each member to the success of a coalition. See for instance Binmore, Rubinstein and Wolinsky (1986) and Owen (1995) for details.

22. *Ex-ante* symmetric refers to the assumption that all countries have the same payoff function though they may receive different payoffs depending on whether they become a signatory or remain a non-signatory (or in the general context, which coalition they join).

23. In the case of symmetric countries, the Nash-bargaining, the Shapley value and probably any other bargaining rule implies no redistribution of the initial payoff allocation. However, strictly speaking, despite the assumption of symmetric countries, any asymmetric allocation of payoffs cannot be ruled out *a priori*, though it would probably require some additional motivation that would be endogenous to the model. See Ray and Vohra (1999) for a first attempt to endogenize the choice of transfer scheme in the coalition formation process.

24. See the discussion and observation on consensus in Section 2.

25. 'New' concepts which take possible chain reactions into consideration are for instance Chwe's concept of farsighted coalitional stability (Chwe 1994) and Ray and Vohra's concept of equilibrium binding agreement (Ray and Vohra 1997). These concepts are discussed in Finus (2001), ch. 15.

26. Under the α- and β-core it is assumed that the remaining players play a minimax and maximin strategy respectively, which constitute harsh and certainly not credible punishments.

27. An extensive exposition and discussion of the core concept may be found in Finus (2001), ch. 13.

28. For differential games in the international pollution context see, e.g. Dockner and van Long (1993) and Tahvonen (1994). To the best of the author's knowledge, difference games have not been used to study international pollution problems yet. Note that structural time independency in repeated games does not imply that there is no strategic time dependency. All dynamic games capture strategic time dependency, which implies that strategies at some point in time depend on strategies played in the past.

29. The interested reader is referred to Finus (2001) for the analysis of finitely repeated games.

30. Simply speaking, a subgame-perfect equilibrium is a dynamic strategy combination which is a Nash equilibrium for the rest of the game at each point in time. For a definition see Finus (2001), chapter 4 and the literature cited there.

31. The average discounted payoff is the payoff a player receives on average in one period if he/she receives a payoff stream over a certain time span. For details on discounting see Finus (2001), ch. 4 and 5 and the literature cited there.

32. This definition stresses that an IEA can be approximated as an infinitely repeated game. By the time a country decides whether to comply it suffices if the end of the game is not known. That is, $p_i > 0$, though p_i may be close to zero.

33. In contrast, for instance in the context of a Cournot oligopoly (competition in output quantities) a natural candidate for the minimax payoff is $\pi_i^{\min\max} = 0$. For a sufficiently high output quantity the market price is zero, implying zero profits.

34. One can easily perceive that the discount rate changes over time and is particularly high prior to elections. In the following we ignore this complication and follow the standard assumption in the literature by assuming a constant discount rate.

35. For an intensive discussion of these conditions in the context of global environmental problems see Endres and Finus (1998a) and Finus and Rundshagen (1998b). We restrict attention here to the weak version of the concept. Strongly renegotiation-proof equilibria are discussed in Finus (2001), chapters 7 and 12.

36. The equivalence sign in C_4 holds because

substituting $\pi_j^{P2} = (1-\delta_j^{t_i^P})\pi_j^R(e_i^l, e_{-i}^l) + \delta_j^{t_i^P}\pi_j^*(e_i^*, e_{-i}^*)$ in $\pi_j^* \le \pi_j^{P2}$ gives $\pi_j^* \le \pi_j^R$.

37. For example, some years ago the USA threatened China that it would not prolong its 'most favored nation status' if it would not legally protect patents and copyrights. Since China knew that US trade depends heavily on exports to China, China concluded that the threat was empty and did not take any serious actions. Another example is the (unsuccessful) grain embargo which was imposed on the former Soviet Union some years ago. US, New Zealand and Australian farmers lobbied their governments to lift the embargo because of substantial profit losses. On the credibility of sanctions see Miyagawa (1992).

38. The fact that abatement costs of the punishers also decrease by such a punishment constitutes a *theoretical* possibility that condition C_4 may, nevertheless, be satisfied. However, this requires that the violator reduces its emissions during the repentance phase sufficiently below Nash equilibrium levels, i.e., $e_i^l << e_i^N = e_i(e_{-i}^N)$, so that $\pi_j^* < \pi_j^R \ \forall \ j$ is possible. This explains our cautious phrasing.

39. For instance, changing the standards of catalytic converters of cars or the level of a fuel tax requires that governments pass a new law in Parliament, which is usually a time-consuming process in democracies.

40. For discount factors close to one, the corridor reduces to one point: $E^{*,\delta} = \{e^N\}$ ($\bar{\Pi}^{*,\delta} = \{\bar{\pi}^N\}$) (Finus and Rundshagen 1998b).

41. For details see Finus (2001), ch. 12.

42. In an IRG where there is no obvious sequence of moves (does the donor or the recipient countries move first?) one may well assume that on average all players move simultaneously. It is easily checked that all qualitative results derived below would also hold for sequential moves, irrespective of who is the first mover.
43. Such measures are sometimes referred to as 'technological exchange'.
44. Formally, this may be demonstrated by considering the non-cooperative maximization task of a donor country j. From $\max_{T_j} b_j(\Sigma T_k) - T_j$ the first order condition in the Nash equilibrium

   is $b_j'(\Sigma T_k^N) = 1$ where b_j denotes the benefit from transfers (e.g. in the form of higher

   stability of an IEA). For any transfer under a cooperative arrangement for which $\Sigma T_k^N < \Sigma T_k^*$

   is true, $b_j'(\Sigma T_k^K) > 1$, implying a free-rider incentive of the second type. See Barrett (1994a), who analyzes in an IRG whether the group of donors can form a stable coalition. His setting resembles that of Section 6.2.
45. In particular, it seems that some of the arguments also apply to the design of IEAs in general.
46. Though Cesar and de Zeeuw (1996) cover renegotiation-proof strategies, their proof is incomplete and only applies to prisoners' dilemmas. The subsequent discussion will show that the result applies to a broader class of games.
47. In Appendix 2 we show that Result 4 also holds for renegotiation-proof strategies.
48. We also implicitly assumed that payoffs in the linked game receive equal weight. In van Mouche (2000) it is shown that Result 4 also applies to additive payoffs with different weights and to any linear transformation of payoffs through issue linkage.
49. For instance, the reduction of SO_x is regulated in the Helsinki Protocol (1985) and the successor agreement the Oslo Protocol (1994). The Sofia Protocol (1988) aims at reducing NO_x.
50. These are methane (CH_4), nitrous oxide (N_2O), hydrofluorocarbons (HFCs), perfluorocarbons (PFCs), sulfur hexafluoride (SF_6).
51. See Finus (2001, ch. 8) and Spagnolo (1996) in the context of international environmental agreements. New insights are provided in Spagnolo (1999 and forthcoming) though in the context of other economic problems.
52. See the examples cited at the beginning of this section and Ragland, Bennett and Yolles (1996).
53. National monitoring is required, for instance, under the 'Convention on International Trade in Endangered Species of Wild Fauna and Flora' (CITES, Washington, 1973), the 'International Tropical Timber Agreement' (ITTA, Geneva, 1994) or the 'Convention on the Conservation of Antarctic Marine Living Resources' (CCAMLR, Canberra, 1980). See Birnie and Boyle (1992, pp. 236ff), Boyle (1991, pp. 166ff), Fischer (1991), Ladenburger (1996, pp. 24ff), Maruahn (1996, pp. 707ff) and Sachariew (1992, p. 31) on this point.
54. Some IEAs have a provision to implement agreed abatement duties into national law as for instance the Waigani Convention ('Convention to Ban the Importation into Forum Island Countries of Hazardous and Radioactive Wastes and to Control the Transboundary Movement and Management of Hazardous Wastes within the South Pacific Region', Waigani, 1995). For details, see Bergesen and Parmann (1997, p. 106) and Sands (1996, pp. 52ff).
55. For instance, the Framework Convention on Climate Change (Rio de Janeiro, 1992) has a provision requiring member states to conduct research on the effects of global warming.
56. The list of examples of uniform emission reduction quotas is long and includes the 'Montreal Protocol on Substances that Deplete the Ozone Layer', which specified an emission reduction of CFCs and halons by 20 per cent based on 1986 emission levels, which had to be accomplished by 1998. Uniform emission quotas are also part of the amendments

signed in London (1990) and in Copenhagen (1992). Another example is the Helsinki Protocol, which suggested a reduction of sulfur dioxide from 1980 levels by 30 per cent by 1993. Moreover, the 'Sofia Protocol Concerning the Control of Emissions of Nitrogen Oxides or Their Transboundary Fluxes' signed in 1988, called on countries to *uniformly* freeze their emissions at 1987 levels by 1995 and the 'Geneva Protocol Concerning the Control of Emissions of Volatile Organic Compounds or Their Fluxes' signed in 1991, required parties to reduce 1988 emissions by 30 per cent by 1999.

57. Due to the transfers involved in permit trading, the welfare implications of a permit system cannot be visualized in Figure 2.1.

58. A proposal, r_i, follows from maximizing $\beta_i((1-r_i)\cdot e_i^N)-\phi_i((1-r_i)\cdot \Sigma e_j^N)$ with respect to r_i.

59. Under a tax regime a proposal, t_i, follows from maximizing $\beta_i(e_i(t_i))-\phi_i(e_1(t_i)+...+e_N(t_i))$ with respect to t_i where $e_i(t_i)$ follows from $\beta_i'(e_i)=t_i$. Under a permit proposal, a proposal r_i, is derived from maximizing $\beta_i(e_i(r_i))-\phi_i(\Sigma e_j^N(1-r_i))-p\cdot(e_i(r_i)-e_i^N(1-r_i))$ with respect to r_i where $\beta_1'(e_1(r_1))=...=\beta_N'(e_N(r_N))=p$. See Endres and Finus (1999) for details.

60. The assumption of strict concavity may be relaxed. It suffices if payoff functions are single peaked (Endres and Finus 1998b). It can be shown that under the fixed uniform quota regime, payoff functions are strictly concave with respect to the policy level for the standard properties of the payoff functions assumed in [2.2]. For the tradable quota and the tax regime, additional assumptions are necessary, which hold for most payoff functions used in the literature (Endres and Finus 1998b and 1999).

61. Though some models (e.g. Barrett 1994b and Hoel 1992) are formulated in reduction space, they can be reformulated straightforwardly in emission space to fit into one of the two categories of payoff functions.

62. We use the phrasing 'is at least as high' instead of 'greater' in Result 8 since for welfare functions of type 2 there are no leakage effects.

63. Bauer (1992) and Hoel (1992) assume no transfers. Barrett (1997b) and Botteon and Carraro (1997) assume either that the gains from cooperation are distributed according to the Nash bargaining solution or the Shaply value.

64. For instance, though China would like to join the WTO and some governments support its application in order to stabilize relations with China in other policy fields, the USA has vetoed any such attempts for a long time.

65. The BAU-scenario is a prediction of how emissions would increase if no actions were taken and the economies grow at a steady path.

66. See Chapter 3 and Endres, Finus and Rundshagen (2000) and the literature cited there.

67. This problem is important for example in the Whaling Convention, where it is difficult to monitor the catch of whales. One cannot (unambiguously) infer the stock of whales from the catch due natural fluctuations of the stock.

68. For details see Endres and Ohl (2000) and Finus (2001, ch. 16).

69. Examples in the context of acid rain include Germain, Toint and Tulkens (1996), Kaitala, Mäler and Tulkens (1995), Kaitala, Pohjola and Tahvonen (1991) and Mäler (1989). In the context of global warming Tahvonen (1994) and Welsch (1995) may be mentioned.

70. Exceptions are for instance Eyckmans (2000) and Eyckmans and Tulkens (1999), Finus and Tjøtta (1998) and Murdoch and Sandler (1997).

71. Hoel and Schneider (1997) and Jeppesen and Andersen (1998) are the first to have considered reputation effects. Endres (1997) and Endres and Finus (1998c) look at the effect of environmental consciousness on the success of an IEA and the demand of environmentally concerned voters that their government should reduce emissions unilaterally in order to give a good example to other countries. However, all these papers analyze these

effects in a traditional welfare economic context by including an additional variable but not in a proper public choice framework.

APPENDIX 1

We prove Result 4 for renegotiation-proof strategies. According to [2.8] and [2.9] in the text, omitting strategies for convenience,

$$(1 - \delta_i^{t_i^P}) \pi_{ik}^R + \delta_i^{t_i^P} \pi_{ik}^* - \pi_{ik}^{P_1} \geq 0$$

$$\pi_{ik}^* - (1 - \delta_i) \pi_{ik}^F - \delta_i \pi_{ik}^{P_1} \geq 0 \quad \text{s.t.} \quad \pi_{jk}^* \leq \pi_{jk}^R \quad \forall \ i, j \text{ and } k \in \{1, 2\} \quad [2.A_1]$$

must hold in the isolated games to sustain both issues in a renegotiation-proof way whereas in the linked game

$$(1 - \delta_i^{t_i^P}) \sum_{k=1}^{2} \pi_{ik}^R + \delta_i^{t_i^P} \sum_{k=1}^{2} \pi_{ik}^* - \sum_{k=1}^{2} \pi_{ik}^{P_1} \geq 0$$

$$\sum_{k=1}^{2} \pi_{ik}^* - (1 - \delta_i) \sum_{k=1}^{2} \pi_{ik}^F - \delta_i \sum_{k=1}^{2} \pi_{ik}^{P_1} \geq 0 \quad \text{s.t.} \quad \sum_{k=1}^{2} \pi_{jk}^* \leq \sum_{k=1}^{2} \pi_{jk}^R \quad \forall \ i \text{ and } j \quad [2.A_2]$$

must be true. Since [2.A$_2$] is implied by [2.A$_1$], Result 4 also applies to renegotiation-proof strategies (q.e.d.).

APPENDIX 2

The consideration of the detection rate k and the frequency of monitoring f in subsection 4.5 have no effect on [2.8] and C$_4$ since both conditions assume that punishment has already started. However, considering $f \in \{1, ...T\}$, [2.9] becomes

$$\sum_{t=0}^{\infty} \delta_i^t \pi_i^* \geq \sum_{t=0}^{f-1} \delta_i^t \pi_i^F + \sum_{t=f}^{\infty} \delta_i^t \pi_i^{P_1} \Leftrightarrow \delta_i \geq \left[\frac{\pi_i^F - \pi_i^*}{\pi_i^F - \pi_i^{P_1}} \right]^{1/f}. \qquad [2.A_3]$$

Considering $k \in [0, 1]$, [2.9] becomes

$$\sum_{t=0}^{\infty} \delta_i^t \pi_i^* \geq \pi_i^F + \delta_i[(1-k) \cdot \pi_i^F + k \cdot \pi_i^{P_1}] + \delta_i^2[(1-k)^2 \cdot \pi_i^F + (1-(1-k)^2) \cdot \pi_i^{P_1} + \ldots]$$

$$\Leftrightarrow \delta_i \geq \frac{\pi_i^F - \pi_i^*}{\pi_i^F - \pi_i^{P_1} - (1-k)(\pi_i^* - \pi_i^{P_1})} \qquad [2.A_4]$$

and hence [2.18] follows from which it is evident that $\partial \delta_i^{\min} / \partial f > 0$ and $\partial \delta_i^{\min} / \partial k < 0$ hold (q.e.d.).

APPENDIX 3

We only sketch the proof since most elements have been proved elsewhere (Endres and Finus 1998b and 1999). Recall that we assume for convenience payoff functions to be strictly convex in policy levels, though this assumption may be relaxed.

1. Fixed and Tradable Quota Regime

By construction of these regimes, any positive quota implies lower global emissions than in the Nash equilibrium. By strict concavity of the payoff functions, all countries must gain from moderate quotas and in particular under the SCD-decision rule. Without loss of generality, suppose proposals to be given by $0 \leq r_1 \leq r_2 \leq \ldots \leq r_N$ and therefore countries agree on r_1. Then r_1 maximizes country 1's welfare if r_1 is applied and all other countries are at the ascending part of their payoff function. Consequently, if all countries gain from moderate emission reductions and particularly from those emission reductions agreed under the SCD-decision rule, global welfare is higher than in the Nash equilibrium.

2. Tax

Any proposal which implies that global emissions are higher than in the Nash equilibrium cannot be individually rational for at least one country i. (1) Suppose all countries increase emissions compared to the Nash equilibrium. By the strict concavity of indifference curves and by the definition of a (unique) Nash equilibrium, this would imply a welfare loss to all countries (see Figure 2.1). (2) Country i reduces emissions compared to the Nash equilibrium and therefore has lower benefits than in the Nash equilibrium but faces higher damages. Thus country i would lose.

Now suppose that global emissions under the tax regime are gradually reduced from Nash equilibrium emissions towards the social optimum. Since payoff functions are strictly concave by assumption, the sum of all payoff functions (global welfare) will also be strictly concave. Consequently, the move from Nash equilibrium emissions towards the global optimum implies a global welfare gain, in particular since emissions are reduced efficiently.

3. Equal Proposals

Equal proposals under the SCD-decision rule are a necessary condition for global welfare to be at the globally optimal level. The reason is simple. 1) Suppose proposals can be ordered according to $\psi_1 \leq \psi_2 \leq ... \leq \psi_N$ where ψ_i is either a fixed quota, tradable quota or tax proposal. 2) A proposal maximizes a country's welfare if it is applied. 3) For the policy level which maximizes global welfare under a policy regime, ψ^*, $\psi_1 \leq \psi^* \leq \psi_N$ must be true since it is derived from maximizing the sum of all payoff functions. Thus, as long as $\psi_1 < \psi_N$, $\psi_1 < \psi^*$ will be true. This has two implications: 1) Since the tradable quota and the tax regime are efficient, equal proposals are a necessary and sufficient condition for global optimal welfare to be obtained. Under the fixed quota regime, equal proposals are only a necessary condition because this policy instrument is inefficient. 2) Under the tax and tradable policy regime $\psi_1 = \psi^*$ implies the same and $\psi_1 < \psi^*$ higher global emissions than in the global optimum since both regimes imply efficient emission reductions. However, under the fixed quota regime emission reductions are generally inefficient and ψ^* maximizes only global welfare given the constraint of uniform reductions. Therefore, conclusions with respect to a comparison of global emissions under the fixed quota regime and the social optimum cannot be drawn.

REFERENCES

Ausubel, J. H. and D. G. Victor (1992), 'Verification of International Environmental Agreements', *Annual Review of Energy and Environment*, **17**, 1–43.

Barratt-Brown, E. P. (1991), 'Building a Monitoring and Compliance Regime under the Montreal Protocol', *Yale Journal of International Law*, **16**, 519–570.

Barrett, S. (1994a), 'The Biodiversity Supergame', *Environmental and Resource Economics*, **4**, 111–122.

Barrett, S. (1994b), 'Self-Enforcing International Environmental Agreements', *Oxford Economic Papers*, **46**, 804–878.

Barrett, S. (1997a), 'Toward a Theory of International Environmental Cooperation', in Carlo Carraro and Dominico Siniscalco (eds), *New Directions in the Economic Theory of the Environment*, Cambridge, UK: Cambridge University Press, 239–280.

Barrett, S. (1997b), 'Heterogenous International Agreements', in Carlo Carraro (ed.), *International Environmental Negotiations: Strategic Policy Issues*, Cheltenham, UK and Lyme, US: Edward Elgar, 9–25.

Barrett, S. (1997c), 'The Strategy of Trade Sanctions in International Environmental Agreements', *Resource and Energy Economics*, **19**, 345–361.

Basar, T. and G. Olsder (1982), *Dynamic Non-Cooperative Game Theory*, London, UK: Academic Press.

Bauer, A. (1992), *International Cooperation over Greenhouse Gas Abatement*, Munich, Germany: Mimeo of the Seminar für empirische Wirtschaftsforschung, University of Munich.

Benedick, R. E. (1991), 'Protecting the Ozone Layer: New Directions in Diplomacy', in J. Mathews (ed.), *Preserving the Global Environment: The Challenge of Shared Leadership*, New York, US and London, UK: Norton & Company, 112–153.

Bergesen, H. O. and G. Parmann (eds) (1997), *Green Globe Yearbook 1997*, New York, US: Oxford University Press.

Beyerlin, U. (1996), 'State Community Interests and Institution-Building in International Environmental Law', *Zeitschrift für ausländisches öffentliches Recht und Völkerrecht*, **56**, 602–627.

Binmore, K., A. Rubinstein and A. Wolinsky (1986), 'The Nash Bargaining Solution in Economic Modelling', *RAND Journal of Economics*, **17**, 176–188.

Birnie, P. W. and A. E. Boyle (1992), *International Law and the Environment*, London, UK: Clarendon Press.

Blackhurst, R. and A. Subramanian (1992), 'Promoting Multilateral Cooperation on the Environment', in K. Anderson and R. Blackhurst (eds), *The Greening of the World Trade Issue*, New York, US: Harvester Wheatsheaf, 247–268.

Bloch, F. (1997), 'Non-Cooperative Models of Coalition Formation in Games with Spillovers', in Carlo Carraro and Dominico Siniscalco (eds), *New Directions in the Economic Theory of the Environment*, Cambridge, UK: Cambridge University Press, 311–352.

Bohm, P. (1993), 'Incomplete International Cooperation to Reduce CO$_2$ Emissions: Alternative Policies', *Journal of Environmental Economics and Managment*, **24**, 258–271.

Bohm, P. and B. Larsen (1993), 'Fairness in a Tradeable-Permit Treaty for Carbon Emissions Reductions in Europe and the Former Soviet Union', *Environmental and Resource Economics*, **4**, 219–239.

Böhringer, C. (2000), 'Cooling Down Hot Air: A Global CGE Analysis of Post-Kyoto Carbon Abatement Strategies', *Energy Policy*, **28**, 779–789.

Bothe, M. (1996), 'The Evaluation of Enforcement Mechanisms in International Environmental Law', in R. Wolfrum (ed.), *Enforcing Environmental Standards: Economic Mechanisms as Viable Means?* Berlin, Germany: Springer, 13–38.

Botteon, M. and C. Carraro (1997), 'Burden-Sharing and Coalition Stability in Environmental Negotiations with Asymmetric Countries', in Carlo Carraro (ed.), *International Environmental Negotiations: Strategic Policy Issues*, Cheltenham, UK and Brookfield, US: Edward Elgar, 26–55.

Botteon, M. and C. Carraro (1998), 'Strategies for Environmental Negotiations: Issue Linkage with Heterogenous Countries', in N. Hanley and Henk Folmer (eds), *Game Theory and the Global Environment*, Cheltenham, UK and Brookfield, US: Edward Elgar, 180–200.

Boyle, A. E. (1991), 'Saving the World? Implementation and Enforcement of International Environmental Law through International Institutions', *Journal of Environmental Law*, **3**, 229–245.

Brown Weiss, E. and H. K. Jacobson (1997), 'Compliance with International Environmental Accords', in M. Role, H. Sjöberg and U. Svedin (eds.), *International Governance on Environmental Issues*, Dordrecht, The Netherlands: Kluwer, 78–110.

Carraro, C. (1997), *The Structure of International Environmental Agreements*, Working Paper, Milan, Italy: Fondazione Eni Enrico Mattei, April.

Carraro C. and C. Marchiori (2001), *Endogenous Strategic Issue Linkage in International Negotiations*, Paper presented at the Workshop on Coalition Theory, January 2001, Louvain-la-Neuve, Belgium.

Carraro C. and F. Moriconi (1997), *International Games on Climate Change Control*, Working Paper, Milan, Italy: Fondazione Eni Enrico Mattei, September.

Carraro, C. and D. Siniscalco (1991), *Strategies for the International Protection of the Environment*, Working Paper, Milan, Italy: Fondazione Eni Enrico Mattei, March.

Carraro, C. and D. Siniscalco (1993), 'Strategies for the International Protection of the Environment', *Journal of Public Economics*, **52**, 309–328.

Carraro, C. and D. Siniscalco (1997), 'R&D Cooperation and the Stability of International Environmental Agreements', in Carlo Carraro (ed.), *International Environmental Negotiations: Strategic Policy Issues*, Cheltenham, UK and Brookfield, US: Edward Elgar, 71–96.

Carraro, C. and D. Siniscalco (1998), 'International Environmental Agreements: Incentives and Political Economy', *European Economic Review*, **42**, 561–572.

Cesar, H. and A. de Zeeuw (1996), 'Issue Linkage in Global Environmental Problems', in A. Xepapadeas, *Economic Policy for the Environment and Natural Resources: Techniques for the Management and Control of Pollution*, Cheltenham, UK and Brookfield, US: Edward Elgar, 158–173.

Chander, P. and H. Tulkens (1995), 'A Core-Theoretic Solution for the Design of Cooperative Agreements on Transfrontier Pollution', *International Tax and Public Finance*, **2**, 279–293.

Chander, P. and H. Tulkens (1997), 'The Core of an Economy with Multilateral Environmental Externalities', *International Journal of Game Theory*, **26**, 379–401.

Chander, P., H. Tulkens, J.-P Van Ypersele, and S. Willems (1999), *The Kyoto Protocol: An Economic and Game Theoretic Interpretation*, Working Paper no. 12, Louvain-la-Neuve, Belgium: CLIMNEG.

Chayes, A. H. and A. Chayes (1993), 'On Compliance'. *International Organization*, **47**, 175–205.

Chwe, M. S.-Y. (1994), 'Farsighted Coalitional Stability', *Journal of Economic Theory*, **63**, 299–325.

DeSombre, E. R. and J. Kauffman (1996), 'The Montreal Protocol Multilateral Fund: Partial Success Story', in R. O. Keohane and M. A. Levy (eds), *Institutions for Environmental Aid: Pitfalls and Promise*, Cambridge, US and London, UK: MIT Press, 89–126.

de Zeeuw, A. J. and F. van der Ploeg (1991), 'Difference Games and Policy Evaluation: A Conceptual Framework', *Oxford Economic Papers*, **43**, 612–636.

Eichberger, J. (1993), *Game Theory for Economists*, San Diego, US: Academic Press.

Endres, A. (1993), 'Internationale Vereinbarungen zum Schutz der globalen Umweltressourcen: der Fall proportionaler Emmissionsreduktion. Außenwirtschaft', *The Swiss Review of International Economic Relations*, **48**, 51–76.

Endres, A. (1995), 'Zur Ökonomie internationaler Umweltschutzvereinbarungen', *Zeitschrift für Umweltpolitik*, **8**, 143–178.

Endres, A. (1997a), 'Increasing Environmental Awareness to Protect the Global Commons: A Curmudgeon's View', *Kyklos*, **50**, 3–27.

Endres, A. (1997b), 'Negotiating a Climate Convention: The Role of Prices and Quantities', *International Review of Law and Economics*, 17, 147–156.

Endres, A. and M. Finus (1998a), 'Renegotiation-Proof Equilibria in a Bargaining Game over Global Emission Reductions: Does the Instrumental Framework Matter?' in N. Hanley and Henk Folmer (eds), *Game Theory and the Global Environment*, Cheltenham, UK and Brookfield, US: Edward Elgar, 135–164.

Endres, A. and M. Finus (1998b), *Quotas May Beat Taxes in a Global Emission Game*, Hagen, Germany: University of Hagen (Preliminary Draft).

Endres, A. and M. Finus (1998c), 'Playing a Better Global Emission Game: Does it Help to be Green?', *Swiss Journal of Economics and Statistics*, **134**, 21–40.

Endres, A. and M. Finus (1999), 'International Environmental Agreements: How the Policy Instrument Affects Equilibrium Emissions and Welfare', *Journal of Institutional and Theoretical Economics*, **155**, 527–550.

Endres, A., M. Finus and B. Rundshagen (2000), *EOLSS-Level Writing in Financial Resource Policy and Management: Strategic Aspects of Implementing the International Agreement on Climate Change*, in M. K. Tolba (ed.), *Our Fragile World: Challenges and Opportunities for Sustainable Development*, Vol. II, Eolss Publishers, Oxford.

Endres, A. and C. Ohl (2000), 'Das Kooperationsverhalten der Staaten bei der Begrenzung globaler Umweltrisiken: Zur Integration stochastischer und strategischer Unsicherheitsaspekte', *Swiss Journal of Economics*, **136**, 1–26.

Eyckmans, J. (2000), *On the Farsighted Stability of the Kyoto Protocol: Some Simulations*, Leuven, Belgium: University of Leuven (Preliminary Draft).

Eyckmans, J. and H. Tulkens (1999), *Simulating with RICE Coalitionally Stable Burden Sharing Agreements for Climate Change Problem*, Leuven, Belgium: University of Leuven (Preliminary Draft).

Falkinger, J., F. Hackl and G. J. Pruckner (1996), 'A Fair Mechanism for Efficient Reduction of Global CO_2-emissions', *Finanzarchiv*, **53**, 308–331.

Fankhauser, S. and S. Kverndokk (1996), 'The Global Warming Game: Simulations of a CO_2 Reduction Agreement', *Resource and Energy Economics*, **18**, 83–102.

Farrell, J. and E. Maskin (1989a), 'Renegotiation in Repeated Games', *Games and Economic Behavior*, **1**, 327–360.

Farrell, J. and E. Maskin (1989b), 'Renegotiation-Proof Equilibrium: Reply', *Journal of Economic Theory*, **49**, 376–378.

Felder, S. and T. F. Rutherford (1993), 'Unilateral Reductions and Carbon Leakage: The Consequences of International Trade in Oil and Basic Materials', *Journal of Environmental Economics and Management*, **25**, 162–176.

Finus, M. (1997), 'Eine spieltheoretische Betrachtung internationaler Umweltprobleme: Eine Einführung', in P. Weis (ed.), *Nachhaltigkeit in der ökonomischen Theorie: Ökonomie und Gesellschaft*, Frankfurt, Germany: Campus, 239–300.

Finus, M. (2001), *Game Theory and International Environmental Cooperation*, Cheltenham, UK and Brookfield, US: Edward Elgar.

Finus, M. and B. Rundshagen (1998a), 'Toward a Positive Theory of Coalition Formation and Endogenous Instrumental Choice in Global Pollution Control', *Public Choice*, **96**, 145–186.

Finus, M. and B. Rundshagen (1998b), 'Renegotiation-Proof Equilibria in a Global Emission Game When Players Are Impatient', *Environmental and Resource Economics*, **12**, 275–306.

Finus, M. and B. Rundshagen (2000), *Strategic Links between Environmental and Trade Policies if Plant Location Is Endogenous*, Working Paper No. 283, Hagen, Germany: University of Hagen.

Finus, M. and B. Rundshagen (2001), *Endogeneous Coalition Formation in Global Pollution Control: A Partition Function Approach*. Working Paper No. 307, Hagen, Germany: University of Hagen.

Finus, M. and S. Tjøtta (1998), *The Oslo Agreement on Sulfur Reduction in Europe: The Great Leap Forward?* Working Paper 1898, Bergen, Norway: University of Bergen.

Fischer, W. (1991), *The Verification of International Conventions on the Protection of the Environment and Common Resources*, Forschungsbericht 2495, Jülich, Germany: Forschungszentrum Jülich.

Folmer, H. and P. van Mouche (1994), 'Interconnected Games and International Environmental Problems II', *Annals of Operations Research*, **54**, 97–117.

Folmer, H. and P. van Mouche (2000a), 'The Acid Rain Game: A Mathematically Rigorous Analysis', in P. Dasgupta, B. Kristroem and K.-G. Loefgren (eds), *Festschrift in Honor of Karl Göran Mäler*, Cheltenham, UK and Brookfield, US: Edward Elgar.

Folmer, H. and P. van Mouche (2000b), 'Transboundary Pollution and International Cooperation', in T. Tietenberg and Henk Folmer (eds), *The International Yearbook of Environmental and Resource Economics*, Cheltenham, UK and Brookfield, US: Edward Elgar.

Folmer, H., P. van Mouche and S. Ragland (1993), 'Interconnected Games and International Environmental Problems', *Environmental and Resource Economics*, **3**, 313–335.

GAO (1992), *International Environmental Agreements Are Not Well Monitored*, Washington D.C., US: United States General Accounting Office, RCED **92–43**.

Germain, M., P. L. Toint and H. Tulkens (1996), 'Calcul économique itératif et stratégique pour les négociations internationales sur les pluies acides entre la Finlande, la Russie et l'Estonie', *Annales d'Économie et Statistique*, **43**, 101–127.

Gibbons, R. (1992), *A Primer in Game Theory*, New York, US: Harvester Wheatsheaf.

Golombek, R., C. Hagem and M. Hoel (1995), 'Efficient Incomplete International Agreements', *Resource and Energy Economics*, **17**, 25–46.

Hahn, R. W. (1989), *A Primer on Environmental Policy Design*, Chur, Switzerland: Harwood Academic Publishers.

Heister, J. (1997), *Der internationale CO$_2$-Vertrag: Strategien zur Stabilisierung multilateraler Kooperation zwischen souveränen Staaten*, Tübingen, Germany: J. C. B. Mohr.

Hoel, M. (1992), 'International Environment Conventions: The Case of Uniform Reductions of Emissions', *Environmental and Resource Economics*, **2**, 141–159.

Hoel, M. (1994), 'Efficient Climate Policy in the Presence of Free Riders', *Journal of Environmental Economics and Management*, **27**, 259–274.

Hoel, M. and K. Schneider (1997), 'Incentives to Participate in an International Environmental Agreement', *Environmental and Resource Economics*, **9**, 153–170.

Ierland, E. C. van and E. C. Schmieman (1999), 'Sustainability and Joint Abatement Strategies under Multiple Pollutants and Multiple Targets: the Case of Tropospheric Ozone and Acidification in Europe', in J. Koehn, J. Gowdy, F. Hinterberger and J. van der Straaten (eds), *Sustainability in Question: The Search for a Conceptual Framework*, Cheltenham, UK and Brookfield, US: Edward Elgar, 209–228.

Jenkins, L. (1996), 'Trade Sanctions: Effective Enforcement Tools', in J. Cameron, J. Werksman and P. Roderick (eds), *Improving Compliance with International Environmental Law*, London, UK: Earthscan, 221–228.

Jeppesen, T. and P. Andersen (1998), 'Commitment and Fairness in Environmental Games', in N. Hanley and Henk Folmer (eds), *Game Theory and the Environment*, Cheltenham, UK and Brookfield, US: Edward Elgar, 65–83.

Jordan, A. and J. Werksman (1996), 'Financing Global Environmental Protection', in J. Cameron, J. Werksman and P. Roderick (eds), *Improving Compliance with International Environmental Law*, London, UK: Earthscan, 247–255.

Kaitala, V., K.-G. Mäler and H. Tulkens (1995), 'The Acid Rain Game as a Resource Allocation Process with an Application to the International Cooperation among Finland, Russia and Estonia', *Scandinavian Journal of Economics*, **97**, 325–343.

Kaitala, V., M. Pohjola and O. Tahvonen (1991), 'An Analysis of SO$_2$ Negotiations between Finland and the Soviet Union', *Finnish Economic Papers*, **4**, 104–112.

Kelsen, H. and R. W. Tucker (1967), *Principles of International Law: Second edition*, Holt, Rinehart and Winston, New York et al.

Keohane, R. O. (1995), 'Compliance with International Standards: Environmental Case Studies', in J. L. Hargrove (ed.), *Proceedings of the Eighty-Ninth Annual Meeting of the American Society of International Law*, Buffalo, NY: ASIL, 206–224.

Kneese, A. V. (1975), 'The International Columbia River Treaty: An Economic Evaluation', in A. V. Kneese and S.C. Smith (eds), *Water Research*, Baltimore, MD: Johns Hopkins Press, 69–97.

Kneese, A. V. (1988), *Environmental Stress and Political Conflicts: Salinity in the Colorado River*, Paper presented at the Conference Environmental Stress and Security, Stockholm, Sweden.

Kummer, K. (1994), 'Providing Incentives to Comply with Multilateral Environmental Agreements: An Alternative to Sanctions?', *European Environmental Law Review*, **3**, 256–263.

Ladenburger, F. (1996), *Durchsetzungsmechanismen im Umweltvölkerrecht: Enforcement gegenüber den Staaten*, Tübingen, Germany: Zeeb-Druck.

Lanchberry, J. (1998), 'Long-term Trends in Systems for Implementation Review in International Agreements on Fauna and Flora', in D. G. Victor, K. Raustiala and E. B. Skolnikoff (eds), *Proceedings of the Eighty-ninth Annual Meeting of the American Society of International Law*, New York, US: ASIL, 206–210.

Lang, W. (1996), 'Trade Restrictions as a Means of Enforcing Compliance with International Law', in R. Wolfrum (ed.), *Enforcing Environmental Standards: Economic Mechanisms as Viable Means?* Berlin, Germany: Springer, 265–283.

Mäler, K.-G. (1989), 'The Acid Rain Game', in Henk Folmer and E. van Ierland (eds), *Valuation Methods and Policy Making in Environmental Economics*, Amsterdam, The Netherlands: Elsevier, 231–252.

Mäler, K.-G. (1990), 'International Environmental Problems', *Oxford Review of Economic Policy*, **6**, 80–108.

Marauhn, T. (1996), 'Towards a Procedural Law of Compliance Control in International Environmental Relations', *Zeitschrift für ausländisches öffentliches Recht und Völkerrecht*, **56**, 696–731.

Miyagawa, M. (1992), *Do Economic Sanctions Work?*, Basingstoke, UK: Macmillan Press.

Murdoch, J.C. and T. Sandler, (1997), 'Voluntary Cutbacks and Pretreaty Behavior: The Helsinki Protocol and Sulfur Emissions', *Public Finance Review*, **25**, 139–162.

Nentjes, A. and Z. X. Zhang (1997), 'International Tradeable Carbon Permits as a Strong Form of Joint Implementation', Working paper, Groningen, The Netherlands. Also forthcoming in J. Skea (ed.), *Tradeable Permits, Tradeable Quotas and Joint Implementation*, Cheltenham, UK and Brookfield, US: Edward Elgar.

O'Connell, M. E. (1992), 'Enforcing the New International Law of the Environment', *German Yearbook of International Law*, **35**, 293–332.

Osborne, M. J. and A. Rubinstein (1994), *A Course in Game Theory*, Cambridge, US: MIT Press.

Owen, G. (1995), *Game Theory*, third edition, New York, US: Academic Press.

Ragland, S. E., L. L. Bennett and P. Yolles (1996), 'Unidirectional Problems with International River Basins: A Game Theoretic Approach', Lisbon, Portugal: Paper presented at the European Meeting of Resource and Environmental Economists, 26–29 June.

Ray, D. and R. Vohra (1997), 'Equilibrium Binding Agreements', *Journal of Economic Theory*, **73**, 30–78.

Ray, D. and R. Vohra (1999), 'A Theory of Endogenous Coalition Structures', *Games and Economic Behavior*, **26**, 286–336.

Sabourian, H. (1989), 'Repeated Games: a Survey', in F. Hahn (ed.), *The Economics of Missing Markets, Information, and Games*, Oxford, UK: Clarendon Press, 62–105.

Sachariew, K. (1992), 'Promoting Compliance with International Environmental Legal Standards: Reflections on Monitoring and Reporting Mechanisms', *Yearbook of International Environmental Law*, **2**, 31–52.

Sand, P. H. (1991), 'International Cooperation: The Environmental Experience', in J. T. Mathews (ed.), *Preserving the Global Environment*, New York, US and London, UK: W. W. Norton, 236–278.

Sand, P. H. (ed.) (1992), 'The Effectiveness of International Environmental Agreements', Cambridge, UK: Grotius Publications.

Sand, P. H. (1996), 'Institution-building to Assist Compliance with International Environmental Law: Perspectives', *Zeitschrift für ausländisches öffentliches Recht und Völkerrecht*, **56**, 774–795.

Sand, P. H. (1997), 'Commodity or Taboo? International Regulation of Trade in Endangered Species'. in: H.O. Bergensen and G. Parmann (eds), *The Green Globe Year Book 1997*, New York, US: Oxford University Press, 19–36.

Sands, P. (1996), 'Compliance with International Environmental Obligations: Existing International Legal Agreements', in J. Cameron, J. Werksman and P. Roderick (eds), *Improving Compliance with International Environmental Law*, London, UK: Earthscan, 48–82.

Schmieman, E. C. and E. C. van Ierland (1999), 'Joint Abatement Strategies: a Dynamic Analysis of Acidification and Tropospheric Ozone', in I. Ring, B. Klauer, F. Waetzold and B. Mansson (eds), *Regional Sustainability*, Berlin, Germany: Physica Verlag, 107–125.

Shihata, I. F. I. (1996), 'Implementation, Enforcement, and Compliance with International Environmental Agreements', *The Georgetown International Environmental Law Review*, **9**, 37–51.

Spagnolo, G. (1996), 'Issue Linkage, Delegation and International Policy Coordination', Working Paper Economics, Energy, Environment, No. 49.96, Milan, Italy: Fondazione Eni Enrico Mattei.

Spagnolo, G. (1999), 'Social Relations and Cooperation in Organizations', *Journal of Economic Behavior and Organization*, **38**, 1–25.

Spagnolo, G. (forthcoming), 'On Interdependent Supergames: Multimarket Contact, Concavity and Collusion', *Journal of Economic Theory*.

Stähler, F. (1996), 'Reflections on Multilateral Environmental Agreements', in A. Xepapadeas (ed.), *Economic Policy for the Environment and Natural Resources: Techniques for the Management and Control of Pollution*, Cheltenham, UK and Brookfield, US: Edward Elgar, 174–196.

Széll, P. (1995), 'The Development of Multilateral Mechanisms of Monitoring Compliance', in W. Lang (ed.), *Sustainable Development and International Law*, London, UK: Graham and Trotman, 97–109.

Tahvonen, O. (1994), 'Carbon Dioxide Abatement as a Differential Game', *European Journal of Political Economy*, **10**, 685–705.

van Mouche, P. (2000), *Théorie formelle des jeux tensoriels*, Wageningen, The Netherlands: University of Wageningen (Preliminary Draft).

van Mouche, P. (2001), *Formal Transboundary Pollution Games: A Non-cooperative Analysis*, Wageningen, The Netherlands: University of Wageningen, Preliminary Draft.

Welsch, H. (1993), 'An Equilibrium Framework for Global Pollution Problems', *Journal of Environmental Economics and Management*, **25**, 64–79.

Welsch, H. (1995), 'Incentives for Forty-Five Countries to Join Various Forms of Carbon Reduction Agreements', *Resource and Energy Economics*, **17**, 213–237.

Werksman, J. (1997), *Five MEAs, Five Years since Rio: Recent Lessons on the Effectiveness of Multilateral Agreements*, Special Focus Report, London, UK: FIELD (Foundation for International Environmental Law and Development).

Yi, S.-S. (1997), 'Stable Coalition Structures with Externalities', *Games and Economic Behavior*, **20**, 201–237.

3. Economic impacts of carbon abatement strategies

Christoph Böhringer and Andreas Löschel

1. INTRODUCTION

Despite the withdrawal of the USA under President Bush in March 2001, the Kyoto Protocol marks a milestone in climate policy history. For the first time, industrialized countries as listed in Annex B of the Protocol have agreed on quantified emissions limitations and reduction objectives. The negotiations around the Protocol have been dominated by two fundamental issues whose reconciliation is crucial for any substantial international agreement on climate protection: efficiency in terms of overall abatement costs, and equity in terms of a 'fair' distribution of these costs across countries. These issues are relevant in other fields of international environmental policy as well, but their importance in the greenhouse context is unique, given the potential magnitude of abatement costs at stake.

With regard to efficiency, the Kyoto Protocol allows for the use of emissions trading, joint implementation (JI) or the clean development mechanism (CDM) in order to reduce total costs of abatement. However, the permissible scope and institutional design of these flexible instruments are controversial among signatory parties. Several Annex B parties, such as the EU, are concerned that the extensive use of flexible instruments will negatively affect the environmental effectiveness of the Kyoto Protocol.

They stress the principle of supplementarity and call for ceilings on the amount by which national reduction targets can be achieved through the use of flexible instruments foreseen by the Kyoto Protocol (Baron et al. 1999). Other Annex B parties, such as the USA, have been strongly opposed to any ceiling plans throughout the negotiations.

With respect to equity, the Convention on Climate Change states that 'Parties should protect the climate system ... on the basis of equity and in accordance with their common but differentiated responsibilities and respective capabilities' (UNFCCC 1997, Article 3.1). The Kyoto Protocol backs this proposition, though concepts of equity have remained rather vague during the negotiation process. Industrialized countries and economies in transition – both referred to as Annex B countries – have committed themselves to reducing greenhouse gas emissions to varying degrees, apparently meaning to reflect differences in the 'ability to pay'. Equity has also been invoked to justify the fact that developing countries have, as yet, not made any commitment to greenhouse gas abatement because they carry only minor historical responsibility for the increase of global greenhouse concentrations in the atmosphere.

A naïve assessment of the Kyoto Protocol may suggest that the adoption of concrete reduction commitments for Annex B countries reflects a careful balancing of efficiency and equity issues. However, the subsequent controversial Conferences of Parties, as well as the fact that no Annex B country has ratified the Protocol so far, indicate the opposite. Policy makers are obviously aware that the concrete – yet undefined – implementation of the Protocol will have important implications for the magnitude and regional distribution of compliance costs. Unresolved policy questions surrounding the implementation of the Kyoto Protocol deal with the implications of flexibility on the economic costs of abatement for Annex B countries, international spillovers to non-abating regions and global environmental effectiveness. Answers to these questions demand quantitative assessment, i.e. the use of analytical economic models. Obviously, models of complex socio-economic systems require simplifying assumptions on system boundaries and system relationships. These assumptions determine the model results and the derived policy conclusions. A major challenge of economic modeling is, therefore, to capture the key entities and relationships of the policy issue at hand. Given some inevitable ambiguity in this process, a careful check of the underlying assumptions is necessary: how do differences in perspectives affect the outcome and what are the implications for the choice of policy options?

There is meanwhile an extensive literature providing quantitative evidence on the economic effects of the Kyoto Protocol. Various studies have been incorporated into recent summary reports (Weyant 1999, IPCC 2001) with the explicit goal of identifying policy-relevant insights and providing explanations for differences in model results. While this is an important contribution, one major shortcoming remains: the models underlying the economic analysis still come as black boxes to non-expert readers. Without knowing the theoretical model, all they can do is believe or not believe the numerical results. Our modest objective here is to open this black box to some extent. We introduce a generic analytical framework which can address the economic and environmental implications of emission abatement strategies in a consistent way. Key features of the model are motivated by the nature of economic issues surrounding carbon abatement policies. Applications to open questions of the Kyoto Protocol will demonstrate how the model can be used for policy analysis, and complementary sensitivity analysis will identify the importance of the key assumptions underlying our calculations.

This chapter is organized as follows: Section 2 provides a short summary of relevant policy issues and presents the main results from applied modeling. Section 3 discusses in further detail computable general equilibrium (CGE) models, which have become the prevailing approach for the economy-wide analysis of climate policy measures. We will outline a blueprint of a comparative-static multi-region, multi-sector CGE model designed for the analysis of alternative Kyoto implementation policies. Section 4 provides applications of this model to selected issues of the international climate policy debate. Section 5 summarizes and concludes.

2. POLICY ISSUES

An economic assessment of climate change has to make a trade-off between costs and benefits. More specifically, rational climate policy making should weigh the benefits from avoided undesirable consequences of global warming against the costs of greenhouse gas emission abatement. To this end, the established technique of cost–benefit analysis (see e.g. Mishan 1975, Maddison 1995, Pearce 1998) provides the appropriate framework for measuring all negative and positive policy impacts and resource uses in the form of monetary costs and benefits. An economically efficient policy for emissions reduction maximizes net benefits, i.e. the benefits of slowed climate change minus the associated costs of emissions reductions. Net benefit maximization requires that emissions reduction efforts are taken up to the level where the marginal benefit of reduced warming equals the marginal cost of emissions reduction.

Given complete information, cost–benefit analysis could tell us how much greenhouse gas (GHG) emissions should be abated, when and by whom. However, neither costs nor benefits of GHG abatement are easy to quantify. In particular, there are large uncertainties in external cost estimates for climate change. The chain of causality – from GHG emissions to ambient concentrations of GHGs in the atmosphere, from temperature increase to physical effects such as climatic and sea level changes – is highly complex. Little agreement exists, therefore, on the desirable level of greenhouse gas emission concentrations in the atmosphere and the scope and timing of emission mitigation measures.

The large uncertainties in external cost estimates are reflected in the current climate policy debate. Emissions reduction objectives are not the outcome of a rigorous cost–benefit analysis, but must rather be seen as a first response to recommendations from natural science on tolerable emission levels. In this vein, we restrict our subsequent analysis of emission abatement strategies to a cost-effectiveness approach. Cost-effectiveness analysis aims at identifying the least expensive way of achieving a given environmental quality target.[1] Only the costs are assessed in relation to an environmental goal; the policy target which represents the level of benefits is taken as given. In climate policy, targets may be formulated with respect to different bases, such as the stabilization of GHG emissions in a certain year, a long-run stabilization of atmospheric concentrations of particular greenhouse gases or the prevention of physical consequences (e.g. sea level rise). For the cost-effectiveness analysis in Section 4, we simply adopt the short-term GHG emissions reduction targets as formulated in the Kyoto Protocol. That is, we measure the economic costs of alternative policy strategies to meet the emissions reduction objectives which Annex B countries have committed to.

In the remainder of this section, we address key issues in the climate policy debate and summarize evidence from quantitative studies without discussing the details of the underlying models. Our objective is twofold. First, we want to justify the choice of the analytical framework described in Section 3. Secondly, we want to motivate the choice of policy scenarios and the design of sensitivity analysis, both of which are discussed in detail in Section 4. For the reasons mentioned, we do not enter the scientific debate on the benefits associated with GHG emissions reduction. Starting from some exogenous global emissions reduction objective, the policy debate comes down to the magnitude and the distribution of abatement costs across regions for alternative policy strategies. The ongoing negotiations around the Kyoto Protocol provide a prime example of the issues at stake. Individual contributions of the Annex B Parties to the Protocol were determined by two basic considerations. On the one hand, the potential costs of the committed reduction had to be 'sufficiently low'. Even voters in wealthy industrialized countries reveal a rather modest willingness to pay for climate protection whose benefits are unclear and of long-term nature (Böhringer and Vogt 2001). On the other hand, the expected pattern of costs across Parties had to comply with basic fairness principles (see e.g. Lange and Vogt 2001). The latter inevitably involves ethically-based equity criteria (see IPCC 1996 and 2001).

The standard approach of positive economics is to separate efficiency and equity considerations. Economics cares for the minimization of the total costs to reach some exogenous reduction target. It is then left to other disciplines as to how these costs should be allocated across agents through lump-sum transfers in order to meet some equity criteria. In the structure of this section, we will take up the traditional distinction between efficiency and equity issues. It should be noted, however, that both issues are closely linked when lump-sum instruments are not available, which is typically the case in political practice.

Our short summary is far from being comprehensive. The informed reader will notice that we have omitted several topics which are not necessarily less important than those explicitly addressed. Among these topics are offsets from CO_2 sinks (see Reilly et al. 1999, Stavins 1999), the incorporation of non-CO_2 GHG mitigation options (see MacCracken et al. 1999, Burniaux and Martins 2000, Reilly et al. 1999), implications from intertemporal flexibility (see Richels and Sturm 1996, Richels et al. 1996, Tol 1999), and quantitative limits to trade (see Criqui et al. 1999, Ellerman and Wing 2000).

2.1   The Magnitude of Abatement Costs

People who search for empirical evidence on the economic impacts of GHG abatement policies are often puzzled about the diverging results across quantitative studies. Not only are there differences in the order of magnitude for abatement costs, but also the sign in reported costs may be opposite. In other words, while one study suggests that an abatement policy results in economy-wide losses, another one indicates economic gains. This 'battle over numbers' explains reservations with respect to the usefulness of quantitative modeling. The constructive approach to this problem is not to renounce insights from applied modeling but to develop some understanding of differences in results. Most of these differences can be traced back to different assumption on the status quo, i.e. the baseline, of the economic system without exogenous policy interference (see Section 2.1.1). Another major source for deviations in cost estimates are differences in the scope of economic interactions that are captured by the studies (see Section 2.1.2). The awareness of these determinants for economic impacts of exogenous policy changes is a prerequisite to properly understanding model results and drawing appropriate conclusions (Böhringer 1999). Hence, a major task for applied modeling is to reveal the importance of subjective judgements, which are implicit in the choice of the baseline, system boundaries and system relationships, for quantitative model results by means of sensitivity analysis.

2.1.1 Baseline assumptions

2.1.1.1 Projections The economic effects of future emission constraints depend crucially on the extent to which quantified emission limitation and reduction objectives will bind the respective economies. In other words, the magnitude of costs associated with the implementation of future emission constraints depends on the Business-as-Usual (BaU) projections for GDP, fuel prices, energy efficiency improvements etc. High economic growth alone, for example, leads to high energy demands and emissions. In the context of the Kyoto Protocol, this would increase the effective abatement requirement, as the Kyoto targets refer to 1990 emissions levels and higher economic growth will therefore imply higher total abatement costs. The importance of baseline projections generally receives little attention in the literature. Most modelers are typically careful in specifying their BaU assumptions but they rarely report results from sensitivity analyses. One exception is Böhringer, Jensen and Rutherford (2000), who study the implications of alternative baseline projections on the magnitude and distribution of emission abatement costs under the Kyoto Protocol within the EU.

2.1.1.2 Market imperfections The incorporation of existing market imperfections is a key factor in explaining why economic adjustments towards more stringent emission constraints might lead to economic gains even when we ignore the benefits of avoided GHG emissions. If policy measures induce reactions that weaken existing distortions, the net outcome might be beneficial even if the policy measure standing alone, i.e. without initial market imperfections, were to cause economic adjustment costs. In the climate change debate, this phenomenon is sometimes referred to as a no-regrets option for abatement policies.

No-regrets options are, by definition, actions to reduce GHG emissions that have negative net costs because they generate direct or indirect benefits large enough to offset their implementation costs. The existence of no-regrets potentials implies that market forces are not operating perfectly. Market imperfections may be due to imperfect information, lack of competition or distortionary fiscal systems and limited financial markets. It should be noted, however, that the removal of market failures and market barriers can cause significant transaction costs (Grubb et al. 1993). Taking transaction costs into account, no-regrets options may be significantly reduced or even non-existent (see Jaffe and Stavins 1991). This explains why economists are rather skeptical about the magnitude of the no-regrets options reported in bottom-up technology-based studies (Krause et al. 1999). These studies assume large initial 'efficiency gaps' between the best available technologies and the equipment actually in use, but they do not incorporate the transaction costs of removing these inefficiencies.

The debate on a double dividend from environmental regulation also builds on the notion of no-regrets policies. Instruments such as carbon taxes or auctioned tradable permits generate revenues to the government. If these revenues are used to reduce existing tax distortions, emission abatement policies may yield a double dividend, i.e., simultaneously improve environmental quality (first dividend) and offset at least part of the welfare losses of climate policies by reducing the overall costs of raising public funds (second dividend). The literature distinguishes two forms of double dividend (Goulder 1995b). In its weak form, a double dividend occurs as long as the gross costs of environmental policies are systematically lower when revenues are recycled via cuts in existing distortionary taxes, rather than being returned as a lump sum. In its strong form, the existence of a double dividend requires that the net cost of the environmental policy is negative (for theoretical analyses see Goulder 1995b or Bovenberg 1999). The weak double dividend is confirmed by many theoretical and numerical studies (e.g. EMF-16 1999). Evidence on the strong double dividend is rather mixed. In public finance terms, a strong double dividend occurs when the marginal distortionary effect of a carbon tax is lower than the marginal distortionary effect of the substituted taxes, given some constant level of tax revenues (Hourcade and Robinson 1996). The existence of a strong double dividend thus depends on a number of factors, such as pre-existing inefficiencies of the tax system along non-environmental dimensions, the type of tax cuts (reductions in payroll taxes, value added taxes (VAT), capital taxes, or other indirect taxes), labor market conditions (level of unemployment and functioning of labor markets), the method of recycling and the level of environmental taxes (i.e. the environmental target). Environmental taxes may well exacerbate rather than alleviate pre-existing tax distortions. This is because environmental taxes induce not only market distortions similar to those of the replaced taxes but also new distortions in intermediate and final consumption. The negative impacts from levying additional environmental taxes (tax interaction effect) can dominate the positive impacts of using additional revenues for cuts in existing distortionary taxes (revenue recycling effect). This result is suggested by the stylized numerical and theoretical studies of Bovenberg and de Mooij (1994) and Parry et al. (1999). Applied studies of economies with few distortions such as the USA find no strong double dividend, but cost reductions as compared to lump-sum recycling up to 30 to 50 per cent (Jorgenson and Wilcoxen 1993, Goulder 1995a). Complementary analysis for EU countries with more distortionary tax systems and substantial labor market imperfections are more optimistic on the prospects for a strong double dividend (Barker 1998 and 1999). In general, it can be argued that existing market imperfections provide an opportunity for beneficial policy reforms independent of environmental policies. In this vein, the second dividend may not be fully attributable to environmental regulation. On the other hand, the taxation of pollution can be seen as a second-best instrument, given growing political constraints on traditional non-environmental taxes (Hourcade 1993).

2.1.2 System boundaries

The choice of system boundaries determines the extent to which the cost-effectiveness analysis accounts for policy-induced adjustment costs. The main challenge of modeling is to select only those system elements and their relationships which really matter for the question at hand. To put it differently: the exclusion of cost components that are outside the chosen system boundaries should not significantly affect the order of magnitude of quantitative results nor the ranking of alternative policy options. In modeling practice, this rule of thumb can hardly be kept because one often does not know beforehand if simplifications that are, after all, a key element of modeling, may turn out to be too simple. Obviously, there is a trade off between the scope of the system to be captured and the level of detail. In our discussion of system boundaries, we start with the widespread distinction between energy-system analysis (bottom-up) and macroeconomic impact analysis (top-down) of emission abatement strategies. Another important issue in the choice of system boundaries is the degree to which international spillovers from domestic policies are taken into account. The common distinction made here is between single-country models and multi-region models. Finally, we point out that system boundaries do not necessarily have a spatial or temporal dimension, but refer – more generally – to the degree of adopted endogeneity for system relationships. We illustrate the latter in the discussion of technological change.

2.1.2.1 Bottom-up versus top-down   There are two broad approaches for modeling the interaction between energy, the environment and the economy. They differ mainly with respect to the emphasis placed on (1) a detailed, technologically based treatment of the energy system, and (2) a theoretically consistent description of the general economy. The models placing emphasis on (1) are purely partial models of the energy sector, lacking interaction with the rest of the economy.[2] In general, they are bottom-up engineering-based linear activity models with a large number of energy technologies to capture substitution of energy carriers on the primary and final energy level, process substitution, process improvements (gross efficiency improvement, emission reduction) or energy savings. They are mostly used to compute the least-cost method of meeting a given demand for final energy or energy services subject to various system constraints such as exogenous emission reduction targets. The models emphasizing (2) are general economic models with only rudimentary treatment of the energy system. Following the top-down approach, they describe the energy system (similar to the other sectors) in a highly aggregated way by means of neoclassical production functions, which capture substitution possibilities by means of substitution elasticities. These models may be classified as open (demand driven Keynesian) or closed (general equilibrium) models (for a model classification see for example Weyant 1999) and capture feedback effects of energy policies on non-energy markets such as price changes for factors or intermediate goods.

In the literature it is often overlooked that the differences between top-down models and bottom-up models are less of a theoretical nature; rather, simply relate to the level of aggregation and the scope of *ceteris paribus* assumptions.[3]

2.1.2.2 International spillovers   Since world economies are increasingly linked through international trade, capital flows and technology transfers, emission abatement by one country has spillovers on other countries. In the policy debate over climate change, spillovers from Annex B countries' abatement to non-abating developing countries play an important role. The Kyoto Protocol explicitly acknowledges the importance of international spillovers in stipulating that unilateral abatement policies should minimize adverse trade effects on developing countries (UNFCCC 1997, Article 2.3). Even more, the UNFCCC guarantees compensation by Annex B to the developing world for induced economic costs under Articles 4.8 and 4.9. On the other hand, the developed Annex B countries fear adverse impacts from unilateral abatement, because their energy use will be taxed, while there will be no taxes in the developing world, hence they can expect to lose competitiveness in energy-intensive production. In a more dynamic perspective, important spillovers may also stem from technology transfers. In the presence of induced technological change, cleaner technologies developed as a response to abatement policies in industrialized countries may diffuse internationally, generating positive spillovers for non-abating countries. The diffusion of cleaner technologies may offset some or all of the negative leakage effects (Grubb 2000). Environmental implications of international spillovers concern the phenomenon of carbon leakage due to sub-global action, which may have important consequences for the design of unilateral abatement strategies (Böhringer, Rutherford and Voss 1998). The following paragraphs discuss the implications of spillovers on regional adjustment costs, industrial competitiveness and global environmental effectiveness in more detail.

Carbon abatement in large open economies not only causes adjustment of domestic production and consumption patterns, but it also influences international prices via changes in exports and imports. Changes in international prices, i.e. the terms of trade (TOT),[4] imply a secondary benefit or burden that can significantly alter the economic implications of the primary domestic policy.[5] Some countries may shift part of their domestic abatement costs to trading partners, while other abating countries face welfare losses from a deterioration of their terms of trade.

With respect to the aggregate terms-of-trade effects, the most important are changes in international fuel markets. The cutback in global demand for fossil fuels due to carbon emission constraints implies a significant drop of their prices, providing economic gains to fossil fuel importers and losses to fossil fuel exporters (van der Mensbrugghe 1998, Tulpulé et al. 1999, McKibbin et al. 1999, Bernstein et al. 1999, Montgomery and Bernstein 2000, Böhringer and Rutherford 2001).

The economic implications of international price changes on non-energy markets are more complex. Higher energy costs implied by carbon taxes raise the prices of non-energy goods (in particular energy-intensive goods) produced in abating countries. Countries that import these goods suffer from higher prices to the extent that they cannot substitute them with cheaper imports from non-abating countries. The ease of substitution – captured by the Armington elasticity – not only determines the implicit burden shifting of carbon taxes via non-energy exports from abating countries, but also the extent to which non-abating countries achieve a competitive advantage *vis-à-vis* abating exporters. The gain in market shares due to substitution effects may be partially offset by an opposite scale effect: due to reduced economic activity and income effects, import demand by the industrialized world declines, and this exerts a downward pressure on the prices of developing country exports. On average, non-abating regions or countries with very low carbon taxes gain comparative advantage on non-energy markets that, however, may not be large enough to offset potentially negative spillovers from international fuel markets.

Terms-of-trade changes affect the pattern of comparative advantage. This refers to the relative cost of producing goods in a particular country compared to the relative cost of producing these goods elsewhere. Since, in the neoclassical view, the location of production is determined by these relative cost differences, competitiveness and comparative advantage can be used interchangeably. Carbon taxes increase production costs and reduce international competitiveness, depending on the size of the carbon tax and the carbon intensity of the product. Particularly, energy-intensive industries such as chemicals, steel or cement in mitigating countries are negatively affected. However, surveys on the impacts of carbon abatement policies on international competitiveness have found only minor effects so far, which might be due to rather modest emission taxes and wide-ranging exemption schemes for energy-intensive production (Ekins and Speck 1998 and Barker and Johnstone 1998). The use of flexibility instruments reduces the competitive advantage of non-Annex B countries (Böhringer and Rutherford 2001; see also Section 4.2.2).

Sub-global abatement may lead to an increase in emissions in non-abating regions, reducing the global environmental effectiveness. This phenomenon is referred to as 'leakage'. Emission leakage is measured as the increase in non-Annex B emissions relative to the reduction in Annex B emissions. There are three basic channels through which carbon leakage can occur. First, leakage can arise when, in countries undertaking emission limitations, energy-intensive industries lose in competitiveness and the production of emission-intensive goods relocates, raising emission levels in the non-participating regions (trade channel). Secondly, cut-backs of energy demands in a large region due to emission constraints may depress the demand for fossil fuels and thus induce a significant drop in world energy prices. This, in turn, could lead to an increase in the level of demand (and its composition) in other regions (energy channel). Thirdly, carbon leakage may be induced by changes in regional income (and thus energy demand) due to terms of trade changes (Rutherford 1995b). Leakage rates reflect the impact of sub-global emission abatement strategies on comparative advantage. Model-based results on carbon leakage depend crucially on the assumed degree of substitutability between imports and domestic production in the formulation of international trade (see for example Böhringer, Ferris and Rutherford 1998, Böhringer 1998a). Other major factors influencing the leakage rates are the assumed degree of competitiveness in the world oil market, the supply elasticities of fossil fuels, the substitution elasticity between energy and other inputs in the production of abating regions and the level of emissions trading (see Oliveira-Martins et al. 1992, Pezzey 1992, Manne and Oliveira-Martins 1994, Bernstein et al. 1999, Burniaux and Martins 2000 and Paltsev 2000a).

2.1.3 Technological change

Technological change is an important determinant of the economic costs induced by mid- and long-run GHG emission constraints, as it may significantly alter production possibilities over time. Löschel (2001) provides an overview of how technological change is represented in applied environment-economy models. These usually account for technical progress through an exogenous technical coefficient called the autonomous energy efficiency improvement (AEEI) (e.g. Capros et al. 1997).[6] The AEEI reflects the rate of change in energy intensity, i.e. the ratio of energy consumption over gross domestic product, holding energy prices constant (IPCC 1996). It is a measure of all non-price induced changes in gross energy intensity, including technical developments that increase energy efficiency, as well as structural changes. The higher (lower) the AEEI, the lower (higher) the baseline emissions, and the lower (higher) the costs to reach a climate target relative to a given base year. Estimates for AEEI rates range from 0.4 per cent to 1.5 per cent (Dean and Hoeller 1992, Kram 1998 and Weyant 1998). Sensitivity studies demonstrate the crucial importance of the AEEI parameter. Even small differences in the number chosen for the AEEI result in large differences in energy demand and emissions in the baseline and, hence, the total costs of emissions reductions (Manne and Richels 1990 and 1992).

The implication of the treatment of technological change using AEEIs in prevalent models is that technological progress is assumed to be invariant with respect to climate policy interference. The modeling of the rate and direction of technical change in climate policy models as exogenous must be considered as a severe limitation (Anderson 1999). If climate policies lead to improvements in technology, then the total costs of abatement may be substantially lower as compared to results from conventional models with exogenous technical change. However, at present, the theory of induced technological change (ITC) is still in development. The main elements in models of technological innovation are (1) corporate investment such as research and development (R&D) as well as learning by doing (LBD) in response to market conditions, and (2) spillovers from R&D. Innovation as a product of explicit private investment incentives in the knowledge sector has its origin in firm level innovation theory, which focuses on private profit incentives from (at least partly) appropriable innovations. With learning by doing in technologies, the technology costs are modeled explicitly as a function of cumulative investment or of installed capacity in that technology. Spillover effects stem from macro-level endogenous or 'new' growth theory. Investments in human capital and technology result in positive externalities (spillovers).

Investment in R&D is presented in models by Goulder and Schneider (1999), Buonanno et al. (2000) and Goulder and Mathai (2000). Quantitative results from these models indicate only weak impacts of induced technical change on the gross costs of abatement. Concerning LBD, it is found that marginal returns from LBD vary greatly between industries at different stages of development. For example, learning-by-doing effects in the mature conventional energy industries may be rather small compared to renewable energy industries (Anderson 1999, Goulder and Mathai 2000). Knowledge spillovers from R&D are analyzed by Goulder and Schneider (1999), Weyant and Olavson (1999) and Goulder and Mathai (2000). They found that R&D market failures (knowledge spillovers) justify R&D subsidies as a second policy instrument in addition to a carbon tax. A counter-example is given by Kverndokk et al. (2000).

With endogenous technological change, the derivation of the shape of the least-cost mitigation pathway becomes more complex (Grubb 1997).[7] ITC from investments in R&D makes it preferable to concentrate more abatement efforts in the future since it lowers the relative costs of future abatement. Early emissions-reduction measures are more preferable when LBD is considered, since current abatement contributes to a learning process that reduces the costs of future abatement (Goulder and Mathai 2000).

2.2   Equity: Burden Sharing

The establishment of international trade in emission rights requires a decision on the initial allocation of these emission rights among nations. From the Coase Theorem we know that the allocation of permits and the implied wealth transfer have only minor effects on the global costs of abatement. When trading concludes, each country will hold the economically efficient (cost-effective) amount of permits (i.e. marginal abatement costs across countries will be equalized), independent of the initial allocation of permits (Manne and Richels 1995). However, the initial allocation of emission rights has major effects on the distribution of gains and losses and thus on the perceived equity of the agreement. Since there is no unique definition of equity or the objectives to which it should be applied, it is a political issue that requires the solution of serious political differences on burden sharing between industrialized countries on the one hand, and between developed and developing countries on the other hand.

Several alternative equity criteria can be found in the literature (see Kverndokk 1995, Rose and Stevens 1998 and Rose et al. 1998): under the egalitarian criterion it is assumed that all nations have an equal right to pollute or be protected from pollution. Emission rights are distributed in proportion to current emissions ('grandfathered'). Under the egalitarian fairness criterion, all people have an equal right to pollute or be protected from pollution. Emission rights are allocated in proportion to population ('equal per capita emissions'). The no-harm criterion states that some (poor) nations should not incur costs. Emission rights are distributed to these countries according to their baseline emissions. The Kyoto Protocol may be seen as yet another *ad hoc* equity criterion. The differentiation in commitments follows some implicit equity considerations (UNFCC 1997, Article 3.1).

There are several modeling studies that analyze the effects of different schemes for allocating emission rights (Manne and Richels 1995, Edmonds et al. 1995, Rose and Stevens 1998, Rose et al. 1998, Böhringer, Harrison and Rutherford, forthcoming and Böhringer and Welsch 1999). Most of these studies deal with global abatement strategies beyond Kyoto and impose emission constraints on developing countries to assure long-term reduction of global GHG emissions. A robust policy conclusion from these studies is that the problem of burden sharing implicit in alternative permit allocation schemes (i.e. equity rules) will be significantly relaxed through efficiency gains from world-wide emissions trading. Complementary analysis suggests that for very different allocations of emission rights, essentially the same cost pattern emerges when efficiency gains from trade in emission rights are not distributed via the market mechanism, but instead according to rules derived from fair division theory (Böhringer and Helm 2001). The latter may be far less controversial than equity rules applied to the initial allocation of emission rights.

The separability of efficiency and equity under marketable permits allows us to concentrate on the former in our model simulations in Section 4. Equilibrium abatement costs are unaffected by different permit distributions. However, as was previously pointed out, in international treaties such as the Kyoto Protocol, equity considerations may be crucial (Rose 1990). The pursuit of equity consideration may even promote efficiency, since more parties with relatively lower abatement costs may be enticed into the agreement if it is perceived to be fair, which, in the case of many developing countries, may be an equal per capita allocation of permits (see for example Morrisette and Plantinga 1991, Bohm and Larsen 1994).

3. A GENERIC CGE MODEL FOR CARBON ABATEMENT POLICY ANALYSIS

Carbon abatement policies not only cause direct adjustments of fossil fuel markets, but they produce indirect spillovers to other markets that, in turn, feed back to the economy. General equilibrium provides a consistent framework for studying price-dependent interactions between the energy system and the rest of the economy. The simultaneous explanation of the origin and spending of the income of the economic agents makes it possible to address both economy-wide efficiency as well as the equity implications of abatement policy interference. Therefore, computable general equilibrium (CGE) models have become the standard tool for the analysis of the economy-wide impacts of greenhouse gas abatement policies on resource allocation and the associated implications for incomes of economic agents (Bergmann 1990, Grubb et al. 1993, Weyant 1999).[8]

This section outlines the main characteristics of a generic static general equilibrium model of the world economy designed for the medium-run economic analysis of carbon abatement constraints (see Böhringer and

Rutherford 2001). It is a well-known Arrow-Debreu model that concerns the interaction of consumers and producers in markets. Consumers in the model have a primary exogenous endowment of the commodities and a set of preferences giving demand functions for each commodity. The demands depend on all prices; they are continuous and non-negative, homogeneous of degree zero in factor prices and satisfy Walras' Law, i.e. the total value of consumer expenditure equals consumer income at any set of prices. Market demands are the sum of final and intermediate demands. Producers maximize profits given constant returns to scale production technology. Because of the homogeneity of degree zero of the demand functions and the linear homogeneity of the profit functions in prices, only relative prices matter in such a model. Two classes of conditions characterize the competitive equilibrium in the model: market clearance conditions and zero profit conditions. In equilibrium, price levels and production levels in each industry are such that market demand equals market supply for each commodity. Profit maximization under constant returns to scale technology implies that no activity does any better than break even at equilibrium prices (Shoven and Whalley 1984). The model is a system of simultaneous, non-linear equations with the number of equations equal to the number of variables.

The concrete specification of the model, with respect to the impact analysis of the Kyoto Protocol, covers 11 regions, eight sectors and three factors. The regional aggregation includes Annex B parties as well as major non-Annex B regions that are central to our analysis. Our model thus accounts for potential terms-of-trade effects triggered by carbon abatement policies. The sectoral aggregation in the model has been chosen to distinguish carbon-intensive sectors from the rest of the economy as far as possible given data availability. It captures key dimensions in the analysis of greenhouse gas abatement, such as differences in carbon intensities and the degree of substitutability across carbon-intensive goods. The energy goods identified in the model are coal, natural gas, crude oil, refined oil products and electricity. The non-energy sectors include important carbon-intensive and energy-intensive industries that are potentially most affected by carbon abatement policies, such as transportation services and an aggregate energy-intensive sector. The rest of the economy is divided into other machinery, construction and other manufactures and services. The primary factors in the model include labor, physical capital and fossil-fuel resources. Factor markets are assumed to be perfectly competitive. In our baseline scenario, labor and physical capital are treated as perfectly mobile across sectors. Fossil-fuel resources are sector-specific. All factors are immobile between regions. Table 3.1 summarizes the regional, sectoral, and factor aggregation of the model.

3.1   Production

Within each region (indexed by the subscript r), each producing sector (indexed interchangeably by i and j) is represented by a single-output producing firm which chooses input and output quantities in order to maximize profits. Firm behavior can be construed as a two-stage procedure in which the firm selects the optimal quantities of primary factors k (indexed by f) and intermediate inputs x from other sectors in order to minimize production costs, given input prices and some production level Y, with $Y = \varphi\,(k,x)$ the production functions. The second stage, given an exogenous output price, is the selection of the output level Y to maximize profits. The firm's problem is then:

$$\underset{y_{jir},x_{jir},k_{fir}}{Max} \quad \Pi_{ir} = p_{ir} \cdot Y_{ir} - C_{ir}\left(p_{jr},w_{fr},Y_{ir}\right) \; s.t. \; Y_{ir} = \varphi_{ir}\left(x_{jir},k_{fir}\right) \quad [3.1]$$

where Π denotes the profit functions, C the cost functions which relate the minimum possible total costs of producing Y to the positive input prices, technology parameters, and the output quantity Y, and p and w are the prices for goods and factors, respectively.

In the model, production of each good takes place according to constant elasticity of substitution (CES) production functions, which exhibit constant returns to scale. Therefore, the output price equals the per-unit cost in each sector, and firms make zero profits in equilibrium (Euler's Theorem).

Profit maximization under constant returns to scale implies the equilibrium condition:

$$\pi_{ir} = p_{ir} - c_{ir}(p_{jr},w_{fr}) = 0 \quad \text{(zero profit condition)} \quad [3.2]$$

where c and π are the unit cost and profit functions, respectively.

Demand functions for goods and factors can be derived by Shepard's Lemma. It suggests that the first-order differentiation of the cost function with respect to an input price yields the cost-minimizing demand function for the corresponding input.

Table 3.1 Model dimensions

Countries and Regions

Annex B
CEA　　　Central European Associates
EUR　　　Europe (EU15 and EFTA)
FSU　　　Former Soviet Union (Russian Federation and Ukraine)
JPN　　　Japan
OOE　　　Other OECD (Australia and New Zealand)
USA　　　United States

Non-Annex B
ASI　　　Other Asia (except for China and India)
CHN　　　China (including Hong Kong and Taiwan)
IND　　　India
MPC　　　Mexico and OPEC
ROW　　　Rest of World

Production sectors

Energy
COL　　　Coal
CRU　　　Crude oil
GAS　　　Natural gas
OIL　　　Refined oil products
ELE　　　Electricity

Non-Energy
AGR　　　Agricultural production
EIS　　　Energy-intensive sectors
OTH　　　Other manufactures and services
CGD　　　Savings good

Primary factors

L　　　Labor
K　　　Capital
R　　　Fixed factor resources for coal, oil and gas

Hence, the intermediate demand for good j in sector i is:

$$x_{jir} = \frac{\partial C_{ir}}{\partial p_{jr}} = Y_{ir} \cdot \frac{\partial c_{ir}}{\partial p_{jr}} \qquad [3.3]$$

and the demand for factor f in sector i is:

$$k_{fir} = \frac{\partial C_{ir}}{\partial w_{fr}} = Y_{ir} \cdot \frac{\partial c_{ir}}{\partial w_{fr}} . \qquad [3.4]$$

The profit functions possess a corresponding derivative property (Hotelling's Lemma):

$$x_{jir} = \frac{\partial \Pi_{ir}}{\partial p_{jr}} = Y_{ir} \cdot \frac{\partial \pi_{ir}}{\partial p_{jr}} \quad \text{and} \quad k_{fir} = \frac{\partial \Pi_{ir}}{\partial w_{fr}} = Y_{ir} \cdot \frac{\partial \pi_{ir}}{\partial w_{fr}} . \qquad [3.5]$$

The variable, price dependent input coefficients, which appear subsequently in the market clearance conditions, are thus:

$$a^x_{jir} = \frac{\partial c_{ir}}{\partial p_{jr}} = \frac{\partial \pi_{ir}}{\partial p_{jr}} \quad \text{and} \quad a^k_{fir} = \frac{\partial c_{ir}}{\partial w_{fr}} = \frac{\partial \pi_{ir}}{\partial w_{fr}} . \qquad [3.6]$$

The model captures the production of commodities by aggregate, hierarchical (or nested) CES production functions that characterize the technology through substitution possibilities between capital, labor, energy and material (non-energy) intermediate inputs (KLEM). Two types of production functions are employed: those for fossil fuels (v = COL, CRU, GAS) and those for non-fossil fuels (n = AGR, EIS, ELE, OIL, OTH).

Figure 3.1 illustrates the nesting structure in non-fossil fuel production. In the production of non-fossil fuels nr, non-energy intermediate inputs M (used in fixed coefficients among themselves) are employed in (Leontief) fixed proportions with an aggregate of capital, labor and energy at the top level.

At the second level, a CES function describes the substitution possibilities between the aggregate energy input E and the value-added aggregate KL:[9]

$$Y_{nr} = \min\left\{ (1-\theta_{nr}) M_{nr}, \theta_{nr}\phi_{nr} \left[\alpha_{nr} E_{nr}^{\rho^{KLE}} + \beta_{nr} KL_{nr}^{\rho^{KLE}} \right]^{1/\rho^{KLE}} \right\} \qquad [3.7]$$

with $\sigma^{KLE} = 1/(1-\rho^{KLE})$ the elasticity of substitution between energy and the primary factor aggregate and θ the input (Leontief) coefficient. Finally, at the third level, capital and labor factor inputs trade off with a constant elasticity of substitution σ^{KL} ($\sigma^{KL} = 1/(1-\rho^{KL})$):

$$
KL_{nr} = \phi_{nr}\left[\alpha_{nr}K_{nr}^{\rho^{KL}} + \beta_{nr}L_{nr}^{\rho^{KL}}\right]^{1/\rho^{KL}}. \tag{3.8}
$$

As to the formation of the energy aggregate E, we employ several levels of nesting to represent differences in substitution possibilities between primary fossil fuel types as well as substitution between the primary fossil fuel composite and secondary energy, i.e. electricity. The energy aggregate is a CES composite of electricity and primary energy inputs FF with elasticity $\sigma^E = 1/(1-\rho^E)$ at the top nest:

$$
E_{nr} = \phi_{nr}\left[\alpha_{nr}ELE_{nr}^{\rho^E} + \beta_{nr}FF_{nr}^{\rho^E}\right]^{1/\rho^E}. \tag{3.9}
$$

The primary energy composite is defined as a CES function of coal and the composite of refined oil and natural gas with elasticity $\sigma^{COA} = 1/(1-\rho^{COA})$. The oil–gas composite is assumed to have a simple Cobb-Douglas functional form with value shares of oil and gas given by θ and $1-\theta$, respectively :

$$
FF_{nr} = \phi_{nr}\left[\alpha_{nr}COA_{nr}^{\rho^{COA}} + \beta_{nr}\left(OIL^{\theta_{nr}}\cdot GAS^{1-\theta_{nr}}\right)^{\rho^{COA}}\right]^{1/\rho^{COA}}. \tag{3.10}
$$

Fossil fuel resources v are modeled as graded resources. The structure of production of fossil fuels is given in Figure 3.2. It is characterized by the presence of a fossil fuel resource in fixed supply. All inputs, except for the sector-specific resource R, are aggregated in fixed proportions at the lower nest. Mine managers minimize production costs subject to the technology constraint:

$$
Y_{vr} = \phi_{vr}\left[\alpha_{vr}R_{vr}^{\rho_{vr}^f} + \beta_{vr}\left[\min\left(\theta_{vr}^K K_{vr}, \theta_{vr}^L L_{vr}, \theta_{vr}^E E_{vr}, \theta_{vr}^M M_{jvr}\right)\right]^{\rho_{vr}^f}\right]^{1/\rho_{vr}^f} \tag{3.11}
$$

The resource grade structure is reflected by the elasticity of substitution between the fossil fuel resource and the capital–labor–energy–material aggregate in production. The substitution elasticity between the specific factor and the Leontief composite at the top level is $\sigma_{vr}^f = 1/(1-\rho_{vr}^f)$. This substitution elasticity is calibrated consistently with an exogenously given supply elasticity of fossil fuel ε_{vr} according to

$$\varepsilon_{vr} = \frac{1-\gamma_{vr}}{\gamma_{vr}} \sigma_{vr}^f \qquad [3.12]$$

with γ_{vr} the resource value share (Rutherford 1998). The resource value share represents major differences between fossil fuel sectors across regions. The resource cost share is rather high, e.g. in oil-exporting MPC, while its share is low in regions with less accessible resources (Babiker et al. 2001).

We now turn to the derivation of the factor demand functions for the nested CES production functions, taking into account the duality between the production function and the cost function. The total cost function that reflects the same production technology as the CES production function, for example, for value added KL in non-fossil fuel production given by [3.8], is:

$$C_{nr}^{KL} = \frac{1}{\phi_{nr}} \left[\alpha_{nr}^{\sigma^{KL}} PK_{nr}^{1-\sigma^{KL}} + \beta_{nr}^{\sigma^{KL}} PL_{nr}^{1-\sigma^{KL}} \right]^{1/(1-\sigma^{KL})} \cdot KL_{nr} \quad [3.13]$$

where PK and PL are the per-unit factor costs for the industry, including factor taxes if applicable. The price function for the value-added aggregate at the third level is:

$$PKL_{nr} = \frac{1}{\phi_{nr}} \left[\alpha_{nr}^{\sigma^{KL}} PK_{nr}^{1-\sigma^{KL}} + \beta_{nr}^{\sigma^{KL}} PL_{nr}^{1-\sigma^{KL}} \right]^{1/(1-\sigma^{KL})} = c_{nr}^{KL} . \quad [3.14]$$

Shepard's Lemma gives the price-dependent composition of the value-added aggregate as:

$$\frac{K_{nr}}{KL_{nr}} = \phi_{nr}^{\sigma^{KL}-1} \left(\alpha_{nr} \cdot \frac{PKL_{nr}}{PK_{nr}} \right)^{\sigma^{KL}} , \quad \frac{L_{nr}}{KL_{nr}} = \phi_{nr}^{\sigma^{KL}-1} \left(\beta_{nr} \cdot \frac{PKL_{nr}}{PL_{nr}} \right)^{\sigma^{KL}}$$

$$[3.15]$$

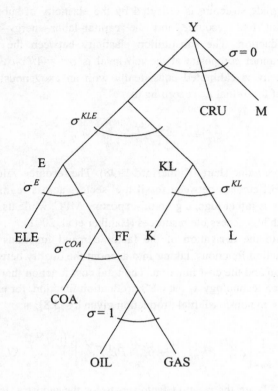

Figure 3.1 Nesting structure of non-fossil fuel production

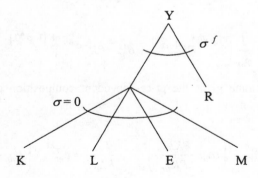

Figure 3.2 Nesting structure for fossil fuel production

In order to determine the variable input coefficient for capital and labor $a_{nr}^K = K_{nr} / Y_{nr}$ and $a_{nr}^L = L_{nr} / Y_{nr}$, one has to multiply

[3.15] with the per unit demand for the value added aggregate KL_{nr} / Y_{nr}, which can be derived in an analogous manner. The unit cost function associated with the production function [3.7] is:

$$PY_{nr} = \left(1 - \theta_{nr}\right) PM_{nr} + \frac{\theta_{nr}}{\hat{\phi}_{nr}} \left[\hat{\alpha}_{nr}^{\sigma^{KLE}} PE_{nr}^{1-\sigma^{KLE}} + \hat{\beta}_{nr}^{\sigma^{KLE}} PKL_{nr}^{1-\sigma^{KLE}} \right]^{\frac{1}{1-\sigma^{KLE}}}$$

[3.16]

and

$$\frac{KL_{nr}}{Y_{nr}} = \theta_{nr} \hat{\phi}_{nr}^{\sigma^{KLE}-1} \left(\hat{\beta}_{nr} \cdot \frac{PY_{nr}}{PKL_{nr}} \right)^{\sigma^{KLE}}$$

[3.17]

with θ_{nr} the *KLE* cost share in total production. The variable input coefficient for labor is then:

$$a_{nr}^L = \theta_{nr} \phi_{nr}^{\sigma^{KL}-1} \hat{\phi}_{nr}^{\sigma^{KLE}-1} \left(\beta_{nr} \cdot \frac{PKL_{nr}}{PL_{nr}} \right)^{\sigma^{KL}} \left(\hat{\beta}_{nr} \cdot \frac{PY_{nr}}{PKL_{nr}} \right)^{\sigma^{KLE}}. \quad [3.18]$$

3.2 Households

In each region, private demand for goods and services is derived from utility maximization of a representative household subject to a budget constraint given by the income level *INC*. The agent is endowed with the supplies of the primary factors of production (natural resources used for fossil fuel production, labor and capital) and tax revenues. In our comparative-static framework, overall investment demand is fixed at the reference level. The household's problem is then:

$$\underset{d_{ir}}{Max} \ W_r\left(d_{ir}\right) \ s.t. \ INC_r = \sum_f w_{fr} \bar{k}_{fr} + TR_r = \sum_i p_{ir} d_{ir} \quad [3.19]$$

where W is the welfare of the representative household in region r, d denotes the final demand for commodities, $\bar{k}$ is the aggregate factor endowment of the representative agent and TR are total tax revenues. Household preferences are characterized by a CES utility function.

As in production, the maximization problem in [3.1] can thus be expressed in the form of a unit expenditure function e or welfare price index pw, given by:

$$pw_r = e_r\left(p_{ir}\right).$$ [3.20]

Compensated final demand functions are derived from Roy's Identity as:

$$d_{ir} = \overline{INC}_r \frac{\partial e_r}{\partial p_{ir}}$$ [3.21]

with $\overline{INC}$ the initial level of expenditure.

In the model, welfare of the representative agent is represented as a CES composite of a fossil fuel aggregate and a non-fossil fuel consumption bundle. Substitution patterns within the latter are reflected via a Cobb-Douglas function. The fossil fuel aggregate in final demand consists of the various fossil fuels (fe = COL, OIL, GAS) trading off at a constant elasticity of substitution. The CES utility function is:

$$U_r = \left[\alpha_r \left(\sum_{fe} \beta_{fe,r} C_{fe,r}^{\rho^F} \right)^{\rho^C / \rho^F} + \phi_r \left(\prod_{j \notin fe} C_{jr}^{\theta_j} \right)^{\rho^C} \right]^{1/\rho^C}$$ [3.22]

where the elasticity of substitution between energy and non-energy composites is given by $\sigma_C = 1/(1-\rho_C)$, the elasticity of substitution within the fossil fuel aggregate by $\sigma_{FE} = 1/(1-\rho_{FE})$, and θ_j are the value shares in non-fossil fuel consumption. The structure of final demand is presented in Figure 3.3.

Total income of the representative agent consists of factor income, revenues from taxes levied on output, intermediate inputs, exports and imports and final demand, as well as tax revenues from CO_2 taxes (TR) and a baseline exogenous capital flow representing the balance of payment deficits B less expenses for exogenous total investment demand $PI \cdot I$. The government activity is financed through lump-sum levies. It does not enter the utility function and is hence exogenous in the model. The budget constraint is then given by:

$$PC_r \cdot C_r = PL_r \cdot \overline{L}_r + PK_r \cdot \overline{K}_r + \sum_v PR_{vr} \cdot \overline{R}_{vr} + TR_r + \overline{B}_r - PI_r \cdot I_r$$ [3.23]

with C the aggregate household consumption in region r and PC its associated price.

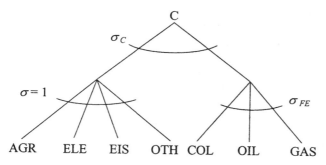

Figure 3.3   Structure of household demand

3.3   Foreign Trade

All commodities are traded in world markets. Crude oil and coal are imported and exported as a homogeneous product, reflecting empirical evidence that these fossil fuel markets are fairly integrated due to cheap shipping possibilities. All other goods are characterized by product differentiation. There is imperfect transformability (between exports and domestic sales of domestic output) and imperfect substitutability (between imports and domestically sold domestic output). Bilateral trade flows are subject to export taxes, tariffs and transportation costs and calibrated to the base year 1995. There is an imposed balance of payment constraint to ensure trade balance, which is warranted through flexible exchange rates, incorporating the benchmark trade deficit or surplus for each region.

On the output side, two types of differentiated goods are produced as joint products for sale in the domestic markets and the export markets respectively. The allocation of output between domestic sales D and international sales X is characterized by a constant elasticity of transformation (CET) function. Hence, firms maximize profits subject to the constraint:

$$Y_{ir} = \phi_{ir}\left[\alpha_{ir} D_{ir}^{\eta} + \beta_{ir} X_{ir}^{\eta} \right]^{1/\eta} \qquad [3.24]$$

with $\sigma^{tr} = 1/(1 + \eta)$ the transformation elasticity.

Regarding imports, the standard Armington convention is adopted in the sense that imported and domestically produced goods of the same kind are treated as incomplete substitutes (i.e. wine from France is different from Italian wine). The aggregate amount of each (Armington) good A is divided among imports and domestic production:

$$A_{ir} = \phi_{ir} \left[\alpha_{ir} D_{ir}^{\rho^D} + \beta_{ir} M_{ir}^{\rho^D} \right]^{1/\rho^D} . \qquad [3.25]$$

In this expression, $\sigma^D = 1/(1-\rho^D)$ is the Armington elasticity between domestic and imported varieties. Imports M are allocated between import regions s according to a CES function:

$$M_{ir} = \phi_{ir} \left[\sum_s \alpha_{ir} X_{isr}^{\rho^M} \right]^{1/\rho^M} \qquad [3.26]$$

with X the amount of exports from region s to region r and $\sigma^M = 1/(1-\rho^M)$ the Armington elasticity among imported varieties. Intermediate as well as final demands are, hence, (nested CES) Armington composites of domestic and imported varieties.

The assumption of product differentiation permits the model to match bilateral trade with cross-hauling of trade and avoids unrealistically strong specialization effects in response to exogenous changes in trade (tax) policy. On the other hand, the results may then be sensitive to the particular commodity and regional aggregation chosen in the model as indicated by Table 3.1 (Lloyd 1994).

3.4   Carbon emissions

GHGs and related gases have direct radiative forcing effects in the atmosphere. The various gases result from industrial production, fossil fuel consumption and household activities. The Kyoto Protocol includes carbon dioxide (CO_2), methane (CH_4), nitrous oxide (N_2O), hydrofluorocarbons (HFCs), perfluorocarbons (PFCs), and sulfur hexafluoride (SF_6) as gases subject to control.

We do not consider the abatement of a complete basket of GHG emissions from all energy-related sources as in the Kyoto Protocol, but instead, focus on carbon dioxide abatement from fossil fuel consumption, since it constitutes the largest part of the contribution to global warming. Carbon emissions are associated with fossil fuel consumption in production, investment, government and private demand. Carbon is treated as a Leontief (fixed coefficient) input into production and consumption activities. Each unit of a fuel emits a known amount of carbon, where different fuels have different carbon intensities. The applied carbon coefficients are 25 MT carbon per EJ for coal, 14 MT carbon per EJ for gas and 20 MT carbon per EJ for refined oil.

Carbon policies are introduced via an additional constraint that holds carbon emissions to a specified limit. The solution of the model gives a shadow value on carbon associated with this carbon constraint. This dual variable or shadow price can be interpreted as the price of carbon permits in a carbon permit system or as the CO_2 tax that would induce the carbon constraint in the model. The shadow value of the carbon constraint equals the marginal cost of reduction; it indicates the incremental cost of reducing carbon at the carbon constraint.

The total costs represent the resource cost or dead-weight loss to the economy of imposing carbon constraints. When reconciling different cost estimates, it should be noted that marginal cost is significant higher than average cost (Nordhaus 1991). Carbon emission constraints induce substitution of fossil fuels with less expensive energy sources (fuel switching) or employment of less energy-intensive manufacturing and production techniques (energy savings). The only means of abatement are hence inter-fuel and fuel-/non-fuel substitution or the reduction of intermediate and final consumption.

Given an emission constraint, producers as well as consumers must pay this price of the emissions resulting from the production and consumption processes. Revenues coming from the imposition of the carbon constraint are given to the representative agent. The total cost of Armington inputs in production and consumption that reflects the CES production technology in [3.25] but takes CO_2 emission restrictions into account is:

$$C_{ir}^A = \left[\left(\alpha_{ir}^{\sigma^D} PD_{ir}^{1-\sigma^D} + \beta_{ir}^{\sigma^A} PM_{ir}^{1-\sigma^D} \right)^{1/(1-\sigma^D)} + \tau_r \cdot a_i \right] \cdot A_{ir} \quad [3.27]$$

with a_i the carbon emissions coefficient for fossil fuel i and τ the shadow price of CO_2 in region r associated with the carbon emission restriction:

$$\overline{CO2}_r = \sum_i A_{ir} \cdot a_i \qquad\qquad [3.28]$$

where $\overline{CO2}$ is the endowment of carbon emission rights in region r.

3.5   Zero Profit and Market Clearance Conditions

The equilibrium conditions in the model are zero profit and market clearance conditions. Zero profit conditions as derived in [3.2] require that no producer earns an 'excess' profit in equilibrium. The value of inputs per unit activity must be equal to the value of outputs. The zero profit conditions for production, using the variable input coefficient derived above, is:

$$PK \cdot a_{ir}^K \cdot Y_{ir} + PL \cdot a_{ir}^L \cdot Y_{ir} + \sum_j PA_j \cdot a_{jir}^M \cdot Y_{ir} = PY_{ir} \cdot Y_{ir}. \qquad [3.29]$$

The market clearance conditions state that market demand equals market supply for all inputs and outputs. Market clearance conditions have to hold in equilibrium. Domestic markets clear, equating aggregate domestic output plus imports, i.e. total Armington good supply, to aggregate demand, which consists of intermediate demand, final demand, investment and government demand:

$$A_{ir} = \sum_j Y_{jr} \frac{\partial \pi_{jr}^Y}{\partial PA_{ir}} + C_r \frac{\partial e_r}{\partial PA_{ir}} \qquad\qquad [3.30]$$

with PA the price of the Armington composite. π_{ir}^Z is the per unit profit function with Z the name assigned to the associated production activity. The derivation of π_{ir}^Z with respect to input and output prices, yields the compensated demand and supply coefficients, e.g. $\partial \pi_{jr}^Y / \partial PA_{ir} = a_{ijr}^A$, the intermediate demand for Armington good i in sector j of region r per unit of output Y. Output for the domestic market equals total domestic demand:

$$Y_{ir} \frac{\partial \pi_{ir}^Y}{\partial PD_{ir}} = \sum_j A_{jr} \frac{\partial \pi_{jr}^A}{\partial PD_{ir}} \qquad\qquad [3.31]$$

with *PD* the domestic commodity price. Export supply equals import demand across all trading partners:

$$Y_{ir} \frac{\partial \pi_{ir}^Y}{\partial PX_{ir}} = \sum_s M_{is} \frac{\partial \pi_{is}^M}{\partial PX_{ir}}$$ [3.32]

with *PX* the export price. Aggregate import supply equals total import demand:

$$M_{ir} = A_{ir} \frac{\partial \pi_{ir}^A}{\partial PM_{ir}}$$ [3.33]

where *PM* is the import price.

Primary factor endowment equals primary factor demand:

$$\overline{L_r} = \sum_i Y_{ir} \frac{\partial \pi_{ir}^Y}{\partial PL_r},$$ [3.34]

$$\overline{K_r} = \sum_i Y_{ir} \frac{\partial \pi_{ir}^Y}{\partial PK_r},$$ [3.35]

$$\overline{R_{vr}} = Y_{vr} \frac{\partial \pi_{vr}^Y}{\partial PR_{vr}}.$$ [3.36]

An equilibrium is characterized by a set of prices in the different goods and factor markets such that the zero profit and market clearance conditions stated above hold.

3.6   Data and Calibration

The model is based on a Social Accounting Matrix (SAM), i.e. a comprehensive, economy-wide data framework, typically representing the economy of a nation (see, for example, Reinert and Roland-Holst 1997). The main data source underlying the model is the GTAP version 4 database that represents global production and trade data for 45 countries and regions, 50 commodities and five primary factors (McDougall 1998). In addition, we use OECD/IEA energy statistics (IEA 1996) for 1995. Reconciliation of these data sources yields the benchmark data of our model (see Babiker and

Rutherford 1997). For this application, the data set has been aggregated as shown in Table 3.1.

In order to perform simulations with our model, we need parameter values for the function parameters. Our large-scale model has many functional parameters that must be specified with relatively few observations. This prevents the econometric estimation of the model parameters as an econometric system of simultaneous equations. The estimation of the parameters using single-equation methods, on the other hand, would not produce an equilibrium solution for the model that matches the benchmark data. The conventional approach is to determine parameters for the equations in the model using a non-stochastic calibration method (Mansur and Whalley 1984). The model is calibrated to a single base-year equilibrium, such that the base solution to the model exactly reproduces the values of the adjusted data. Since we use CES utility and production functions, the assumptions of cost minimization and utility maximization leave us with one free parameter. Therefore, exogenously specified elasticity values from econometric literature estimates are also required. The other parameter values follow from the restrictions imposed by cost minimization and utility maximization. The given set of benchmark quantities and prices, together with the substitution elasticities given in Table 3.2, completely specify the benchmark equilibrium. The substitution elasticities determine the curvature of isoquants and indifference surfaces, while their position is given by the benchmark equilibrium data.

For example, consider again the value-added aggregate *KL* in non-fossil fuel production given by [3.8]. Deriving the first order conditions for cost minimization and solving for α gives:

$$\alpha_{nr} = \frac{PK_{nr} \cdot K_{nr}^{1/\sigma^{KL}} \Big/ PL_{nr} \cdot L_{nr}^{1/\sigma^{KL}}}{1 + PK_{nr} \cdot K_{nr}^{1/\sigma^{KL}} \Big/ PL_{nr} \cdot L_{nr}^{1/\sigma^{KL}}} \qquad [3.37]$$

with $PL = PL^* (1+tl)$ and $PK = PK^* (1+tk)$ the cost of capital and labor including taxes *tl* and *tk*, respectively. Since benchmark data are given in value terms, we have to choose units for goods and factors to separate price and quantity observations. A commonly used units convention is to choose units for both goods and factors such that they have a price of unity in the benchmark. The benchmark net-of-tax factor prices PL^* and PK^* are thus set equal to one and [3.37] can be written as:

$$\alpha_{nr} = \frac{\left(1 + tl_{nr}\right) \cdot K_{nr}^{1/\sigma^{KL}} \Big/ \left(1 + tk_{nr}\right) \cdot L_{nr}^{1/\sigma^{KL}}}{1 + \left(1 + tl_{nr}\right) \cdot K_{nr}^{1/\sigma^{KL}} \Big/ \left(1 + tk_{nr}\right) \cdot L_{nr}^{1/\sigma^{KL}}} \qquad [3.38]$$

The unit conventions further imply that the number of units of each factor equals the net of tax value of factor use. For each industry n the values of L, tl, K and tk are available from the underlying input–output tables and α can be calculated according to [3.38] given an exogenous value for the substitution elasticity σ^{KL} and thus ρ^{KL}. β_{nr} is $(1 - \alpha_{nr})$. When we know α, β and ρ, we can calculate ϕ using the zero-profit condition:

$$PK_{nr} \cdot K_{nr} + PL_{nr} \cdot L_{nr} = KL_{nr} \qquad [3.39]$$

or

$$\phi_{nr} = \frac{\left(1 + tk_{nr}\right) \cdot K_{nr} + \left(1 + tl_{nr}\right) \cdot L_{nr}}{\left[\alpha_{nr} K_{nr}^{\rho^{KL}} + \beta_{nr} L_{nr}^{\rho^{KL}}\right]^{1/\rho^{KL}}}. \qquad [3.40]$$

In a second step, we do the forward calibration of the 1995 economies to the target year, which is 2010 in our case, employing baseline estimates by the US Department of Energy (DOE 1998) for GDP growth, energy demand and future energy prices. The economic effects of carbon abatement policies depend on the extent to which emissions reduction targets constrain the respective economies.

In other words, the magnitude and distribution of costs associated with the implementation of future emission constraints depend on the baseline (BaU) projections for GDP, fuel prices, energy efficiency improvements etc. In our comparative-static framework, we infer the BaU structure of the model regions for the target year using recent projections for economic development. We then measure the costs of abatement relative to that baseline.

Numerically, the model is formulated and solved as a mixed complementarity problem (MCP) using the Mathematical Programming Subsystem for General Equilibrium (MPSGE) described in Rutherford (1995a, 1999) within the Generalized Algebraic Modelling System (GAMS) mathematical modeling language (Brooke et al. 1996).

Table 3.2   Default values of key substitution and supply elasticities

Description	Value
Substitution elasticities in non-fossil fuel production	
σ^{KLE} Energy vs. value added	0.8
σ^{KL} Capital vs. labor	1.0
σ^{E} Electricity vs. primary energy inputs	0.3
σ^{COL} Coal vs. gas-oil	0.5
Substitution elasticities in final demand	
σ_{C} Fossil fuels vs. non-fossil fuels	0.8
σ_{FE} Fossil fuels vs. fossil fuels	0.3
Elasticities in international trade (Armington)	
σ^{D} Substitution elasticity between imports vs. domestic inputs	4.0
σ^{M} Substitution elasticity between imports vs. imports	8.0
σ^{tr} Transformation elasticity domestic vs. export	2.0
Exogenous supply elasticities of fossil fuels ε	
Crude oil	1.0
Coal	0.5
Natural gas	1.0

4.   QUANTITATIVE ASSESSMENT OF CARBON ABATEMENT POLICIES

This section presents quantitative estimates for the economic impacts of carbon abatement restrictions under the Kyoto Protocol. Our main objective is to show how our static general equilibrium model of the global economy can be used to identify important determinants of adjustment costs across various regions. These determinants can be grouped into three categories. First, there are the policy settings such as the initial endowment with carbon emission rights or the degree of coordinated policies that characterize the design of any global abatement scenario. Second, there are assumptions underlying the basic model structure – most notably elasticities – which reflect the sensitivity of demand-side and supply-side responses to exogenous policy changes. Third, a larger part of the differences in the marginal and inframarginal costs of carbon emission constraints across regions may be traced back to structural differences in their economic and energy systems.

We will illustrate in the following how a shift in the policy design or changes in the model parametrization affect the model results. Although such a sensitivity analysis can clearly not be exhaustive, it is an indispensable step in any credible CGE analysis of policy interference, as it conveys important information on the robustness of results.

In our core simulations, we examine three different scenarios on the degree of international emissions trading:

[NOTRADE] Annex B countries can trade emission rights as allocated under the Kyoto Protocol only within domestic borders. There is no international trade in permit rights. This scenario is equivalent to a situation where Annex B countries apply domestic carbon taxes that are high enough to meet their individual Kyoto commitments.

[ANNEXB] All Annex B countries including FSU and CEA are allowed to trade emissions with each other.

[GLOBAL] There are no regional restrictions to emissions trading. Non-Annex B countries participate in global emissions trading with initial permit endowments which are equal to their Business-as-Usual emission level.

A fourth policy scenario accounts for the recent withdrawal of the USA as stated by President Bush in March 2001:

[NOUSA] The Kyoto Protocol is implemented without participation of the USA. All remaining countries meet their individual targets through strictly domestic action.

We then assess how changes in key model parameters affect our results. The objective is to strengthen the thinking of non-technical readers on major drivers of the model results. The first set of runs deals with the question about the extent transaction costs reduce the efficiency gains from 'where' – flexibility provided by the use of flexible instruments:

[TCOST] In the global trading scenario we have not incorporated any additional costs that might result from the setup and control (costs for monitoring, verification, certification, etc.) of flexible instruments. Many people believe that these costs can be substantial, particularly if some sort of emissions trading takes place between Annex B and non-Annex B countries. In the TCOST runs, we assess how the level of transaction costs affects the efficiency properties of the GLOBAL trading scenario. We assume that transaction costs apply to carbon exports from non-Annex B countries only, and will be incurred by them, also.

The next scenario examines the importance of the underlying baseline projections on economic growth and emissions under Business-as-Usual:

[BASELINE] As compared to the reference case, we adopt more optimistic assumptions on economic growth, which implies – *ceteris paribus* – higher demands for fossil fuels and higher BaU carbon emissions.

Finally, we assess the sensitivity of results with respect to changes in key assumptions underlying our core simulations: ease of substitution between domestic and imported goods (ARMINGTON), oil price responses (OIL), and the inefficiency of raising public funds (MCF):

[ARMINGTON] As described in Section 3, we represent trade in goods with an Armington structure. Imports are imperfect substitutes for domestically produced goods. The elasticity of substitution between imports and domestically produced goods, referred to as the Armington elasticity, measures how easily imports can substitute for domestic goods. In the scenario ARMINGTON, we vary the values of Armington elasticities to quantify the induced changes in the trade impacts of carbon abatement policies.

[OIL] The supply elasticity for oil determines how the world oil price responds to changes in world oil demand. We employ alternative values for the oil supply elasticity to investigate the economic implications on oil-exporting and oil-importing regions.

[MCF] The issue of revenue recycling has received lots of attention in the scientific and policy debate during the last decade. Environmental policies that raise public revenues can be complemented by revenue-neutral cuts of distortionary fiscal taxes. This provides prospects for the well-known double-dividend hypothesis from environmental taxation (see, for example, Pezzey 1992, Goulder 1995a). In our core simulations, we assume that revenues from carbon taxes or permit sales are recycled lump-sum to the representative agent in each region. In the scenario MCF we analyze how reductions in distortionary fiscal taxes will affect the gross costs of carbon abatement policies, i.e. the costs excluding environmental benefits.

All simulations are measured against the BaU scenario where no carbon emission restrictions apply. For the sake of brevity, we restrict sensitivity analyses to the NOTRADE policy setting in which emission targets are met through strictly domestic action. The NOTRADE reference setting is denoted as REF in Tables 3.12 to 3.39 below, summarizing the results of our sensitivity analysis.[10]

4.1   Effective Reduction Requirements

An important feature of any international agreement on greenhouse gas abatement is the extent to which it binds the involved economies in the future; the magnitude and distribution of costs associated with the implementation of future emission constraints depend on the Business-as-Usual (BaU) projections for gross domestic product, fuel prices, energy efficiency improvements etc. As outlined in Section 3, we infer the BaU structure of the model's regions for 2010 based on recent expert projections on economic development (DOE 1998). In our comparative static analysis, we measure the economic effects associated with abatement policies relative to the BaU in 2010.

It is important to notice that the nominal reduction targets to which Annex B countries have committed themselves under the Kyoto Protocol may substantially differ from the effective reduction requirements they face under BaU in 2010. Emissions of most Annex B countries have grown significantly along the baseline compared to 1990 levels. The Kyoto targets which are stated with respect to 1990 then translate into much higher effective carbon requirements with respect to BaU emission levels in 2010. Table 3.3 reports both the nominal Kyoto commitments as well as the effective reduction requirements across Annex B countries in 2010.

We see, for example, that the USA, which committed itself to a 7% reduction target with respect to 1990 levels, would have an effective cutback requirement of more than 30% as compared to the 2010 BaU level if it were to ratify the Protocol.[11]

Table 3.3 Nominal and effective CO$_2$ reduction requirements (in %)

Region	Nominal reduction (wrt 1990)	Effective reduction (wrt 2010)
CEA	7.00	−4.21
EUR	7.73	16.60
FSU	0.00	−31.74
JPN	6.00	23.05
OOE	0.91	22.68
USA	7.00	33.19

OOE is allowed to increase emissions under the Kyoto Protocol by 7% over 1990 levels, while it effectively faces the need for a decrease by more than 20% from BaU emissions in 2010. On the other hand, regions CEA and particularly FSU will stay below their 1990 emission levels due to major structural breaks between 1990 and 2000.

4.2 NOTRADE: Domestic Abatement Policies

4.2.1 Marginal abatement costs and welfare impacts

Table 3.4 reports the marginal abatement costs and welfare changes emerging from the implementation of the Kyoto targets through strictly domestic carbon abatement policies. In this framework, the marginal abatement costs are equivalent to the domestic carbon tax, which must be levied in order to achieve the exogenous emissions reduction target.

Obviously, the marginal abatement costs for non-Annex B countries are zero, because they have not committed themselves to any emission limitation. Among Annex B countries, the Kyoto targets do not become binding for CEA and FSU. All other Annex B parties, i.e. OECD countries, must cut back their BaU emissions substantially, which is reflected in the level of marginal abatement costs. Partial equilibrium analysis suggests that the level of abatement is a major determinant of the marginal abatement costs. The further out we are on the abatement cost curve, the more costly it is at the margin to replace carbon in production and consumption.

However, cross-country comparison of reduction requirements and marginal abatement costs in Table 3.4 reveals that the relative cutback requirements are only one determinant of marginal abatement costs. The latter depend also on the BaU energy price levels.

Table 3.4 Marginal abatement costs and welfare effects

Region	Marginal abatement cost*	Welfare effect**
CEA	-	0.29
EUR	112.76	−0.18
FSU	-	−0.25
JPN	229.36	−0.32
OOE	106.74	−0.66
USA	159.53	−0.60
ASI	-	0.03
CHN	-	0.22
IND	-	0.20
MPC	-	−0.48
ROW	-	−0.06

Notes: * $US95 per ton of carbon
** in % change of real consumption as compared to BaU

Typically, a country with higher BaU energy prices will require larger carbon taxes to achieve the same percentage emissions reduction than countries with lower BaU energy prices.[12] Differences in carbon intensities of sectors across countries play another important role in explaining the variation in marginal abatement costs. Countries which use carbon-intensive coal heavily in activities where fuel switching to less carbon-intensive oil or gas comes relatively cheap, face lower marginal abatement costs to meet the same reduction than countries which use relatively little carbon in sectors with low-cost substitution options.

These features explain, for example, why JPN faces much higher carbon taxes compared to USA, although its percentage reduction target is smaller: BaU energy prices in JPN are considerably higher than in USA. In addition, JPN has little scope for cheap inter-fuel substitution in electricity generation, which is largely nuclear-power based.

4.2.2 Welfare effects

The static welfare impacts are measured as the percentage change in real consumption with respect to BaU. Two things should be kept in mind when interpreting these numbers: First, we report only the gross economic impact of carbon emission constraints without accounting for environmental benefits.

Therefore, losses in real consumption cannot be construed as an argument against environmental action in cost-benefit terms. Second, in our core simulations, we do not incorporate second-best considerations which might raise the scope for a double dividend from environmental taxation.[13] Under these conditions, the implications of emission constraints on the global economy are straightforward. At the global level, adjustment of production and consumption patterns towards less carbon intensity implies a less productive use of resources, which translates into a decline of real income, i.e. less consumption, given fixed investment. At the single-country level, however, the welfare implications are ambiguous. Carbon abatement in large open economies not only causes adjustment of domestic production and consumption patterns, but also influences international prices via changes in exports and imports. Changes in international prices (terms-of-trade impacts) imply a secondary benefit or burden which may alter the economic implications of the primary domestic abatement policy. Some countries may shift part of their domestic abatement costs to trading partners, while other abating countries face additional welfare losses from a deterioration of their terms of trade. These international spillovers also explain why countries which do not face any emission restriction under the Kyoto Protocol may nevertheless be significantly affected by the abatement of Annex B countries.[14]

Table 3.4 suggests that for OECD countries, the unambiguous primary domestic policy effect is not dominated by secondary terms-of-trade effects, which is not surprising given the stringency of the respective emission constraints. For countries that do not face a binding emission constraint, the secondary terms-of-trade effect is equal to the total welfare effect as reported in Table 3.4. Given our core model parametrization, we see that spillover effects harm FSU, MPC and ROW, whereas they are beneficial to developing regions ASI, CHN and IND, as well as the economies in transition CEA.

Among international spillovers that result from trade in goods, most important are the adjustments on international energy markets. The cut-back in demands for fossil fuels from abating OECD countries depresses the international energy prices. Lower world energy prices harm energy exporting countries and benefit energy importing countries. In this vein, spillover effects from energy markets cause welfare losses for fuel exporters FSU, MPC and ROW, because the prices of energy exports decline and, therefore, export revenues fall. CEA as well as developing regions ASI, CHN and IND are net importers of fuels and therefore benefit from the depression of world energy prices.

The welfare implications of international price changes in non-energy markets, where traded goods are differentiated by region of origin, are more complex. Higher energy costs raise prices of non-energy goods produced in Annex B countries. Countries that import these goods suffer from higher prices to the extent that they cannot easily move away from more expensive imports towards cheaper imports from non-abating countries. The implicit burden shifting of carbon taxes on non-energy markets not only applies between abating and non-abating countries but also within the group of abating Annex B regions; for example, OOE, which has relatively low marginal abatement costs, suffers from the increased export prices of trading partners with high marginal abatement costs, such as Japan.

Due to reduced economic activity (productivity) in abating developed regions, trading partners face a negative scale or income effect as the import demand by the industrialized world declines, which exerts a downward pressure on the prices of demanded goods. On the other hand, this effect may be (partially) offset by an opposite substitution effect. Developing countries may gain market shares because their exports become more competitive. As reported in Table 3.4, all non-Annex B countries, apart from MPC and ROW, improve their terms of trade. It should be noted that this result is rather sensitive to the representation of price responses on the world crude oil and coal market. When larger cuts in oil and coal demand cause only a small decrease in world fuel prices, the positive spillover for oil and coal importing developing countries is significantly reduced and may be offset by negative spillovers on other (non-energy) markets.

Moreover, our choice of a comparative-static framework potentially overstates the gains from unilateral action by Annex B countries for developing countries. We do not account for the effects of reduced investment on the economic growth and import demand of industrialized countries. As complementary analysis in a dynamic framework shows (see, for example, Böhringer and Rutherford 2001), the additional income losses for developing countries may then have the effect that most of them lose on balance from trade distortions caused by emission constraints in the industrialized countries.

4.2.3 Comparative advantage and the pattern of trade

In the conventional economic paradigm, comparative advantage refers to the relative cost of producing goods in a particular country in comparison to the relative cost of producing the same goods elsewhere. Unilateral action has important implications for comparative advantage, i.e. the competitiveness of industrial sectors across regions. Carbon emission constraints increase the cost of production, particularly for those sectors in which energy represents a significant share of direct and indirect costs. At the sectoral level, policy makers in Annex B countries are, therefore, concerned about the negative repercussions of emission constraints on production and employment in energy-intensive sectors. Tables 3.5 and 3.7 indicate why.[15]

Due to unilateral abatement, energy-intensive sectors in Annex B countries, which face binding emissions constraints, lose competitiveness. Most affected is energy-intensive production in the USA, which experiences the highest increase among Annex B countries, given the low US energy costs under BaU. CEA and FSU, as well as all developing non-Annex B countries, face a cost advantage because they do not have to levy domestic carbon taxes.

Even though energy costs do not constitute a large share of value-added in energy-intensive production, the cost increase in OECD countries changes comparative advantage sufficiently to induce large changes in trade flows. As we can see from Table 3.7, the EU exports to FSU drop by nearly 10%, whereas imports from FSU to EU increase by roughly 9%.

Table 3.5 Impacts on energy-intensive production (% change)

Region	
CEA	1.93
EUR	−0.53
FSU	4.87
JPN	−0.82
OOE	−1.33
USA	−2.33
ASI	1.47
CHN	2.08
IND	2.24
MPC	3.50
ROW	1.17

4.2.4 Environmental Effectiveness and Leakage

Given the global nature of the carbon externality, sub-global abatement action induces efficiency losses due to carbon leakage. Under the Kyoto Protocol, emissions reduction in Annex B countries can be offset by increased emissions elsewhere through the relocation of energy-intensive production or depressed prices of fossil fuels. This effect is measured by the leakage rate, which – in general terms – is defined as the ratio of the emissions increase in non-abating countries to the total emissions reduction in abating countries. If leakage is significant, the design of unilateral abatement policies may be altered to avoid leakage and increase the efficiency of sub-global abatement strategies. One approach would be to lower the abatement burden on emission-intensive industries via (partial) exemptions or grandfathered permits (see, for example, Böhringer 1998a, Böhringer, Ferris and Rutherford 1998, Böhringer, Rutherford and Voss 1998).

Table 3.6 summarizes the leakage rates at the regional and global level for the NOTRADE scenario. In total, the emissions reduction of Annex B countries are offset by more than 20% through emission increases by non-Annex B countries, with CHN as the main source for leakage.

The magnitude of the leakage rate can be traced back to our treatment of fossil energy markets. We assume that oil and coal markets are homogeneous due to relatively low transport costs. A drop in oil and coal demand by Annex B countries then reduces world prices for coal and oil more than if we had assumed heterogeneity of these goods. This induces a larger increase of oil and coal consumption in non-Annex B countries.

There are several other factors that determine the leakage rate and, hence, the effectiveness of sub-global abatement policies. Among these are the assumed degree of the scope of international carbon trading (see Section 4.3) or the substitutability between imported and domestic production (see Section 4.7).

4.3 ANNEX B and GLOBAL: The Impacts of Emissions Trading

One major controversial issue of the Kyoto Protocol is the extent to which emissions reduction commitments by individual countries can be met through the use of flexible instruments such as emissions trading. In principle, the Kyoto Protocol allows emissions trading across signatory countries; however the rules are vague, and have yet to be defined.[16] With respect to the scope of tradable permits, the Kyoto Protocol states that any trading shall be 'supplemental' to domestic action for the purpose of meeting obligations. The principle of supplementarity was inserted mainly due to concerns in the EU about hot air.

Table 3.6 Leakage rates (in %)

Region	Leakage rate
ASI	0.97
CHN	14.15
IND	2.40
MPC	1.55
ROW	2.82
TOTAL	21.90

This increases the effective emissions compared to strictly domestic action because regions with BaU emissions below target levels can trade in their abundant emission rights. This will be particularly relevant for FSU, where projected emissions are far below the Kyoto entitlements.

Estimates of hot air range up to 500–650 million tons of CO_2, which corresponds to 70–90% of the total Annex B reduction commitment (Herold 1998, Böhringer 2000).

First of all, we see that Annex B emissions trading substantially reduces the negative impacts of meeting Kyoto targets for the global economy. Compliance costs are reduced to roughly a third of the cost figure in the NOTRADE reference case. Note that global welfare gains stem from two different sources. First, there are gains from the equalization of marginal abatement costs across Annex B countries. Second, there are gains from an implicit relaxation of the NOTRADE emission constraints due to hot air. In fact, CEA and, in particular, FSU, sell larger amounts of formerly abundant emission rights.

Even more disputed than emissions trading within the block of Annex B countries is the implicit extension of emissions trading to non-Annex B countries via the Clean Development Mechanism. While this has a clear economic efficiency rationale, opponents of global emissions trading systems such as the EU refer to potential loopholes associated with the problems of defining credible emission baselines and the lack of regulations regarding monitoring or verification.

In this context, estimates of the magnitude of efficiency gains from trade provide a useful reference point against which one can count transaction costs for the institutional set-up and control of emissions trading (see Section 4.5).

Table 3.7 Trade in energy-intensive production (% change)

Imports from Row region to Column region

	CEA	EUR	FSU	JPN	OOE	USA
CEA	1.51	3.59	−5.69	6.34	5.96	8.67
EUR	−2.36	−0.36	−9.88	2.29	1.91	4.56
FSU	6.77	8.89	−1.14	11.81	11.31	14.19
JPN	−3.54	−1.59	−11.04	0.82	0.58	3.17
OOE	−6.11	−4.29	−13.57	−1.69	−1.99	0.37
USA	−5.69	−3.79	−13.15	−1.23	−1.71	−2.33
ASI	1.24	3.35	−6.38	6.11	5.67	8.42
CHN	2.31	4.37	−5.42	7.13	6.71	9.46
IND	3.38	5.45	−4.38	8.23	7.82	10.61
MPC	2.45	4.52	−5.29	7.27	6.83	9.59
ROW	0.85	2.90	−6.83	5.57	5.25	7.97
	ASI	CHN	IND	MPC	ROW	
CEA	1.58	−0.22	−1.96	0.75	0.67	
EUR	−2.28	−4.03	−5.62	−3.08	−3.14	
FSU	6.72	4.86	3.33	5.88	5.80	
JPN	−3.45	−5.12	−6.66	−4.27	−4.39	
OOE	−6.10	−7.71	−9.28	−6.86	−6.93	
USA	−5.59	−7.23	−8.64	−6.44	−6.39	
ASI	1.32	−0.44	−2.08	0.53	0.43	
CHN	2.34	0.54	−1.11	1.53	1.44	
IND	3.39	1.59	2.24	2.58	2.50	
MPC	2.47	0.66	−1.02	1.64	1.59	
ROW	0.86	−0.92	−2.49	0.08	0.01	

Tables 3.8 and 3.9 summarize the changes in marginal and inframarginal abatement costs when we move from NOTRADE to policies which allow for trade in permits among Annex B countries (ANNEXB) or all world regions (GLOBAL).

Table 3.8 Marginal abatement costs (in $US95 per ton of carbon)

Region	NOTRADE	ANNEXB	GLOBAL
CEA	-	57	31
EUR	113	57	31
FSU	-	57	31
JPN	229	57	31
OOE	107	57	31
USA	160	57	31
ASI	-	-	31
CHN	-	-	31
IND	-	-	31
MPC	-	-	31
ROW	-	-	31

Table 3.9 Welfare impacts (in % change of real consumption)

REGION	NOTRADE	ANNEXB	GLOBAL
CEA	0.29	0.87	0.37
EUR	−0.18	−0.11	−0.03
FSU	−0.25	5.16	2.58
JPN	−0.32	−0.09	−0.01
OOE	−0.66	−0.53	−0.46
USA	−0.60	−0.38	−0.24
ASI	0.03	0.03	0.08
CHN	0.22	0.15	0.25
IND	0.20	0.15	0.03
MPC	−0.48	−0.38	−0.44
ROW	−0.06	−0.05	−0.09
TOTAL	−0.29	−0.09	−0.06

The pattern of permit trade is determined by the level of marginal abatement costs under NOTRADE compared to the equalized marginal abatement costs for tradable permits. Countries whose marginal abatement costs under NOTRADE are below the uniform permit price will sell permits and abate more emissions. In turn, countries whose marginal abatement costs are above the uniform permit price rate will buy permits and abate fewer emissions.

Table 3.10 Leakage rates (in %)

Region	NOTRADE	ANNEXB
ASI	0.97	0.71
CHN	14.15	9.85
IND	2.40	1.70
MPC	1.55	1.15
ROW	2.82	2.39
TOTAL	21.90	15.79

Table 3.11 Carbon emissions (in Gt)

Region	BASELINE	NOTRADE	ANNEXB	GLOBAL
CEA	0.25	0.26	0.20	0.23
EUR	1.16	1.01	1.10	1.16
FSU	0.82	0.94	0.70	0.77
JPN	0.45	0.34	0.41	0.43
OOE	0.27	0.22	0.24	0.26
USA	2.07	1.41	1.75	1.92
ASI	0.36	0.37	0.37	0.34
CHN	1.35	1.62	1.57	1.24
IND	0.32	0.36	0.35	0.30
MPC	0.62	0.65	0.65	0.59
ROW	0.66	0.70	0.69	0.63
TOTAL	8.33	7.88	8.03	7.87

All Annex B countries benefit substantially from Annex B trade in permits.[17] There are huge monetary transfers from emission sales to FSU, which turns the region's welfare loss under NOTRADE into huge welfare gains as compared to BaU. CEA further improves welfare beyond BaU levels through the sales of emissions. OECD countries face much smaller marginal abatement costs due to additional supplies of emission rights from FSU and CEA. The drop in marginal abatement costs is reflected in the decrease of inframarginal consumption losses. International spillovers to non-Annex B countries are reduced for Annex B trading as the changes in comparative advantage, i.e. the terms of trade, become less pronounced.

As expected, global emissions trading further reduces the world-wide costs of Kyoto. However, the implied cost reduction associated with a shift from ANNEXB to GLOBAL is much smaller than that generated by the move from NOTRADE to ANNEXB (see also the respective changes in marginal abatement costs). Hot air from CEA and FSU obviously accounts for a larger share of welfare gains achievable through permit trading. Among Annex B countries, only the OECD regions benefit from global emissions trading as compared to the ANNEXB scenario. The reason for this is obvious: global trading increases the supply of emission abatement from abroad, which further relaxes the Kyoto emission constraint on OECD countries and decreases the price of tradable emission permits. On the other hand, both FSU and CEA suffer from the decline in the permit price, which implies a substantial loss of their income from permit sales.

The leakage rate under ANNEXB drops by a fourth compared to the NOTRADE case. Emissions trading reduces the cost increase for energy-intensive sectors in OECD countries, which diminishes counterproductive relocation of 'dirty' industries to non-abating countries. Nevertheless, global emissions rise under ANNEXB trading compared to the NOTRADE scenario: the decline in leakage gets more than offset by hot air from FSU and CEA. In the GLOBAL trading scenario, leakage becomes zero by definition. Global carbon emissions are at the same level as under NOTRADE. This indicates that, under GLOBAL, avoided leakage is just offset by hot air.

4.4   NOUSA: Kyoto without USA

In March 2001, the USA under President Bush switched its attitude towards the Kyoto Protocol and declared 'We have no interest in implementing this treaty'. Since then, other major Annex B countries have emphasized their willingness to implement Kyoto even without US participation. The scenario NOUSA reflects this policy situation in assuming that the USA does not face any emission constraint on its economy, whereas all other ANNEXB countries meet their Kyoto commitments through domestic action. Tables 3.12 through 3.15 summarize the economic and environmental implications of this scenario.

Without emission constraint, the US economy is more or less unaffected by the carbon abatement policies of the other Annex B regions. However, the higher fossil fuel demand by the US economy has important implications for spillovers from international energy markets. Prices for coal and oil do not fall as much, which is beneficial for energy exporting regions MPC and ROW, but harmful to energy importers such as EUR, JPN or developing regions CHN, IND and ASI. Non-compliance of the USA results in significantly higher global carbon emissions than in the reference case. The USA becomes more competitive in the production of energy-intensive goods. This increases the global carbon leakage up to 28%, with CHN and USA accounting for the largest part of it.

Table 3.12 Welfare impacts (in % change of real consumption)

Region	REF	NOUSA
CEA	0.29	0.16
EUR	−0.18	−0.22
FSU	−0.25	−0.46
JPN	−0.32	−0.36
OOE	−0.66	−0.44
USA	−0.60	0.01
ASI	0.03	−0.02
CHN	0.22	0.03
IND	0.20	0.04
MPC	−0.48	−0.15
ROW	−0.06	−0.03
TOTAL	−0.29	−0.14

4.5   TCOST: The Effects of Transaction Costs

A common assumption of CGE models is that all decisions are made under certainty. In the case of climate change this is doubtful.

If a country or company uses one of the flexible instruments to achieve its reduction target, it must be certain that purchased emission rights will be valid.Otherwise, it will bear the risk of non-compliance and corresponding sanctions. Incorporating this uncertainty into the modeling framework might change the optimal choice between domestic and foreign actions, since reduction measures abroad might bear higher risks, shifting the relative advantage to domestic actions.

Closely linked to the risk problem is the issue of transaction costs. To reduce or avoid risks, the purchasing party might insure the projects or diversify through carbon funds. Further options would be more stringent rules for project verification and certification. All these strategies are associated with higher transactions costs. Model simulations that neglect the existence of transaction costs overestimate the potential benefit from the international trade of emission permits.

Table 3.13 Marginal abatement costs (in $US95 per ton of carbon)

Region	REF	NOUSA
CEA	-	-
EUR	113	107
FSU	-	-
JPN	229	224
OOE	107	98
USA	160	-
ASI	-	-
CHN	-	-
IND	-	-
MPC	-	-
ROW	-	-

Table 3.14 Leakage rates (in %)

Region	REF	NOUSA
USA	0.00	10.28
ASI	0.97	0.88
CHN	14.15	10.77
IND	2.40	1.83
MPC	1.55	1.54
ROW	2.82	2.83
TOTAL	21.90	28.13

These considerations show the need to assess the effects of transaction costs. In the scenario GLOBAL, we assume that the transaction costs for transferring abatement from non-Annex B countries to Annex B countries equal zero. We now impose transaction costs of $US5 (CDM05), $US10

(CDM10) or $US20 (CDM20) on every ton of carbon that is sold from non-Annex B countries to Annex B countries. Transaction costs are represented as resource use which does not generate revenues for the partners involved in emissions trading. In the model, we incorporate transaction costs as a requirement for human resources (i.e. labor) to monitor and verify trade in emission abatement.[18]

Table 3.15 Carbon emissions (in Gt)

Region	REF	NOUSA
CEA	0.26	0.26
EUR	1.01	1.01
FSU	0.94	0.90
JPN	0.34	0.34
OOE	0.22	0.22
USA	1.41	2.14
ASI	0.37	0.37
CHN	1.62	1.51
IND	0.36	0.34
MPC	0.65	0.64
ROW	0.70	0.68
TOTAL	7.88	8.41

Tables 3.16–3.18 report the economic implications of transaction costs. Not surprisingly, they reduce the magnitude of efficiency gains from emissions trading with non-Annex B countries. The higher the transaction costs are, the higher the global effective permit prices are (as indicated by the marginal abatement costs of Annex B countries) and the lower the overall level of permit trading. The payment received by non-Annex B countries for any ton of carbon abated domestically equals the difference between the global permit price Annex B countries perceive and the assumed transaction costs. Transaction costs that apply to emissions trading with non-Annex B countries but not to emission sales from Annex B countries are beneficial to CEA and FSU. These countries can now sell their permits at higher prices than in the GLOBAL scenario without any transaction costs. Due to this implied 'mark-up' for FSU and CEA, OECD countries do worse than under the scenario GLOBAL because they move to higher marginal abatement costs. Except for CHN, the largest non-Annex B supplier of emission permits

in absolute terms, transaction costs hardly affect welfare for the other non-Annex B countries simply because their level of trade is already rather small under GLOBAL without any transaction cost.[19]

Table 3.16 Welfare impact (in % change of real consumption)

Region	GLOBAL	CDM05	CDM10	CDM20
CEA	0.37	0.40	0.44	0.53
EUR	−0.03	−0.04	−0.05	−0.06
FSU	2.58	2.80	3.02	3.52
JPN	−0.01	−0.01	−0.02	−0.03
OOE	−0.46	−0.47	−0.48	−0.51
USA	−0.24	−0.25	−0.27	−0.30
ASI	0.08	0.07	0.07	0.06
CHN	0.25	0.22	0.20	0.16
IND	0.03	0.02	0.02	0.02
MPC	−0.44	−0.44	−0.45	−0.45
ROW	−0.09	−0.09	−0.09	−0.09
TOTAL	−0.06	−0.07	−0.07	−0.08

Table 3.17 Marginal abatement costs (in $US95 per ton of carbon)

Region	GLOBAL	CDM05	CDM10	CDM20
CEA	31	33	36	41
EUR	31	33	36	41
FSU	31	33	36	41
JPN	31	33	36	41
OOE	31	33	36	41
USA	31	33	36	41
ASI	31	28	26	21
CHN	31	28	26	21
IND	31	28	26	21
MPC	31	28	26	21
ROW	31	28	26	21

4.6 BASELINE: Higher Growth Projections

The cost estimates for carbon abatement depend crucially on BaU projections for gross domestic production, energy efficiency improvements, fuel prices etc. High economic growth, for example, increases the effective abatement requirement; and because the Kyoto commitments refer to 1990 emissions levels, this will imply higher total abatement costs.

Table 3.18 Carbon emissions (in Gt)

Region	GLOBAL	CDM05	CDM10	CDM20
CEA	0.23	0.22	0.22	0.22
EUR	1.16	1.15	1.14	1.13
FSU	0.77	0.77	0.76	0.74
JPN	0.43	0.42	0.42	0.42
OOE	0.26	0.26	0.26	0.26
USA	1.92	1.91	1.89	1.85
ASI	0.34	0.34	0.34	0.35
CHN	1.24	1.26	1.28	1.33
IND	0.30	0.31	0.31	0.32
MPC	0.59	0.59	0.60	0.61
ROW	0.63	0.63	0.64	0.65
TOTAL	7.87	7.87	7.87	7.87

Table 3.19 Effective CO_2 emission cut-back requirements under BASELINE (in % with respect to 2010)

Region	REF	BASELINE
CEA	−4.21	1.19
EUR	16.60	21.03
FSU	−31.74	−28.78
JPN	23.05	27.33
OOE	22.68	26.40
USA	33.19	33.48

Our sensitivity analysis below illustrates the importance of baseline assumptions, which generally receive little attention in the literature.[20] Based on projections by the DOE for alternative economic growth paths (DOE 1998), we adopt higher GDP growth rates that are linked to higher demands in fossil fuels as compared to our reference case. In the higher growth scenario, Table 3.19 reports the increase in the effective cut-back requirements of Annex B countries as compared to the reference case.

Table 3.20 Welfare impacts (in % change of real consumption)

Region	REF	HI
CEA	0.29	0.48
EUR	−0.18	−0.46
FSU	−0.25	−0.53
JPN	−0.32	−0.63
OOE	−0.66	−1.09
USA	−0.60	−0.76
ASI	0.03	0.08
CHN	0.22	0.31
IND	0.20	0.32
MPC	−0.48	−0.77
ROW	−0.06	−0.11
TOTAL	−0.29	−0.49

Table 3.21 Marginal abatement costs (in $US95 per ton of carbon)

Region	REF	HI
CEA	-	14
EUR	113	204
FSU	-	-
JPN	229	379
OOE	107	167
USA	160	207
ASI	-	-
CHN	-	-
IND	-	-
MPC	-	-
ROW	-	-

The increase in projected BaU emissions and effective cutback requirements causes a steep rise in marginal and inframarginal abatement costs (Tables 3.20 and 3.21).

International spillovers to non-abating countries from abatement policies in Annex B countries are substantially magnified. As expected, higher effective reduction requirements in Annex B countries lead to larger changes in comparative advantage for energy-intensive industries (Table 3.22) and a higher leakage rate of sub-global action as compared to the reference case (Table 3.23).

Table 3.22 Energy-intensive production (% change)

Region	REF	HI
CEA	1.93	2.07
EUR	−0.53	−1.22
FSU	4.87	6.95
JPN	−0.82	−1.37
OOE	−1.33	−2.89
USA	−2.33	−3.03
ASI	1.47	2.41
CHN	2.08	3.05
IND	2.24	3.21
MPC	3.50	6.22
ROW	1.17	1.98

Table 3.23 Leakage rates (in %)

Region	REF	HI
ASI	0.97	1.31
CHN	14.15	17.40
IND	2.40	2.76
MPC	1.55	2.35
ROW	2.82	3.48
TOTAL	21.90	27.29

Table 3.24 Carbon emissions (in Gt)

Region	REF	HI
CEA	0.26	0.27
EUR	1.01	1.01
FSU	0.94	0.97
JPN	0.34	0.34
OOE	0.22	0.22
USA	1.41	1.41
ASI	0.37	0.45
CHN	1.62	2.02
IND	0.36	0.42
MPC	0.65	0.76
ROW	0.70	0.84
TOTAL	7.88	8.70

4.7 ARMINGTON: Low-and High-Trade Impact Cases

Apart from crude oil and coal, which are represented as homogeneous goods across regions, imported and domestically produced varieties of the same good are treated as imperfect substitutes. The trade-off between the two varieties is captured by the Armington elasticity. In our policy simulations, this trade elasticity affects, for example, the extent to which OECD's domestically produced goods are displaced by non-OECD imports when a carbon abatement policy raises the cost of OECD production. In the reference case, the elasticity of substitution between the domestic good and the import aggregate is set to 4, and the elasticity of imports from different regions within the import aggregate is set to 8. In the sensitivity analysis, we either halve (LOARM) or double (HIARM) these values.

From the perspective of a small open economy that faces fixed world market prices, the cost of its carbon abatement policy moves inversely with trade elasticities. When domestic and imported goods are closer substitutes, countries can more easily move away from carbon-intensive inputs into production and consumption (see Table 3.26). This primary effect of changes in the trade elasticities must be combined with secondary terms-of-trade effects. At the global level, terms-of-trade effects cancel out such that the welfare impact of higher trade elasticities is unambiguous: the welfare costs of emission constraints on the global economy decline (see Table 3.25). At the single-country level, the terms-of-trade effects may strengthen, weaken or even outweigh the unambiguous primary welfare effect associated with a change in trade elasticities.

Table 3.25 Welfare impacts (in % change of real consumption)

Region	LOARM	REF	HIARM
CEA	0.30	0.29	0.30
EUR	−0.18	−0.18	−0.18
FSU	−0.42	−0.25	−0.15
JPN	−0.32	−0.32	−0.33
OOE	−0.75	−0.66	−0.63
USA	−0.56	−0.60	−0.62
ASI	0.03	0.03	0.02
CHN	0.16	0.22	0.26
IND	0.19	0.20	0.20
MPC	−0.68	−0.48	−0.40
ROW	−0.09	−0.06	−0.05
TOTAL	−0.30	−0.29	−0.29

Table 3.26 Marginal abatement costs (in $US95 per ton of carbon)

Region	LOARM	REF	HIARM
CEA	-	-	-
EUR	121	113	108
FSU	-	-	-
JPN	255	229	216
OOE	114	107	102
USA	161	160	158
ASI	-	-	-
CHN	-	-	-
IND	-	-	-
MPC	-	-	-
ROW	-	-	-

Controlling global warming

In general, lower trade elasticities imply that cost advantages of countries with low or zero abatement costs translate into smaller gains in market shares. In other words, the trade elasticity determines the extent to which domestic abatement costs can be passed further to trading partners ('beggar-thy-neighbor'). With lower elasticities, a country importing carbon-intensive goods from a trading partner with high domestic abatement costs is less able to change from the expensive imports to cheaper domestically produced goods. As expected, higher trade elasticities enforce the adverse impacts on energy-intensive industries in abating OECD countries (Table 3.27) which causes an increase in the global leakage rate (Table 3.28).

Table 3.27 Energy-intensive production (% change)

Region	LOARM	REF	HIARM
CEA	1.12	1.93	3.35
EUR	−0.47	−0.53	−0.66
FSU	4.21	4.87	5.90
JPN	−0.75	−0.82	−1.01
OOE	−0.67	−1.33	−2.57
USA	−1.88	−2.33	−3.11
ASI	0.85	1.47	2.66
CHN	1.52	2.08	3.15
IND	1.64	2.24	3.34
MPC	2.84	3.50	4.69
ROW	0.89	1.17	1.75

Table 3.28 Leakage rates (in %)

Region	LOARM	REF	HIARM
ASI	0.94	0.97	1.05
CHN	13.69	14.15	14.72
IND	2.31	2.40	2.51
MPC	1.42	1.55	1.70
ROW	2.85	2.82	2.88
TOTAL	21.21	21.90	22.85

Table 3.29 Carbon emissions (in Gt)

Region	LOARM	REF	HIARM
CEA	0.26	0.26	0.26
EUR	1.01	1.01	1.01
FSU	0.95	0.94	0.93
JPN	0.34	0.34	0.34
OOE	0.22	0.22	0.22
USA	1.41	1.41	1.41
ASI	0.37	0.37	0.37
CHN	1.59	1.62	1.64
IND	0.36	0.36	0.36
MPC	0.64	0.65	0.66
ROW	0.69	0.70	0.70
TOTAL	7.84	7.88	7.91

4.8   OIL: Responsiveness of crude oil prices

In the reference case, the crude oil supply elasticity is set to 1. In our sensitivity analysis, we double this value for the high elasticity case (HI_OIL) and halve it for the low elasticity case (LO_OIL).

Table 3.30 Welfare impacts (in % change of real consumption)

Region	LO_OIL	REF	HI_OIL
CEA	0.38	0.29	0.23
EUR	−0.15	−0.18	−0.21
FSU	−0.26	−0.25	−0.23
JPN	−0.31	−0.32	−0.34
OOE	−0.66	−0.66	−0.66
USA	−0.58	−0.60	−0.62
ASI	0.08	0.03	0.01
CHN	0.25	0.22	0.21
IND	0.27	0.20	0.15
MPC	−0.69	−0.48	−0.33
ROW	−0.06	−0.06	−0.06
TOTAL	−0.28	−0.29	−0.30

Lower elasticities imply that the crude oil price is more responsive to a change in demand. Therefore, when the OECD reduces its demand for crude oil, the price drops more for lower elasticity values than for higher values. Increasing the price response causes oil exporting nations to suffer more when a carbon abatement policy is enacted.

Table 3.31 Marginal abatement costs (in $US95 per ton of carbon)

Region	LO_OIL	REF	HI_OIL
CEA	-	-	-
EUR	114	113	112
FSU	-	-	-
JPN	231	229	228
OOE	108	107	106
USA	161	160	159
ASI	-	-	-
CHN	-	-	-
IND	-	-	-
MPC	-	-	-
ROW	-	-	-

Table 3.32 Energy-intensive production (% change)

Region	LO_OIL	REF	HI_OIL
CEA	2.00	1.93	1.88
EUR	−0.53	−0.53	−0.53
FSU	4.93	4.87	4.82
JPN	−0.83	−0.82	−0.81
OOE	−1.31	−1.33	−1.37
USA	−2.35	−2.33	−2.32
ASI	1.47	1.47	1.47
CHN	2.09	2.08	2.08
IND	2.26	2.24	2.23
MPC	3.67	3.50	3.38
ROW	1.16	1.17	1.19

Conversely, higher price responses lead to greater benefits for oil-importing countries. This explains why oil-importing OECD countries and developing countries do worse for higher oil supply elasticities. The opposite applies to oil-exporting regions such as FSU and MPC.[21] As expected, leakage through adjustments in international oil markets declines with higher oil supply elasticities. However, the induced changes are rather small.

Table 3.33 Leakage rates (in %)

Region	LO_OIL	REF	HI_OIL
ASI	1.09	0.97	0.89
CHN	14.21	14.15	14.12
IND	2.48	2.40	2.35
MPC	1.79	1.55	1.40
ROW	2.94	2.82	2.74
TOTAL	22.50	21.90	21.50

Table 3.34 Carbon emissions (in Gt)

Region	LO_OIL	REF	HI_OIL
CEA	0.26	0.26	0.26
EUR	1.01	1.01	1.01
FSU	0.94	0.94	0.94
JPN	0.34	0.34	0.34
OOE	0.22	0.22	0.22
USA	1.41	1.41	1.41
ASI	0.37	0.37	0.37
CHN	1.62	1.62	1.62
IND	0.36	0.36	0.36
MPC	0.65	0.65	0.65
ROW	0.70	0.70	0.70
TOTAL	7.89	7.88	7.87

4.9 MCF: The Gains from Revenue Recycling

In our core simulations, the revenues of carbon taxes are recycled lump-sum to the representative agent in each region. We do not capture therefore the welfare effects of swapping carbon taxes for distortionary existing taxes. In

Controlling global warming

our global model of the world economy, we are not able to represent country-specific tax distortions, due to the level of aggregation and the lack of appropriate data.

Table 3.35 Welfare impacts (in % change of real consumption)

Region	REF	MCF05	MCF10	MCF25
CEA	0.29	0.29	0.30	0.30
EUR	−0.18	−0.12	−0.06	0.12
FSU	−0.25	−0.24	−0.24	−0.24
JPN	−0.32	−0.25	−0.17	0.07
OOE	−0.66	−0.55	−0.43	−0.07
USA	−0.60	−0.46	−0.32	0.10
ASI	0.03	0.04	0.04	0.05
CHN	0.22	0.23	0.23	0.24
IND	0.20	0.20	0.20	0.20
MPC	−0.48	−0.47	−0.47	−0.45
ROW	−0.06	−0.06	−0.05	−0.05
TOTAL	−0.29	−0.22	−0.15	0.06

Table 3.36 Marginal abatement costs (in $US95 per ton of carbon)

Region	REF	MCF05	MCF10	MCF25
CEA	-	-	-	-
EUR	113	113	113	115
FSU	-	-	-	-
JPN	229	230	231	233
OOE	107	107	108	109
USA	160	160	161	163
ASI	-	-	-	-
CHN	-	-	-	-
IND	-	-	-	-
MPC	-	-	-	-
ROW	-	-	-	-

Therefore, we can address the issue of revenue recycling only in a very stylized way. We adopt uniform estimates for the marginal costs of public funds (MCF) (see Böhringer, Ruocco and Wiegard 2001a, 2001b) across regions and calculate to what extent revenues from carbon taxes in abating countries reduce the welfare costs of carbon emission constraints. As a simple shortcut, we multiply the carbon tax revenue with the MCF and place the resulting amount to the credit of the representative agent in the respective region.

We study the implications of revenue recycling for cases where MCFs in Annex B countries equal 0% (the reference case), 10% and 25%. Not surprisingly, we find that our stylized representation of MCFs dramatically reduces the costs for abating OECD countries. For an MCF of 25%, domestic carbon tax policies may even yield net welfare gains.

The latter result should be treated with some caution, because we exclude the welfare-reducing tax interaction effects of existing distortionary taxes with carbon taxes (see Goulder 1995b). Non-abating countries are hardly affected by the recycling policies; neither is global environmental effectiveness.

Table 3.37 Energy-intensive production (% change)

Region	REF	MCF05	MCF10	MCF25
CEA	1.93	1.93	1.93	1.93
EUR	−0.53	−0.48	−0.43	−0.27
FSU	4.87	4.87	4.88	4.90
JPN	−0.82	−0.77	−0.72	−0.56
OOE	−1.33	−1.25	−1.16	−0.89
USA	−2.33	−2.23	−2.13	−1.83
ASI	1.47	1.47	1.47	1.48
CHN	2.08	2.08	2.08	2.09
IND	2.24	2.24	2.24	2.25
MPC	3.50	3.49	3.48	3.46
ROW	1.17	1.17	1.17	1.17

Table 3.38 Leakage rates (in %)

Region	REF	MCF05	MCF10	MCF25
ASI	0.97	0.97	0.97	0.97
CHN	14.15	14.17	14.19	14.24
IND	2.40	2.41	2.41	2.41
MPC	1.55	1.55	1.55	1.54
ROW	2.82	2.82	2.82	2.81
TOTAL	21.90	21.92	21.93	21.97

Table 3.39 Carbon emissions (in Gt)

Region	REF	MCF05	MCF10	MCF25
CEA	0.26	0.26	0.26	0.26
EUR	1.01	1.01	1.01	1.01
FSU	0.94	0.94	0.94	0.94
JPN	0.34	0.34	0.34	0.34
OOE	0.22	0.22	0.22	0.22
USA	1.41	1.41	1.41	1.41
ASI	0.37	0.37	0.37	0.37
CHN	1.62	1.62	1.62	1.62
IND	0.36	0.36	0.36	0.36
MPC	0.65	0.65	0.65	0.65
ROW	0.70	0.70	0.70	0.70
TOTAL	7.88	7.88	7.88	7.88

5.   CONCLUDING REMARKS

There are two fundamental issues whose reconciliation is crucial for any international agreement on greenhouse gas emission abatement strategies: efficiency in terms of overall abatement costs, and equity in terms of a 'fair' distribution of these costs across countries. Consequently, the climate policy debate requires quantitative estimates of the magnitude and regional distribution of costs that are associated with alternative policy strategies to reach some given emissions reduction targets. In this context, analytical models of economic adjustment to emission constraints provide an important tool for gaining policy-relevant insights since they accommodate the systematic and consistent assessment of how changes in the policy design or structural assumptions may affect simulation results and policy conclusions.

It is sometimes asserted that quantitative economic models do not provide useful information because they produce different results. This is a false perception of the role of economic modeling: differences in results do not weaken, but rather strengthen, the need for rigorous model-based analysis, in order to identify and critically discuss the sources for these differences. One approach to doing so is by comparing results from alternative modeling systems, as undertaken by the Economic Modeling Forum in Stanford (see for example Weyant 1999). One potential shortcoming of the cross-model comparison is that it overstrains the non-technical reader, who needs to be familiar with not only one but various models, including the respective differences in parametrization, which are often not very transparent.

In this chapter we have taken a different approach. We endorsed the use of a *single* analytical framework, in our case the computable general equilibrium (CGE) approach. We then laid out in detail a generic multi-sector, multi-region CGE model of the world economy to study the economic and environmental impacts of alternative emission abatement scenarios. Simulations focused on the implementation of the Kyoto Protocol, but the issues addressed are relevant for any future agreements on quantified emission limitation and reduction objectives. An extensive sensitivity analysis has been performed to provide insights as to how differences in underlying assumptions affect the model results. The main conclusions emerging from our modeling exercise on the implementation of the Kyoto Protocol can be summarized as follows:

1. Emission constraints as mandated under the Kyoto Protocol induce non-negligible adjustment costs to OECD countries. The main reason is that the emissions of these countries have grown significantly along the baseline compared to 1990 levels. The Kyoto targets, which are stated with respect to 1990, therefore translate into much higher effective carbon abatement requirements with respect to BaU emission levels in 2010. At the domestic level, OECD countries must impose rather high carbon taxes to comply with their commitments; the tax-induced reallocation of resources such as fuel shifting or energy savings causes efficiency costs, which translates into a loss in real income for households in industrialized countries. These mechanisms highlight the importance of the underlying

baseline on economic and emission growth, as it defines the size of the reduction and the magnitude of the abatement costs required for meeting a particular target.

2. Abatement in OECD countries produces significant spillovers to non-abating regions through induced changes in international prices, i.e. the terms of trade. Most important are adjustments in international markets for crude oil and coal. The cut-back in global demand for these fossil fuels implies a significant drop in their prices, providing economic gains to fossil fuel importers and losses to fossil fuel exporters. These effects explain most of the welfare impacts on developing countries.

3. Sub-global action on behalf of Annex B countries has important implications for comparative advantage and the pattern of trade for energy-intensive goods. Even though energy costs do not constitute a large share of value-added in energy-intensive production, the unilateral cost increase in OECD countries diminishes competitiveness sufficiently to induce large changes in trade flows.

4. The drop in international fuel prices and changes in the pattern of trade for energy-intensive goods induces global leakage of more than 20% for the NOTRADE scenario in which Annex B countries meet their Kyoto reduction targets solely by domestic action. The magnitude of leakage is very sensitive to the representation of fossil fuel markets. In our analysis, we assumed homogeneity of crude oil and coal from different origins based on empirical evidence of low transport costs. This significantly increases leakage, as compared to a setting in which crude oil and coal are distinguished as imperfect substitutes by region of origin.

5. Not surprisingly, international trade in emissions significantly reduces the global costs of compliance to Kyoto through the equalization of marginal abatement costs across regions. What is surprising, however, is that the cost reduction associated with a shift from Annex B trading to global emissions trading is much smaller than that generated by the move from the no-trade scenario to Annex B trading. The reasoning behind this, is that hot air from CEA and FSU accounts for a larger share of welfare gains achievable through permit trading. In particular, FSU can trade in huge amounts of abundant emission rights since its BaU emissions are far below its Kyoto commitment. Trade in emission rights makes FSU substantially better off even as compared to the BaU. Among Annex B countries, only the OECD regions benefit from global emissions trading as compared to restricted Annex B trading. Global trading increases the supply of

emission abatement from abroad, which further relieves the Kyoto emission constraint on OECD countries. FSU and CEA suffer from a decline in the permit price, which implies a substantial loss in their income from permit sales. If we include transaction costs for permit sales from non-Annex B countries to Annex B regions, the welfare implications of global trading for OECD countries on the one hand and FSU as well as CEA on the other hand, become attenuated. In terms of environmental effectiveness, it is interesting to see that avoided leakage through global trading is just compensated by hot air as compared to the no-trade case.

6. It is now commonly accepted that the gross costs of emission abatement can be substantially reduced when revenues accruing from emission taxes or permit sales are used for revenue-neutral cuts in existing distortionary taxes. In our simulations, we addressed this issue in a very stylized way, indicating the scope for a double dividend of GHG abatement policies.

7. Sensitivity analyses on the values of key elasticities confirm economic intuition that global economic adjustment to emission constraints is cheaper, the better the indirect substitution possibilities for fossil fuels. The more enlightening insight from this section of sensitivity analyses is that the distributional impacts across regions may be quite different. If we were to believe, for example, that crude oil supply reacts in a more price-elastic way to cuts in global oil demand, this would imply smaller gains for crude oil importers but smaller losses to oil exporters. Trade elasticities on non-energy markets are also a major determinant of the secondary terms-of-trade effect, which may significantly alter the direct (primary) economic impacts of abatement policies. Furthermore, the choice of these elasticities affects the environmental effectiveness of sub-global abatement action, which may have important implications for the design of unilateral abatement policies, such as tax exemptions or tax cuts for energy-intensive industries to reduce leakage.

Most of the insights listed above may not be new to those readers who have followed the scientific and policy debate on climate change during the last few years. However, we hope that they have nevertheless benefited from the concise and stringent treatment of key policy issues within one single transparent modeling framework.

We close with several caveats. Although our model captures important aspects of economic responses to global carbon emission constraints, it is nonetheless only a crude approximation of the real world's technologies, preferences, factor endowments etc. We therefore caution against too literal an interpretation of the numerical results. Second, there are several aspects missing from the analytical framework presented above that are potentially important, such as the incorporation of non-CO_2 gases and sinks, the incorporation of endogenous investment responses in a dynamic setting with rational expectations, global capital mobility or induced technological change. Finally, we want to stress that quantitative economic models are not at all truth machines, but simply a means of comparing various options along with their price tags. They cannot resolve fundamental political or philosophical conflicts; in the end, it is up to society and governments to decide what to do. Nonetheless, we are convinced that quantitative estimates based on the rigorous and deliberate use of economic models can provide useful decision support for the climate policy debate.

NOTES

1. The equivalent (dual) formulation is to achieve the greatest improvement in some environmental target for a given expenditure of resources.
2. One exception is ETA-MACRO (Manne 1981) and its derivatives. It combines a fairly detailed linear technology model of energy supply with a highly aggregated (one-sector) macroeconomic model.
3. In fact, recent developments in the solution of nonlinear systems of inequalities (Dirkse and Ferris 1995) have promoted the synthesis of bottom-up and top-down models within one consistent general equilibrium framework (see Böhringer 1998b).
4. The terms of trade are generally measured as the ratio of a country's exports to its imports in value terms.
5. Böhringer and Rutherford (forthcoming) provide a method for decomposing the primary and secondary effects in a multi-regional general equilibrium framework.
6. In bottom-up models, technological innovation can be captured through explicit technologies. However, the evolution of future technologies is typically taken as exogenous inputs from expert projections and not treated as an endogenous variable.
7. With exogenous technical change, it is generally cheaper to wait for better technologies to come along.
8. For surveys on the use of numerical models in other fields, see Shoven and Whalley (1992), Peireira and Shoven (1992), Kehoe and Kehoe (1994), or Fehr and Wiegard (1996).
9. For the sake of simplicity, the symbols α, β, ϕ and θ are used throughout the model description to denote the technology coefficients.
10. The one exception is the TCOST scenario, in which we allow for global carbon trading, in order to have a meaningful base for comparison.
11. Among other reasons, this may have motivated the recent withdrawal of the USA from the Kyoto Protocol.
12. The simple reason is that the higher the BaU energy prices, the larger the required absolute price increases to achieve a given percentage change in prices.
13. We address this question in a very crude manner in Section 4.8.

14. The Kyoto Protocol explicitly acknowledges the importance of international spillovers in stipulating that unilateral abatement policies should minimize adverse trade effects on other Parties (UNFCCC 1997, Article 2, 3). Böhringer and Rutherford (2001) present a simple decomposition technique of the total welfare effect of carbon abatement policies into a primary domestic market effect (at constant international prices) and a secondary international spillover impact as a result of changes in international prices.

15. These concerns may be justified on cost-effectiveness grounds when the relocation of energy-intensive industries to non-abating countries significantly reduces the environmental effectiveness of sub-global abatement policies. However, a natural consequence of decreasing carbon emissions is to reduce carbon-intensive production (and consumption) – an obvious point often missed by policy makers.

16. Unresolved issues are, *inter alia*, the time when trading might start, the definition of participants and gases that might be traded, the establishment of the rules and procedures for trading, the institutional set-up and the regulations regarding monitoring, verification and an ultimate enforcement of the rules.

17. Note that – in contrast to textbook partial equilibrium analysis – this need not be the case in a general equilibrium framework where, at the single country level, direct gains from emissions trading can be more than offset from indirect losses through the deterioration of a country's terms of trade (see e.g. Böhringer 2001).

18. More specifically, we use the US labor market as the resource input involved and scale time requirement such that the additional cost of trading is equal to $US5, $US10 and $US20 respectively. The 'closure' of transaction costs via the huge US labor market has only negligible general equilibrium effects on the aggregate labor demand and thus the equilibrium price for US labor.

19. Remember that the larger part of potential efficiency gains from trading is due to sales from FSU and CEA – see Section 4.3.

20. One notable exception is Böhringer, Jensen and Rutherford (2000), who focus on the economic implications of alternative BaU assumptions on the magnitude and distribution of abatement costs across EU countries.

21. The implications of changes in coal supply elasticities are analogous. For the sake of brevity, the respective results are omitted here.

REFERENCES

Anderson, D. (1999), *Technical Progress and Pollution Abatement: An Economic Review of Selected Technologies and Practices*, Working Paper, London: Imperial College.

Armington, P. A. (1969), 'A Theory of Demand for Products Distinguished by Place of Production', *IMF Staff Papers*, **16** (1), 159–178.

Babiker, M. H., J. M. Reilly, M. Mayer, R. S. Eckaus, I. S. Wing and R. C. Hyman (2001), 'The MIT Emissions Prediction and Policy Analysis (EPPA) Model: Revisions, Sensitivities, and Comparisons of Results', *MIT Joint Program on the Science and Policy of Global Change Report* **71**.

Babiker, M. H. and T. F. Rutherford (1997), *Input-Output and General Equilibrium Estimates of Embodied Carbon: A Dataset and Static Framework for Assessment*, Working Paper 97-2, Boulder: University of Colorado.

Barker, T. (1998), 'The Effects on Competitiveness of Coordinated Versus Unilateral Fiscal Policies Reducing GHG Emissions in the EU: An Assessment of a 10% Reduction by 2010 Using the E3ME Model', *Energy Policy*, **26** (14), 1083–1098.

Barker, T. (1999), 'Achieving a 10% Cut in Europe's CO_2 Emissions Using Additional Excise Duties: Coordinated, Uncoordinated and Unilateral Action Using the Econometric Model E3ME', *Economic Systems Research*, **11** (4), 401–421.

Barker, T. and N. Johnstone (1998), 'International Competitiveness and Carbon Taxation', in T. Barker and J. Köhler (eds), *International Competitiveness and Environmental Policies*, Cheltenham: Edward Elgar, 71–127.

Baron, R., M. Bosi, A. Lanza and J. Pershing (1999), *A Preliminary Analysis of the EU Proposals on the Kyoto Mechanisms*, Energy and Environment Division, International Energy Agency.

Bergmann, L. (1990), 'The Development of Computable General Equilibrium Models', in L. Bergman, D. W. Jorgenson and E. Zalai (eds), *General Equilibrium Modeling and Economic Policy Analysis*, Oxford: Blackwell, 3–30.

Bernstein, P., D. Montgomery and T. F. Rutherford (1999), 'Global Impacts of the Kyoto Agreement: Results from the MS-MRT Model', *Resource and Energy Economics*, **21** (3–4), 375–413.

Bohm, P. and B. Larsen (1994), 'Fairness in a Tradable Permit Treaty for Carbon Emissions Reductions in Europe and the Former Soviet Union', *Environmental and Resource Economics*, **4**, 219–239.

Böhringer, C. (1998a), 'Unilateral Taxation of International Environmental Externalities and Sectoral Exemptions', in A. Fossati and J. Hutton (eds), *Policy Simulations in the European Union*, London: Routledge, 140–155.

Böhringer, C. (1998b), 'The Synthesis of Bottom-Up and Top-Down in Energy Policy Modeling', *Energy Economics*, **20** (3), 233–248.

Böhringer, C. (1999), 'Die Kosten von Klimaschutz: Eine Interpretationshilfe für die mit quantitativen Wirtschaftsmodellen ermittelten Kostenschätzungen', *Journal of Environmental Law and Policy*, **22** (3), 369–384.

Böhringer, C. (2000), 'Cooling Down Hot Air: A Global CGE Analysis of Post-Kyoto Carbon Abatement Strategies', *Energy Policy*, **28**, 779–789.

Böhringer, C. (2001), 'Industry-Level Emission Trading Between Power Producers in the EU', *Applied Economics*, **34** (4), 523–533.

Böhringer, C., M. Ferris and T. F. Rutherford (1998), 'Alternative CO_2 Abatement Strategies for the European Union', in J. Braden and S. Proost (eds), *Climate Change, Transport and Environmental Policy*, Cheltenham: Edward Elgar, 16–47.

Böhringer, C., G. W. Harrison and T. F. Rutherford (forthcoming), 'Sharing the Burden of Carbon Abatement in the European Union', in C. Böhringer und A. Löschel (eds), *Empirical Modeling of the Economy and the Environment*, Heidelberg: ZEW Economic Studies, Physica.

Böhringer, C. and C. Helm (2001), 'Fair Division with General Equilibrium Effects and International Climate Politics', *ZEW Discussion Paper* 01-67, Mannheim.

Böhringer, C., J. Jensen and T. F. Rutherford (2000), 'Energy Market Projections and Differentiated Carbon Abatement in the European Union', in C. Carraro (ed.), *Efficiency and Equity of Climate Change Policy*, Dordrecht: Kluwer Academic Publishers, 199–220.

Böhringer, C., A. Ruocco and W. Wiegard (2001a), 'Energiesteuern und Beschäftigung: Ein Simulationsmodell zum Selberrechnen', *WISU*, **30** (1), 117–123.

Böhringer, C., A. Ruocco and W. Wiegard (2001b), 'Energiesteuern und Beschäftigung: Einige Simulationsergebnisse', *WISU*, **30** (4), 596–612.

Böhringer, C. and T. F. Rutherford (forthcoming), 'Carbon Abatement and International Spillovers', *Environmental and Resource Economics*.

Böhringer, C. and T. F. Rutherford (2001), 'World Economic Impacts of the Kyoto Protocol', in P. J. J. Welfens (ed.), *Internalization of the Economy and Environmental Policy Options*, Berlin: Springer, 161–180.

Böhringer, C., T. F. Rutherford and A. Voss (1998), 'Global CO_2 Emissions and Unilateral Action: Policy Implications of Induced Trade Effects', *International Journal of Global Energy Issues*, 18–22.

Böhringer C. and C. Vogt (2001), 'Internationaler Klimaschutz: nicht mehr als symbolische Politik?', *Aussenwirtschaft* **56** (II), 139–155.

Böhringer, C. and H. Welsch (1999), 'C&C–Contraction and Convergence of Carbon Emissions: The Economic Implications of Permit Trading', *ZEW Discussion Paper* 99-13, Mannheim.

Bovenberg, A. L. (1999), 'Green Tax Reforms and the Double Dividend: An Updated Reader's Guide', *International Tax and Public Finance*, **6**, 421–443.

Bovenberg, A. L. and R. A. de Mooij (1994), 'Environmental Levies and Distortionary Taxation', *American Economic Review*, **84** (4), 1085–1089.

Brooke, A., D. Kendrick and A. Meeraus (1996), *GAMS: A User's Guide*, Washington DC: GAMS Development Corp.

Buonanno, P., C. Carraro and M. Galeotti (2000), 'Endogenous Induced Technical Change', Working paper, Fondazione ENI Enrico Mattei.

Burniaux J-M., and J. O. Martins (2000), 'Carbon Emission Leakages: A General Equilibrium View', Working Paper 242, Organisation for Cooperation and Development (OECD), Economics Department.

Capros, P., T. Georgakopoulos, D. van Regemorter, S. Proost, T. F. N Schmidt and K. Conrad (1997), 'European Union: the GEM-E3 General Equilibrium Model', *Economic and Financial Modelling*, Special Double Issue, **4** (2/3).

Criqui, P., S. Mima and L. Viguer (1999), 'Marginal Abatement Costs of CO_2 Emission Reductions, Geographical Flexibility and Concrete Ceilings: An Assessment Using the POLES Model', *Energy Policy*, **27** (10), 585–602.

Dean, A. and P. Hoeller (1992), 'Costs of Reducing CO_2 Emissions: Evidence from Six Global Models', *OECD Economic Studies* **19** (Winter).

Dirkse, S. and M. Ferris (1995), 'The PATH Solver: A Non-monotone Stabilization Scheme for Mixed Complementarity Problems', *Optimization Methods and Software*, **5**, 123–156.

Dixit, A. and V. Norman (1984), *Theory of International Trade: A Dual General Equilibrium Approach*, Cambridge: Cambridge University Press.

DOE (Department of Energy) (1998), *Annual Energy Outlook*, Energy Information Administration http://www.eia.doe.gov/.

Edmonds, J., M. Wise and D. Barns (1995), 'Carbon Coalitions: The Cost and Effectiveness of Energy Agreements to Alter Trajectories of Atmospheric Carbon Dioxide Emissions', *Energy Policy*, **23**, 309–335.

Ekins, P. and S. Speck (1998), 'The Impacts of Environmental Policy on Competitiveness: Theory and Evidence', in T. Barker and J. Köhler (eds), *International Competitiveness and Environmental Policies*, Cheltenham: Edward Elgar, 33–70.

Ellerman, A. D. and I. S. Wing (2000), 'Supplementarity: An Invitation for Monopsony', *The Energy Journal*, **21** (4), 29–59.

EMF-16 Working Group (1999), *Economic and Energy System Impacts of the Kyoto Protocol: Results from the Energy Modeling Forum Study*, Stanford Energy Modeling Forum, Stanford University.

Fehr, F. and W. Wiegard (1996), Numerische Gleichgewichtsmodelle: Grundstruktur, Anwendungen und Erkenntnisgehalt, *Ökonomie und Gesellschaft, Jahrbuch 13: Experiments in Economics*, Frankfurt: Campus-Verlag, 297–339.

Goulder, L. H. (1995a), 'Effects of Carbon Taxes in an Economy with Prior Tax Distortions: An Intertemporal General Equilibrium Analysis', *Journal of Environmental Economics and Management*, **29**, 271–297.

Goulder, L. H. (1995b), 'Environmental Taxation and the Double Dividend: A Reader's Guide', *International Tax and Public Finance*, **2**, 157–183.

Goulder, L. H. and K. Mathai (2000), 'Optimal CO_2 Abatement in the Presence of Induced Technological Change', *Journal of Environmental Economics and Management*, **39** (1), 1–38.

Goulder, L. H. and S. Schneider (1999), 'Induced Technological Change, Crowding Out, and the Attractiveness of CO_2 Emissions Abatement', *Resource and Environmental Economics*, **21** (3–4), 211–253.

Grubb, M. (1997), 'Technologies, Energy Systems, and the Timing of CO_2 Abatement: An Overview of Economic Issues', *Energy Policy*, **25**, 159–172.

Grubb, M. (2000), 'Economic Dimensions of Technological and Global Responses to the Kyoto Protocol', *Journal of Economic Studies*, **27** (1/2), 111–125.

Grubb, M., J. Edmonds, P. ten Brink and M. Morrison (1993), 'The Costs of Limiting Fossil-fuel CO_2 Emissions: A Survey and Analysis', *Annual Review of Energy and Environment*, **18**, 397–478.

Herold, A. (1998), 'Hot Air and the Kyoto Protocol', in WWF/Forum on Environment and Development, *Emissions Trading in International Climate Protection*, Bonn, 50–53.

Hourcade, J-C. (1993), 'Modelling Long-run Scenarios: Methodology Lessons from a Prospective Study on a Low CO_2 Intensive Country', *Energy Policy*, **21** (3), 309–311.

Hourcade, J-C. and J. Robinson (1996), 'Mitigating Factors: Assessing the Cost of Reducing GHG Emissions', *Energy Policy*, **24** (10/11), 863–873.

IEA (International Energy Agency) (1996), *Energy Prices and Taxes: Energy Balances of OECD and Non-OECD-Countries*, Paris: IEA publications.

IPCC (International Panel on Climate Change) (1996), *Climate Change 1995: Economic and Social Dimensions of Climate Change*, Contribution of Working Group III to the Second Assessment Report of the Intergovernmental Panel on Climate Change, Cambridge: Cambridge University Press.

IPCC (International Panel on Climate Change) (2001), *Climate Change 2001: Mitigation*, Contribution of Working Group III to the Third Assessment Report of the Intergovernmental Panel on Climate Change, Cambridge: Cambridge University Press.

Jaffe, B. and R. N. Stavins (1991), 'The Energy-Efficiency Gap: What Does it Mean?', *Energy Policy*, **22** (10), 804–810.

Jorgenson, D. W. and P. J. Wilcoxen (1993), 'Reducing U.S. Carbon Emissions: An Econometric General Equilibrium Assessment', *Resource and Energy Economics*, **15**, 7–25.

Kehoe, P. J. and T. J. Kehoe (1994), 'A Primer on Static Applied General Equilibrium Models', *Federal Reserve Bank of Minneapolis Quarterly Review*, Spring.

Kram, J. (1998), 'The Costs of Greenhouse Gas Abatement', in W. Nordhaus (ed.), *Economics and Policy Issues in Climate Change*, Washington, DC: Resources for the Future, 167–189.

Krause, F., J. Koomey and D. Olivier (1999), 'Cutting Carbon Emissions while Saving Money: Low Risk Strategies for the European Union: Executive Summary', in F. Krause et al. (eds), *Energy Policy in the Greenhouse*, Vol. II, Part 2, El Cerrito, USA: IPSEP.

Kverndokk, S. (1995), 'Tradable CO_2 Permits: Initial Distribution as a Justice Problem', *Environmental Values*, 4 (2), 129–148.

Kverndokk, S., K. E. Rosendahl and T. F. Rutherford (2000), *Climate Policies and Induced Technological Change, Which to Choose: the Carrot or the Stick?*, Boulder: University of Colorado.

Lange, A. and C. Vogt (2001), 'Cooperation in International Environmental Negotiations due to a Preference for Equity', *ZEW Discussion Paper* 01-14, Mannheim.

Lloyd, P. (1994), 'Aggregation by Industry in High-dimensional Models', *Review of International Economics*, 2 (2), 97–111.

Löschel, A. (2001), 'Technological change in economic models of environmental policy: a survey', *ZEW Discussion Paper* 01-62, Mannheim.

MacCracken, C.N., J.A. Edmonds, S.H. Kim, and R.D. Sands. 'The Economics of the Kyoto Protocol', in John Weyant (ed.), *The Costs of the Kyoto Protocol: A Multi-Model Evaluation*, special issue of The Energy Journal, 1999.

Maddison, D. (1995), 'A Cost-Benefit Analysis of Slowing Climate Change', *Energy Policy*, 23 (4/5), 337–346.

Manne, A. S. (1981), *ETA-MACRO: A User's Guide*, EA-1724, Palo Alto, CA: Electric Power Research Institute.

Manne, A. S. and J. Oliveira-Martins (1994), 'Comparisons of Model Structure and Policy Scenarios: GREEN and 12RT', in OECD, *Policy Response to the Threat of Global Warming*, Paris: OECD.

Manne, A. S. and R. G. Richels (1990), 'The Costs of Reducing CO_2 Emission: A Further Sensitivity Analysis', *Energy Journal*, 11 (4), 69–78.

Manne, A. S. and R. G. Richels (1992), *Buying Greenhouse Insurance: The Economic Costs of CO_2 Emission Limits*, Cambridge, MA: MIT Press.

Manne, A. S. and R. G. Richels (1995), 'The Greenhouse Debate: Economic Efficiency Burden Sharing and Hedging Strategies', *Energy Journal*, 16 (4), 1–37.

Mansur, A. and J. Whalley (1984), 'Numerical Specification of Applied General Equilibrium Models: Estimation, Calibration, and Data', in H. E. Scarf and J. B. Shoven (eds), *Applied General Equilibrium Analysis*, New York: Cambridge University Press, 69–127.

McDougall, R. A., A. Elbehri and T. P. Truong (1998), *Global Trade, Assistance and Protection: The GTAP 4 Data Base*, West Lafayette: Center for Global Trade Analysis, Purdue University.

McKibbin, W., M. Ross, R. Shackleton and P. Wilcoxen (1999), 'Emissions Trading, Capital Flows and the Kyoto Protocol', *The Energy Journal*, Special Issue, 287–333.

Mishan, E. J. (1975), *Cost-Benefit Analysis*, London: Allen & Unwin.

Montgomery, D. W. and P. Bernstein (2000), *Insights on the Kyoto Protocol: Impact on Trade Patterns and Economic Growth in 25 Countries*, Charles River Associates.

Morrisette, P. and A. Plantinga (1991), 'The Global Warming Issue: Viewpoints of Different Countries', *Resources*, 103, 2–6.

Nordhaus, W. D. (1991), 'The Cost of Slowing Climate Change: A Survey', *The Energy Journal*, **12** (1), 37–65.

Oliveira-Martins, J., J.-M. Burniaux and J. P. Martin (1992), 'Trade and the Effectiveness of Unilateral CO2 Abatement Policies: Evidence from GREEN', *OECD Economic Studies*, **19**, 123–140.

Palmer, K., W. Oates and P. Portney (1995), 'Tightening Environmental Standards: The Benefit-Cost of the No-Cost Paradigm?', *Journal of Economic Perspectives*, **9**, 119–132.

Paltsev, S. V. (2000a), *The Kyoto Agreement: Regional and Sectoral Contributions to the Carbon Leakage*, Working Paper 00-5, Boulder: University of Colorado.

Paltsev, S. V. (2000b), *The Kyoto Protocol: 'Hot air' for Russia?*, Working Paper 00-9, Boulder: University of Colorado.

Parry, I. W. H., R. Williams and L. H. Goulder (1999), 'When Can Carbon Abatement Policies Increase Welfare? The Fundamental Role of Distorted Factor Markets', *Journal of Environmental Economics and Management*, **37** (1), 52–84.

Pearce, D. (1998), 'Cost-Benefit Analysis and Environmental Policy', *Oxford Review of Economic Studies*, **14** (4), 84–100.

Peireira, A. M and J. B. Shoven (1992), 'Survey of Dynamic Computational General Equilibrium Models for Tax Policy Evaluation', *Journal of Policy Modeling*, **10**, 401–426.

Pezzey, J. (1992), 'Analysis of Unilateral CO2 Control in the European Community and OECD', *The Energy Journal*, **13**, 159–171.

Porter, M. and C. van der Linde (1995), 'Towards a New Conception of the Environment-Competitiveness Relationship', *Journal of Economic Perspectives*, **9** (4), 97–118.

Reilly, J., R. Prinn, J. Harnisch, J. Fitzmaurice, H. Jacoby, D. Kicklighter, J. Melillo, P. Stone, A. Sokolov, and C. Wang. 1999: 'Multi-Gas Assessment of the Kyoto Protocol', *Nature*, **401**, 549-555.

Reinert, K. A., and D. W. Roland-Holst (1997), 'Social Accounting Matrices', in J. F. Francois and K. A. Reinert (eds), *Applied Methods for Trade Policy Analysis: A Handbook*, New York: Cambridge University Press, 94–121.

Richels, R., J. Edmonds, H. Gruenspecht and T. Wigley (1996), 'The Berlin Mandate: The Design of Cost Effective Mitigation Strategies', *Energy Modeling Forum 14, Working Paper*.

Richels, R. and P. Sturm (1996), 'The Cost of CO_2 Emissions Reductions: Some Insights from Global Analyses', *Energy Policy*, **24** (10/11), 875–887.

Rose, A. (1990), 'Reducing Conflict in Global Warming Policy: The Potential of Equity as a Unifying Principle', *Energy Policy* **18**, 927–935.

Rose, A. and B. Stevens (1998), 'A Dynamic Analysis of Fairness in Global Warming Policy: Kyoto, Buenos Aires, and Beyond', *Journal of Applied Economics* **1** (2), 329–362.

Rose, A., B. Stevens, J. Edmonds and M. Wise (1998), 'International Equity and Differentiation in Global Warming Policy', *Environmental and Resource Economics*, **12**, 25–51.

Rutherford, T.F. (1995a), *Carbon Dioxide Emission Restrictions in the Global Economy: Leakage, Competitiveness and the Implications for Policy Design*, Washington, DC: American Council for Capital Formation.

Rutherford, T. F. (1995b), 'Extensions of GAMS for Complementarity Problems Arising in Applied Economics', *Journal of Economic Dynamics and Control*, **19**, 1299–1324.

Rutherford, T. F. (1998), *Economic Equilibrium Modelling with GAMS: An Introduction to GAMS/MCP and GAMS/MPSGE*, Washington DC: GAMS Development Corp.

Rutherford, T. F. (1999), 'Applied General Equilibrium Modelling with MPSGE as a GAMS Subsystem: An Overview of the Modelling Framework and Syntax', *Computational Economics*, **14**, 1–46.

Shoven, J. B. and J. Whalley (1984), 'Applied General Equilibrium Models of Taxation and International Trade: An Introduction and Survey', *Journal of Economic Literature*, **22**, 1007–1051.

Shoven, J. B. and J. Whalley (1992), *Applying General Equilibrium*, Cambridge: Cambridge University Press.

Stavins, R. (1999), 'The Costs of Carbon Sequestration: A Revealed-Preference Approach', *American Economic Review*, **89** (4), 994–1009.

Tol, R. S. J. (1999), 'Spatial and Temporal Efficiency in Climate Policy: Applications of FUND', *Environmental and Resource Economics*, **14** (1), 33–49.

Tulpulé, V., S. Brown, J. Lim, C. Polidano, H. Pant and B. Fisher (1999), 'An Economic Assessment of the Kyoto Protocol Using the Global Trade and Environment Model', *The Energy Journal*, Special Issue, 257–285.

UNFCCC (United Nations Framework Convention on Climate Change) (1997), *Kyoto Protocol to the United Nations Framework Convention on Climate Change*, FCCC/CP/L.7/Add.1, Kyoto.

van der Mensbrugghe, D. (1998), 'A (Preliminary) Analysis of the Kyoto Protocol, Using the OECD GREEN model', in OECD, *Economic Modelling of Climate Change*, Paris: OECD, 173–204.

Weyant, J. (1998), 'The Costs of Carbon Emissions Reductions', in W. Nordhaus (ed.), *Economics and Policy Issues in Climate Change*, Washington, DC: Resources for the Future, 191–214.

Weyant, J. (ed.) (1999), 'The Costs of the Kyoto Protocol: A Multi-Model Evaluation', *The Energy Journal*, Special Issue.

Weyant, J. and T. Olavson (1999), 'Issues in Modeling Induced Technological Change in Energy, Environment, and Climate Policy', *Journal of Environmental Management and Assessment*, **1**, 67–85.

4. On the political economy of international environmental agreements – some theoretical considerations and empirical findings

Carsten Vogt

1. INTRODUCTION

The problem of international cooperation in environmental affairs has been addressed during the last decade in a couple of models. Predominantly, the problem has been analyzed in a game-theoretic framework in which the main focus is on the underlying pure economic incentives for sovereign states to enter into international environmental agreements (IEAs).[1] Combating global warming clearly constitutes the problem of providing a pure public good. Greenhouse gas emissions from one state are equally distributed in the atmosphere. Reductions in these emissions, thus not only benefit the country that undertakes the reduction, but also all other countries in the world that might otherwise suffer from more severe global warming.[2] Thus, climate protection is a non-excludable good. Moreover, the consumption of one unit of climate protection by one country does not lower the consumption of other countries of this good; thus, climate protection is also a non-rival good.

As is well known from standard economic theory, pure public goods are faced with severe incentive problems. Any rational acting country that only pursues its own interest will not take into account the positive externalities its reduction measures will have on other countries. Thus, the level of greenhouse gas (GHG)-emission reductions will be too low. The real tragedy that countries face is the fact that all countries would be better off if all of them behaved in a cooperative way, i.e. if all of them took into account the benefits they confer on others. But if countries realized this Pareto efficient outcome, each one would face an incentive to deviate from this solution, because profiting from the reduction measures of all others while not contributing oneself is always preferable. Since all countries face this free-riding incentive equally, the public good climate protection will not be provided at all or only at a Pareto inferior level.

However, this argument is based upon the assumption that governments involved in international environmental negotiations try solely to maximize national net benefits; here, 'net benefits' is used in its narrow, pure economic sense, i.e. governments are supposed to act as national welfare maximizers. But, clearly, any real government is at least to some extent also motivated by the objective of maximizing its political income.

In a standard political economy model, this means that governments try to maximize their chance of being re-elected. In order to do so, they have to obey the preferences of their pivotal voter, who may be approximately identical to the median voter in a democracy. Thus, national median voters clearly impose a restriction on what would be acceptable to a government in international environmental negotiations (IEN). Ultimately, one would expect a government only to enter into agreements that would be acceptable to the relevant pivotal voter.[3] Surprisingly, this fact has been widely ignored in the literature. Particularly, one would expect 'green preferences' of national pivotal voters to lead to more ambitious contributions to global public goods than would be predicted by standard models. The following paragraphs are dedicated to the investigation of this conjecture.

The chapter is organized as follows. Section 2 derives the demand of the pivotal voter for environmental regulation in a global context. The resulting allocation is compared to those obtained by national and global welfare maximization. Section 3 refers to empirical findings concerning public awareness of climate change and willingness to pay for combating global warming. While the European public seems mostly to be very concerned about the greenhouse effect, willingness to pay for substantial climate policy seems to be rather low for a vast majority. This leaves us with the conclusion that we should expect any observable climate treaty to be more symbolic than substantial. Section 4 is dedicated to the question of how the history of climate policy and particularly the Framework Convention of Climate Change and the Kyoto Protocol fit into this prediction.

2. THE PIVOTAL VOTER'S DEMAND FOR A GLOBAL PUBLIC GOOD

In order to get an idea of how the pivotal voter's preferences may influence the outcome of IEN, we must derive the pivotal voter's demand for environmental quality in an international context. The following model is a simplified version of Congleton (1992) [4]. Suppose individuals derive utility from the consumption of private goods, C_i, and from *global* environmental quality, E, i.e.

$$U^i = U^i \left(C_i, E \right). \qquad [4.1]$$

Let the consumption of individual i be a constant fraction of national income Y, i.e. $C_i = \alpha_i Y$. National income may depend on a variety of factors. For our purposes, let us assume that it depends on the national degree of environmental regulation, R. Congleton assumes a non-monotonic relationship between R and Y, i.e. according to him there may be an initial range in which an increase in regulation influences national income positively. Indeed, there seems to be some evidence that very fundamental regulatory activities concerning public health, for example, may have helped improve labor productivity (cf. Congleton 1992, footnote 5) and thus may have led to higher national income. However, for most modern industrialized countries, a decreasing concave relationship between environmental regulation and income level seems more appropriate. Any further improvement on environmental quality cannot be achieved without cost but has to be paid for with some sacrifice of national income; it also seems highly plausible to assume that additional improvements can only be achieved at increasing marginal costs. Thus, the geometry of the relationship between R and Y, and E and Y respectively could be summarized by the familiar economic trade-off curve, as given in Figure 4.1.

For environmental quality E, it seems natural to assume that it depends on national and worldwide regulation standards, as well as on national and global income. Since the consideration of income effects on environmental quality only adds algebraic complications without leading to new insights, for simplicity, we assume that global environmental quality depends solely on regulation levels.[5]

Let there be $j=1,...,N$ countries, let j be the country under consideration and $-j$ denote all other $N-1$ countries. Then,

$$E = E\left(R^{j}, R^{-j}\right)$$

[4.2]

summarizes the influence of regulation standards on global environmental quality, where R^{j}, R^{-j} denote regulation standards adopted by country j and the 'rest of the world', respectively.

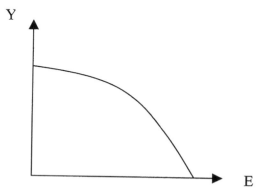

Figure 4.1   Trade-off between income and environmental quality

It seems plausible to assume that an increase in environmental regulation at both the national and the worldwide level leads to a higher global environmental quality, i.e.

$$E_{R^{j}}, E_{R^{-j}} > 0.$$

However, as usual in environmental economics, we assume decreasing marginal returns from environmental regulation, i.e.

$$E_{R^{j}R^{j}}, E_{R^{j}R^{-j}} < 0.$$

The pivotal voter then prefers that level of environmental regulation that maximizes his utility, which can now be written as

$$U^{P} = U^{P}\left(\alpha_{P}Y^{j}\left(R^{j}\right), \ E\left(R^{j}, R^{-j}\right)\right).$$

[4.3]

Any rational government trying to get the approval of its pivotal voter would have to maximize [4.3] by an appropriate choice of national regulation level. Differentiating [4.3] with respect to R^j leads to the first order condition:

$$U^P_{R^j} = U^P_{C_P} \alpha_P Y^j_{R^j} + U^P_E E_{R^j} = 0 \Leftrightarrow$$

$$\frac{Y^j_{R^j}}{E_{R^j}} = -\frac{U^P_E}{U^P_{C_P} \alpha_P}. \qquad [4.4]$$

Obviously, the optimal regulatory degree is characterized by the equality of the absolute value of marginal utility losses due to more stringent regulation, thus leading to an income loss and the marginal benefits from an improved environmental quality. The pivotal voter will approve of a strengthening of environmental regulation as long as the additional benefits outweigh the additional costs to him of a more ambitious international environmental policy. This result hardly comes as a surprise.

Equation [4.4] implicitly defines the demand for national environmental regulation. Relying on the implicit function theorem, one can formulate the pivotal voter's demand for national regulation as:

$$R^P = R^P\left(\alpha_P, R^{-j}\right). \qquad [4.5]$$

Taking α_P as fixed, demand for environmental regulation of the pivotal voter of country j therefore depends solely on regulation standards adopted by all other countries. It can easily be verified that any additional effort undertaken by the other countries will be, at least partly, offset by country j. Applying the implicit function theorem to [4.4] leads to

$$\frac{dR^j}{dR^{-j}} = -\frac{U^P_{C_P} \alpha_P Y^j_{R^j R^j} + U^P_E E_{R^j R^j}}{U^P_E E_{R^j R^{-j}}}. \qquad [4.6]$$

Since we assumed a concave trade-off between national income and environmental regulation,

$$Y^j_{R^j R^j} < 0 \,.$$

Since we further assumed $E_{R^j R^j} < 0$, $E_{R^j R^{-j}} < 0$,

$$\frac{dR^j}{dR^{-j}} < 0 \,.$$

Thus, higher environmental regulation standards set by other countries will be followed by a decrease of regulation in country j. This resembles the familiar free-rider incentive in standard models. As we will see below, however, in a political economy context, this incentive does not necessarily imply underprovision of the global public good. However, [4.6] may help to explain why it is obviously so difficult to reach agreement in international environmental negotiations.

Now let us study how the optimal degree of environmental regulation from the view of a national pivotal voter compares to the regulation standard that would maximize *national* and *global* welfare. Any national government trying to maximize national welfare would have to take the utility of all citizens into account, not only of its pivotal voter. For the sake of simplicity, let us assume that the government is maximizing a Bergson-Samuelson welfare function, and for further simplicity, assume that it puts equal weight on all utilities, i.e. it behaves as a utilitarian welfare maximizer. Stated in formal terms, the government solves

$$\sum_i U^i\left(\alpha_i Y^j\left(R^j\right),\ E\left(R^j, R^{-j}\right)\right) \to \max_{R^j} \,. \qquad [4.7]$$

The first order condition to this problem is obtained as

$$\sum_i U^i_{C_i} \alpha_i Y^j_{R^j} + \sum_i U^i_E E_{R^j} = 0 \Leftrightarrow$$

$$\frac{Y^j_{R^j}}{E_{R^j}} = -\frac{\sum_i U^i_E}{\sum_i U^i_{C_i}\alpha_i} . \qquad [4.8]$$

Now let us compare equations [4.4] and [4.8]. The right-hand side of [4.4] gives us the pivotal voter's marginal rate of substitution (MRS) between environmental quality and private consumption, while the right-hand side of [4.8] is some kind of average MRS.[6] Thus, whenever the pivotal voter's marginal willingness to pay is higher than the average (as defined below), i.e.

$$\left|MRS^P\right| \equiv \left|-\frac{U^P_E}{U^P_{C_P}\alpha_P}\right| > \left|-\frac{\sum_i U^i_E}{\sum_i U^i_{C_i}\alpha_i}\right| \equiv \left|\overline{MRS^j}\right| \qquad [4.9]$$

holds, the amount of environmental quality implied by [4.4] will be higher than that implied by [4.8]. Thus, green voter preferences may indeed help to improve upon the non-cooperative Nash-Cournot outcome in a standard public good game.

It may even be possible that the public good will be provided at levels that would be equal to or above the optimal amount from a global point of view. To see this, look at the optimization problem of a (fictitious, non-existing) world government trying to maximize global welfare. Let us again assume that this fictitious government aims to maximize a utilitarian welfare function:

$$\sum_j\sum_i U^i\left(\alpha_i Y^j\left(R^j\right), \ E\left(R^j,R^{-j}\right)\right) \to \max_{R^j} .$$

The necessary condition for a maximum of global welfare is derived as

$$\sum_j\left[\sum_{i\in j} U^i_{C_i}\alpha_i Y^j_{R^j} + \sum_{i\in j} U^i_E E_{R^j} + \sum_{-j}\sum_{i\in -j} U^i_E E_{R^j}\right] = 0 . \qquad [4.10]$$

As expected, [4.10] recognizes the positive externalities conferred on all other countries $-j$ by any country j, as indicated by the term

$$\sum_{-j}\sum_{i\in -j} U_E^i E_{R^j} \, .$$

For simplicity, let us assume identical countries, i.e. $Y_1 = Y_2 = ... = Y_N = Y$. Clearly, identical countries will choose identical regulation standards $R_1 = R_2 = ... = R_N = R$. Then, [4.10] simplifies to

$$N\left[\left[\sum_i U_{C_i}^i \alpha_i Y_R + \sum_i U_E^i E_R + (N-1)\sum_i U_E^i E_R\right]\right] = 0 \, ,$$

which transforms into

$$\frac{Y_R}{E_R} = -N\frac{\sum_i U_E^i}{\sum_i U_{C_i}^i \alpha_i} \equiv -N\overline{MRS^j} \equiv MRS^G . \qquad [4.11]$$

A comparison of the right-hand sides of [4.11] and [4.8] immediately reveals

$$\left|MRS^G\right| > \left|\overline{MRS^j}\right| , \qquad [4.12]$$

indicating that the degree of environmental regulation from a global welfare point of view has to be higher than that implied by [4.8]. This result, again, does not come as a surprise.

While the ranking of the results for global and national welfare maximization is clear cut, a similar unambiguous ordering with respect to a government obeying its pivotal voter's preferences is not possible. *A priori*, even the case

$$\left|MRS^P\right| > \left|MRS^G\right| \qquad\qquad [4.13]$$

cannot be ruled out. Note, however, that for [4.13] to hold, the marginal willingness to pay of the pivotal voter must exceed the average marginal willingness multiplied by N, which is a much more restrictive condition than [4.9]. Thus, one might expect overprovision of the public good to be unlikely to happen.

One may characterize [4.13] as a more-or-less hypothetical case for a further reason. For the major countries actively engaged in international climate policy, such as the United States or the European countries, pivotal voters may be thought of as being roughly identical to the corresponding median voters. These, furthermore, may be approximated by the median income recipients, as is usually argued in the literature. An empirical investigation would presumably reveal that for most countries, median income is well below the average income. Relying on the assumption that global environmental quality is a normal good, for empirical reasons one might argue

$$\left|MRS^G\right| > \left|\overline{MRS}\right| > \left|MRS^P\right| \qquad\qquad [4.14]$$

to be the relevant relationship. Hence, obedience to median voters' environmental preferences may lead to an even worse outcome compared to a public good game where governments act as national welfare maximizers.

To sum up, the above basic theoretical considerations have shown that pivotal voters' preferences do matter in international environmental affairs, such as combating climate change. Our reference case is a standard public good model where governments are assumed to maximize national welfare. It can easily be verified that governments always fail to provide the public good at a globally optimal level. However, taking into account political economy aspects may change this view substantially. For sufficiently 'green' preferences, the amount of the global public good provided by governments obeying the preferences of their national pivotal voters will have to be higher than in the reference case. Moreover, even the case that the good is supplied at or above the globally optimal level cannot be ruled out *a priori*. But this will only be the case if the preferences of the pivotal voter are much greener.

For empirical reasons, one may argue that this case is presumably of little relevance.

Clearly, it must be stressed that the above considerations are very basic and much of a political economy theory of international environmental negotiations is still missing. Particularly, a theory of the negotiation process and how voters' preferences may influence the negotiation outcome are completely lacking. Furthermore, the welfare analysis above was carried out under the simplifying assumption of identical countries. Despite these obvious shortcomings, the point is that voters' environmental attitudes may have an impact on international environmental agreements (IEAs). Rational governments will only enter such IEAs as they perceive to be acceptable to their decisive voters at home, thus ensuring their approval.

3. EMPIRICAL FINDINGS

In the section above, we argued that in a political economy context, governments are obliged to keep the preferences of their voters in mind and will not agree upon treaties that would not find the support of the pivotal voter at home. Thus, in order to investigate the prospects of combating climate change, it would be interesting to know how much climate protection is actually demanded by the national median voters of countries that are engaged in the climate change negotiations.

However, empirical estimates of the demand for mitigating the greenhouse effect are sparse in the literature. There are essentially two methods which would generally allow the measurement of environmental preferences with respect to climate change. First, one could try to estimate the demand for climate protection from some theoretical model, e.g. a public good model. This approach is taken by Murdoch and Sandler (1997) for the case of the similar problem of ozone layer depletion. However, this excellent study stands as a rare, if not unique attempt to measure environmental demand in the context of a global public good. Second, one could try to detect people's preferences by asking them directly, e.g. by using the framework of a contingent valuation (CV) study. Unfortunately, this type of study has also been used extremely seldom to address the question of environmental demand in an international context. A great deal of effort has been spent during the last two decades investigating how people value environmental resources in their local or regional neighborhood or, at best, at the national level.[7] Often, CV studies try to determine the value of some recreational or wildlife area.

Clearly, it is much easier to value a highly visible good, like a certain landscape, than the highly abstract and invisible good 'protection of the earth's climate', in which benefits are highly uncertain and may not arise until far in the future. This might be the major reason why the CV technique, at least to my knowledge, has not been applied to the problem of mitigating climate change with the exception of a Swiss study, which will be referred to in Section 3.1.[8]

In so far as empirical evidence from econometric and CV studies is very scarce, it seems to be appropriate to rely additionally on public opinion polls. In Section 3.2, we refer to the results of a few polls conducted both in the US and in several European countries. Clearly, this type of study does not usually meet the high methodological standards of CV studies and is thus normally not an economist's first choice. Nevertheless, some questions can count as a rough indicator of people's willingness to pay (WTP) for addressing the problem of climate change. As we will see below, there seems to be a gap between people's awareness of climate change and the need to take action on the one side and their willingness to pay on the other side. People believe that climate change is a severe problem and that governments should address it. But if asked to sacrifice personal income for combating the greenhouse effect, vast majorities show little enthusiasm. Thus, while there is a high demand for symbolic policy, the demand for effective action seems to be rather low, casting doubts on whether a substantial international treaty on climate change will ever be implemented.

3.1   WTP for Combating Climate Change in Switzerland

For Switzerland, there is a single study in existence (Ledergerber et al. 1994) that explicitly addresses the question of people's willingness to pay for climate protection. The study was based on interviews with a total of 901 individuals. The participants of the survey were confronted with a business-as-usual scenario of the greenhouse effect based on the IPCC (1990) report. They were then asked which amount of money they were willing to spend for a 'halfway' and a full solution, respectively, of the greenhouse problem. The participants were told that payments were given to an international fund to which all other countries would also contribute in a similar way.

Most surprisingly, less than half of the individuals reported a positive WTP at all; 41% of them reported a positive WTP for a full solution of the greenhouse problem, while 36% reported a positive WTP for the 'halfway solution'. In addition, the study asked for people's willingness to accept

(WTA) income losses. An additional 6% told the interviewers they would be willing to incur income losses for a solution of the climate problem. All in all, only 46.9% of all subjects reported a positive WTP or WTA. The average WTP of all individuals turned out to be 27 Swiss Francs per month. After the respondents had announced their WTP, they were given the opportunity to adjust their statement. People were asked to think about their total budget and imagine where exactly they wanted to save the money for the climate fund. After these adjustments, the average WTP turned out to be 22 SF. Moreover, the answers showed a large variance. A small number of people stated a very (presumably unrealistically) high WTP of up to 2000 SF per month. When correcting for these outliers, the WTP was even lower. Most of the respondents stated WTPs from 10 to 100 SF per month.

The same study also attempted to figure out the WTP for fighting the depletion of the ozone layer and for improving air quality. The WTP for all issues was about the same, with the WTP for improving air quality slightly higher. When summed up, the total average WTP for a full solution of all three problems together amounted to 67 SF. However, when individuals were asked directly (and not issue by issue) how much they were willing to spend on all three problems, WTP decreased to a mere 47 SF. This is a well-known phenomenon in many other contingent valuation studies, known as the embedding effect (cf. Svedsäter 2000 and the literature cited there). There is evidence from experimental economics (Selten and Ockenfels 1998) that people define for themselves a fixed total amount they are willing to sacrifice for some purpose, such as giving to charities or improving environmental quality. This amount does not substantially change with the number of issues subjects are confronted with. This clearly implies that with an increasing number of issues, the WTP per issue declines. As the number of issues grows further, single WTP declines to zero. Since there is a large number of important issues on the environmental agenda, the average WTP of 22 SF measured by Ledergerber et al. must be considered as a high number.

The study also tried to identify variables that significantly influence the WTP. A multiple regression analysis showed that the WTP increases with household income, decreases with the age of individuals, and increases with educational attainment. The study also asked about acceptance of various environmental policy measures. As expected and supported by the findings in the next section, subjects favor policies such as subsidizing measures to save energy, but they are strongly opposed to taxes and charges.

To sum up, the Swiss study contains some interesting and important results. First and probably most important in a political economy context, the median WTP equals zero. Thus, there is no political majority for an ambitious, i.e. costly, climate policy in Switzerland. Next, the overall average WTP is rather low. The WTP of 22 SF per month must probably be considered to be a high number due to the embedding effect. Thus, if people were confronted with an even longer list of environmental problems than those studied by Ledergerber et al., the average WTP would probably be even lower.

Although the Swiss results obviously cannot be generalized to other countries, they are nevertheless remarkable in so far as they have been obtained in a high income country with well educated people. Since these are the variables that have turned out to determine WTP and that, throughout the literature, are usually suspected to determine demand for environmental protection, one might conjecture that similar results would be obtained in countries with similar characteristics with respect to the corresponding variables.

3.2 Findings From Opinion Polls

3.2.1 Public concern about global warming
In Europe, the issue of global warming climbed on the public agenda at the beginning of the 1990s. While at the end of the 1980s, relatively few people in Europe had heard of or were concerned about the greenhouse effect, these numbers rose considerably during the first half of the nineties. The results summarized in table 4.1 indicate that public concern on climate change reached a peak in the year 1991. Note that the polls used slightly different questions, which are described in the notes to the tables. The corresponding answers are indicated by the letters A, B, C and D, and are explained below.

The developments of public opinion in three major European countries resemble each other to a remarkable extent. The percentage of people who were very concerned about the greenhouse effect rose to about two-thirds of the population or higher, while the fraction of people who were not very concerned dropped to 5% or lower. In the following years, there were some smaller shifts, but all in all public concern remains stable at a high level.

Table 4.1 Public concern about global warming in France, United Kingdom and Germany (answers in percent)

Answer	April 1988 Question 1	March 1991 Question 2	April 1992 Question 3	June 1995 Question 3	November 1996 Question 2
France					
A	37.5	64.6	55.1	43.7	73.1
B	32.3	30.2	29.7	33.9	22.5
C	21.7	5.2	11.8	17.6	4.4
D	8.5	-	3.4	4.8	-
United Kingdom					
A	41.9	66.8	59.2	51.6	64.5
B	32.3	30.2	29.7	33.9	22.5
C	15.6	6.1	7.9	11.7	5.0
D	8.0	-	2.0	3.8	-
Germany (West/East)					
A	50.6	79.4 / 77.5	67.8 / 65.8	58.4 / 58.2	70.7 / 76.2
B	35.3	18.5 / 20.9	26.0 / 27.2	30.3 / 31.9	25.9 / 22.9
C	11.6	2.1 / 1.6	5.6 / 6.7	9.8 / 8.3	3.4 / 0.9
D	2.5		0.7 / 0.2	1.4 / 1.6	

Question 1: How concerned are you about the possible damage to the atmosphere caused by CO_2 emissions due to the burning of coal and oil?
Answers: A=very concerned, B=fairly concerned, C=not very concerned, D=not at all concerned
Question 2: Could you please tell me whether the greenhouse effect is a very serious, a fairly serious or not a serious problem to you?
Answers: A=very serious, B=fairly serious, C=not serious
Question 3: Are you very concerned, somewhat concerned, not very concerned or not concerned at all about global warming?
Answers: A=very concerned, B=somewhat concerned, C=not very concerned, D=not concerned at all
Source: Eurobarometer (1988, p. 190, 1991, p. 148, 1992, p.466, 1995, p.91, 1996, p. 269)

In contrast to Europe, no similar development regarding public consciousness on the climate topic can be observed in the US. Since the late 1980s, the Gallup Organization has conducted polls which ask for people's attitudes towards global warming. As Table 4.2 shows, there was a slight increase in public concern about the issue during the early 1990s, but it is not comparable in size to the increase happening in the same time period in

Europe. Moreover, in 1997, the fraction of people who were very concerned about the greenhouse effect fell even below the 1989 level.

Table 4.2 Public concern in the US about global warming (percentages of all responses)

	May 1989	April 1990	April 1991	May 1993	Oct 1997
Great deal	35	30	35	47	24
Fair amount	28	27	27	31	26
A little	18	20	22	7	29
Not at all	12	16	12	3	17
Don't know	7	6	5	12	4

Question: I'm going to read you a list of environmental problems. As I read each one, please tell me if you personally worry about this problem a great deal, a fair amount, only a little, or not at all. How much do you worry about the 'greenhouse effect' or 'global warming'?
Source: Gallup (2001a, p.7)

These observations may very well help to explain why the European Community at the beginning of the 1990s began to claim environmental leadership on the topic of global warming and pushed for an international agreement to combat climate change, while the United States hesitated to take action in this new policy area.

The US government did not feel the urge to show activity in the field of global warming the way the European governments did. This observation gains additional support when we look at the relative ranking of environmental topics with respect to other topics, such as, for example education, medical care or 'the economy' (Table 4.3).

It is more than obvious that American people are mostly concerned about issues like 'ethics', education, and violence and crime. This pattern of ranking is robust throughout the 1990s. Only 1–4 per cent of the respondents in Gallup polls said that the environment would be the most important problem to them (cf. Gallup 2000, p.2).

Table 4.3 Relative ranking of 'environment' in the US

Problem	April 2000	January 2001
Ethics/moral/family decline/ dishonesty/lack of integrity	7	13
Education	11	12
Crime/violence	12	9
Drugs	5	7
Health care	6	7
The economy (general)	4	7
Taxes	3	5
Poverty/hunger/homelessness	6	4
Environment/pollution	2	2
Lack of military defense	1	2

Question: What do you think is the most important problem facing this country today?
Source: Gallup (2001b, p.4)

Moreover, if we look at the ranking of global warming within a list of severe environmental problems, the picture gets even worse (Table 4.4). As one can clearly see, global warming ranks at the bottom of the list. Obviously, Americans are much more concerned about environmental damage that is more visible than the greenhouse effect. Taken together, environmental problems rank low in relation to other topics like medical care, education or crime, but within a list of the most important environmental problems, global warming is ranked lowest.

3.2.2   Willingness to pay for combating global warming: some findings from polls

3.2.2.1 The United States   So far, we have seen that there is some concern about global warming in the US but much higher concern by the European public. However, the facts presented up to now only explain why climate change entered the public agenda and, subsequently, the agenda of high international politics, but they do not allow for a prediction about the amount of climate protection voters prefer.

Table 4.4 Ranking of different environmental topics in the US

	May 1989	April 1990	April 1991	Oct 1997	April 1999	April 2000
Pollution of lakes, rivers and reservoirs	72	64	67		61	66
Contamination of soil and water by toxic waste	69	63	62		63	64
Air pollution	63	58	59	42	52	59
Loss of natural habitat for wildlife	58	51	53		49	51
Ocean and beach pollution	60	52	53		50	54
Damage to the ozone layer	51	43	49	33	44	49
Loss of tropical rain forests	42	40	42		49	51
Acid rain	41	34	34		29	34
Global warming	35	30	35	24	34	40

Question: I'm going to read you a list of environmental problems. As I read each one, please tell me if you personally worry about this problem a great deal, a fair amount, only a little, or not at all?
The table shows the percentage of respondents who worried a great deal.
Source: Gallup (2000, p.4)

From a theoretical point of view, this is clearly the most interesting question, since voters' demand for climate protection ultimately drives the outcome of international environmental negotiations. Thus, we have to look at voters' willingness to pay in order to get an idea of whether people prefer strong, 'substantive' treaties, which may imply some measurable personal income loss, or weak, 'symbolic' agreements.

However, as already mentioned earlier, there is a lack of studies on this topic. Public opinion polls sometimes address the question of WTP, but do it in a very unsatisfactory manner. Gallup, for example, has asked whether people are willing to sacrifice economic growth for the sake of the environment. Astonishingly, about two-thirds of the respondents in the US give the environment priority over economic growth. A closer look, however, shows that a vast majority of respondents does not recognize the fundamental trade-off familiar to any economist between growth and environmental protection. Thus, people presumably do not realize that more ambitious environmental protection implies personal income losses.

However, a few studies exist that address the question of willingness to pay in a more direct manner. The Mellman Group conducted a poll for the Worldwide Fund for Nature (WWF 1997) in September 1997, prior to the Kyoto Conference in December 1997. They explored whether American people were prepared to pay higher taxes on gasoline in order to discourage car use, leading to lower carbon dioxide emissions. Interestingly, the question coupled the idea of higher gasoline prices with a compensation for the income loss suffered. Precisely, individuals were asked whether they were willing to pay a gasoline tax that is 50 cents per gallon higher, given that they would receive a $250 rebate on their income tax. A vast majority rejected this proposal: 46% of the respondents told the interviewers they were strongly opposed to that idea, while 12% said they were somewhat opposed to it. Only 17% were somewhat in favor of a higher tax, and merely 14% strongly favored this idea. Not surprisingly, higher tax proposals led to higher degree of refusal. When asked whether they were willing to pay a tax mark-up of 75 cents per gallon (with a $375 rebate), 52% were strongly and 14% were somewhat opposed to that idea. Even an increase in taxes by only 10 cents per gallon, combined with the proposal to earmark the money for the development of alternative fuels and technologies, was opposed strongly by 36% and opposed somewhat by 13% of the respondents. Clearly, a majority of American people opposes even slightly higher taxes in order to reduce traffic emissions. These results are obviously much more suited to giving us an idea about people's willingness to pay for mitigating climate change than non-binding questions about an abstract trade-off between environmental protection and economic growth, which most people do not realize, anyway.

3.2.2.2 Europe   Since Europeans are more concerned about the greenhouse effect, one might be tempted to conjecture that they are also more willing to pay for environmental improvements.

Table 4.5 Acceptance of 'eco taxes' in a variety of European
countries (%)

	G (W)	G (E)	GB	I	IRL	NIRL
vw	5.0	1.6	6.0	5.7	3.5	4.2
fw	28.8	17.8	32.6	32.7	20.4	27.5
nwnu	24.8	23.6	27.0	12.5	8.0	30.0
fuw	24.7	31.1	19.5	23.2	24.6	20.4
vu	16.8	26.0	14.9	25.9	43.4	17.9
vw+fw	**33.8**	**19.4**	**38.6**	**38.4**	**23.9**	**31.7**

	NL	N	CZ	PL	BG	SLO	H
vw	4.7	4.3	3.1	5.6	17.1	5.4	4.4
fw	43.8	26.9	13.8	28.0	22.1	27.9	12.1
nwnu	24.3	28.5	25.3	19.7	14.6	36.8	20.8
fuw	14.3	24.5	32.8	28.9	25.0	12.5	25.6
vu	13.0	15.8	25.1	17.8	21.1	17.3	37.1
vw+fw	**48.5**	**31.2**	**16.9**	**33.6**	**39.2**	**33.3**	**16.5**

Notes: G(W)=Germany(West), G(E)=Germany(East), GB=Great Britain,
I=Italy, IRL=Ireland, NIRL=Northern Ireland, NL=The Netherlands,
N=Norway,   CZ=Czech   Republic,   PL=Poland,   BG=Bulgaria,
SLO=Slovenia, H=Hungary

Question: How willing would you be to pay much higher taxes in order to protect
the environment? vw= very willing, fw= fairly willing, nwnu= neither
willing nor unwilling, fuw= fairly unwilling, vuw= very unwilling

Source: ISSP (1993) (A follow-up study was conducted in 1999. Unfortunately
the data of this study were not available when preparing this chapter.)

But this view is pretty optimistic. Unfortunately, we were not able to find
any study which explicitly asked for voters' willingness to pay for climate
protection. However, some studies ordered by the European Commission ask
for voters' willingness to pay for environmental protection in general. Since
there are no better data available, we had to rely on them. As Table 4.5
shows, European voters would not be overwhelmingly enthusiastic about eco-
taxes. The fraction of respondents that are strongly or somewhat in favor of

high environmental taxes lies around one-third, with the single exception of the Netherlands, where this percentage is significantly higher.

Table 4.6 Acceptance of cuts in standard of living (%)

	G (W)	G (E)	GB	I	IRL	NIRL
vw	9.5	6.3	5.2	7.9	4.6	3.5
fw	45.0	33.9	24.7	44.3	24.9	22.4
nwnu	21.8	24.4	24.7	16.5	10.7	23.9
fuw	15.9	21.8	25.5	20.5	23.5	27.8
vu	7.8	13.6	20.0	10.8	36.3	22.4
vw+fw	**54.5**	**40.2**	**29.9**	**52.2**	**29.5**	**25.9**

	NL	N	CZ	PL	BG	SLO	H
vw	6.6	9.0	3.1	3.5	16.1	4.7	3.4
fw	41.6	41.7	16.4	21.9	17.8	26.9	8.9
nwnu	25.2	26.4	23.8	21.1	16.0	38.9	18.4
fuw	17.3	15.6	29.6	33.1	25.7	14.2	28.7
vu	9.3	7.4	27.0	20.4	24.4	15.3	40.6
vw+fw	**48.2**	**50.7**	**19.5**	**25.4**	**33.9**	**31.6**	**12.3**

Question: And how willing would you be to accept cuts in your standard of living in order to protect the environment? vw=very willing, fw=fairly willing, nwnu=neither willing nor unwilling, fuw=fairly unwilling, vuw=very unwilling

Source: ISSP (1993)

Since a number of eastern European countries are expected to join the European Community in the near future and then would have to sustain a common European policy on environmental issues, the corresponding results are also given.

Some difficulties arise as to how to interpret responses that fall into the somewhat obscure category 'neither willing nor unwilling'. Since it lies between 'fairly willing' and 'fairly unwilling', the responses in this category seem to indicate that these respondents wanted to express that they do not want a change of the status quo. If interpreted in this way, Table 4.5 clearly shows that the vast majority of European people (60–80%) is opposed to the idea of introducing high taxes in order to protect the environment. The picture is only slightly more optimistic if one asks for the willingness to accept cuts in personal living standards in order to protect the environment.

But even here we see that, with the exception of Norway and Italy, a majority does not want to see its way of life restricted. Consistent with Table 3.5, vast majorities also reject the idea of imposing energy or gasoline taxes as is shown for completeness in Tables 4.7 and 4.8.

Table 4.7 Acceptance of energy taxes (%)

	G (W)	G (E)	GB	I	IRL	NL
vw	11.5	6.2	3.8	2.6	3.7	3.2
fw	24.8	18.8	15.7	11.9	15.2	17.6
nwnu	19.0	17.7	16.8	12.4	8.6	25.2
fuw	26.7	30.2	33.5	23.8	35.0	42.4
vu	18.0	27.1	30.2	49.3	37.4	11.5
vw+fw	**36.3**	**25.0**	**19.5**	**14.5**	**18.9**	**20.8**
fuw+vu	**44.7**	**57.3**	**63.7**	**73.1**	**72.4**	**53.9**

Question: There are various ways governments might try to get people to use less
              energy, for the sake of the environment. For the sake of the environment,
              the government should put up energy taxes each year for the next ten
              years to get people to use less energy. vw=very willing, fw=fairly
              willing, nwnu=neither willing nor unwilling, fuw=fairly unwilling,
              vuw=very unwilling
Source: ISSP 1993

Even if we count only those respondents that explicitly stated that they would be unwilling to bear taxes on energy use or gasoline, the picture is as clear as it could be: most people (60 to 80%) are opposed to gasoline taxes, while only very few state an explicit approval (10 to 20%). The only exception is Germany, where approval rates are higher. But even there, the number of opponents of environmental taxes is significantly higher than the number of proponents.

One remark on these results is in order. Interestingly, but from an economist's point of view not surprisingly, people are more prepared to accept sacrifices for the environment the less specific the targets are. When asked for cuts in their standard of living, which is pretty nebulous, nearly half of all respondents indicate their willingness. Clearly, the western standard of living depends heavily on the (excessive) use of energy, and driving cars presumably also contributes to individual well-being to a remarkable extent. But when asked for policy measures that are suited to reduce energy use and driving, approval is very low.

Table 4.8 Acceptance of taxes on gasoline (%)

	G (W)	G (E)	GB	I	IRL	NL
vw	14.1	9.7	4.1	3.1	2.0	4.5
fw	25.3	24.4	15.1	9.5	9.5	19.6
nwnu	15.4	14.8	15.8	8.4	7.7	19.4
fuw	24.3	24.7	31.8	22.2	26.0	39.6
vu	20.9	26.4	33.1	56.9	54.8	16.8
vw+fw	**39.4**	**34.1**	**19.2**	**12.6**	**11.5**	**24.1**
fuw+vu	**45.2**	**51.1**	**64.9**	**79.1**	**80.8**	**56.4**

Question: There are various ways governments might try to get people to cut back on driving for the sake of the environment. For the sake of the environment, the government should put up taxes on petrol each year for the next ten years to get people to cut back on driving. vw=very willing, fw=fairly willing, nwnu=neither willing nor unwilling, fuw=fairly unwilling, vuw=very unwilling

Source: ISSP 1993

Despite the low willingness to pay for climate protection both in the US and Europe, people want to see their governments take action in this field. The WWF study finds that 56% of the respondents wanted President Clinton to take action on climate change, while only 30% agreed with the statement that 'President Clinton should not take action on global warming because there are too many real problems that need attention'. Even higher fractions of people in Europe want their political leaders to address the problem of global warming.

All in all, the results from opinion polls suggest the following picture. In Europe, people are highly concerned about global warming and want their governments to pay attention to this problem. However, the willingness of a vast majority of the population to pay for climate policy measures seems to be rather low. In the US, both people's concern and their willingness to pay for climate protection is low, but still a considerable number of people want the federal government to address the problem. These stylized facts, in combination with our theoretical considerations above, suggest the following qualitative predictions: (1) Since people are concerned about the greenhouse effect, we should see political activity in this area and governments trying to reach some international agreement. But, (2), since the willingness to pay of a majority of voters is low both in the US and in Europe, we should not expect such a treaty to be a substantive one, i.e. a treaty that goes far beyond the non-cooperative status without any agreement. Thus the question arises, how the history of climate policy fits into our explanatory scheme.

3.3   What Do We Observe – Substantive or Symbolic Policy?

3.3.1 The Climate Change Convention

Clearly, (1) is easily confirmed. The nineties have seen a great deal of effort in the field of climate policy, leading first to the United Nations Framework Convention on Climate Change (UNFCCC) in 1992 at the Rio Conference. For the part of the Framework Convention, (2) is also readily confirmed. The Rio treaty does not contain any quantified emission targets or any timetables. It only sets out some fundamental objectives and principles, such as the 'stabilisation of greenhouse gas concentrations in the atmosphere at a level that would prevent dangerous anthropogenic interference with the climate system', as stated in Article 2 of the UNFCCC, or the principle of 'common but differentiated responsibilities' for developed and developing countries laid down in Article 3. Since these principles are not accompanied by any quantitative statement about what level of greenhouse gas concentrations would be consistent with Article 2, or whether burden sharing between developed and developing countries would meet the aim of Article 3, they will have hardly any legal consequences.

Thus, the Convention may be characterized as a symbolic treaty. Not surprisingly, a large number of countries signed and ratified the Convention not long after it was drafted. By March 2001, 186 states had ratified the document, including the major players in climate policy, especially the US, the EC, China, India and the Russian Federation. Moreover, consistent with our empirical findings described above, it was the EC and not the US that pushed for the treaty.

3.3.2 The Kyoto Protocol

However, the climate change negotiating process proceeded after Rio, leading ultimately to the well-known Kyoto Protocol adopted by the Conference of the Parties to the UNFCCC in December 1997. This treaty, unlike the UNFCCC, specifies quantified reduction targets for a basket of six major greenhouse gases for industrialized countries. The United States, for example, is bound to reduce its emissions by 7% compared to the 1990 levels. Moreover, the Kyoto Protocol also specifies a deadline for the fulfillment of obligations. Signatories must verify fulfillment of their commitments during the period 2008–2012. How does the existence of this apparently substantive treaty fit into our political economy prediction of symbolic policy?

3.3.2.1 The open question of ratification   First, it should be observed that the Kyoto Protocol, up to now, has not been ratified by any of the major players involved in the climate change negotiations.[9] Particularly, the United States has stated repeatedly that it will not put the treaty into force in its present state. A couple of months prior to the Kyoto Conference, the US Senate unanimously passed the Byrd–Hagel–resolution,[10] which makes 'meaningful participation' of developing countries a *conditio sine qua non* for ratification of the Kyoto Protocol. The Senate made clear that it will not accept any treaty on climate change 'unless the protocol or other agreement also mandates new specific scheduled commitments to limit or reduce greenhouse gas emissions for Developing Country Parties within the same compliance period' (Oberthür and Ott 1999, p.70).

This decision constituted a clear attempt to restrict the US government's leeway in the Kyoto negotiations. As had become apparent prior to the Conference, President Clinton and especially his Vice-President, Al Gore, were in favor of a substantive, to some degree ambitious, agreement. Despite their own preferences, Clinton and Gore were very well aware that the American public was not prepared for a 'green' Kyoto agreement. Thus, they raised their efforts to a remarkable extent to influence public opinion and to gain more domestic support. Oberthür and Ott (1999, p.69) give a brief summary of these attempts:

> The US administration designed a campaign, the White House Initiative on Global Climate Change, to raise public awareness about the issue and generate support for action. The starting point was a meeting of President Clinton and Vice President Gore with seven scientists, including three Nobel Laureates, on 24 July 1997 at the White House. The campaign included regional conferences held across the United States on the probable impacts of climate change, which generated wide media

coverage of the issue. In October 1997, the President himself toured the US to explain the need to act. The campaign culminated in a White House Conference on climate change in Washington, D.C., on 6 October 1997. It was attended by some 200 politicians and representatives of civil society, and broadcast live over the internet and via satellite to 32 locations across the country.

The campaign just described nicely supports our thesis that the median voters' preferences towards climate change do matter. Obviously, Clinton and Gore recognized that the American public was not supportive enough for a strong Kyoto agreement, and they tried hard to change people's minds. Were they successful? The answer depends on the definition of success. If we only look at public awareness of the problem of climate change, the campaign succeeded (cf. Oberthür and Ott, 1999, p.69). However, if we look at the problem of burden sharing – the main issue of the Byrd–Hagel resolution, the public seems to be much more supportive to the Senate's position, as is indicated by the numbers given in Table 4.9.

Table 4.9 US opinion on burden sharing (%)

All countries the same changes	70
Developing countries less burden	19
Don't know	8
Both/ neither	3

Question: Some people say that since poorer countries did not cause much pollution, they should not have to bear as much of the burden in dealing with global warming. Others say that every country, rich or poor, should make the same changes in order to limit future global warming. Which of these views comes closer to your own?
Source: Princeton Survey Research/ Pew 1997, cited in: http://www.publicagenda.org/issues/angles_graph.cfm?issue_type= environment&id=93&graph=mp9.gif

A survey conducted by Wirthlin in the US in September 1998 (Wirthlin 1998) yields very similar results. When confronted with the statement: 'I do not support the Kyoto Protocol because it unfairly forces developed countries to reduce pollutants, while allowing other countries to continue polluting', 25% of the respondents agreed strongly and 43% told the interviewers they agreed somewhat. Only 30% agreed to the following statement: 'It is only fair that undeveloped countries should not be held to the same pollution standards, since they still need to catch up with the rest of the developed countries' (Wirthlin 1998, p.6).

Thus, public support for the Senate's position on the Kyoto Protocol seems to be rather strong, giving the threat of non-ratification some credibility. This threat has not missed its target. Not only did the US administration adapt its negotiation position at the Kyoto conference 'to the Senate's request', as is mentioned by Oberthür and Ott (1999, p.70), but the follow-up negotiations have also been strongly influenced by the Senate's move. As has become evident at the sixth Conference of The Parties at The Hague in November 2000, the US delegation, under its chief negotiator, Frank Loy, negotiated hard for far-reaching concessions from the European delegations. A number of topics left open at the Kyoto Conference still await a solution, including the important question of carbon sinks. These are natural reservoirs, such as oceans and forests, that are capable of storing carbon for a period of time. The Kyoto Protocol in principle allows for the accounting of such sinks, but leaves the question of how much largely open. Clearly, the question of how carbon sinks are accounted for in a climate change treaty directly affects the amount of emissions reductions that must be undertaken 'effectively' by industry, households and the traffic sector. As became evident at the Hague Conference, the US delegation demanded a wide definition of carbon sinks and their generous accounting, thus trying to lower its effective reduction target. Actually, what can be observed since the 1997 Kyoto Conference is not only the clarification of some technical details previously left open, but also the substantial re-negotiation of the reduction targets laid down in the Protocol, with the US striving for less ambitious targets and their implementation at minimum cost. Thus, the behavior of the US fits fairly well into our political economic story of satisfying some public demand for action on global warming while doing this without substantial costs.

3.3.2.2 Europe: A Credible Climate Policy Leader?   It must be conceded that the behavior of the European Community (EC) does not fit so easily. From the start, the EC strove for a much more ambitious climate policy than the US. Early on, when global warming had just climbed the public and political agenda, Europe demanded a binding agreement with targets and timetables. It is not easy to explain European climate policy, and a serious approach would take much more space than a few paragraphs in this chapter. But some critical remarks on the self-declared climate leadership of the EC seem to be in order.

First, it should be mentioned that since the EC started to push for a climate treaty, there has been a discrepancy between its letters of intent and appropriate action. The EC had already in 1990 committed itself to stabilizing its CO_2 emissions by the year 2000. As is evident, it failed to reach this target. The reason was that 'the stabilization target was not built upon a careful, systematic review of actually existing and future means for controlling CO_2 emissions within the EC. Rather, after a pledge-and-review round in which member countries described their expected energy use and trajectories of greenhouse gas emissions until 2000, it simply seemed feasible to stabilize total EC emissions by that time' (Ringius 1999, p.8). Thus, at least for the early period of European climate policy, a lack of systematic evaluation had to be stated, causing a severe lack of credibility of the EC in climate negotiations and thus weakening the EC's bargaining power. This weakness was perhaps most apparent at the first Conference of the Parties to the UNFCCC, which took place in 1995 in Berlin:

> Svend Auken, Denmark's environment minister, stated 'that we see a twenty percent reduction [in OECD countries] by 2005 as a necessary and also realistic target.' John Gummer, the UK environment minister, who prior to the Berlin Conference had proposed cutting emissions to a level 5–10 percent below 1990 levels by 2010, declared: 'We are sure that a commitment to reduce total greenhouse gas emissions on a comprehensive basis below their 1990 levels is essential. [...]'. [But:] As it did in Rio and later in Kyoto, the EC was struggling with a credibility problem in Berlin. It was widely believed that the political goals outlined by the political leaders of member countries were unrealistic and unachievable. As it seemed uncertain whether most member countries would even be able to achieve the stabilization target, these declarations did not convince governments and observers that the EC member countries were able to achieve future reductions. (Ringius 1999, p.11)

This lack of credibility prevailed even at the Kyoto Conference. At Kyoto, the EC started negotiations with a reduction target of 15% below 1990 emission levels. However, it was only able to reach an agreement on internal burden sharing for an EC-wide reduction target of 10%. Not surprisingly, the EC did not succeed with its ambitious reduction plan. An agreement with the US was reached on reduction targets far below 15 per cent (8% of 1990 emission levels for the EC, 7% for the US).

Second, and related to the first point, the credibility gap of the EC was underlined by the Community's failure to implement common policies and measures. Most prominently, this inability is evidenced by the Commission's plan for the introduction of a community-wide CO_2 tax, which was heavily opposed by Germany, Denmark, Italy, Luxembourg and The Netherlands prior to the Rio Conference in 1992. In 1994, the idea of a common tax was officially abandoned once and for all.

Table 4.10 European burden sharing agreement

Member State	Emission reduction by 2008–2012 (%)
Austria	– 13.0
Belgium	–7.5
Denmark	– 21.0
Finland	0.0
France	0.0
Germany	– 21.0
Greece	– 25.0
Ireland	– 13.0
Italy	–6.5
Luxembourg	– 28.0
Netherlands	–6.0
Portugal	– 27.0
Spain	– 15.0
Sweden	– 4.0
United Kingdom	– 12.5

Without measures for the implementation of ambitious targets, one may ask whether the announcement of such targets is meant as a serious proposal or is nothing more than an attempt to demonstrate to the public politicians' will to address the problem of climate change.

Next, it must be observed that the Community is not a unitary actor, as one might suppose at first sight. The common climate policy of the EC is the result of an internal burden sharing agreement. Reduction targets within the EC are highly differentiated (Table 4.10).

According to Ringius (1999), three groups of countries within the EC can be identified. The Cohesion Countries are the poorest member states within the Community and usually show less green preferences (therefore termed 'poor and less green'). These countries mostly worry about their further economic development and fear the burdens ambitious environmental policies may put on their economies. Thus, in line with our theoretical considerations, these countries have largely been exempted from contributing substantially to the European climate target.

A second group of countries, termed the 'rich and less green', can also be identified. These countries are less concerned about environmental issues and thus only contribute to a moderate extent. Belgium, France and Italy may be seen as typical members of this category.

A real challenge is the explanation of the very ambitious reduction targets for Denmark, Germany, and, to a lesser extent, the United Kingdom. With respect to the UK, it must be taken into account that a substantial restructuring of the energy sector in Great Britain took place in the late eighties and early nineties, the so-called 'dash for gas'. The UK shifted its production structure heavily from the burning of coal and oil to gas, thus leading to a noticeable decline in CO_2 emissions. Therefore, it has been much easier for the UK to agree on a fairly ambitious policy.

Similarly, Germany would not have been able to adopt such an aspiring goal without its so-called 'wall fall profits'. The economic breakdown of eastern Germany and the subsequent restructuring of the industrial sector, which implied dramatic increases in the efficiency of energy use, led to a sharp decline in CO_2 emissions of more than 10 per cent between 1990 and 1993. But clearly, this can only be part of the whole story. 'Wall fall profits' alone do not fully explain the challenging German target. Presumably, further factors, such as the long-standing tradition of an environmental movement in Germany as well as the long-standing existence of a strong green party, may contribute to an explanation. However, a detailed exploration of these factors is beyond the scope of this chapter.

Altogether, it seems that the EC's position on climate policy is not fully capable of rationalization within a simple political economy approach. Yet we have to be cautious with final conclusions. Data on voters' demand for climate protection are very scarce. Good contingent valuation studies on the willingness to pay for mitigating climate change are not available for most countries, and the few results from opinion polls clearly do not meet the far higher methodological standards of contingent valuation studies. Thus, a careful examination might lead to the conclusion that the varying positions on combating global warming may be due to differing WTP in different countries. This seems to be a fruitful field for future research.

All in all, the question of what we have observed so far – substantive or symbolic climate policy – must be left open. There is evidence that the US is trying to push the Kyoto Protocol into the direction of a symbolic treaty. On the other hand, the EC policy does not seem to fit perfectly into the theoretical prediction of symbolic climate policy. Thus, a concluding evaluation of the climate policy observed so far and of the Kyoto Protocol in particular must be suspended until some future date when it will become evident whether the Protocol will be implemented at all and whether it will be implemented as a substantive or a symbolic treaty.

3.4   Lessons from the Montreal Protocol

Since the available data do not allow for a rigorous empirical investigation of our theoretical predictions with respect to climate policy, it might be appropriate to look at similar policy areas with comparable incentive problems. One such area is the fight against the depletion of the earth's ozone layer. As is well known, in September 1987, the 'Montreal Protocol on Substances that Deplete the Ozone Layer' was finally agreed upon. It entered into force on 1 January 1989. Ratifiers of the Montreal Protocol were obliged to reduce the emission of ozone depleting substances to their 1986 levels by 1 July 1993. In a further step, until 1 July 1998, the annual production and consumption must not exceed 80% of 1986 levels. Thereafter, it must not exceed 50% of 1986 levels.

Reducing the emissions of ozone depleting substances can be regarded as a contribution to a global public good. Chlorofluorocarbons (CFCs) display their disastrous impact regardless of where they are emitted. Thus, the 'thinning [of the ozone layer] has consequences for countries worldwide and is, thus, nonexcludable. Furthermore, one nation's increased exposure to enhanced ultraviolet radiation does not lessen the risks to any other nation; hence, nonrivalry is clearly present' (Murdoch and Sandler 1997, p. 332). Therefore, the fundamental incentive problems with respect to the ozone hole and global warming are identical.

Murdoch and Sandler investigate the question of whether observable emission cut-backs of CFCs can be explained as voluntary contributions to the production of a pure public good. In order to do so, they focus on cut-backs that preceded the ratification of the Montreal Protocol. In a qualitative assessment of the data they find that the Montreal Protocol presumably does not constitute the case of a cooperative solution, but instead appears to be consistent with non-cooperative Nash behavior. This is confirmed by the fact that emission reductions during the observation period 1986–1989 did not significantly differ for countries that ratified the Montreal Protocol and for those which did not. Thus, it is highly plausible to argue that the observed behavior simply implies reductions that countries were already prepared to undertake in the absence of the Protocol. Moreover, the Protocol called for reductions to 1986 levels only until 1993. But the observed abatement efforts went far beyond this target. The average percentage reduction in CFCs from 1986 to 1989 compared to 1986 was greater than 41%. Two further facts point in the same direction: (1) The Montreal Protocol called for equal percentage reductions. If the observed abatement behavior was due to the existence of the treaty, one would have expected countries to keep to the equal percentage target. But actual emission reductions show a standard deviation of 17%. (2) Each developing country was allowed to become a so-called Article 5 country, which implied a ten-year delay for the fulfillment of the treaty obligations. Thus, if the Montreal Protocol was solely responsible for emissions reductions, Article 5 countries had no incentive for early fulfillment. But surprisingly, 22 of these countries show considerable abatement efforts with an average reduction of 45% compared to 1986 levels.

Moreover, Murdoch and Sandler (1997) test the public good model of Andreoni (1988). This model introduces an additional parameter that accounts for countries' different tastes for the public good. This parameter may be considered as a vector of different exogenous influences, such as, for example, geographical position or political institutions. The latter point is of special interest in our context. As Congleton (1992) pointed out, the environmental demand of the pivotal voter may differ according to the constitution of a country. This becomes immediately apparent in a comparison of democracy versus dictatorship. In a democracy, the pivotal voter is clearly the median voter, which is roughly approximated by the voter with median share of national income. In a dictatorship, however, the pivotal voter usually enjoys a far greater share of national income, thus leading to a different demand for environmental quality.[11] The regression results confirm the theoretical predictions derived from the extended public good model. This means that if the model controls for heterogeneous tastes, countries' observable emissions reductions are consistent with the model prediction of non-cooperative Nash behavior. Moreover, political constitution has a significant impact on contribution levels. The degree of political freedom is positively correlated with the amount of emissions reductions. This can be counted as indirect support for the median voter hypothesis.

Taken together, Murdoch and Sandler conclude that 'the Montreal Protocol may be more symbolic than a true instance of a cooperative equilibrium', since 'it codified reductions in CFC emissions that polluters were voluntarily prepared to accomplish' (Murdoch and Sandler 1997, p. 332).

4. SUMMARY OF EMPIRICAL FINDINGS

From a political-economic point of view, governments engaged in international environmental negotiations such as the climate talks must take note of their national pivotal voter's demand for environmental quality. Any rational government maximizing its chance of re-election should not agree on any treaty not acceptable to its pivotal voter at home. Thus, the national pivotal voter's demand for climate protection ultimately drives the outcomes of international negotiations. In order to evaluate the prospects of climate policy, therefore, it is necessary to investigate empirically voters' preferences towards climate protection.

However, contingent valuation studies, which explicitly try to elicit peoples' willingness to pay for mitigating the impacts of climate change, are very rare. A sole study for Switzerland (Ledergerber et al. 1994) has been found which addressed this question. The study suggests that people's preferences for combating climate change differ substantially. While there is a positive mean WTP, more than half of the respondents declared a WTP of zero, indicating that a majority of people were not in favor of a substantive, i.e. costly climate policy. However, this is a single observation for one country at one point in time. In order to get an idea of people's WTP for climate policy both in the US and the EC, much future research has to be done.

However, results from several opinion polls cast doubt on whether people approve of an ambitious climate policy. While people are concerned about climate change, particularly in Europe, but to a lesser extent also in the United States, the poll results suggest that people are not very enthusiastic about measures that are likely to lead to personal income losses. Vast majorities reject, for example, the introduction of eco-taxes, such as taxes on gasoline or energy use.

Thus, we are left with the somewhat schizophrenic situation that people want their governments to take action with respect to climate change, but not at a substantial cost. Hence, from a political-economic view, we should expect climate policy to be more symbolic than substantial. This prediction is easily confirmed in the case of the Framework Convention on Climate Change, which eloquently addresses the problem of global warming and the urgent need to act, but contains no targets and timetables. However, the Kyoto Protocol seems to be a much more substantial climate treaty since it obliges signatories to reduce their greenhouse gas emissions to substantial amounts below 1990 levels. A final evaluation of the Kyoto Protocol is clearly not possible until the mid-future shows whether the treaty was implemented and in which way. However, tough renegotiating efforts since the Kyoto Conference indicate that the US wants to push the treaty into the direction of a more symbolic agreement, with reduction targets watered down through the generous accounting of carbon sinks.

The prediction of symbolic climate policy gains support if we look at related problems like the depletion of the ozone layer. The study by Murdoch and Sandler suggests that the treaty just codified emission reductions that countries were prepared to undertake voluntarily in the absence of any treaty, thus confirming the theoretical prediction of non-cooperative Nash behavior in a public good model. However, Murdoch and Sandler also find that political circumstances influence a country's decision to contribute to a public good and to what amount, thus providing some empirical support for the Congleton model.

NOTES

1. The basic model of international coalition formation stems from Barrett (1994). Further basic references are Carraro and Siniscalco (1991) and Hoel (1991).
2. We exclude the possibility that some countries may indeed benefit from global warming.
3. The main focus of this chapter is on the influence of voter preferences on the negotiation positions of governments. Clearly, it is not the government itself that carries out the bargaining, but the administration. Thus, principal–agent problems may arise. Note, however, that even a highly green bureaucracy would only agree on an international treaty that had a good chance of being ratified and implemented at the national level. Thus, green but rational bureaucrats also have to obey voter preferences. For a paper explicitly addressing principal–agent issues in international environmental affairs see Congleton (1995).
4. Note, however, that Congleton does not provide a welfare economic evaluation.

5. In the more general formulation, $E = E\left(R^j, Y^j, R^{-j}, Y^{-j}\right)$, and hence, $U^P = U^P\left(\alpha_p Y^j\left(R^j\right), E\left(R^j, Y^j\left(R^j\right), R^{-j}\left(Y^{-j}\right), Y^{-j}\right)\right)$. Thus, benefits from higher environmental quality accrue not only due to a direct effect of regulation, but also to an indirect effect via lower national income.

6. Clearly, the average MRS as defined by [4.9] is not identical to the average MRS, as it is usually defined, since in general

$$\frac{\sum_i U_E^i}{\sum_i U_{C_i}^i \alpha_i} \neq \frac{1}{I} \sum_i \frac{U_E^i}{U_{C_i}^i}.$$

7. Compare, for example, the range of topics covered in Navrud (1992). This includes the value of different uses of a water reservoir in France; the value of traffic noise reductions in Germany and Switzerland; valuation of outdoor recreation in Finland; valuing of a clean environment in The Netherlands; valuation of water and air quality in Norway and Sweden; and the valuation of different environmental goods in the United Kingdom, including water and air quality, forest and beach recreation.

8. There is one recent study by Svedsäter (2000) that also asks the participants for their willingness to pay (WTP) for mitigating the greenhouse effect. But the focus of this paper is mainly on measuring different types of embedding effects, not on figuring out some empirically meaningful measure of WTP. Note, however, that the median WTP of the sample for combating climate change – when evaluated together with three other environmental issues – turned out to be £20 per annum, which is even below the WTP found in the Swiss study by Ledergerber et al. (1994).

9. The current state of ratification can be found at http://www.unfccc.org/.

10. Named after its initiators, Republican Senators Robert Byrd and Charles Hagel.

11. Whether the demand of the decisive voter in an authoritarian regime is lower or higher than that of the median voter in a democracy depends on the relative strength of two effects: a relative price effect, and an income effect. According to Congleton (1992, p. 416), an 'increase in the fraction of national income going to the individual of interest increases the marginal cost of environmental standards faced by him, since he will now bear a larger fraction of associated reductions in national income. On the other hand, his income is higher for any given standard and thus, would, except for the relative price effect, opt for greater expected environmental quality.' Thus, an increase of the national income share accruing to the pivotal voter leads to a lower demand for environmental regulation if the relative price effect dominates the income effect.

REFERENCES

Andreoni, J. (1988), 'Privately Provided Public Goods in a Large Economy: The Limits of Altruism', *Journal of Public Economics*, **35** (1), 57–73.

Barrett, S. (1994), 'Self-enforcing Environmental Agreements', *Oxford Economic Papers*, **46**, 804–878.

Carraro, C. and D. Siniscalco (1991), 'Strategies for the International Protection of the Environment', working paper, Milan: Fondazione Eni Enrico Mattei

Congleton, R.D. (1992), 'Political Institutions and Pollution Control', *Review of Economics and Statistics*, **74** (3), 412–421.

Congleton, R.D. (1995), 'Return to Rio: Agency Problems and the Political Economy of Environmental Treaties', working paper, Series II-No.261 Faculty of Law and Faculty of Economics and Statistics, University of Konstanz, Germany

Eurobarometer 29 (1988), *Environmental Problems and Cancer*, Central Archive for Empirical Social Research at the University of Cologne, http://www.gesis.org/ZA/

Eurobarometer 35.0 (1991), *Foreign Relations, the Common Agricultural Policy and Environmental Concerns*, Central Archive for Empirical Social Research at the University of Cologne, http://www.gesis.org/ZA/

Eurobarometer 37.0 (1992), *Awareness and Importance of Maastricht and the Future of the European Community*, Central Archive for Empirical Social Research at the University of Cologne, http://www.gesis.org/ZA/

Eurobarometer 43.1 (1995), *Regional Development, Consumer and Environmental Issues*, Central Archive for Empirical Social Research at the University of Cologne, http://www.gesis.org/ZA/

Eurobarometer 46.0 (1996), *Personal Health, Energy, Development Aid, and the Common European Currency*, Central Archive for Empirical Social Research at the University of Cologne, http://www.gesis.org/ZA/

Gallup (2000), *Poll Releases September 25 2000*, Princeton: The Gallup Organization, http://www.gallup.com/poll/releases/pr000925.asp

Gallup (2001a), *Poll Releases February 20 2001*, Princeton: The Gallup Organization, http://www.gallup.com/poll/releases/pr010220.asp

Gallup (2001b), *Poll Releases February 5 2001*, Princeton: The Gallup Organization, http://www.gallup.com/poll/releases/pr010205.asp

Greenpeace (2000), 'Cheating the Kyoto Protocol: Loopholes and Environmental Effectiveness', paper distributed at the COP 6 in The Hague, November

Hoel, M. (1991), 'Global Environmental Problems: The Effects of Unilateral Actions Taken by One Country', *Journal of Environmental Economics and Management*, **20**, 55–70.

IPCC (Intergovernmental Panel on Climate Change) (1990), *Climate Change: The IPCC Scientific Assessment*, Cambridge Massachusetts: Cambridge University Press.

ISSP (International Social Science Panel) (1993), *Environment I*, Codebook ZA Study 2450, Central Archive for Empirical Social Research at the University of Cologne, http://www.gesis.org/ZA/

Ledergerber, Elmar, Walter Ott, Rolf Iten, Daniel Peter and Barbara Jäggin (1994), *Zahlungsbereitschaft für die Verhinderung einer globalen Klimaänderung [The Willingness to Pay for Prevention of Global Climate Change]*, Bern: Bundesamt für Energiewirtschaft

Mueller, D. (1989), *Public Choice II*, Cambridge Massachusetts: Cambridge University Press.

Murdoch, J.C. and T. Sandler (1997), 'The Voluntary Provision of a Pure Public Good: The Case of Reduced CFCs Emissions and the Montreal Protocol', *Journal of Public Economics*, **63**, 331–349.

Navrud, S. (ed.) (1992), *Pricing the European Environment*, Oxford: Oxford University Press,

Oberthür, S. and H. Ott (1999), *The Kyoto Protocol: International Climate Policy for the 21st Century*, Berlin: Springer.

Ringius, L. (1999), 'The European Community and Climate Protection: What's Behind the Empty Rhetoric?', report 1999:8, Oslo: Cicero.

Selten, R. and A. Ockenfels (1998), 'An Experimental Solidarity Game', *Journal of Economic Behavior and Organization,* **34**, 517–539.

Svedsäter, H. (2000), 'Contingent Valuation of Global Environmental Resources: Test of Perfect and Regular Embedding', *Journal of Economic Psychology,* **21**, 605–623.

Wirthlin (1998), *The Wirthlin Report September 1998*, Wirthlin Worldwide, http://209.204.197.52/publicns/report/wr9809.html

WWF (Worldwide Fund for Nature) (1997), *Climate Change Opinion Poll*, http://www.panda.org/climate/climate_event/poll_download.htm

5. Interest group preference for instruments of environmental policy: an overview

Jan-Tjeerd Boom

1. INTRODUCTION

In environmental politics, two things have to be decided: the level of abatement and the method of implementation. Economists have tried to shed light on both issues. The standard economic answer to the first question is: one should abate up to the level where marginal social costs are equal to marginal social benefits. However, this answer is not always of much help, mainly because the marginal benefits are unknown. But economists have also taken up this challenge by trying to measure the value of what was previously immeasurable (see Hanemann 1994).

So far, economists seem to have contributed more to answering the second question. Already more than a century ago, Sidgwick (1883) proposed using taxes to correct for negative externalities. This concept was later popularized by Pigou (1920), hence the name Pigouvian taxes. In the 1960s another instrument was added to the economist's toolbox: tradable permits, a concept proposed by Crocker (1966) and Dales (1968a, 1968b) and formalized by Montgomery (1972). Since the rise of environmental policy in the 1960s and 1970s, economists have advocated, dare one say lobbied for, these instruments. Despite their efforts, not much has been gained. True, both taxes and tradable permit systems have been implemented (see Stavins 2000).

However, taxes have often been set at such a low level that they have had no effect other than supplying government with revenue. Tradable permit systems are being used more and more, but in comparison to forms of direct regulation, their use has been limited (OECD 1994).

The natural question to ask then is why certain instruments are implemented and others not. As will be clear from the above, the main riddle for the economist is why direct regulation is so popular. The case for taxes and tradable permits seems clear; they are efficient and hence maximize welfare. Direct regulation on the other hand tends to be very crude and will create differences in marginal abatement costs between sources.

Positive political economic theory tries to give an answer to this. In essence, it says that economic agents will try to capture the rents created, deliberately or accidentally, by government action (Krueger 1974). This will also be the case in environmental policy. Every instrument has certain characteristics that make it more-or-less advantageous to different groups. Hence, every group will have its preferred instrument and will be willing to spend time and money to have it implemented.

But how do we know which instrument will be preferred by which group? To answer that question, we need to know what motivates the members of the groups, and if they are represented by interest groups, what the motives of the management of these interest groups are. This seems to be an often forgotten part of the public choice literature on instrument choice. Assumptions about interest group motivation are made in a rather *ad hoc* way, without much reference to the literature in this field.

In this survey, we will give an overview of both the motives and the preferences for policy instrument of the interest groups involved in and affected by environmental policy. We will then assess whether the public choice literature on interest group preference for environmental policy instrument takes the motives fully into account. As this is not always the case, we will also discuss how the results may change when all motives are taken into account.

This chapter only deals with instrument choice at the national level; we analyze the preferences of interest groups for international emissions trading schemes in the next chapter. However, the current survey has considerable relevance for the analysis of preferences for international instruments. First of all, the motives behind the preferences of the various interest groups will be the same, whether they have to make a choice between national or international instruments. The discussion in this chapter therefore forms the basis for the analysis in the next chapter. Furthermore, as will become clear later, the choice of international emissions trading scheme is related to the choice of national instrument. A discussion of preferences for national instruments is therefore necessary before proceeding with a discussion of preferences for international emissions trading schemes.

This chapter is organized as follows. In Section 2, we give a short description of the main instruments of environmental policy, which fall into two groups: economic instruments and direct regulation instruments. The next step is to identify the main actors in the rent-seeking game (Section 3). Having identified the main actors, we continue by discussing their motivations (Section 4). A large part of this literature stems from the 1960s and 1970s. Especially important in this respect is the paper by Alchian and Demsetz (1972), who model the relationship between the owners or donors of an organization and its management as a principle–agent problem. In Section 5, we give an overview of the political economy literature on environmental policy instrument choice. An assessment of this literature is given in Section 6. Here special emphasis is given to the assumptions about the motivations of the different interest groups. Finally, in Section 7 some conclusions are given.

2.   ENVIRONMENTAL POLICY INSTRUMENTS

Environmental policy instruments are normally divided into two broad categories (Bohm and Russell 1985, Barde 1995 and Russell and Powell 1999): direct regulation instruments and market-based instruments. Direct regulation consists of the implementation and enforcement of laws and regulations prescribing objectives, standards and technologies polluters must comply with (Barde 1995). Various direct regulation instruments exist, most in the form of standards. Examples are emission standards, process standards and product standards. Emission standards can be absolute, specifying a maximum level of emissions for the plant or firm, or relative, where the total level of emissions is allowed to vary with some variable, mostly production. Voluntary agreements can also be counted as direct regulation. Here, the environmental goals are negotiated between government and industry. The regulated industry is thereafter free to determine how these goals are realized. Although the industry could decide to implement market-based instruments, this has not happened so far. Hence, in most cases, voluntary agreements result in a standard for the individual firm. Market-based, or economic, instruments use financial incentives to induce abatement by polluters. Examples are taxes, charges, subsidies, tradable permits, deposit refund systems and liability provisions.

Economists often argue that market-based instruments are more efficient than other instruments (see Baumol and Oates 1988). However, Russell and Powell (1999) argue that in general, one cannot say that market-based instruments are more efficient than other instruments. This only holds for greenhouse gases and ozone depleting substances, since these are global pollutants that mix fully in the atmosphere. In all other cases, direct regulation may be more efficient than market-based instruments.

Although the distinction between instruments that prescribe something, and those that do not is helpful in some ways, it is also oversimplified; the group of direct regulation instruments in particular is enormously diverse. Therefore, Russell and Powell (1999) propose another taxonomy of environmental policy instruments. They suggest two criteria for classifying instruments: whether the instrument specifies what is to be achieved or not and whether the instrument specifies how to achieve whatever is achieved. In this classification, all market-based instruments fall in the category 'not specifying what is to be achieved and not specifying how to achieve whatever is achieved'. Hence, these instruments leave the polluter free in the choice of emission level and abatement level. With direct regulation instruments, at least one of these things is specified.

However, since the division into direct regulation and economic instruments is the one most used in the literature, we will also use it in this overview. It is important though, as Dijkstra (1999) notes, to specify which instrument of direct regulation is analyzed. In the following, we will do so as much as possible.

3. ACTORS

The literature describes many actors and their interest groups that are involved in, or affected by environmental policy. An important group is formed by regulators. This group in turn can be subdivided into politicians and bureaucrats. Another group is formed by those who are regulated. In much of the literature, it is assumed that it is industry that is regulated. Industry is, however, not a unitary actor. It consists of the providers of risk bearing capital (the owners), the managers and the workers. Besides regulators and industry, a third group is affected by environmental policy: consumers.

To have some influence on policy, affected actors combine in interest groups. The more effective a group is in organizing, the more influence it will have on policy. Here groups consisting of many individual actors with diverging interests are at a disadvantage, since it will be harder for such a group to organize than for a small and homogeneous group (Olson 1965). This tendency is also visible in the groups mentioned above.

Although industry consists of many individual units, it is usually well organized. One reason for this is that it is a rather homogeneous group. Furthermore, government regulation often makes it compulsory for firms within a sector of industry to organize in branch organizations.

Although organizations of shareholders do exist, they are often not present in the debate on environmental policy. Shareholder organizations organize shareholders from many different branches. These are affected in different ways by environmental policy. However, through their influence on firm policy, they do affect the behavior of firms. Workers are organized in labor unions. The degree of organization, however, varies considerably between countries and between sectors within a country. Differences in organization between countries are often caused by differences in government policy.

Because of their large number and divergence in interests, consumers are hard to organize. Most policy affects the average consumer only very little. Therefore, the individual benefit of lobbying for a specific policy instrument is too small compared with the costs. However, environmentally concerned consumers are organized in environmental organizations. These organizations are highly present in the environmental debate.

So we end up with a number of actors that are important in the environmental policy game. On the side of the regulators, both politicians and the environmental bureaucracy will have an influence. Industry will be directly affected and will therefore try to influence environmental policy. Within industry, three groups can be identified, each with different motives: shareholders, managers and labor unions. Finally, there is a large and diverse group of consumers. However, they are too weak to organize effectively. Therefore, only the environmentally concerned consumers will be represented by environmental organizations.

4. MOTIVATIONS

Before one can analyze the preferences of the different actors involved in and affected by environmental policy, it is necessary to know their motivations. As we will see, the motives of the various individual actors are not that different. After all, they are all just versions of economic man. Besides motives, it is also important to analyze the constraints placed on the behavior of the individual actors within the organizations that affect environmental policy. These two, motives and constraints, result in the behavior of the individuals and organizations.

4.1 Legislators

4.1.1 Politicians

There are two basic assumptions in the literature about the motivation of politicians (Persson and Tabellini 2000). In the public choice literature, the standard assumption is that politicians are opportunistic, i.e., they behave in purely self-interested way. In this kind of model, politicians do not derive utility from the policy outcomes, but only from being in office. One version of opportunistic behavior is that politicians are only interested in winning elections (Downs 1957). Such an assumption implies that candidates converge to the same policies.

Another version of opportunistic behavior is that politicians are rent seekers. They try to exploit their political power to receive rents at the expense of the voters (Brennan and Buchanan 1980). In essence, this means that there is a principal–agent problem between the voters (principals) and the politicians (agents). Wittman (1989, 1995), however, shows that political competition will bring out an optimal outcome for voters, an idea already voiced by Stigler (1972) and Becker (1983). Hence, as long as there is competition between politicians, the principal–agent problem will not be very large.

The other basic assumption is that politicians have certain ideological preferences. That is, they derive utility directly from policy outcomes (see Wittman 1977, 1983 and Calvert 1985). In this kind of model, the preferences of the politicians determine the outcome.

In all the above models, lobbying by interest groups can alter the outcome. By providing funds to a candidate, interest groups can increase that candidate's chance of winning. In return they will demand regulation that provides them with rents.

It is quite likely that politicians are risk-averse. In environmental policy, they set certain goals. If these goals are realized, the politicians can expect to benefit from this. However, when the objectives are not met, they may be punished by the voters. For this reason, politicians have an incentive to delegate decisions to agencies, i.e. the bureaucracy, when the expected damage from not realizing the objective is larger than the expected gain from realizing them (Fiorina 1982a, 1982b).

The economic literature is in general not very benign to politicians. They are seen as risk-averse opportunists whose main objective is to be re-elected. In some cases however, they are endowed with a conscience in the form of ideology. Often, not even these assumptions are made, and the policy outcome is decided by the relative strength of the interest groups. In that case, the politician is at best seen as the mouthpiece of the winning interest group.

4.1.2 Environmental bureaucracy

The most influential study of bureaucracies is without doubt Niskanen's *Bureaucracy and Representative Government* (1971). Although there had been analyses of bureaucratic behavior before, notably Simon (1947), March and Simon (1957), Tullock (1965) and Downs (1967), Niskanen was the first to provide a formal model of bureaucracies on which future work could be based. Niskanen's main assumption is that bureaucrats are budget maximizers. The reason for this is that income, prestige, power and perquisites of the office, which are items entering the bureaucrat's utility function, are positively related to the size of the bureau's budget. In his model, Niskanen assumes that there are only two actors, the (head of the) bureau and the sponsor. In the relationship, the bureau has some distinct advantages over the sponsor in that it has a monopoly of information on production costs and because it can control the agenda. Furthermore, it knows the value the sponsor attaches to every level of output. The result is that the bureaucracy has enormous powers and can force the sponsor to accept a large budget.

Niskanen's analysis has been criticized on many grounds. Much of it has centered on the power of bureaucracies. The ability of bureaucrats to control the agenda has been questioned (see Romer and Rosenthal 1978 and Miller and Moe 1983). Another critique centered around the assumption that the bureau had a monopoly on information. In later analyses, the relationship between sponsor and bureau was modeled as a principal–agent problem, where the sponsor as principal has several methods of monitoring and controlling the bureau, either *ex post* or *ex ante* (see Breton and Wintrobe 1975, Bendor et al. 1985, 1987, Banks 1989 and Banks and Weingast 1992).

Johnson and Libecap (1989) test empirically whether the salary of the incumbent personnel at government bureaux increases with an increase in the total number of employees. They found that there was no such relationship. Hence, the quest for a larger bureaucracy does not give higher salary to the incumbent bureaucrats. It is still possible that the utility of the bureau management increases with the bureau size, but then mainly because it gives more prestige and status.

Migué and Bélanger (1974) argue that bureaucrats cannot simultaneously pursue maximum budget, prestige, output and salary. Instead of budget maximization, Migué and Bélanger suggest that bureaucrats maximize the discretionary budget, defined as the difference between the total budget and the minimum costs of production. Niskanen has accepted this critique (Niskanen 1975, 1991). Both Migué and Bélanger (1974) and Niskanen (1991) argue that bureaucrats can have a decided preference for the output of their department. The type of bureaucrat that does so has been dubbed 'zealot' by Downs (1967). Frey (1983) gives an overview of a large number of studies that empirically test the difference in cost efficiency between private and public production. In general, the studies show that public production of a good is more costly than private production of the same good. This can be interpreted as evidence for the hypothesis that bureaucrats can secure discretionary budgets for themselves.

Another view on bureaucracy is offered by Stigler (1971) and Peltzman (1976), which builds on the work by Olson (1965). Stigler and Peltzman argue that interest groups and politicians stand to gain from each other. Politicians want to be re-elected. To be re-elected, they need to maximize support. Interest groups will be willing to provide such support in return for favorable legislation. The result, according to Stigler and Peltzman, is that politicians set up bureaux to serve the interest groups. Hence, the bureaucracy is 'captured' by interest groups by design. Elaborations on this theory are given by Becker (1983) and Wilson (1980). They show that capture of bureaucracies is only a special case with many other outcomes possible. Furthermore, other groups such as voters have more influence than Stigler gives them.

Kelman (1981) asserts that the environmental bureaucracy is averse to a new instrument, because it would have to bear the brunt of the organizational learning that a switch to a new system would imply. Rees (1988) also stresses this point. He states that agency resistance to change cannot only be explained by conservatism or management self-interest. There are, often considerable, transitional costs, such as information collection, staff retraining or recruitment and departmental reorganization. These learning costs do at least partly explain why there is bureaucratic inertia (see Hanley et al. 1990). Another factor that can be connected with learning costs is that the preferences of bureaucrats may differ according to their training background.

It is argued that those with a legal or technical background have a predisposition to command and control instruments, while those with an economic background favor market-based instruments. Both groups would incur learning costs if the instrument implemented is different from the one they were taught about.

Another problem is that the management of a bureaucracy has several objectives. Rees (1988) mentions a large number of objectives. Most of these can be categorized either as part of supplying the service the bureau is set up to deliver, as maximizing discretionary spending or as diminishing the interference of the outside world (politicians and interest groups) with the daily business of the bureau. Any policy instrument fulfills these objectives to a different degree. Changing instruments will therefore produce conflicts with the organizational goals. Furthermore, change increases the visibility of the bureau and the amount of public flack it receives (see also Savornin Lohman 1994). Rees (1988) asserts that the losers under the status quo are only imperfectly aware of their disadvantage and of the benefits they could derive under a different system. Those whose relative position is affected negatively by change are clearly much more aware of it. This implies that the bureau takes the effect of a change in regulation on the regulated industry into account.

Several authors argue that the environmental bureaucracy is risk-averse (Nentjes and Dijkstra 1994 and Savornin Lohman 1994). Savornin Lohman (1994) argues that environmental regulators are averse to the environmental effectiveness risk because society has given them the job of attaining physical environmental results. If the goals are not realized, the bureaucracy will be heavily criticized for being ineffective. In the worst case, this could result in the dismissal of the bureaucrats involved. Also, an over-realization of the goals can affect the bureaucracy negatively. The adversely affected parties will in that case demand compensation.

To conclude, bureaucrats have their own agenda. Although there are several checks on the self-interested behavior of bureaucrats, it is likely that they will be able to pursue their goal of discretionary budget maximization to some degree. It is also likely that bureaucrats take the effects of regulation on the regulated industry into account, either because they are captured by the industry or because they want to minimize flack. Furthermore, the bureaucracy has an incentive to stick to the policy instruments currently in use, although the background of the bureaucrats may give them a preference for a certain instrument. Last but not least, bureaucrats will be risk-averse because both not realizing and over-realizing the goals set will result in criticisms from interest groups.

4.2 Industry

Often, industry is taken as a unitary actor. However, within industry, several actors with diverging objectives can be distinguished. Here we will discuss three actors: owners, managers, and labor unions.

4.2.1 Owners

Owners provide the firm with risk-bearing capital and expect some return on their investment. More specifically, they will want to maximize profits. If the return is too low, they can withdraw their money and invest it in another way which gives higher profits. Alternatively, they can replace the managers of the firm with some new managers.

Under two circumstances, the owners of the firm may not want to maximize profits (Tirole 1988 and Mas-Colell et al. 1995). When profits are uncertain and the owners are risk-averse, expected profit maximization is not optimal. Production plans that are risky may now not be implemented although their expected profit is positive. Another factor that may affect the preference of the owners is that the firm may have an influence on the price and the owners are consumers of the good. In this case, the owners may have an incentive to overproduce to lower the price of the good.

These two cases will often play a minor role. First of all, it is easier to insure against risks by diversifying the portfolio than by letting every firm restrain from risk-bearing investments. Secondly, it is unlikely that the owner (of a share of) the firm consumes so much of the good produced that he wants to lower the price of it. Therefore, in the following, we assume that owners want the firm to maximize profits.

4.2.2 Managers

In many cases, the owners of the firm will not form the management. The shareholders will still be interested in maximum profit, but it might be that the managers have other objectives. Although some parts of the management effort, such as number of hours worked, can be monitored with relative ease, it is less easy to ascertain that whether the efforts of the management have been directed to profit maximization. Hence, a principal–agent problem arises where the manager (the agent) has some opportunities to realize his own objectives at the expense of the shareholders (the principals). However, there are some disciplining factors that restrict the managers in their pursuit of pure self-realization.

Several models of managerial behavior have been put forward. A part of the literature endows the manager with a single objective, often under the constraint of a minimum level of profit. In other studies, several objectives enter the utility function of the managers (see also Marris and Mueller 1980 for an overview).

If the compensation of the managers is more dependent on sales volume than on profits, a manager may try to maximize the sales level at the expense of profits (Baumol 1962 and 1966). Later, Baumol changed the hypothesis of sales maximization to maximization of the growth rate of sales. Empirical work by McGuire et al. (1962) lends some support to the hypothesis that managers' incomes are more closely correlated to sales than to profits. Werden and Hirschey (1980) show that management income is related to both sales and profits. However, other empirical work is less supportive (see Bevars and Siders 1967, Hall 1967 and Baker 1969).

Another hypothesis is that managers maximize the rate of growth of sales revenues (Marris 1963, 1964). Mueller (1972) has put forward an amended version of this thesis. He states that only mature firms are affected by a growth maximization objective of the management.

Managers may also be interested in increasing the number of staff beyond the profit maximizing level. Several reasons can exist for this. First, an increase in the number of staff may increase the chances of promotion for the incumbent staff (Williamson 1963). Second, the management can spread the workload over more people, leading to a lower workload per manager.

One could also expect that managers want to maximize the organizational slack. With this is meant that managers are interested in maximizing the means that they can use in a discretionary way (Williamson 1963).

The previous models replace profit in the objectives of managers by another single variable. Another approach is to include a number of arguments in the objective. Williamson (1963) gives an exact specification of the utility function. The items entering the utility function are salary, security, dominance and professional excellence. Dominance consists of three sub-motives: status, power and prestige. He argues that managers have a preference for some types of expense that enhance the objectives of the managers; these expense preferences do not have to be productive. From the utility function, Williamson derives assumptions on the maximizing behavior of managers. First of all, he assumes that managers have a positive preference for staff for the reasons mentioned above. Williamson also assumes that managers have a preference for emoluments. Finally, managers have a positive preference for discretionary profit. With this is meant the profit above the minimum performance constraint set by the market and stockholders. Managers can use this part of the profits in a rather discretionary way.

Does the above mean that management will have its way, and pursue its own goals at the expense of the owners? If the management is not restricted in any way, the answer is yes. However, there are several factors external to the firm that restrict the management in its actions. Holmstrom and Tirole (1989) mention three external disciplining factors: the labor market, the product market and capital markets. The first factor works through the reputation of the management. If profits are consistently low, the reputation of the management will also be low and their value in the labor market will then decrease. The second factor is concerned with the level of competition in the product market. When the product market the firm is operating in is highly competitive, the possibilities for non-profit maximizing behavior are few. In that case, the management has to strive for profit maximization purely to survive. Only when the firm has a certain monopoly power, can management pursue goals other than profit maximization. This does, however, only hold for individual firms in a sector. With environmental policy, the whole sector is typically regulated with the same instrument. Here, the sector may collectively lobby for an instrument that is not profit maximizing. The third disciplining factor is the threat of take-over in which the incumbent management would be replaced (Marris 1963, 1964). Furthermore, the owners can devise incentive schemes to keep management on the track of profit maximization. The income of the managers could, for example, be made dependent on the profit earned.

In all, managers seem to have incentives to pursue goals other than profit maximization. However, several constraints, external and internal, will prevent the management from wandering too far astray. There is still reason to believe that the objectives of managers are reflected in the behavior of firms. Clarkson and Miller (1982), for example, conclude from a large body of literature that both profits and firm size are important explanatory variables of firm behavior.

4.2.3 Labor unions
Workers can be affected in several ways by environmental policy. On the positive side, environmental regulation can improve working conditions.

However, environmental regulation can also result in plant closures and lower wages. The representatives of workers, the labor unions, can be expected to oppose measures that affect workers negatively. One major question here, is what the objectives of unions are.

Within the literature, the goals of the unions have been a hotly debated issue. A debate already existed in the 1940s on whether unions could be seen as the maximizers of some objective, as Dunlop (1944) asserted, or whether they could not, but should be seen as political organizations, as put forward by Ross (1948).

Building on Dunlop, several maximizing models have been proposed (see Sapsford and Tzannatos 1993, Pencavel 1991 and Booth 1995 for an overview). Early studies assumed a single maximand such as wages, employment, union membership or rents. However, these models invariably ran into problems, always leaving the labor union with only one member.

More recent theoretical studies endow the labor union with a utility function. A common specification of the union utility function is that it contains both wages and employment. This specification makes it possible to model wage maximization and employment maximization as special cases. Different kind of unions can emphasize one of the objectives more than the other. The result is an intermediary outcome between maximum wage and maximum employment. Alternatively, the union utility can be modeled as the sum of the utilities of the individual members (Oswald 1982 and Mayhew and Turnbull 1989).

Following Ross (1948), unions can also be viewed as political organizations. The leadership of unions is elected and the results of the negotiations with employers are subject to approval by the members of the union. Therefore, it might be appropriate to model the union in the same way as a political party. Booth (1984) presents a model in which the union managers are concerned with maximizing the probability of re-election as well as wage and employment levels. Union members are only concerned about wages and employment. Booth uses a median voter model to describe the behavior of the management. In this kind of model, under certain conditions, the management will maximize the utility of the median voter (see also Grossman 1983 and Booth and Chatterji 1993).

The leadership of the union may have objectives of their own. Pemberton (1988) includes the preferences of the management in the union's utility function. He argues that the union management has a preference for a large membership because this gives the leadership greater influence and/or wealth.

The union leader may also be concerned with his or her tenure, being an elected official (Pencavel 1991). As in any organization where there is a division between donors and management, a principal–agent problem exists within unions. This allows the management to pursue their own agenda. In comparison with firms, the principal–agent problem in unions will be bigger. It is very hard to monitor whether the output of the union is the maximum output possible. Therefore, there should be ample possibilities for managers to pursue their own objectives.

Burton (1984) presents a model in which the utility of the union leadership is a function of power, social status, income and job security. The first three items are in turn a function of the membership of the union, while the last item is a function of the wages of the union members.

There are only a few empirical studies on union objectives. Farber (1978a, 1978b) analyzes the objectives of the United Mineworkers' Union in the US, while Carruth and Oswald (1985) do the same for the British National Union of Mineworkers. Other studies are by Dertouzos and Pencavel (1981) and Pencavel (1984), who examine the objectives of the International Typographical Union. In the two industries covered, both employment and wages matter to labor unions. There is, however, a large difference in preferences within these industries.

The above shows that labor unions have at least a dual objective. It seems reasonable to assume that unions are not only interested in high wages for their members, but also in a high level of employment. Since managers are difficult to monitor, their preferences will be reflected in the behavior of the union. Hence, it is likely that management will try to increase the membership of the union. As Bain and Elsheikh (1976) and Ashenfelter and Pencavel (1969) show, union membership rises with employment. We would therefore expect that union management is more interested in a high level of employment than in a high wage level for their members.

4.3 Environmental Organizations

Not much has been written in the scientific literature on the behavioral assumptions of environmental organizations. Most studies go no further than to remark that environmental organizations want to improve environmental quality. Undoubtedly, provision of environmental quality is the main objective of environmental organizations, but how is this done and do they have other objectives?

In most cases, environmental protection is not provided directly by environmental organizations, but indirectly. They try to induce others, mainly the government, to improve the quality of the environment. Environmental organizations can lobby either through spending money to influence policy makers, or by convincing politicians that taking measures to improve the environment will lead to more votes. The latter will be easier, the higher the membership of the environmental organization (Svendsen 1998b). To raise the level of contributions per member and to raise the level of membership, the environmental organization has essentially two strategies. Organizations that are successful, i.e. organizations that provide a high level of environmental quality, will see their membership and contributions increased. Furthermore, direct fundraising will also increase both factors. If the management of the environmental organization only has the interests of the donors at heart, it will engage in fundraising up to the point where the marginal benefits equal the marginal costs.

However, managers may have their own objectives, although it is likely that they do have a preference for high environmental quality. The question is whether managers of environmental organizations have opportunities to realize their own objectives, and what those objectives are.

Most, if not all, environmental organizations are non-profit organizations. There are three main reasons for organizing in this way (Rose-Ackerman 1996). First of all, by choosing the form of a non-profit organization, gifts cannot be converted into profits for the owners. In this way, the donors are assured that it is their interests that are being served with the donated funds (Hewitt and Brown 2000). Second, non-profit organizations may have less incentive to misrepresent the quality of the service provided than for-profit organizations do. Third, non-profit organzations may foster experimentation and provide the possibility of putting into practice unpopular or extreme ideologies. The first factor means that non-profit orgaizations are better at competing for gifts than for-profit organizations. The second and third factors are important in the case of environmental organizations, because the product provided by them can to a large degree be characterized as a public good. Moreover, it is a public good of which it is hard to determine both quantity and quality.

Although their organizational form should lead people to trust environmental organizations, it also leads to some problems. Non-profit managers have little incentive to manage their organizations in an efficient manner since no one has a claim on the profits. Hence we can expect that shirking is more likely to occur in non-profit organizations than in for-profit organizations (Alchian and Demsetz 1972 and Rose-Ackerman 1996). In general, we can expect the principal–agent problem to be highly acute. Not only are there few methods for disciplining the managers, but as mentioned before, the output of environmental organizations is hard to monitor.

As with bureaucrats, it is very likely that the managers of environmental organizations will maximize the discretionary budget (Niskanen 1971 and Migué and Bélanger 1974). Furthermore, as with labor unions, it is likely that the managers of environmental organizations have a preference for a high level of membership. This will give them status and more influence in the political arena. If the management is only interested in discretionary spending, fundraising will occur up to the point where the marginal benefit of fundraising is equal to zero.

However, it is also likely that many of the managers themselves have a preference for the output of their organization; they are so called 'zealots'. In that case, fundraising may be done beyond the point where the marginal benefit is equal to the marginal costs, but not to the point where it is zero.

Hewitt and Brown (2000) have tested whether managers of environmental organization are only interested in discretionary spending, or whether they also derive utility from the output of the organization. They find that managers of environmental organizations derive positive marginal utility from discretionary spending. Although they do not go so far as to conclude that the managers maximize discretionary spending, they mention that their results could be explained as such.

Environmental organizations always press for lower levels of pollution. Indeed, they have always maintained a symbolic goal of zero pollution (Svendsen 1998b). This implies that any emission level above the policy goal will be unacceptable to environmental organizations. The result is that they are risk-averse (Nentjes and Dijkstra 1994). To be more specific, they are downward risk-averse, since an emission level below the goal can be explained as a success for the environmental organization.

To be effective at lobbying for environmental protection, environmental organizations need a large number of donors and a high level of income. The organization can attract donors by being successful and by engaging in fundraising. Since environmental organizations can expect to be confronted by industry, they may have more success by supporting the same policy instrument as industry does (Svendsen 1998b). If the management has a preference for discretionary spending, it will show up in excessive expenditure on fundraising. This will increase membership, but will decrease the level of services provided. To conclude, the objectives of the environmental organization are to provide environmental quality and to increase membership. On top of this, they are risk-averse.

The literature discussed in this section shows some clear tendencies, which run through almost all interest groups. First of all, managers have a preference for discretionary spending and for the size of the organization they work for. Second, there is a principal–agent problem in all organizations. The level of manager discretion then depends on how well the principals, i.e. owners or donors of the organization, can monitor and control the manager. Hence, managers will have a large influence on the policy of the organization in labor unions and environmental organizations and least in firms operating in perfectly competitive markets.

5.   PREFERENCES

We described above the behavioral assumptions of the different actors in the environmental rent-seeking game. In this section, we give an overview of the literature that discusses the preferences of interest groups for environmental policy instruments. The aim of this literature is to explain which instruments are used, as opposed to much of the environmental economics literature, that analyzes which instrument is the most optimal to use.

5.1 Legislators

5.1.1 Politicians
In most analyses of instrument choice, the preferences of politicians are not taken into account. The implicit assumption is that the policy is determined in a contest between interest groups. The interest group that is best at rent seeking wins the contest and will see its preferred instrument implemented. However, there are a few studies that do analyze the preferences of politicians and how these preferences affect the outcome.

Verbruggen (1991) assumes that the main interest of politicians is to maximize public support in order to be re-elected. Since environmental issues are of high concern to the public, politicians will wish to attain certain environmental goals. However, in doing this they are constrained by two conditions. First, the policy should have no harmful adverse effects on income distribution and employment. Second, the international competitiveness of domestic industry should not be adversely affected. Furthermore, to set environmental policy, the government will need information that can only be provided by the polluters. This creates a discussion and negotiation platform. Therefore, Verbruggen argues that the industry lobby will be very effective. The result is that politicians will choose direct regulation or voluntary agreements with industry. If emission charges are used, the revenue is often recycled to the regulated industry.

Hochman and Zilberman (1978) conclude that because relative standards result in higher output and lower prices, they contribute less to unemployment and inflation while achieving an acceptable environmental threshold. For these reasons, politicians may prefer relative standards to emissions charges.

In their analysis, Nentjes and Dijkstra (1994) split the group of politicians into Members of Parliament and the minister. The description of the political process in their study relates strongly to the situation in the Netherlands, although it is also applicable to other countries with similar political systems. Since in the Netherlands, voters vote for a party and not a single candidate, Nentjes and Dijkstra do not take the single candidate, but the political party as the decision-making unit. The assumption is that political parties want to maximize the number of parliamentary seats. Besides this, Nentjes and Dijkstra also assume that ideology is important in politicians' preference of environmental policy instruments. They identify four political blocks with different emphases on the welfare of workers, wealth holders and the environment. The final ordering of instruments of a party is then equal to the preference of the interest group that comes first in the political party's ordering. This is a rather crude method of assigning a preference for environmental policy instruments to political parties. Furthermore, although Nentjes and Dijkstra explicitly mention that parties aim to maximize seats in parliament, they assign preferences purely with regard to ideology.

Nentjes and Dijkstra (1994) endow the minister with only one objective: to translate the government policy programme into concrete proposals. Government in the Netherlands always consists of a coalition of parties. Therefore, Nentjes and Dijkstra construct from the preferences of the parties, preferences of possible coalitions. Furthermore, they argue that the environmental bureaucracy has considerable power in a system such as the Dutch one. In this way, Nentjes and Dijkstra show that it is very likely that industry will be regulated through direct regulation.

An extensive overview of the preferences of legislators is given by Keohane et al. (1997). However, they do not always distinguish between politicians and bureaucrats. A first argument given by Keohane et al. is that legislators and their staff are predisposed to favor direct regulation by their predominantly legal training. Furthermore, unfamiliar instruments require legislators to invest time in learning about them. This gives a bias in favor of existing instruments, which are mostly command and control instruments.

Another factor important for the preference of politicians is uncertainty. Here, we not only refer to uncertainty about the level of emissions, but also about the distribution of costs and benefits among the affected parties. Here the flexibility of market-based instruments is a disadvantage, since they give uncertainty about the distributional effects and may create hot spots (McCubbins and Page 1986). Especially in countries where politicians represent a certain geographical area, they may be more concerned with the distribution of costs and benefits than with overall efficiency (Hahn and Stavins 1991). The costs also include the possibility of closure and relocation of firms and the local unemployment associated with it (Hahn and Noll 1990). If legislators want a certain distribution of benefits and costs, they will have greater opportunity to do so with direct regulation. This after all gives them the possibility of prescribing rules and procedures that favor one group over another (McCubbins et al. 1987 and Keohane et al. 1997).

A divergence from current policies creates both winners and losers. However, the losers will be more aware of their loss than the winners of their gain. Moreover, it is not the real costs and benefits that are important, but the perceived costs and benefits (Hahn 1987). For this reason, politicians are likely to prefer direct regulation because they tend to hide the costs of regulation, whereas market-based instruments tend to give a focus on the costs (Keohane et al. 1997).

Keohane et al. (1997) also stress the importance of ideology. Here they cite Kelman (1981), who finds that Republicans support the concept of charges, perhaps not so much for their efficiency, but more because they use markets and give less intervention from government. Democrats on the other hand, did not support charges, again largely on ideological grounds.

In most analyses, politicians are non-existent. Which policy instrument is implemented is then determined in a contest between interest groups. If politicians are present in the analysis, they are mostly depicted as support-maximizing and risk-averse. On the basis of these assumptions, most authors conclude that politicians will prefer direct regulation. Endowing politicians with an ideology can either reinforce this conclusion, or weaken it.

5.1.2 Environmental bureaucracy

We concluded above that the environmental bureaucracy has a set of preferences. The set included budget and discretionary costs. Furthermore, it is likely that at least some of the bureaucrats have a preference for environmental quality, but at the same time take the effect of the regulation on the polluters into account. The background of the bureaucrat, legal or technical on the one side or economic on the other, may have an influence on the bureaucrat's preference of instruments. Last but not least, bureaucrats are risk-averse. Several of these preferences are mentioned in the literature on the choice of environmental policy instrument.

From several Dutch government reports, Nentjes (1988) concludes that the main objective of the environmental bureaucracy is certainty of effectiveness. This objective can be seen as a result of the risk-aversion of the bureaucrats. Direct regulation gives a clear prescription of either the measures to take or the level of abatement to attain and furthermore gives the bureaucracy a high level of control over the regulated industry. Therefore, the environmental bureaucracy will prefer direct regulation (see also Frey 1993 and DeClerq 1996).

Nentjes and Dijkstra (1994) give the most comprehensive analysis of environmental bureaucrats' preferences. They assume that the main objective of the bureaucrats is the certainty of realizing the environmental target. Next to this, two secondary objectives are identified. Nentjes and Dijkstra argue that the bureau cannot be ignorant of the costs of the regulation to polluters. Furthermore, bureaucrats may have internal goals such as organizational slack, which is reflected in a preference for a large input of bureaucratic labor.

For each of the objectives, they rank the instruments. They argue that emission ceilings give the bureau the largest level of control, with grandfathered tradable permits taking second place. Although tradable permits give certainty of realizing the overall objective, they do not give the bureaucracy control over the pollution per firm. With regard to cost for the regulated industry, Nentjes and Dijkstra assess that all market-based instruments give the same costs to industry. Only emission ceilings will give lower costs. Finally, on the issue of labor input, they rank charges and grandfathered tradable permits highest. Overall, they conclude that the environmental bureaucracy will prefer emission ceilings to all other instruments.

Keohane et al. (1997) also arrive at the conclusion that the environmental bureaucracy will prefer direct regulation. As reasons they state that the bureau will be familiar with this form of regulation, and shifting to another instrument will require them to gather much new information about the working of these instruments. Moreover, their current knowledge may become obsolete when a new instrument is chosen, which leads to job insecurity. Finally, market-based instruments imply a scale down in the role of the agency by shifting decision making from the bureau to the firms. This undermines the prestige of the agency and the job security of the bureaucrats (see also Hahn and Stavins 1991).

Liroff (1986) finds that the environmental bureaucracy is not a homogeneous group. Instead, two groups can be distinguished: the command minimalists and the command expansionists. Command minimalists will support economic instruments because they give most freedom to industry, both in determining how much to abate and how to abate. Command expansionists on the other hand want to have as much control over the polluters as possible. Therefore, they will support direct regulation. Note that the same disposition was found among politicians.

Christoffersen and Svendsen (2000) argue that bureaux have influence on the spending of the taxes that are collected by the bureau. If this is the case, bureaucrats may be more inclined to use revenue-raising instruments such as taxes and auctioned tradable permits.

Dijkstra (1999) presents some empirical evidence on the preferences of Dutch environmental bureaucrats. He notes that there is considerable disagreement within the bureaucracy on the issue of instrument choice. A general tendency seems to be that the bureaux see no need for large changes in the use of instruments. At most, the current instruments can be made more flexible. However, there is a large division between the two groups within the bureaux. The main issue is how much responsibility industry can handle in reducing emissions. One group only wants to set emission levels and leave the implementation to industry, while the other group stresses that this responsibility cannot be left to industry. It is not certain whether these differences in opinion are correlated with educational background. The level of contact with the regulated industry may also play a role. The closer the contacts, the more 'captured' the bureaucrat is.

The literature that discusses bureaucratic preferences sees bureaux as important in the setting of environmental policy. They are however, mostly seen as conservative in that they have a preference for the status quo. Because of the high costs of adapting to new instruments and the uncertainty connected to economic instruments, bureaucrats prefer direct regulation. The survey of Dijkstra (1999) however, shows that there may be diverging opinions within the bureaucracy, with one group supporting economic instruments and the other direct regulation.

5.2 Industry

Industry is usually assumed to be one entity with one unified goal: profit maximization. In some cases, workers are treated separately. However to our knowledge, the distinction between shareholders and management has never been made explicitly.

5.2.1 Shareholders

If one assumes that firms maximize profits, the positive political economy explanations of the demand for regulation by industry can be divided into three categories (Keohane et al. 1997): (1) preference for an instrument can arise from lower aggregate costs to industry, (2) the instrument awards industry with rents and places a barrier to entry, and (3) There are differences in the costs of compliance across firms within the industry.

In general, industry will prefer instruments that have low aggregate costs. Although market-based instruments are most cost-effective, it is not certain that they will be preferred by industry (Keohane et al. 1997). Taxes and auctioned tradable permits give high costs to industry because with both instruments a price is paid for residual emissions. This is not the case with grandfathered tradable permits and direct regulation, which is why industry will prefer these instruments.

Another factor may also make industry prefer direct regulation. It is often argued that industry has more influence on policy with direct regulation than with other instruments. According to Bohm and Russell (1985), direct regulation is more uncompromising. Therefore, the government is more inclined to listen to the views of the polluters before any action is taken. Industry influence will be especially large when information about abatement costs is needed by the government. This would be the case when regulation is firm-specific or when an aggregate emission target has to be translated into a tax. A firm then has a certain bargaining power, which it can use to obtain a more lenient standard or tax. However, since the precise setting of a tax requires a large amount of information, this is never done. Mostly, the level of a tax is based on rather crude calculations. This is not to say that firms will have no influence on an environmental tax. As is shown by Andersen (1996), DeClerq (1996) and Svendsen (1998a), industry often has a large influence on the design and level of a tax.

The above suggests that industry will prefer direct regulation and perhaps grandfathered tradable permits. The advantage of the latter is that they are efficient, give industry a free choice in how to abate and do not give firms the cost of residual emissions. Although direct regulation is not efficient, and in many cases does not give firms a free choice of abatement technology, it gives low costs to industry and may be prone to industry influence.

Several studies have addressed the question of preference for environmental policy instrument directly. The first to do so were Buchanan and Tullock (1975). They showed that, in a partial equilibrium model with perfect competition, the profits of the polluting industry are higher with direct regulation than with an emission tax. The form of direct regulation used in their model is a cap on emissions. Since they assume that there is no technology to remove the pollution, the cap on emissions effectively becomes a cap on production. In this way, the price of the good produced is increased. In the short run, the firm is better off with the cap than with taxes, because with taxes it has to pay for the residual emissions. The firm may even make a profit with emission ceilings, both in the short run and in the long run. This occurs when the reduction in production causes a proportionally higher rise in the price of the good. Without entry, the firm may even experience profits in the long run.

Dewees (1983) provides another comparison of instruments. Contrary to Buchanan and Tullock (1975), Dewees allows for the possibility that emissions can be reduced per unit of output. His analysis is somewhat out of line with the main body of the literature in that he assumes that the aim of government policy is to reduce emissions per unit of output. Dewees considers three instruments: an emission charge per unit of emissions, tradable permits, and a relative standard. He shows that when capital can be transferred without cost, shareholders will never lose. Moreover, with grandfathered tradable permits, the rent received at the initial distribution of the permits increases the profits. Hence, in this case, shareholders prefer grandfathered tradable permits. Also when capital is immobile, shareholders may prefer grandfathered tradable permits. However, relative standards may perform equally well. The preference for grandfathered tradable permits is based, as in Buchanan and Tullock (1975), on the fact that the firm receives rents from the initial distribution of permits. Although Dewees (1983) is in many regards a step forward in comparison to Buchanan and Tullock (1975), Dijkstra (1999) shows that Dewees's analysis is flawed on many points.

The most comprehensive treatment of preferences for environmental policy instrument is given by Dijkstra (1999). In a partial equilibrium model with perfect competition, he discusses the effects of four instruments: relative standards, emission ceilings, emissions charges and tradable permits (both grandfathered and auctioned). In the model, it is assumed that there are no barriers to entry. Dijkstra finds that in the short run, emission ceilings, charges and tradable permits have the same effect on production and product price. Only relative standards give a different outcome. More specifically, with the same level of pollution, a relative standard gives a higher level of production and consequently a lower product price (see also Hochman and Zilberman 1978, Helfand 1991 and Ebert 1998, 1999). In the long run, market-based instruments give the highest welfare. Dijkstra also arrives at the conclusion that shareholders should prefer grandfathered tradable permits because they present a rent, which is given free.

The conclusion of the formal models is clear. When the goods market is fully competitive and entrance is restricted, both direct regulation and grandfathered tradable permits create a rent, which is awarded free to the shareholders. Therefore, they have a preference for these instruments. With free entry, only grandfathered tradable permits create a rent. Shareholders therefore prefer grandfathered tradable permits to all other instruments. The next instruments in the preference listing are emission ceilings and relative standards. At least in the short run, these create rents. Furthermore, with emission charges and auctioned tradable permits, a price is paid for the residual emissions, while this is not the case with ceilings and relative standards.

The analysis by Dijkstra (1999) clearly shows that with free entry, firms subjected to direct regulation will not receive rents in the long run. Only if the instrument creates a barrier to entry will such rents persist. Such a barrier could exist if new plants were subjected to stricter environmental standards than existing ones. Stricter standards for new plants may be efficient if the cost of abatement for such plants is lower than for existing plants. However, when the standards are very tight for new plants, a real barrier to entry exists. Tietenberg (1985) describes how under the Clean Air Act, new or modified sources are subjected to stricter standards than existing ones (see also Maloney and McCormick 1982 and Svendsen 1998b). It is however, not clear whether existing differences in standards between existing and new firms comprise a barrier to entry, or whether they only reflect differences in costs of abatement.

There is some difference in opinion in the literature on whether grandfathered tradable permits create a barrier to entry. With grandfathering, existing firms receive permits for free while new firms have to pay for them. Hence, incumbent firms do not have to pay for (all) their residual emissions, while new firms do. This would then be an entrance barrier (Keohane et al. 1997 and Svendsen 1998b). However, Koutstaal (1997) and Dijkstra (1999) argue that this in itself does not form a barrier to entry. The grandfathered permits constitute an opportunity cost to the recipient because it could have sold them on the market. Koutstaal and Dijkstra mention that grandfathering will result in an entry barrier when new firms have to incur transaction costs to purchase the permits or when the capital markets work imperfectly.

With tradable permits, existing firms can raise a barrier to entry themselves by colluding. They could agree not to sell permits to new firms or to raise the market price (Tietenberg 1985 and Misiolek and Elder 1989). When there are many firms in the market however, this is unlikely to happen. Furthermore, the government can deter this kind of behavior by selling a certain portion of the permits available each year, as is done in the US sulfur trading program.

Maloney and McCormick (1982) argue that environmental regulation can increase the value of some firms in the regulated industry, while lowering the value of other firms. In general, the value of low-cost firms is expected to increase, while that of high-cost firms will decline. They also provide some empirical evidence showing that this was the case in several cases of environmental regulation.

Because of the differences in costs of abatement, firms that are affected less than average by a particular policy instrument may support it because it gives them a competitive advantage (Leone and Jackson 1981 and Oster 1982). There is some empirical support for this suggestion (see Keohane et al. 1997 for an overview and Maloney and McCormick 1982). However, the paper by Leone and Jackson (1981) found that the intra-industry transfer argument is not very important.

The theoretical literature on industry preferences for environmental policy instrument is not conclusive. It points to both direct regulation and grandfathered tradable permits as the favored instruments of industry. Reasons to prefer direct regulation are: (1) direct regulation leads to lower costs for the polluters. The reason is that with taxes and tradable permits, a price is paid for the residual emissions, which is not the case with direct regulation; (2) industry has more influence on policy with direct regulation than with market-based instruments; (3) direct regulation creates rents that are distributed free to the industry; and (4) because abatement demands are usually less stringent for existing plants than for new ones, direct regulation often leads to a barrier to entry, benefiting the incumbent firms.

Reasons to prefer grandfathered tradable permits are: (1) tradable permits are efficient and hence lead to low costs for the industry as a whole; (2) grandfathered tradable permits create a rent; and (3) they also create a barrier to entry (although this is debatable).

When maximizing profits is the objective, the conclusion derived from formal models is that industry should prefer direct regulation or grandfathered tradable permits, because both create a rent. However, several qualifications should be made. First, the result that direct regulation leads to rents will only hold in the long run if there are barriers to entry. If this is not the case, new entrants to the market will compete the rents away. Second, what is direct regulation? Buchanan and Tullock (1975) and Leidy and Hoekman (1994) take emission ceilings, while Dewees (1983) uses relative standards. Only Dijkstra (1999) analyzes the effect of both forms of direct regulation. Dijkstra (1999) shows that in the long run there is no difference in profitability between ceilings and relative standards. Third, only Dewees (1983) and Dijkstra (1999) analyze some forms of both direct regulation and tradable permits. Both authors conclude that industry should prefer grandfathered tradable permits to direct regulation.

A few surveys exist that try to shed light on interest group preferences for environmental policy instruments. Kelman (1981) was the first to conduct such a survey. In the survey, respondents only had a choice between direct regulation and charges. Kelman found that industry was clearly opposed to charges; 85% of the respondents were against them. At the same time, it showed that industry was not very well informed about charges.

Wallart and Bürgenmeier (1996) did a survey among major Swiss firms, which also concentrated on emissions charges. They found a surprisingly large acceptance of charges by industry. In all, two-thirds of the polluting firms were in favor of charges. However, Dijkstra (1999) conjectures that the survey by Wallart and Bürgenmeier (1996) may have been wrongly designed, leading to the high acceptance of charges.

In a survey of American and Danish interest groups, Svendsen (1998b) finds some differences between the industrial sectors in the two countries. In the US, both industry and public electricity companies favor grandfathered tradable permits because they perceive this instrument as both efficient and flexible. Danish industry on the other hand prefers voluntary agreements; the industry wants to take voluntary action to prevent state intervention. Taxes are rejected because they will bring higher production costs. Grandfathered tradable permits are seen as a compromise solution. In contrast to industry, Danish public electric utilities prefer taxes. In general they prefer market-based instruments, but assess that Denmark is too small to have a viable market in permits. The reason for this difference between industry and public electric utilities is, according to Svendsen, that the utilities, being heavily regulated, share interests with the state.

Dijkstra (1999) conducted a survey among Dutch interest groups in which industry shows a preference for relative targets as opposed to absolute ones. However, in general there is doubt in industry about market-based instruments. Taxes especially are seen as detrimental to the international competitiveness of industry. Industry also expects problems with the initial distribution of tradable permits. The only industrial organization giving a direct preference ordering preferred relative standards.

Grandfathered tradable permits come in second place; charges and auctioned tradable permits get very little support. In comments given to the survey, several industrial organizations express a preference for covenants or voluntary agreements because they are flexible and give a minimum of government interference. Tradable permits are seen as a complement to voluntary agreements.

The outcome of the surveys is that American industry prefers grandfathered tradable permits, while European industry prefers voluntary agreements. Although more attention has been given to voluntary agreements in the economic literature lately, the positive literature on environmental policy choice has mostly ignored them. Voluntary agreements are however very attractive to industry. Through voluntary agreements with the government, industry can influence both the level of emissions and the policy instrument used (Dietz and Straaten 1992). Hence, voluntary agreements provide industry with ample opportunities for rent-seeking (Verbruggen 1991).

In all, the theoretical studies seem to be supported by the surveys. According to the theoretical studies, shareholders should prefer direct regulation or grandfathered tradable permits. The surveys shows that these are the preferred instruments of industry. However, neither the theoretical, nor the empirical analyses give a unanimous result.

5.2.2 Workers

The preferences of workers are not often analyzed. One reason for this is that labor unions are not seen as very influential in the environmental debate. Environmental policy is not the core interest of unions, and hence, they often have no policy on this issue. When the preferences of unions are discussed in the literature on environmental policy choice, it is almost always assumed that unions maximize employment.

Hochman and Zilberman (1978) make a connection between output and employment. They examine the impact of taxes and relative standards and conclude that the latter result in higher output and lower prices. Therefore, workers will prefer relative standards.

Another analysis is offered by Dewees (1983). He assumes that the government wants to reduce emissions per unit of production. Hence, total production and thereby total emissions can vary per instrument. When capital is flexible, Dewees finds that employment will be highest when relative standards are used and lowest when market-based instruments are used. The reason for this is that in the model, a fixed portion of operating costs goes to labor. With market instruments, a part of the firm's revenue is forwarded to the government with taxes, or to the shareholders with tradable permits. With non-flexible capital, there is no difference in the effect on employment between the instruments.

In a model that is essentially the same as that of Buchanan and Tullock (1975), Leidy and Hoekman (1994) include an analysis of the preferences of workers. They argue that workers will prefer emission ceilings. Since output is produced inefficiently in the long run under emission ceilings, industry employment will be higher with this instrument. Furthermore, industry profits are highest under emission ceilings. Workers will try to capture a part of these profits in the form of higher wages. Finally, under direct emission ceilings, possible lay-offs will occur at all firms, while with charges, job losses only occur in connection with firm closures. The first option is seen as more equitable.

Dijkstra (1999) analyzes the preferences of workers in a partial equilibrium model. His assumption about worker preferences is that they are mostly interested in employment. Dijkstra argues that in the short run, employment will be highest with relative standards and lowest with market-based instruments. This follows from the level of production, which is highest under relative standards and lowest under market-based instruments. To compare employment levels in the long run, Dijkstra assumes that labor costs are a fixed percentage of operating costs, hereby following Dewees (1983). The result is that employment will be lowest with market-based instruments. Depending on the elasticity of demand for the produced good, relative standards or emission ceilings give the highest employment in the long run.

Nentjes and Dijkstra (1994) assume that workers prefer the policy instrument that maximizes employment in the regulated industry and the stability of jobs within firms. They furthermore assume that the industry is fully competitive and that there is a constant capital/labor ratio. Nentjes and Dijkstra argue that workers prefer direct regulation to market-based instruments. With direct regulation, total employment in the industry is higher than with market-based instruments and more firms stay in the industry, meaning that fewer workers have to shift firm.

Keohane et al. (1997) use essentially the same assumptions as Nentjes and Dijkstra (1994); unions seek to protect jobs and are therefore opposed to instruments that lead to plant closures or industrial dislocations. Keohane et al. (1997) mention that direct regulation standards have generally been tailored to protect aging plants, which would not be easy with market-based instruments. Hence, they conclude that labor will prefer direct regulation to market-based instruments.

Only Dijkstra (1999) gives empirical evidence on workers unions' preferences for environmental policy instruments. The two Dutch unions included in his survey do not give a unanimous preference ordering. One union (CNV) prefers emission ceilings, with charges taking second place. Tradable permits, whether auctioned or grandfathered are least preferred. The other union (FNV) states a general preference for market-based instruments, although it has some doubts about their practicability. Furthermore, the FNV states that a combination of instruments often works best in practice.

The theoretical studies lead to a clear conclusion. Workers prefer direct regulation because this gives the highest level of employment. The empirical evidence, however, is less conclusive.

5.3 Environmental Organizations

In the literature, environmental organizations are thought of as guardians of the environment. Their main, if not only, objective is to reduce emissions.

In the model by Dewees (1983), the government sets a standard per unit of production. As a result, the instrument that gives the highest output also gives the highest total level of pollution. Since market-based instruments give the lowest output, Dewees argues that environmentalists should prefer these to direct regulation.

Other arguments related to the level of emissions are given by Dijkstra (1999). Environmentalists will be against tradable permits, because they give firms the possibility of selling permits when the firm was going to reduce emissions anyway. This could be in connection with the start of a new plant replacing an older more polluting one, or when the firm goes out of business. In these cases, the environmental movement would argue that total emissions should be reduced.

Most models of environmental policy instrument choice take the target of emissions to be an absolute one. In that case, environmental organizations should be indifferent between instruments. However, if they are risk-averse, they may have a preference ordering for the instruments. Leidy and Hoekman (1994), for example, argue that environmental organizations will prefer emission ceilings. Like Buchanan and Tullock (1975), they assume that emissions can only be reduced by reducing output. In the model, firms will have an incentive to produce more than their ceiling. However, perfect monitoring ensures that they will not. Furthermore, the firms in the industry will receive a rent from regulation, which will increase their profits. Therefore, they will be able to pay for an eventual clean up if they violate the regulation. Contributing to this is that no firm will leave the market as a result of the regulation.

Nentjes and Dijkstra (1994) also assume that environmental organizations are risk-averse. They argue that only emission charges give uncertainty about the aggregate emission level. Nentjes and Dijkstra therefore use another criterion to come to a preference ordering. They argue that if environmental organizations assess that they are rather strong at lobbying, they may have a preference for instruments that give revenue. Therefore, Nentjes and Dijkstra conclude that environmental organizations prefer auctioned tradable permits, since these give both a revenue and a high certainty of realizing the objective.

Besides arguments based on the emission level or risk aversion, many of the arguments used by environmental organizations are moral or ethical.

These arguments are always directed against the use of market-based instruments.

One of these arguments is that it is wrong to use market-based instruments because the environmental problem is caused by a failure of the market (Nentjes 1988). It is furthermore said that marked-based instruments give polluters a license to pollute (Kelman 1981). After all, with tradable permits or taxes, firms can emit as long as they are willing to pay for it. Worst is the situation with grandfathered tradable permits, where the government gives polluters a right to emit for free. Environmental organizations argue that the right to environmental quality belongs to the public and not to the polluters. Furthermore, firms should reduce emissions because it is wrong to pollute, not because they can earn money (or save costs) doing so (Dijkstra 1999). Finally, environmentalists see the environment as priceless. Therefore it is morally wrong to put a price on it through marked-based instruments (Kelman 1981).

Environmental organizations may also oppose market-based instruments for strategic reasons (Keohane et al. 1997 and Dijkstra 1999). When permits are given the status of property rights, it will be very hard to reduce emissions to a lower level in the future without giving compensation to the polluters (Hahn and Noll 1990). This can be remedied by explicitly stating that the permits do not represent a property right, or by making the permits only valid for a specific period of time (Keohane et al. 1997). Taxes will also be hard to increase, since this instrument raises strong resistance from industry.

One reason for environmental organizations to support market-based instruments is that they lower overall costs of compliance. Therefore, it could be easier to reduce emissions to a lower level than with direct regulation. Furthermore, as already mentioned above, taxes and auctioned tradable permits yield a revenue. This could be used, earmarked, for environmental protection (Dijkstra 1999).

Keohane et al. (1997) make a connection between the preference of instrument by environmental organizations and the level of membership and thereby the budgetary resources of the organization. If the support for a particular instrument attracts members, increases donations or increases the visibility and prestige of the organization, it may affect its preference of instrument. Hence, if an environmental organization can distinguish itself by supporting a certain instrument, it may be profitable to do so. Keohane et al. (1997) give the example of the Environmental Defense Fund (EDF), which in contrast to other environmental organizations, supports tradable permits.

Three surveys exist in which the attitudes of environmental organizations toward environmental policy instruments are described. The first one was conducted by Kelman (1981). He finds that environmentalists are far from unanimous on the issue of charges. Of the 19 environmentalists interviewed, 32% supported charges, 16% favored experiments with taxes, while 37% were against charges.

Svendsen (1998b) finds that US environmental organizations support tradable permits. He argues that they have abandoned their philosophical objections to market-based instruments because they need success. Environmental organizations have realized that environmental improvement can only come about with the cooperation of the polluters. Since the (US) polluters prefer tradable permits, so do the environmental organizations (see also Svendsen 1999). Svendsen (1998b) finds that Danish environmental organizations support environmental taxes. However, they remain skeptical about tradable permits. Svendsen attributes this to a lack of knowledge.

In a survey of Dutch interest groups, Dijkstra (1999) finds some support for market-based instruments by environmental organizations. However, as in the survey by Kelman (1981) there is considerable disagreement among environmentalists as to which instrument is best. Furthermore, a mix of instruments is often proposed. However, there is much agreement among environmental organizations that the target of policy should be stated in absolute terms and not in relative ones. This would imply emission ceilings or tradable permits.

The above shows that environmental organizations should either prefer emission ceilings or auctioned tradable permits. Both instruments give a high certainty of realizing the abatement goal set. However, from the point of view of environmental organizations, there are some important differences between them. Tradable permits are less preferred for moral and ethical reasons. On the other hand, auctioned tradable permits give a revenue that could be used for further environmental improvements and grandfathered tradable permits may make it easier to come to an agreement with industry. In contrast to tradable permits, emissions ceilings allow control of individual polluters. The empirical evidence is as inconclusive as the theoretical literature.

The literature discussed in this section gives some indications as to why market-based instruments are not used very much in environmental policy. First of all, none of the groups mentioned has a preference for taxes. Actually, this lack of support for taxes is rather surprising. They are an important source of revenue for the government and it can be expected that politicians and bureaucrats have a large influence on how these revenues are spent. Hence, one would expect them to have a preference for this instrument. Also other interest groups could have an interest in taxes. Labor unions, for example, could argue that the revenue of environmental taxes should be used to lower distortionary taxes on labor. Environmental organizations could try to have the proceeds of environmental taxes earmarked for further environmental improvements. However, such arguments are not put forward in the literature. What is emphasized is that taxes give high uncertainty about the realization of the policy objectives. It is mainly for this reason that taxes are rejected.

Tradable permits only receive support from owners of firms and partly from environmental organizations. It must be noted though that owners support grandfathering of permits, while environmental organizations prefer auctioning of permits. The other interest groups reject tradable permits for several reasons. A prime problem is that tradable permits are a new instrument. Hence, all actors would incur learning costs when this instrument is implemented. Furthermore, tradable permits give almost no possibility for government influence on the polluter. Although this is seen as a blessing by firms, politicians and bureaucrats would prefer to have influence on the level of emissions and the abatement techniques used by individual firms. Although environmental organizations should prefer tradable permits on rational grounds, several moral and ethical objections cause them to reject this instrument. Hence, of all interest groups, only the owners of firms are warm supporters of grandfathered tradable permits. All other interest groups prefer some form of direct regulation.

6.   ASSESSMENT

The different motives for the interest groups discussed in Section 4 are not all taken into account in the public choice literature on preference for environmental policy instruments. More specifically, the motives of the interest groups are almost always equated with the motives of the owners and donors. Managers are virtually non-existent in this literature. In this section, we will assess whether taking all motives into account, including those of managers, as discussed in Section 4, will change the preferences of the interest groups and whether this will affect the outcome of the rent-seeking game. Furthermore, some other factors are discussed that may affect the choice of instrument and some suggestions for further research are given.

Politicians are not often taken into consideration when the choice of environmental policy instrument is analyzed. However, as discussed above, they will have certain preferences, which may alter the outcome of the analysis. Although they are not discussed often, all the motives mentioned in Section 4.1.1 are discussed in the literature. Hence, we can conclude that politicians will mostly support direct regulation.

Most of the motives of bureaucrats as mentioned in Section 4.1.2 are also mentioned in the public choice literature on choice of instrument. A factor that has not received much attention is that environmental bureaucrats may have a preference for the output of their bureau.

Casual evidence from the Netherlands (Volkskrant 1999) shows that environmental bureaucrats see themselves as the guardians of the environment, and not as the executors of ministerial decisions. Hence, the preferences of the environmental bureaucracy may resemble those of environmental organizations to a large degree. Whether this resemblance is a result of capture of the bureau by the environmental organizations, or of self-selection of environmental bureaucrats is not certain. As the discussion in the previous section about environmental organizations shows, this will not lead to a unanimous preference of policy instrument. However, it may be that the environmental bureaucrats share the moral and ethical objections against economic instruments. This would imply that environmental bureaucrats are mostly command expansionists, and therefore prefer direct regulation.

In the literature discussed above, the only objective of industry is to maximize profits. However, as we have seen in Section 4.2, this is the objective of the shareholders. Only a few authors mention this (e.g. Nentjes and Dijkstra 1994 and Dijkstra 1999). When doing so, however, they do not mention that there may be a conflict of interest between shareholders and management.

The question is whether the objectives of managers will change the preference for environmental policy instrument. This could be when managers have a preference for firm size, and more specifically for high levels of production. Section 4.2.2 showed that firm managers will have such preferences. As Dijkstra (1999) shows, relative standards will result in a higher level of production than all other instruments. So managers will prefer relative standards because these give the highest level of production.

It is, however, not certain that managers can lobby for their own preferences. If the influence of shareholders is large, managers will have to choose the profit-maximizing instrument, i.e. grandfathered tradable permits.

If on the other hand, shareholders have little influence, managers will be able to push for relative standards. This may explain the apparent differences between the US and Europe in preference for instrument by industry. In the US, shareholder influence on management seems to be rather large. At the same time, US industry prefers grandfathered tradable permits. In Europe on the other hand, shareholder influence is not so large. As a consequence, managers are able to lobby for their preferred instrument.

The most used assumption about the objective of labor unions is that they maximize employment. Even though as we have seen above, labor unions are more interested in maximizing employment than in maximizing wages, high wages are an important factor in labor union preferences. Only Leidy and Hoekman (1994) mention that unions may prefer instruments which maximize profit, because the union hopes to capture part of the profits as higher wages. If we assume that employment is increasing with production and wages are increasing with profits, labor unions are put in a dilemma. Relative standards cause the highest production level, and thereby the highest level of employment. On the other hand, profits are highest with grandfathered tradable permits.

As was mentioned in Section 4, the leadership of labor unions will have a preference for a large membership of their organizations. Since there is a positive relationship between employment and membership, the union leadership has an incentive to strive for maximum employment. Since most studies take employment maximization as the objective of labor unions, assuming that the leadership has an influence on the policy of the union will not change the outcome. However, it must be noted that the assumption that unions maximize employment is never based on the preferences of the union leadership.

The general assumption about environmental organizations in the public choice literature discussed above is that they are risk-averse and want to maximize environmental quality. Furthermore, they have an anti-economic instrument bias because of moral and ethical reasons. From this it is concluded that environmental organizations prefer direct regulation. The management of environmental organizations, on the other hand, prefers a large membership. One main way of achieving this is by providing environmental quality, i.e. by having success. To realize this, the management may be more willing to compromise with industry. Therefore, they may support grandfathered tradable permits.

A factor that is almost never mentioned in the literature is that governments provide a large part of the funding for non-profit organizations (Rose-Ackerman 1996). The possibility of receiving state funding may change the preferences of environmental organizations. State funding will most likely flow to environmental organizations that are willing to negotiate and compromise; those with extreme and uncompromising opinions will not easily attract state funding. There are two advantages of state funding for the management of environmental organizations. Firstly, it provides them with additional funding, which can be used to improve environmental quality, but also partly as discretionary spending by the management. Secondly, the government is less likely to hold the management accountable for the way the funds are spent than private donors are. Hence, state funds give a greater possibility for discretionary spending than private donations. For these reasons, the management of environmental organizations may be willing to compromise on some of their more extreme positions. A likely candidate is their resistance to tradable permits. Hence, we expect that the possibility of state funding will make the management of environmental organizations more willing to support tradable permits.

Taking into account the motives as discussed in Section 4 can make some difference to the analysis. The clearest alteration in preferences occurs within firms. When the motives of managers are taken to be dominant, instead of those of the owners, the preference of industry shifts from grandfathered tradable permits to relative standards. Hence, now even industry is opposed to market-based instruments. The result would be that all interest groups have a preference for some form of direct regulation, which could explain why market-based instruments are so little used.

Taking more motives into account with bureaucrats and labor unions does not alter the analysis dramatically. Environmental bureaucrats may share some of the moral objections to market-based instruments with environmental organizations. This will make them prefer direct regulation even more. In labor unions, the preference for higher wage by the members is not often taken into account. Such a preference would lead to a greater support for grandfathered tradable permits. However, the preference of the union leadership for a large membership counters this factor. In the end, labor unions are most likely to stress the effects on employment than on wages.

The urge to have success and the possibility of state funding may lead the management of environmental organizations to drop their moral objections to tradable permits. In this way, they make the opposite shift in comparison with firms.

All of the results discussed in the previous section are either derived from qualitative models or from models with perfect competition. It is curious that the choice of environmental instrument is not analyzed in a model of imperfect competition.

As Ulph (1996) shows in an oligopoly model, different instruments can have a different impact on the output of the firm. This is in contrast to perfect competition, where only relative standards give a different output level from all other instruments. Since output has an impact on price, the differences in output will result in differences in profits. Take for example the case of oligopoly. Here, the Cournot equilibrium leads to an outcome that is not optimal, neither from the point of view of the firms, nor of society. For the firms, output is too large. They will therefore prefer an instrument that reduces industry output. Ulph (1996) shows that emission ceilings will lead to the lowest output level. This will then be the preferred instrument of the owners of the firm. Now not even the owners prefer a market-based instrument. For society on the other hand, production is too low under oligopoly. Consumers will therefore prefer relative standards as they give the highest output. It is likely that politicians take this preference at least partly into account. As is clear, in a model of imperfect competition, the outcome may be different from the one in a model of perfect competition. Furthermore, as mentioned earlier, perfect competition does not give the manager much possibility of straying from the narrow path of profit maximization. Imperfect competition in the goods market does give such opportunities.

A factor that seems to be overlooked in the literature discussed in Section 5 is the costs of implementing the policy. It seems obvious that there are large differences in, for example, monitoring costs between the instruments. One would, for example, expect that it would be much cheaper to check whether a firm has implemented some technical device to reduce emissions than to continuously monitor its emission flow. So differences in monitoring costs may be an additional explanatory variable in the analysis of preference for policy instrument.

7. CONCLUSIONS

To understand why certain policy instruments are implemented and others not, insight is needed into the motivations of the agents involved. First of all, the actors that are involved in the process of policy making need to be properly defined. In all instances, managers play an important role. They steer the organization and they lobby for a certain instrument. The preferences of the owners or donors of the organization are important. But these should not be equated with the preferences of the organizations. In all organizations, the managers will have opportunities to act at least partly so as to fulfill their own objectives.

The public choice literature on environmental policy instrument choice most often does not take this aspect into account. This is most problematic in the analysis of firms. Shareholders will want the firm to maximize profits. The instrument that does this is a system of grandfathered tradable permits. The managers of the firm, however, have a preference for a large scale of production. They will therefore lobby for relative standards, which allow the largest production level. In other organizations, the preferences of managers do matter, but do not always have a decisive influence on the preference for instrument. The preference of managers for relative standards can partly explain why market-based instruments are seldom used. Not only the regulator, but also the regulated party, opposes such instruments.

Also, other aspects are sometimes forgotten. Workers will prefer both high employment and high wages. The literature on instrument choice however, almost unanimously connects labor unions with the goal of maximizing employment. Environmental organizations may compromise on their moral objections to tradable permits to receive state funding and to achieve success in supplying environmental quality.

Taking the motivations of managers into account does not in general lead to more unequivocal results. When politicians are allowed to have an ideology, the group falls apart in two sub-groups: those that want to reduce government control over firms and those that want to expand it. The same division is apparent in the environmental bureaucracy. In explaining the outcome of environmental policy, one should therefore investigate which of the two groups was dominant within both politics and the environmental bureaucracy.

This is not to say that the literature on the choice of environmental policy instrument so far has not made any contribution to explaining the dominance of direct regulation. It shows that most organizations have a preference for direct regulation, although for different reasons. Taking the points above into account could, however, lead to some more insight into the process of environmental policy setting.

Most of the literature on environmental policy instrument choice assumes that firms are competing in a perfectly competitive market. It would be interesting to analyze preferences for instruments in a model with imperfect competition, since this may very well lead to some different outcomes.

REFERENCES

Alchian, Armen A. and Demsetz, Harold (1972), 'Production, Information Costs, and Economic Organization', *American Economic Review*, **62** (5), 777–795.

Andersen, Mikael S. (1996), *Governance by Green Taxes: Making Pollution Prevention Pay*, Manchester: Manchester University Press.

Ashenfelter, O. and Pencavel, J.H. (1969), 'American Trade Union Growth, 1900–1960', *Quarterly Journal of Economics*, **83** (3), 434–448.

Bain, G. S. and Elsheikh, F. (1976), *Union Growth and the Business Cycle: An Econometric Analysis*, Oxford: Blackwell.

Baker, Samuel (1969), 'Executives' Incomes, Profits and Revenues: A Comment on Functional Specification', *Southern Economic Journal*, **35**, 379–383.

Banks, Jeffrey S (1989), 'Agency Budgets, Cost Information, and Auditing', *American Journal of Political Science*, **33**, 670–699.

Banks, Jeffrey S. and Weingast, Barry R. (1992), 'The Political Control of Bureaus under Asymmetric Information', *American Journal of Political Science*, **36**, 509–524.

Barde, Jean-Philippe (1995), 'Environmental Policy and Policy Instruments', in H. Folmer, H. L. Gabel and H. Opschoor (eds), *Principles of Environmental and Resource Economics: A Guide for Students and Decision-Makers*, Aldershot: Edward Elgar, 201–227.

Baumol, William J (1962), 'On the Theory of Expansion of the Firm', *American Economic Review*, **52** (5), 1078–1087.

Baumol, William J. (1966), *Business Behavior, Value and Growth*, (rev. edn), Harcourt, Brace & World.

Baumol, William J. and Oates, Wallace E. (1988), *The Theory of Environmental Policy*, (second edn), Cambridge: Cambridge University Press.

Becker, Gary S. (1983), 'A Theory of Competition Among Pressure Groups for Political Influence', *Quarterly Journal of Economics*, **98**, 371–400.

Bendor, Jonathan, Taylor, Serge and Gaalen, Roland van (1985), 'Bureaucratic Expertise vs. Legislative Authority: A Model of Deception and Monitoring in Budgeting', *American Political Science Review*, **79**, 1041–1060.

Bendor, Jonathan, Taylor, Serge and Gaalen, Roland van (1987), 'Politicians, Bureaucrats and Asymmetric Information', *American Journal of Political Science*, **31**, 796–828.

Bevars, D. Mabre and Siders, David L. (1967), 'An Empirical Test of the Sales Maximization Hypothesis', *Southern Economic Journal*, **33**, 367–377.

Bohm, Peter and Russell, Clifford S. (1985), 'Comparative Analysis of Alternative Policy Instruments', in A. V. Kneese and J. L. Sweeney (eds), *Handbook of Natural Resource and Energy Economics*, vol. 1, Amsterdam: Elsevier, 395–460.

Booth, Alison L. (1984), 'A Public Choice Model of Trade Union Behaviour and Membership', *Economic Journal*, **94** (376), 883–898.

Booth, Alison L. (1995), *The Economics of the Trade Union*, Cambridge: Cambridge University Press.

Booth, Alison L. and Chatterji, M. (1993), 'Reputation, Membership and Wages in an Open Shop Trade Union', *Oxford Economic Papers*, **45**, 23–41.

Brennan, Geoffrey and Buchanan, James M. (1980), *The Power to Tax: Analytical Foundations of a Fiscal Constitution*, Cambridge: Cambridge University Press.

Breton, Albert and Wintrobe, Ronald (1975), 'The Equilibrium Size of a Budget Maximizing Bureau: A Note on Niskanen's Theory of Bureaucracy', *Journal of Political Economy*, **82**, 195–207.

Buchanan, J. M. and Tullock, G. (1975), 'Polluters' Profits and Political Response: Direct Control versus Taxes', *American Economic Review*, **65**, 139–147.

Burton, John (1984), 'The Economic Analysis of the Trade Union as a Political Institution', in Jean-Jacques Rosa (ed.), *The Economics of Trade Unions: New Directions*, Dordrecht: Kluwer-Nijhoff, 123–154.

Calvert, Randell L. (1985), 'Robustness of the Multi-Dimensional Voting Model: Candidate Motivations, Uncertainty, and Convergence', *American Journal of Political Science*, **29** (1), 69–95.

Carruth, Alan A. and Oswald, Andrew J. (1985), 'Miners' Wages in Post-war Britain: An Application of a Model of Trade Union Behaviour', *Economic Journal*, **95**, 1003–1120.

Christoffersen, Henrik and Svendsen, Gert Tinggaard (2000), *Bureaucratic Tax-Seeking: The Danish Waste Tax*, Paper Presented at the Public Choice Workshop II (December 1), Aarhus University.

Clarkson, Kenneth W. and Miller, Roger LeRoy (1982), *Industrial Organization: Theory, Evidence and Public Policy*, London: McGraw-Hill.

Coase, R. (1960), 'The Problem of Social Cost', *Journal of Law and Economics*, **3**, 1–44.

Crocker, T. D. (1966), 'The Structuring of Atmospheric Pollution Control Systems', in Harold Wolozin (ed.), *The Economics of Air Pollution*, New York: W.W. Norton.

Dertouzos, James N. and Pencavel, John H. (1981), 'Wage and Employment Determination under Trade Unionism: The International Typographical Union', *Journal of Political Economy*, **89** (6), 1162–1181.

Dewees, D. N. (1983), 'Instrument Choice in Environmental Policy', *Economic Inquiry*, **21**, 53–71.

Dijkstra, Bouwe R. (1999), *The Political Economy of Environmental Policy: A Public Choice Approach to Market Instruments*, Cheltenham: Edward Elgar.

Downs, Anthony (1957), *An Economic Theory of Democracy*, New York: Harper and Row.

Downs, Anthony (1967), *Inside Bureaucracy*, Boston: Little, Brown and Company.

Dunlop, John T. (1944), *Wage Determination under Trade Unions*, New York: Macmillan.

Ebert, Udo (1998), 'Relative Standards: A Positive and Normative Analysis', *Journal of Economics*, **67**, 17–38.

Ebert, Udo (1999), 'Relative Standards as Strategic Instruments in Open Economies', in E. Petrakis, E. Sartzetakis and A. Xepapadeas (eds), *Environmental Regulation and Market Power*, Cheltenham: Edward Elgar, 210–232.

Farber, Henry S. (1978a), 'Individual Preferences and Union Wage Determination: The Case of the United Mine Workers', *Journal of Political Economy*, **86**, 923–942.

Farber, Henry S. (1978b), 'The United Mine Workers and the Demand for Coal: An Econometric Analysis of Union Behavior', *Research in Labor Economics*, **2**, 1–74.

Fiorina, Morris P. (1982a), 'Groups Concentration and the Delegation of Legislative Authority', in Roger G. Noll (ed.), *Regulatory Policy and the Social Sciences*, Berkeley: University of California Press.

Fiorina, Morris P. (1982b), 'Legislative Choice of Regulatory Forms: Legal Process or Administrative Process?', *Public Choice*, **39**, 33–66.

Frey, Bruno S. (1983), *Democratic Economic Policy*, Oxford: Martin Robertson.

Frey, Bruno S. (1992), 'Pricing and Regulating Affect Environmental Ethics', *Environmental and Resource Economics*, **2**, 399–414.

Grossman, Gene M. (1983), 'Union Wages, Temporary Layoffs, and Seniority', *American Economic Review*, **73** (3), 277–290.

Hahn, Robert W. (1987), 'Jobs and Environmental Quality: Some Implications for Instrument Choice', *Policy Sciences*, **20**, 289–306.

Hahn, Robert W. and Noll, Roger R. (1990), 'Environmental Markets in the Year 2000', *Journal of Risk and Uncertainty*, **3**, 351–367.

Hahn, Robert W. and Stavins, Robert N. (1991), 'Incentive-Based Environmental Regulation: A New Era from an Old Idea?', *Ecology Law Quarterly*, **18** (1), 1–42.

Hall, Marshall (1967), 'Sales Revenue Maximization: An Empirical Examination', *Journal of Industrial Economics*, **15** (2), 143–156.

Hanemann, W. Michael (1994), 'Valuing the Environment Through Contingent Valuation', *Journal of Economic Perspectives*, **8** (4), 19–43.

Hanley, N., Hallett, S. and Moffatt, I. (1990), 'Why Is More Notice Not Taken of Economists' Prescriptions for the Control of Pollution', *Environment and Planning A*, **22** (11), 1421–1439.

Helfand, Gloria E. (1991), 'Standards versus Standards: The Effects of Different Pollution Restrictions', *American Economic Review*, **81** (3), 622–634.

Hewitt, Julie A. and Brown, Daniel K. (2000), 'Agency Costs in Environmental Not-for-Profits', *Public Choice*, **103** (1–2), 163–183.

Hochman, Eithan and Zilberman, David (1978), 'Examination of Environmental Policies Using Production and Pollution Microparameter Distributions', *Econometrica*, **46** (4), 739–760.

Holmstrom, Bengt R. and Tirole, Jean (1989), 'The Theory of the Firm', in Richard Schmalensee and Robert D. Willig (eds), *Handbook of Industrial Organization*, Vol. 1, Amsterdam: North-Holland, 61–134.

Johnson, Ronald N. and Libecap, Gary D. (1989), 'Agency Growth, Salaries and the Protected Bureaucrat', *Economic Inquiry*, **27** (3), 431–451.

Kelman, Steven (1981), *What Price Incentives? Economists and the Environment*, Boston: Auburn House.

Keohane, Nathiel O., Revesz, Richard L. and Stavins, Robert N. (1997), 'The Positive Political Economy of Instrument Choice in Environmental Policy', in Paul Portney and Robert Schwab (eds), *Environmental Economics and Public Policy*, Cheltenham: Edward Elgar.

Koutstaal, Paul R. (1997), *Economic Policy and Climate Change: Tradable Permits for Reducing Carbon Emissions*, Cheltenham: Edward Elgar.

Krueger, Anne O. (1974), 'The Political Economy of the Rent-seeking Society', *American Economic Review*, **64** (3), 291–303.

Leidy, Michael and Hoekman, Bernard M. (1994), '"Cleaning Up" While Cleaning Up? Pollution Abatement, Interest Groups, and Contingent Trade Policies', *Public Choice*, **78**, 241–258.

Leone, Robert A. and Jackson, John E. (1981), 'The Political Economy of Federal Regulatory Activity: The Case of Water-Pollution Controls', in Gary Fromm (ed.), *Studies in Public Regulation*, Cambridge, MA: MIT Press, 231–271.

Liroff, Richard A. (1986), *Reforming Air Pollution Regulation: The Toil and Trouble of EPA's Bubble*, Washington, DC: The Conservation Foundation.

Maloney, Michael T. and McCormick, Robert E. (1982), 'A Positive Theory of Environmental Quality Regulation', *Journal of Law and Economics*, **25** (1), 99–123.

March, James G. and Simon, Herbert A. (1957), *Organizations*, New York: John Wiley and Sons.

Marris, Robin (1963), 'A Model of the "Managerial" Enterprise', *Quarterly Journal of Economics*, **77**, 185–209.

Marris, Robin (1964), *The Economic Theory of Managerial Capitalism*, Glencoe, NY: Free Press.

Marris, Robin and Mueller, Dennis C. (1980), 'The Corporation, Competition, and the Invisible Hand', *Journal of Economic Literature*, **18** (1), 32–63.

Mas-Colell, Andreu, Whinston, Michael D. and Green, Jerry R. (1995), *Microeconomic Theory*, Oxford: Oxford University Press.

Mayhew, K. and Turnbull, P. (1989), 'Models of Union Behaviour: A Critique of Recent Literature', in R. Drago and R. Perlman (eds), *Microeconomic Issues in Labour Economics: New Approaches*, London: Harvester Wheatsheaf, 105–129.

McCubbins, Mathew D., Noll, Roger G. and Weingast, Barry R. (1987), 'Administrative Procedures as Instruments of Political Control', *Journal of Law, Economics and Organization*, **3** (2), 243–277.

McGuire, Joseph W., Chiu, John S. and Elbing, Alvar O. (1962), 'Executives' Incomes, Sales, and Profits', *American Economic Review*, **52** (4), 753–761.

Migué, J.-L. and Bélanger, G. (1974), 'Towards a General Theory of Managerial Discretion', *Public Choice*, **17**, 27–47.

Miller, Gary J. and Moe, Terry M. (1983), 'Bureaucrats, Legislators, and the Size of Government', *American Political Science Review*, **77** (2), 297–322.

Misiolek, Walter S. and Elder, Harold W. (1989), 'Exclusionary Manipulation of Markets of Pollution Rights', *Journal of Environmental Economics and Management*, **16**, 156–166.

Montgomery, W. David (1972), 'Markets in Licenses and Efficient Pollution Control Programs', *Journal of Economic Theory*, **5**, 395–418.

Mueller, Dennis (1972), 'A Life Cycle Theory of the Firm', *Journal of Industrial Economics*, **20** (3), 199–219.

Nentjes, Andries (1988), 'Marktconform Milieubeleid', *Economisch Statistische Berichten*, **27** (4), 401–405.

Nentjes, Andries and Dijkstra, Bouwe R. (1994), 'The Political Economy of Instrument Choice in Environmental Policy', in M. Faure, J. Vervaele and A. Weale, (eds), *Environmental Standards in the European Union in an Interdisciplinary Framework*, Antwerp: Maklu, 197–216.

Niskanen, William A. (1971), *Bureaucracy and Representative Government*, Chicago: Aldine-Atherton.

Niskanen, William A. (1975), 'Bureaucrats and Politicians', *Journal of Law and Economics*, **18**, 614–617.

Niskanen, William A. (1991), 'A Reflection on Bureaucracy and Representative Government', in A. Blais and S. Dion (eds), *The Budget-Maximizing Bureaucrat: Appraisals and Evidence*, Pittsburgh: University of Pittsburgh Press.

OECD (1994), *Managing the Environment: The Role of Economic Instruments*, Paris: OECD.

Olson, Mancur (1965), *The Logic of Collective Action*, Cambridge: Cambridge University Press.

Oster, Sharon (1982), 'The Strategic Use of Regulatory Investment by Industry Sub-Groups', *Economic Inquiry*, **20**, 604–618.

Oswald, A. J. (1982), 'The Microeconomic Theory of the Trade Union', *Economic Journal*, **92** (367), 576–595.

Peltzman, Sam (1976), 'Toward a More General Theory of Regulation', *Journal of Law and Economics*, **19**, 211–240.

Pemberton, James (1988), 'A "Managerial" Model of the Trade Union', *Economic Journal*, **98** (392), 755–771.

Pencavel, John H. (1984), 'The Tradeoff between Wages and Employment in Trade Union Objectives', *Quarterly Journal of Economics*, **99** (2), 215–231.

Pencavel, John H. (1991), *Labor Markets under Trade Unionism: Employment, Wages and Hours*, Cambridge, Mass.: Blackwell.

Persson, Torsten and Tabellini, Guido (2000), *Political Economics: Explaining Economic Policy*, Cambridge, MA: MIT Press.

Pigou, Arthur Cecil (1920), *The Economics of Welfare*, London: Macmillan.

Rees, J. (1988), 'Pollution Control Objectives and the Regulatory Framework', in R. Kerry Turner (ed.), *Sustainable Environmental Management: Principles and Practice*, London: Belhaven, 170–189.

Romer, Thomas and Rosenthal, Howard (1978), 'Political Resource Allocation, Controlled Agendas and the Status Quo', *Public Choice*, **33** (4), 27–43.

Rose-Ackerman, Susan (1996), 'Altruism, Nonprofits, and Economic Theory', *Journal of Economic Literature*, **34** (2), 701–728.

Ross, Arthur M. (1948), *Trade Union Wage Policy*, Berkeley: University of California Press.

Russell, Clifford S. and Powell, Philip T. (1999), 'Practical Considerations and Comparison of Instruments of Environmental Policy', in Jeroen C. J. M. van den Bergh (ed.), *Handbook of Environmental and Resource Economics*, Cheltenham: Edward Elgar, 307–328.

Sapsford, David and Tzannatos, Zafiris (1993), *The Economics of the Labour Market*, London: Macmillan.

Savornin Lohman, L. de (1994), 'Economic Incentives in Environmental Policy: Why Are They White Ravens?', in Johannes B. Opschoor and R. Kerry Turner, (eds), *Economic Incentives and Environmental Policies: Principles and Practice*, Dordrecht: Kluwer Academic Publishers, 55–68.

Sidgwick, Henry (1883), *Principles of Political Economy*, London: Macmillan.

Simon, Herbert A. (1947), *Administrative Behavior*, New York: Macmillan.

Stavins, Robert N. (2000), *Experience with Market-Based Environmental Policy Instruments*, Working Paper, Cambridge, MA: Harvard University.

Stigler, George J. (1971), 'The Theory of Economic Regulation', *The Bell Journal of Economics and Management Science*, **2** (1), 3–21.

Stigler, George J. (1972), 'Economic Performance and Political Competition', *Public Choice*, **13**, 91–106.

Svendsen, Gert Tinggaard (1998a), 'A General Model of CO2 Regulation: The Case of Denmark', *Energy Policy*, **26**, 33–44.

Svendsen, Gert Tinggaard (1998b), *Tradable Permit Systems in the United States and CO_2 Taxation in Europe*, Cheltenham: Edward Elgar.

Svendsen, Gert Tinggaard (1999), 'US Interest Groups Prefer Emission Trading: A New Perspective', *Public Choice*, **101** (1/2), 109–128.

Tietenberg, T.H. (1985), *Emissions Trading: An Exercise in Reforming Pollution Policy*, Washington, DC: Resources for the Future.

Tirole, Jean (1988), *The Theory of Industrial Organization*, Cambridge, MA: MIT Press.

Tullock, Gordon (1965), *The Politics of Bureaucracy*, Washington, DC: Public Affairs Press.

Ulph, Alistair (1996), 'Environmental Policy Instruments and Imperfectly Competitive International Trade', *Environmental and Resource Economics*, **7**, 333–355.

Verbruggen, H. (1991), 'Political Economy Aspects of Environmental Policy Instruments', in Frank J. Dietz, Frederick van der Ploeg and Jan van der Straaten (eds), *Environmental Policy and the Economy*, Amsterdam: North Holland, 141–149.

Volkskrant (1999), Ministers Hebben Heiligheid Verloren, *Volkskrant*, 11 June.

Wallart, Nicolas and Bürgenmeier, Beat (1996), 'L'acceptabilité des taxes incitatives en Suisse', *Swiss Journal of Economics and Statistics*, **132**, 3–30.

Werden, Gregory J. and Hirschey, Mark J. (1980), 'An Empirical Analysis of Managerial Incentives', *Industrial Organization Review*, **8**, 66–78.

Williamson, Oliver E. (1963), 'Managerial Discretion and Business Behavior', *American Economic Review*, **53** (5), 1032–1057.

Wilson, James Q. (1980), *The Politics of Regulation*, New York: Basic Books.

Wittman, Donald (1977), 'Candidates with Policy Preferences: A Dynamic Model', *Journal of Economic Theory*, **14**, 180–189.

Wittman, Donald (1983), 'Candidate Motivation: A Synthesis of Alternative Theories', *American Political Science Review*, **77** (1), 142–157.

Wittman, Donald (1989), 'Why Democracies Produce Efficient Results', *Journal of Political Economy*, **97** (6), 1395–1424.

Wittman, Donald (1995), *The Myth of Democratic Failure: Why Political Institutions Are Efficient*, Chicago: University of Chicago Press.

6. Interest group preference for an international emissions trading scheme

Jan-Tjeerd Boom

1. INTRODUCTION

The Kyoto Protocol of 1996 allows emissions trading between the countries that have committed to an emission ceiling (the Annex B countries). However, it does not specify how international emissions trading should be conducted. Basically, there are three possible schemes of international emissions trading: government trading, permit trading and credit trading.

The description of emissions trading in the Kyoto Protocol clearly refers to trade between governments, although private trading has not been dismissed. In the case of government trading, trading can be seen as a bilateral renegotiation of the abatement commitments of the trading countries. After the trade is concluded, the countries involved will have to change their domestic policies to comply with their new commitment.

Permit trading and credit trading are both private trading schemes. This means that under both schemes, individual emission sources will be able to trade directly with each other. Permit trading means that emissions sources are regulated through a system of tradable permits at the national level. International permit trading can then be conducted by linking the national trading schemes. With credit trading, the sources are regulated through some other instrument, most likely a relative standard, and are allowed to trade credits which are obtained through abatement projects.

Several studies have analyzed the advantages and disadvantages of the three international emissions trading systems. Bohm (1999) gives an analysis of a government trading system and concludes that it can, under certain conditions, be quite efficient. Hahn and Stavins (1999) analyze which domestic environmental policy instruments are compatible with the different flexibility instruments under the Kyoto Protocol. They describe international emissions trading as permit trading. Their conclusion is that international emissions trade between private entities is only viable when the trading firms are regulated through a national tradable permit system. Ellerman (1998) and Zhang and Nentjes (1999) arrive at the same conclusion. UNCTAD (1998) mentions both permit and government trading, but does not give an analysis of the two schemes, although it does give an analysis of previous experience with national tradable permit and credit schemes. Boom and Nentjes (2000) give an analysis of government trading and permit trading. They conclude that the choice between private trading and government trading is largely a choice between full efficiency but limited political control of the system, and limited efficiency but full political discretion over the amount of trade and whom to trade with. Finally, Boom (2001) gives an analysis of credit trading. He finds that this is less efficient than permit trading, but is more compatible with different domestic instruments than permit trading is. Furthermore, credit trading makes the trade in hot air impossible and will therefore lead to a lower emission level than permit trading.

Often, interest groups have considerable influence on the implementation of policy. In many countries, governments negotiate with industry both the level of abatement and the instrument to be used. Other interest groups, such as environmental organizations, also exert influence on these decisions through rent seeking. Also, groups within the legislature, such as bureaucrats and politicians, may have their own preferences.

The international emissions trading schemes mentioned above have different characteristics; they have a different impact on factors such as profits, environmental effectiveness, compatibility with domestic instruments etc. It is therefore likely that different interest groups will have different preferences, and will be willing to sacrifice resources to ensure that their most preferred instrument is implemented.

In this chapter, we give both a theoretical analysis and empirical evidence of the preferences of interest groups for an international emissions trading scheme. The same analysis is also given for the preferences for national instrument. The reason for including the latter analysis is that the choice of international emissions trading scheme is dependent on the choice of national instrument. As mentioned above, international permit trading can only take place when the country has already implemented a national scheme of tradable permits. Hence, if an interest group prefers an instrument other than tradable permits at the national level, it cannot logically lobby for permit trading at the international level.

Another important factor in the preference for an international emissions trading scheme is the existence of 'hot air'. Under the Kyoto Protocol, some countries have received a higher emission ceiling than their real emissions. This means that these countries can sell emission quotas without having to reduce emissions. It also implies that if it can be made impossible to trade hot air, aggregate emissions will be lower. Since the different trading schemes have different effects on hot air trading, the choice of trading scheme will also be affected by the preference for emission level.

We analyze the preferences of industry, labor unions, environmental organizations, the environmental bureaucracy and politicians in the theoretical part of the chapter. However, in the empirical part, we only discuss industry and environmental organizations. The reason for this is that these two groups will be most active in rent seeking and will be most visible. Environmental bureaucrats will also be very influential, but have no interest groups that lobby for them. Hence, it will be hard to find information on their preferences.

Since there are no surveys available on the preference of interest groups for an international trading regime, we chose to gather information on the Internet. Because interest groups are also interested in the support of the general public, we expected that they would provide information on their opinions on this medium. In general this was right, although environmental organizations use the Internet more as a platform for distributing information than industry does.

Gathering information in this way may cause some problems. The organizations that present themselves on the Internet may only be a selection of the total number of organizations involved. Although this may be true, it is also an advantage. Only organizations that have formed an opinion and want to influence policy makers and public opinion are present on the Internet. Other groups may be affected, but as long as they do not form an opinion themselves, they will not affect the decision making process and are therefore irrelevant to this study. Another problem that can arise is strategic behavior. It is not certain that interest groups always give their real opinion on some issues for various reasons. This problem is a real one, but is not confined to our method of gathering information. Such behavior can only be detected with certainty by leading members of the organizations. In the analysis below, we mention when organizations may have strategic reasons for not displaying their true preferences or motivations.

The remainder of this chapter is organized as follows: In the next section we discuss the three schemes of international emissions trading. Their weaknesses and strengths will be analyzed briefly to give an impression of the characteristics of the schemes. In Section 3 we make a start with the analysis of the political acceptability of the three schemes. The theoretical analysis of interest group preferences is given in Section 4 and the empirical evidence is discussed in Section 5. Finally, in Section 6 we give some conclusions and policy recommendations.

2.   THREE SYSTEMS OF TRADING

In this section, we give a short overview of the three possible international trading regimes: trade between governments, permit trade between private entities (here called firms) and credit trading between firms. For a more extensive and in-depth review, the reader is referred to Boom and Nentjes (2000) and Boom (2001).

The most likely scheme of government trade to arise is bilateral trade in big quantities, with most trade taking place in the early stage when national policies are designed and just before or during the commitment period 2008–2012. Government trade will be bilateral because this is the easiest way to do business for states and saves transaction costs. In the design phase, governments will want to trade to improve efficiency. In the later stages of the commitment period, governments may discover that they are going to either overcomply or undercomply, which gives an opportunity for trade. For the reasons mentioned above, and because of the limited number of potential traders (the 38 Annex B countries), we expect trade to be infrequent. Because there will only be a restricted number of trades, clustered at the beginning and the end of the period 2000–2012, there will not be a well-performing market with regular price signals.

In a system of permit trading, emission sources will be able to trade emission permits directly with each other. When governments allow international permit trade, they should also set up national permit trade (see Boom and Nentjes 2000, Ellerman 1998, Hahn and Stavins 1999 and Zhang and Nentjes 1999). Hence, a system of international permit emission trade will consist of internationally linked national emissions trading schemes.

Emission sources will also be able to trade directly with each other in a system of credit trading. In this respect, credit trading resembles permit trading. However, with credit trading, a firm cannot sell emission credits until an official agency has approved of the abatement project started by the firm. It is likely that credits will be traded on a fully developed market, just as permits would be.

Table 6.1   A comparison of three schemes of trading

	Government trade	Permit trade	Credit trade
Cost efficiency	+	++	+
Complexity	+	-	-
Preparation time	+	-	-
Political control	+	-	+/-
Political acceptability	+	-	+
Compatibility with other instruments	+	-	+
Information requirements	-	+	+/-
Transaction costs	-	+	+
Flexibility	-	+	+/-
Market Power	-	+	+
Strategic behavior	-	+	+
Monitoring	-	+	+
Enforcement	-	+	+
Compliance	-	+	+
Environmental effectiveness	-	+	?

Notes: – = negative factor
              + = positive factor

Sources: Boom and Nentjes (2000) and Boom (2001).

In the remainder of this section, we will give a comparison of the strengths and weaknesses of the three trading schemes. To make it easier to compare the three systems of permit trade, the different aspects are listed in Table 6.1. Here, a minus means that it is a negative factor for the trading system under which it is listed, while a plus indicates a positive factor. Hence, market power and strategic behavior will be present in a government trading system and pose a problem there, while the reverse is true for a permit trading system.

All systems will improve efficiency when compared to a situation without emissions trading. However, permit trading and credit trading will be more efficient than government trading. The reason for this is that trade will occur regularly in a permit and credit trading scheme, while government trade will be infrequent. Furthermore, in a government trading scheme, there are strategic incentives to misrepresent the costs of abatement during the negotiations with the trading partner, and because of the limited number of traders, certain countries can exert market power. These effects are absent in a permit trading system and in a credit trading system. Below, we argue that there are higher costs connected with credit trading than with permit trading, making the latter more efficient than the former.

Information requirements are expected to be higher in the government and credit trading schemes than in the permit trading scheme. With permit trading, firms only need to know their own marginal abatement costs and the price of permits to decide whether to buy or sell permits. With government trade, governments need to gather a large amount of data to infer the domestic marginal abatement cost, while information about foreign abatement cost is imperfect. The informational requirements of a credit trading system are unevenly distributed among the traders. A buyer of emission credits only has to know its own marginal abatement costs and compare this to the market price of credits. A potential seller must not only know its marginal abatement costs, but must also determine a baseline and report all this to the evaluating agency. The determination of the baseline can be troublesome, especially when instruments are used that do not set a cap on emissions per firm.

One advantage of the government trading scheme over the permit trading scheme is that it has a low complexity. That is, the principle of government trade is easy to understand and explain. A permit and a credit trading scheme, on the other hand, might be hard to understand, especially when derivatives such as options are developed. Furthermore, permit and credit trading may give rise to speculation in emission permits, which will be hard to accept for environmental organizations. On top of this, with the credit trading system, a baseline has to be determined and the abatement project has to be evaluated.

Government trading is also highly compatible with all domestic instruments, while permit trading is only compatible with a system of domestically tradable permits. Credit trading takes an intermediate position, as the baseline for abatement projects is easier to determine with emission ceilings and tradable permits, than with flexible instruments such as taxes and emission standards per unit of product.

Government trade can take place even before national instruments are implemented. In this way, the results from the trade can be taken into account in the setting of national policy. With credit trading and permit trading, the national policy has to be implemented before firms can trade. Hence, only a short preparation time is needed before government trading can take place, while the preparation time for permit and credit trading is longer. Once the national instruments are implemented, permit trading is quickest to execute, while credit trading may take some time, and government trading will be rather slow because of the negotiation process and the translation into national policy. One has to keep in mind that in all three trading schemes, national instruments have to be implemented, not just under a government trading system. Planning and implementation of such national instruments also takes time. Therefore, we should not exaggerate the differences in complexity and preparation time between the three schemes.

The same is true for transaction costs. Although the transaction costs per trade will be higher for government trade, the size of the trade will ensure that transaction costs per emission quota will be quite low.

Monitoring costs might be high with national tradable permits because of the number of sources involved. However, Duijse et al. (1998) and Boom and Nentjes (2000) show that they do not have to be much higher. Credit trading, however, will cause higher monitoring costs. The main reason for this is that it is based on projects that need to be monitored closely. At the international level, the costs of monitoring and enforcement are the same for all systems.

The main advantage of the credit trading scheme is that it excludes trading in hot air. Credit trading is based on abatement projects that reduce emissions below a certain baseline. The baseline consists of the emissions a firm will emit over the relevant period. Hence, hot air is not included in the baseline, and, therefore, the firm cannot sell it under credit trading. Other schemes can also be adjusted to exclude trading in hot air. Zhang and Nentjes (1999) and Boom and Nentjes (2000) state that countries that want to join a permit trading scheme will have to fulfill certain conditions of good enforcement policy. The conditions may keep countries with hot air out of the permit trading scheme. Even though credit trading blocks trade in hot air, it may give rise to another problem, thus weakening environmental effectiveness. When the pollution rights of an emission source are given in some relation to production, i.e. standards per unit of product, a firm may expand its production beyond the normal level to obtain additional emission quotas. These add to the stock of quotas available, reducing the abatement level. Governments will presumably react by setting tighter standards, but this will take time (Boom 2001).

The conclusion of this short summary of the advantages and disadvantages of the three trading schemes is that permit trade offers full efficiency without much possibility of government interference in the permit trading scheme, while government trading gives limited efficiency but enables government influence on trading. Credit trading does not provide full efficiency, either. However, it is compatible with all national instruments and blocks trade in hot air.

3.   POLITICAL ACCEPTABILITY

The previous section makes clear that the three possible international emissions trading schemes have widely different characteristics. In the following sections, we try to shed some light on the political acceptability of these schemes. We do this by analyzing the preferences of interest groups with respect to the three schemes, both theoretically and empirically.

The interest groups discussed are politicians, environmental bureaucrats, industry, labor unions and environmental organizations. With industry we mean the leadership of the firm. As is clear from the previous chapter, industry can be divided into two groups: shareholders and managers. We would like to argue that firm leadership is in the hands of the management. It is they who make decisions, and they also contribute to the industrial interest organizations. Shareholders are important, but more as a constraint on managers' behavior. Depending on the relative power of the two groups, the firm behavior can resemble the preferences of either of these groups.

Two problems arise when analyzing interest group preferences for an international emissions trading scheme. First of all, there is an interdependence between the choice of national instrument and the choice of international trading scheme. International permit trading is, in essence, an international linkage of national tradable permit schemes. Hence tradable permit schemes are a prerequisite for international permit trading. The consequence of this is that if an interest group prefers an instrument other than tradable permits at the national level, it cannot logically choose permit trading at the international level. This also makes it necessary to determine the preferences of interest groups for a national instrument before we can discuss their preferences for an international emissions trading scheme.

A second problem is the existence of 'hot air'. By 'hot air' we mean that some countries have received a higher emission ceiling in the Kyoto Protocol than their real emissions will be. These countries can therefore sell emission quotas without reducing emissions. Although this in itself is seen as a problem by some, it also expands the discussion on the choice of international trading scheme. If one can stop the trade in hot air, total emissions will be lower than with hot air trading. Since the three trading schemes give different opportunities to limit the trade in hot air, the preference of trading scheme now becomes dependent on the preference for emission level.

4.   INTEREST GROUP PREFERENCES: THEORY

4.1 National Instruments

The literature on interest group preferences for environmental policy instruments has been surveyed extensively in the previous chapter. The analysis given here is based on the results of that survey.

Industry
We assume that the managers of the firm have a preference for a large production level. However, they are also bound by the demands of the shareholders for maximum profits. The result is that managers will maximize output subject to the realization of a certain level of profits (Baumol 1966).

As we have seen in the previous chapter, taxes and auctioned tradable permits will give lowest profits to industry because they imply that firms also have to pay for residual emissions. Grandfathered tradable permits will give the highest profit because they create a rent for the recipients. Also, emission ceilings and relative standards can create a rent when new plants have to fulfill stricter standards. With regard to production level, Dijkstra (1999) shows that in a perfect competition model, only relative standards give a different, and higher, output level than the other instruments.

So we are left with two candidates: grandfathered tradable permits and relative standards. Grandfathered permits exhibit the highest profit, while relative standards offer less profit and a higher production level. The final outcome will depend on the relative power of shareholders and managers. Here, we assume that managers are the most influential. Hence, we conclude that industry prefers relative standards.

Labor unions

Workers prefer high income and a high level of employment. However, the managers of labor unions prefer a large membership. It is generally asserted that labor union membership is high when employment is high; hence, managers may want to maximize employment, even at the expense of income for the members.

It is not immediately clear which instrument will maximize employment and which will maximize income, and whether there is an instrument that does both. Dewees (1983), Nentjes and Dijkstra (1994) and Dijkstra (1999) assume that a fixed proportion of operating costs goes to labor. From this they conclude that employment will be highest with relative standards. It is also likely that employment is a function of production. This also leads to the conclusion that relative standards give highest employment. Concerning the level of income, one could assume that labor unions will be able to capture part of the profits for higher wages (Leidy and Hoekman 1994). Since grandfathered tradable permits lead to the highest profits, labor unions should be able to press for higher wages under this instrument than they could under all other instruments.

So, labor unions have to choose between relative standards, which bring about high employment, and grandfathered tradable permits, which offer high income. As mentioned above, managers will have a preference for high employment. This leads us to the conclusion that labor unions prefer relative standards.

Environmental organizations

Environmental organizations want to increase environmental quality and will be risk-averse. Furthermore, the organization, and especially the management, will want a large membership. One way of achieving this is by successfully reducing emissions. In addition to these motives, environmental organizations may have moral objections to market-based instruments.

It is unlikely that environmental organizations will support taxes and relative standards. Both instruments give high uncertainty about the total level of emissions. For the same reason, environmental organizations will be against the setting of relative standards. Instruments that do give certainty about the level of emissions are emission ceilings and tradable permits.

There are now two arguments that lead to different conclusions. On the one hand, the moral objections to market-based instruments will lead environmental organizations to choose emission ceilings. This instrument has the further advantage, at least for environmental organizations, that it gives greater control of the emission level of individual firms. On the other hand, tradable permits present lower costs to industry. They may therefore be induced to abate more under this instrument. The choice between auctioned and grandfathered tradable permits also puts environmental organizations in a dilemma. Auctioned permits raise a revenue that could be used to improve the environment. However, industry will strongly resist this instrument. Grandfathered tradable permits, therefore, have a higher chance of success.

In the end, the result is that environmental organizations will either prefer emission ceilings or grandfathered tradable permits. The more willing the organization is to compromise in order to show to its donors that it achieves emission reductions, the more it will support grandfathered tradable permits.

Environmental bureaucrats
Bureaucrats have several motives. They are risk-averse, and prefer a large bureau. Furthermore, there is bureaucratic inertia, i.e. resistance to new methods, because of the learning costs associated with them. However, as with politicians, two groups of environmental bureaucrats can be found: command minimalists and command expansionists. The command minimalists prefer instruments that leave industry as free as possible in its choice of emission level and method of reducing emissions. The command expansionists, on the other hand, prefer instruments that give them as much control over firms' emissions as possible. Many environmental bureaucrats have motives that coincide with those of environmental organizations, i.e. they see themselves as the guardians of the environment and consequently have a preference for the output of their bureau. Finally, bureaucrats try to minimize resistance to their decisions. Therefore, they will take the costs of abatement of industry into account.

This large array of motives makes it difficult to point to a single instrument as the one preferred by environmental bureaucrats. In general, taxes are not preferred because they give high uncertainty of realizing the abatement goal and high costs to industry, even though they provide revenue. Relative standards also have a high uncertainty, but when these are used, the policy goal is usually set in relative goals too. Tradable permits have a high certainty of realizing the overall goal, as is the case with emission ceilings. The latter instrument has the further advantage that it gives control over the emissions of individual firms.

To increase the size of the office, bureaucrats should support an instrument that demands much bureaucratic labor input. The least labor will be needed with auctioned tradable permits. Here only the total level has to be set and an auction has to be organized. With emission ceilings and grandfathered tradable permits, the initial distribution of the permits has to be taken care of. With tradable permits, the changes in permit holdings per firm as a result of trading have to be administered too. Taxes and relative standards must be designed in such a way that the total abatement goal will be met. When, after some time, it is clear that the goals will not be met, these instruments have to be adjusted. Both with taxes and relative standards, detailed information is needed to set them at the appropriate levels. Taxes also have to be collected, which entails further labor inputs. Finally, with technical standards, information must be gathered on which techniques can be applied for all relevant production processes. At the same time, the standards have to be set so that the overall goal is met. We assess that most labor input is required with technical standards, followed by taxes and grandfathered tradable permits.

The learning costs connected with switching to a new instrument induce bureaucrats to prefer, perhaps amended versions of, well-known instruments. Since environmental policy has so far made extensive use of direct regulation, the environmental bureaucracy will not be eager to switch to market-based instruments, and especially tradable permits. However, as mentioned above, command minimalists may prefer economic instruments.

To reduce flack, the environmental bureaucracy has to take the preferences of industry into account. Above, we showed that costs of compliance are lowest with instruments of direct regulation and highest with auctioned tradable permits and taxes. Grandfathered tradable permits take a special position. Here, the permits represent an opportunity cost. However, because the permits are given free to industry, they also give a rent.

To conclude, taxes will not be favored by the bureaucracy because they produce a large degree of uncertainty. Technical standards and grandfathered tradable permits are therefore the main candidates. Both demand a large amount of bureaucratic labor input, and both give low costs (or high profits) to industry. Technical standards have the advantage that the bureaucracy is familiar with them. Hence, a large part of the environmental bureaucracy will prefer technical standards. However, command minimalists may prefer grandfathered tradable permits.

Politicians
In this analysis we will assume that politicians derive utility both from being re-elected and from certain policy outcomes. This means that politicians strive to maximize support, but that they also have a certain ideology. Furthermore, we assume that politicians are risk-averse.

Politicians are unlikely to favor taxes. Although taxes raise revenue, they provide no certainty about the emission level realized. Furthermore, the introduction of a tax will raise sharp opposition from industry. Instruments that do have a high level of certainty of realizing the overall goal are emission ceilings and tradable permits. Relative standards will also qualify here, as long as the government sets a relative goal, which is not uncommon.

Of these instruments, emission ceilings and relative standards give government a large degree of control over emissions per firm. Tradable permits, on the other hand, leave individual firms free to decide the level of emissions. Therefore, command expansionists will prefer emission ceilings, while command minimalists will prefer tradable permits.

We find that at the national level, interest groups are divided on the choice of instrument for environmental policy, although certain tendencies are clear. No interest group prefers taxes. Only politicians and bureaucrats may have a direct incentive to choose taxes because they gain directly from the revenues. Other interest groups may also gain from taxes if they are strong enough at rent seeking to appropriate a part of the revenue. However, taxes give too much uncertainty about the realized level of emissions and raise too much resistance from industry to be seen as a realistic option.

There is quite a degree of support for grandfathered tradable permits. For shareholders, it is the first choice. Environmental organizations, parts of the environmental bureaucracy and politicians may prefer it too. Whether these three groups as a whole prefer tradable permits depends on several factors. For environmental organizations, the main obstacles to preferring tradable permits are moral and ethical. Within the group of politicians and bureaucrats, only the command minimalists prefer grandfathered tradable permits. Here, the overall preference depends on their relative power versus the power of the other part of the environmental bureaucracy. The main advantages of grandfathered tradable permits are that they give a high certainty of realizing the policy objective but leave firms free in both level of emissions and in choice of abatement technique. Furthermore, they provide industry with a rent for free.

Relative standards also command some support. Managers in industry and labor unions prefer them. Reasons for preferring relative standards are that they result in a large output, give high employment and are a familiar instrument. Furthermore, as long as the policy objective is stated in relative term, they also give a high certainty of realizing these objectives.

Emission ceilings are supported by environmental organizations and politicians. They give a high certainty of realizing the objective and give a high level over control over the emissions of individual firms.

4.2 International Instruments

In this section, we will give an analysis of the preferences of interest groups for an international emissions trading scheme. The three possible schemes are permit trading, credit trading and government trading. Furthermore, we will discuss the position of the interest groups with respect to a cap on trading.

Industry
Above, we concluded that industry prefers relative standards. With relative standards, it cannot choose international permit trading, because this instrument is always based on a national system of tradable permits. Hence, if industry wants some form of private trading, it must choose credit trading.

Of the two private international trading schemes, permit trading will give lower costs to industry than credit trading. The reason for this is that credit trading is based on projects. As mentioned in Section 2, project-based emissions trading leads to higher transaction costs than permit trading. Hence, when both options are open to industry, it will prefer permit trading. However, when neither option is available, as is the case when industry wants relative standards at the national level, industry will still want to use credit trading, because it improves efficiency and hence leads to lower costs of compliance.

Although private emissions trading is more efficient than government trading, industry may prefer the latter. As Boom and Nentjes (1999) mention, government trading is most likely to occur in two periods. The first trading period will be in the phase where governments set their policies. This trade then alters the national commitment, hence the gains to be realized from rent seeking. When the government sells quotas, industry will try to avoid bearing the brunt of the additional abatement burden, and instead shift it to consumers. At the same time, it will try to capture a disproportionately large share of the proceeds of the government trade. Since industry is much better organized than consumers, it will be likely to succeed in this strategy. If the government buys quotas abroad, industry will push for a free initial distribution of the additional permits to industry. Since these are distributed together with the initial permits, this may be quite easy.

The second trading phase will be just before or in the commitment period, when governments discover that they will under- or over-comply. This again provides an ample opportunity for rent seeking for industry. At this stage, policy has been set, and changing it will meet resistance. Moreover, at this stage, there is not enough time to change policy. Hence, if industry does not realize the goals set for it, the government will have to buy quotas abroad and distribute them to industry. It is very likely that this distribution will also be free. If there is over-compliance, industry will point to its achievements and its costs of abatement and demand that a large part of the proceeds of the trade be given to industry.

Hence, government trading will lead to a redistribution from non-organized groups, such as consumers, to industry, which is very well organized. However, it is not certain that the proceeds of rent seeking by industry will be larger than the efficiency gains from private trading. Therefore, industry may prefer a combination of private trading and government trading. This would give it the opportunity of capturing more rents in the initial stage. However, this will reduce rent-seeking possibilities in the later phase. The efficiency gains may well, however, be larger than the rent captured in the later phase.

Another major reason for supporting government trading is that it makes trade in hot air possible. Credit trading excludes hot air trading. To be able to buy hot air anyway, industry will support government trading.

On the issue of restricting international emissions trading by putting a quantitative cap on the amount that can be traded, we can be brief. Such a cap on trading will increase overall costs and is therefore not in the interest of industry.

Hence, industry will prefer a combination of government trading and credit trading. Industry prefers private trading because it is most efficient. However, because of its preference for relative standards at the national level, it can only choose credit trading. Government trading gives industry ample opportunities for rent seeking and allows for hot air trading.

Labor unions

Above, we concluded that labor unions prefer relative standards. Hence, they cannot choose permit trading at the national level. The question, then, is whether they prefer credit trading or government trading, or a combination of these two.

Labor unions may even have a reason to prefer no international emissions trading. If the industry has low abatement costs, international emissions trading may mean a loss of jobs. When a firm wants to reduce emissions, it is likely that it will do so, at least in part, by reducing output. This means that it will need less inputs, of which labor is one ingredient. Hence, in a low cost country, labor unions may reject international emissions trading on the ground that it will lead to higher unemployment. On the other hand, emissions trading will lead to higher profits for industry. This will give labor unions a greater opportunity to press for high wages for their members.

Hence, labor unions, not only in high cost countries, but possibly also in low cost ones, will support emissions trading. More specifically, they will want costs for industry to be as low as possible. Therefore, they will prefer a combination of credit trading and government trading. The reason for this is that credit trading excludes the possibility of hot air trading, but is possible with government trading. For the same reason, labor unions will reject a cap on trading; after all, such a cap will increase the cost of compliance for industry.

Environmental organizations

The main objective of environmental organizations is to reduce pollution. Besides that, they are risk-averse. The latter motive may lead environmental organizations to prefer credit trading, which is based on abatement projects and may therefore lead to more certain abatement than permit trading.

Also, the objective of reducing pollution points to credit trading as the preferred instrument of environmental organizations. Some countries have received hot air under the Kyoto Protocol. This means that these countries can sell emission quotas without having to reduce emissions. Hence, if the trade in hot air could be banned, total emissions would be lower. Credit trading will do precisely this, because credits are only awarded to real emission reductions realized through abatement projects. This then makes it impossible to sell hot air.

So one would expect environmental organizations to prefer credit trading. There is, however, one pitfall with this approach. As mentioned in Section 2, private trading can be combined with government trading. In this way, hot air can be traded anyway. Environmental organizations will realize this and will try to prevent hot air trading through other measures. One such measure, though an imperfect one, is to limit the amount of quotas any country can trade. Although this will not prevent hot air trading totally, it will limit it.

In the end, environmental organizations may press for credit trading. However, since they realize that government trading can take place alongside credit trading, they will also support quantitative caps on trading.

Environmental bureaucrats

The environmental bureaucracy is split over the choice of national instrument. As we saw above, a part of the bureaucracy prefers technical standards, while another part prefers grandfathered tradable permits. We will assume here that all international emissions trading schemes are still open to the environmental bureaucracy.

The bureaucracy has several motives. Bureaucrats will be risk-averse, prefer a large bureau, resist new methods, minimize resistance to their decisions and may have a preference for the output of the bureau. Furthermore, they are split into command minimalists and command expansionists.

The certainty of realizing the environmental policy goal is not dependent on the international trading scheme, but on the national policy. However, with credit trading, over-compliance will occur at the global level. Connected with risk aversion is control over emissions. The more control the bureaucracy has, the more certain it is that the objectives will be met. Although even here the national instrument is more important in determining how much control the bureau has over individual firms, some international trading schemes may offer additional controlling power. Government and permit trading will have no additional options for control. Credit trading will give some control, especially with firms that sell credits. The bureau will monitor these firms extensively to ensure that the predicted abatement level will be realized. Command minimalists will, however, prefer instruments that decrease bureaucratic control. Hence, they will prefer government trading or permit trading.

The amount of bureaucratic labor required will differ between the schemes. Permit trading will require the least labor. Here, only the trade must be administered. With credit trading, this has to be done too, but beside that the projects have to be monitored and controlled, which requires a considerable amount of bureaucratic labor. With government trading, the bureaucracy has to determine the marginal cost of abatement of the country and it has to prepare the negotiations. Furthermore, it has to collect data on possible trading partners. After a trade, the change in the domestic abatement commitment has to be distributed over the emission sources. Although all of this requires a considerable amount of bureaucratic labor, the labor inputs per emission quota may not be that large. Government trading will be very infrequent and the traded amounts will be large.

Government trading has the major advantage that it deviates least from current policy. What government trading actually entails is a bilateral renegotiation of the abatement commitment of two countries. The choice of domestic policy instrument is not affected by this scheme. Credit trading also has some advantages in this respect, since it still allows the use of the usual policy instruments. However, credit trading also means the use of a new instrument. Permit trading is a complete break with the usual policy, hence it will meet the most resistance.

To reduce flack, the bureau will take the preferences of industry into account. As we saw above, industry prefers a combination of private trading and government trading. Hence, it is likely that the bureaucracy will allow for some form of private trading.

Environmental bureaucrats may prefer quantitative caps on trading. Such caps have to be administered, which demands a large input of bureaucratic labor. Furthermore, caps ensure that the total emission level will be lower. This is not to say that these views will be unchallenged within the bureaucracy. Caps will meet resistance from industry and command minimalists.

It is hard to determine the preference of environmental bureaucrats for an international trading scheme. The different motives do not all point in the same direction. However, it is likely that the bureaucracy will prefer credit trading to permit trading. Credit trading excludes trade in hot air, needs more bureaucratic labor, allows for greater control over individual firms, and deviates less from current policy than permit trading. There may, however, still be a fraction of the bureaucracy that prefers permit trading because of the high level of freedom for industry. Government trading has some specific advantages. It exerts control over the trading partner and will decrease the use of private emissions trading. Furthermore, it will rely heavily on bureaucratic labor. All in all, we expect that the environmental bureaucracy will prefer a combination of credit trading and government trading. It is also highly likely that the environmental bureaucracy will prefer caps on trading. Such caps give more work to the bureaucracy and lower total emissions.

Politicians

Politicians are risk-averse, and maximize support, but also have an ideology that makes them prefer certain policy outcomes. Besides these factors, it is likely that politicians will have the same preference for continuing with the instruments currently in use. They would also incur learning costs when switching to a new instrument.

The only international emissions trading scheme which puts politicians in control over the amount traded and over the trading partner is government trading. Politicians may prefer not to trade with countries that have hot air and/or countries that do not monitor and enforce their emission ceiling effectively on their emission sources. If they did this, it would result in heavy criticism from the environmental movement. Not allowing any trading at all, however, would raise criticism from industry. Politicians are also likely to be sensitive to industry's plea for flexibility and cost-effectiveness and may therefore be willing to allow for private emissions trading.

Where politicians stand on the issue of limiting trade is also hard to determine. Command minimalists will probably reject caps, but command expansionists may support them.

As a result, we find that most groups prefer a combination of credit trading and government trading. The reasons for this preference vary greatly, however. For managers in industry and labor unions, credit trading is the only possible form of private trading because they prefer relative standards at the national level. Environmental organizations prefer credit trading because it entails the lowest level of emissions. This is also one of the reasons why the environmental bureaucracy prefers credit trading. Furthermore, credit trading gives more work to the bureaucracy than permit trading.

Industry and labor unions support government trading because this allows for the trade in hot air and thereby lowers compliance costs. For industry, government trading also gives ample opportunities for rent seeking. Environmental bureaucrats will also support government trading. This instrument needs much bureaucratic labor input and diminishes the role of private trading schemes. Politicians will support government trading because it gives them control over trade.

Table 6.2   Preferences of interest groups

	National	International	Caps on trade
Industry	Relative standards	Private trading and government trading	No
Labor unions	Relative standards	Credit trading and government trading	No
Environmental organizations	Emission ceilings or gr. tradable permits	Credit trading	Yes
Bureaucrats	Technical standards or gr. tradable permits	Credit trading and government trading	Yes
Politicians	Emission ceilings or gr. tradable permits	Government and private trading	?

Note: gr. = grandfathered

Since caps on trading increase the costs of compliance, industry and labor unions will reject them. Environmental organizations and the environmental bureaucracy, on the other hand, will support them. Their reasons are that caps on trading limit the use of hot air and that they give more work to the bureaucracy. The preferences of the different groups are summarized in Table 6.2.

5.   INTEREST GROUP PREFERENCES: EMPIRICAL EVIDENCE

In this section we present empirical evidence on the preferences of interest groups for both a national instrument and an international emissions trading scheme. To gather the information, we used the Internet. Interest groups will try to influence public opinion by arguing their case in public. Therefore, we expected that interest groups would also provide information on their opinions on the Internet. In general this was true, although we were not able to find information on all groups. More precisely, we only found information on industrial and environmental organizations.

Environmental bureaucrats have no interest groups that voice their preferences publicly. Hence, we could not find information on their preferences. Labor unions do not seem to be very involved in the debate on international emissions trading and hardly any information on their preferences could be found on the Internet. Therefore, we excluded them from the empirical analysis.

5.1 Industry

5.1.1 National instrument
Most industrial organizations express a preference for voluntary agreements. This is the case for the three global organizations we found information on. Also, US industrial organizations express a preference for voluntary agreements, which is perhaps rather surprising when one considers their warm support for tradable permits in the case of SO_2 abatement (Svendsen 1998b). Noting the history of environmental policy in Canada, Japan and Europe, the support for voluntary agreements in these countries is less surprising. There is, however, also some support for market-based instruments, especially grandfathered tradable permits. Such support is found in the UK, Norway, Denmark, New Zealand, Australia, and partly in other countries.

Several reasons are given by industry for its preference for voluntary agreements. In the first place, as stated by the Edison Electricity Institute, 'the best way to address climate change should be voluntary, cost-effective and flexible' (EEI 1998). In general, industry sees voluntary agreements as cost-effective and flexible (Toyoda et al. 1997, European Chemical Industry Council 1998a). With flexibility, the industry means two things. In voluntary agreements, industry negotiates certain abatement goals with government. How these goals are met is left to the industry to determine. Hence, voluntary agreements give industry a free choice of how to reduce emissions (Meller and Hildebrand 1998). Most of the time, voluntary agreements specify a relative target. In the case of CO_2 emission reduction, the target is often to improve energy efficiency. This is, for example, the case in the agreement between industry and the government in the Netherlands, in which industry commits itself to be in the top 10 per cent efficient firms within their sector (VNO-NCW 1999). This kind of agreements allows industry to increase total emissions when production is increased, although they have to reduce emissions per unit of production. Thus, industry also wants flexibility in the total level of emissions (BRT 1997 and Electric Power Supply Association 1998).

Another reason for supporting voluntary agreements is that they give industry influence over the environmental bureaucracy and politicians. Industry is surprisingly frank on this issue. It is, for example, said that industry should participate in voluntary agreements, because doing nothing would 'diminish electric utility influence on regulators, possibly subjecting companies to government control that tell them what strategies and technologies to use' (Kinsman et al. 1996). Furthermore, voluntary agreements improve 'the dialogue between those who set environmental objectives and the economic actors' (UNIPEDE and EURELECTRIC 1999b).

Industry does not support the use of taxes to reduce greenhouse gas emissions. It should be noted here that only the European industry voices opposition to taxes. Whereas American industry has been able to avoid environmental taxes to a large extent, European industry is regulated heavily through taxes and charges (see Stavins 2000). American industry, therefore, concludes that taxes are not an option in the control of greenhouse gases, while European industry feels that these might be used. The main reason for resisting taxes seems to be that industry is of the opinion that taxes deprive industry of the funds needed to invest in abatement technology (European Chemical Industry Council 1997, 1998b and Meller and Hildenbrand 1998). It is also argued that taxes are far less effective than voluntary agreements (Meller and Hildenbrand 1998). Finally, taxes increase the already high costs of energy in Europe (VBO-FEB 1998).

Emission ceilings are rejected too. According to industry, they are 'tantamount to rationing use of fossil fuels and would thereby entail unacceptable limitations on production' (European Chemical Industry

Council 1998a). Furthermore, absolute emission caps 'could severely threaten industrial competitiveness, employment and growth' (IFIEC 1998).

The support for voluntary agreements is also shown in the large number of agreements already in existence. The Canadian Pulp and Paper Association (CPPA) and the Canadian Electricity Association (CEA) support the Voluntary Challenge and Registry (VCR) Program, a voluntary program to reduce greenhouse gas emissions (Weyerhaeuser 1996, CEA 1999). Dutch industry has likewise made an agreement with the government (VNO-NCW 1999). Voluntary agreements also exist in Australia.

Although voluntary agreements are preferred by the largest number of industrial organizations, there is also some support for (grandfathered) tradable permits. The support is concentrated in Australia, New Zealand, the UK and Scandinavia, but some organizations in other countries also support tradable permits. The main reason for preferring them is their cost-reducing potential (BRT 1999, Confederation of British Industry 1999a, 1999b and NZBR 1996, 1999). Furthermore, tradable permits will reflect the environmental costs in the energy prices (Næringslivets Hovedorganisasjon 1998, 1999) and 'such instruments make sustainable energy more competitive and will move the innovation process in an optimal direction' (Metz 1998). Finally, there is an expectation that private international emissions trading will be allowed. In that case, industry can prepare for this by setting up a national tradable permit system. This seems to be one of the reasons why the Confederation of British Industry (CBI) has designed an industry-wide scheme for emissions trading in cooperation with the British government (Confederation of British Industry 1999a, 1999b). The CBI states that 'The aim of the emissions trading project is to design a scheme for emissions trading in the UK which could then link into a future international emissions trading scheme' (Confederation of British Industry 1999a). Furthermore, it is hoped that the scheme will keep the UK in the 'vanguard of international emissions trading and in a good position to get involved in any future schemes' (Confederation of British Industry 1999b).

However, some objections to tradable permits have also been voiced. For example, the National Association of Manufacturers (NAM) thinks that tradable permits would shoulder a disproportionately large share of the abatement burden on industry. Furthermore, such a scheme would put small manufacturers at a disadvantage (NAM 1999). There is also doubt about the instrument because of the limited experience with it (Fay 1999).

Does the empirical evidence support the theoretical analysis? This concluded that industry would prefer relative standards. The empirical evidence shows that voluntary agreements are the preferred instrument of industry, at least in the case of greenhouse gases. This finding seems to contradict the theory. However, as the industrial organizations often mention themselves, the voluntary agreements almost always contain some relative target. Thereby, they are reduced to relative standards where the level of the standard is set through negotiations between industry and the government. In this way, the theory is confirmed.

Even though the empirical evidence seems to vindicate the theory in general, some findings need further explanation. First of all, the choice of tradable permits by the UK, Norway, Denmark, Australia and partly New Zealand and Sweden needs to be explained. Furthermore, it is surprising, considering their experience with tradable permits, that US industry does not prefer tradable permits, but voluntary agreements.

For some countries, it is expected that they will gain much from international emissions trading. These are the high- and low-cost countries. Norway and Sweden are high-cost countries. They rely on hydro power for a large part of their power generation. Sweden has also decided to phase out its nuclear power stations. These countries will presumably rely heavily on emissions trading to comply with their abatement commitment under the Kyoto Protocol. The UK, New Zealand and Australia on the other hand have negotiated rather high emissions ceilings. In addition, Australia and New Zealand are large energy consumers per capita and per unit of GDP. These countries should therefore have ample possibilities for reducing their emissions. Although the UK does not have the same high level of energy consumption, it received hot air under the Kyoto Protocol. Hence, Australia, New Zealand and the UK are potential sellers of emission permits. Countries that expect to trade permits may want to build experience in emissions trading as soon as possible. This will make it easier for their emission sources to join international emissions trading.

Denmark is a rather special case. The country has set itself the ambitious goal of reducing its greenhouse gas emissions by 21 per cent in the year 2010 compared to 1990. Although Denmark has rather low costs for reducing greenhouse gas emissions, it is not certain that the country can sell permits. The reason for preferring tradable permits may be explained in another way. At this moment, an intricate CO_2 tax system is in use in Denmark directed at industry (Svendsen 1998a). Since taxes are the least preferred instrument of industry, it seems that Danish industry has not been able to convince the Danish government of the usefulness of relative standards. Hence, the choice of instruments is limited to marked-based instruments. Within this class, grandfathered tradable permits are clearly preferred to taxes by industry.

Although the result is in line with the theory as described above, the lack of support for tradable permits in the US is remarkable. Svendsen (1998b) shows that American industry has a preference for grandfathered tradable permits. Furthermore, there is substantial experience with tradable permits in the US. Therefore, one would expect somewhat more support for tradable permits. However, the US has not ratified the Kyoto Protocol and may very well never do so. Industry may therefore be careful not to show too much willingness to reduce emissions, and not to give the impression that it is willing to take on a fixed ceiling.

5.1.2 International trading scheme

In the theoretical analysis, we found that industry will prefer a combination of credit trading and government trading. Furthermore, industry is against a quantitative cap on trading because this will increase the costs of compliance.

In their statements on the Internet, most industrial organizations express support for some system of private international emissions trading. Government trading is, however, hardly discussed. The reaction to a cap on trading is unequivocal; industry clearly rejects any restrictions on international emissions trading.

Industry supports international emissions trading mainly because of the reduction in compliance costs and because of the flexibility that the instrument brings. According to the Business Roundtable (BRT), international emissions trading can 'result in sharply reduced compliance costs, reducing the impact of limiting the levels of these (GHG) emissions' (BRT 1999). In Europe, too, these advantages of international emissions trading are brought forward. UNIPEDE and EURELECTRIC (1999a) argue that 'free and open trading can help to meet emission objectives by lowering compliance costs and by giving a strong signal, via the price of CO_2 permits, on the economic implications of an emission objective'.

When endorsing international emissions trading, most industrial organizations state a preference for trading between private entities. As the World Business Council for Sustainable Development (WBCSD) states, 'governments should foster *a market in which companies can participate directly* in international emissions trading and can trade credits obtained from projects' (WBCSD 1998). Hereby, the WBCSD also states a preference for credit trading because it emphasizes that trading should be based on projects.

The primary reason for preferring private emissions trading is that this will be more effective than government trading. The Pulp and Paper Manufacturers Federation of Australia (PPMFA) states that 'for international emissions trading to work as an efficient market mechanism, it is essential that there are a large number of potential buyers and sellers' (Cribb 1998). According to the International Federation of Industrial Energy Consumers (IFIEC) 'the trading system would operate at company level, as only companies can deliver the agreed efficiency improvements' (IFIEC 1998).

However, international emissions trading is not always met with enthusiasm. Some organizations are doubtful about the instrument, for example, because of the lack of experience with emissions trading at the international level. The Edison Electric Institute (EEI) states that 'until provisions governing emissions trading, joint implementation and CDM are fully fleshed out, the value of these mechanisms cannot be determined' (EEI 1998). Other criticisms have also been voiced. According to the NAM, 'International emissions trading would require U.S. companies to buy "credits" from Russia or ex-Soviet bloc economies, ..., which are really economic-growth rights, at near-monopolistic prices. This private foreign aid will be a huge additional energy tax on American business' (NAM 1999).

Only the Japanese organization Keidanren mentions government trading directly. They state that 'the idea of JI and the emissions trading scheme among governments and so on deserve consideration as approaches that provide flexibility' (Keidanren 1997), which clearly endorses government trading. In most other cases where government trading is mentioned, or even more often hinted at, it is treated as something inevitable. Many industrial organizations therefore plead for governments to allow trading between firms alongside government trading.

Industry is strongly opposed to any restrictions on international emissions trading. Several reasons are mentioned, but the most common objection is that such restrictions will increase costs of compliance for industry. This view is clearly given by the WBCSD, for example: 'Attempts to elaborate supplementarity through national ceilings on trading will increase complexity and cost. It may also erode confidence in a traded commodity relying on parties' commitment to the targets that they have negotiated' (WBCSD 1998). The European organization UNICE also expresses this view: 'it would be environmentally and economically counterproductive to seek to put arbitrary limits on the use of flexibility and trading' (UNICE 1998). Other organizations are also very clear in their rejection of caps on trading. According to the Global Climate Coalition 'We must do everything we can to minimize the damage to the economy.... For that reason, any emissions trading has to be unlimited' (GCC 1999). The EEI is very categorical in its rejection 'there must be no quantitative or qualitative caps or limits, individually or collectively, on the use of the market mechanisms' (EEI et al. 1999). Another reason for rejecting caps on trading is provided by the Swedish industrial organization Industriforbundet. It states that restrictions on trade may jeopardize the ratification of the Kyoto Protocol by certain countries, notably the US (Industriforbundet 1999).

The empirical findings are largely in accordance with the theory. Industry states a clear preference for private emissions trading, and restrictions on international emissions trading are rejected. However, there are some inconsistencies between theory and the empirical data.

First of all, we predicted that industry would prefer credit trading. The reason for this is that industry prefers relative standards at the national level. This excludes the use of permit trading at the international level because this scheme requires that countries have a system of tradable permits at the national level. When industry prefers another instrument than tradable permits at the national level, the only private trading system open for it is credit trading. Although some industrial organizations state a direct preference for credit trading, many do not discuss whether by private emissions trading they mean permit or credit trading. One reason for this could be that industry has no clear insight into the two private trading schemes and into the consequences of their choice at the national level on their options at the international level.

We also expected clear support for government trading. Such support is almost never given. There is, however, an expectancy that trade between governments will take place. It may be for this reason that industry does not bother to mention it. Other reasons for not stating a preference for government trading could be strategic. Most of the reasons for preferring government trading, such as the possibility of buying hot air, and improved possibilities for rent seeking, would not give industry a good image if they were expressed openly. Therefore, industry has every reason not to express them.

Table 6.3 Industry preferences

Organization	Location	National instrument	Int. trading scheme	Caps on trading
ICCA	Global	VA	-	-
ICCP	Global	VA/permits	Private	No
WBCSD	Global	VA/permits	Private	No
WCI	Global	VA/permits	Private	No
BRT	USA	VA/permits	Private	-
EEI	USA	VA	Credit	No
EPSA	USA		-	-
GCC	USA	VA	-	No
NAM	USA	VA	-	-
AMEC	CAN	VA/permits	-	-
CEA	CAN	VA	-	-
CPPA	CAN	VA	-	-
FEPC	J	VA	Credit	No
Keidanren	J	VA	Government	-
CEFIC	Europe	VA/credits	Credit	-
e[5]	Europe	Permits	Permits	-
ERT	Europe	VA/permits	Private	-
Eurelectric	Europe	VA	Credit	No
IFIEC	Europe	VA	Credit	No
UNICE	Europe	VA/credits	Gov./private	No
UNIPEDE	Europe	VA	Credit	No
VNO-NCW	NL	VA	Government	-
VBO-FEB	B	VA	Credit	-
BDI	D	VA	-	-
VDEW	D	VA	Credit	No
CBI	UK	Permits	Permits	-
NHO	N	Permits	Permits	-
DI	DK	Permits	Private	-
Industriforbundet	S	-	Government	No
NZBR	NZ	Permits/taxes	-	-
ESAA	AUS	Permits	-	-
PPMFA	AUS	Permits	Private	-

Notes: A dash indicates that preferences on this issue were not found.
VA = voluntary agreement

Source: Boom and Svendsen (2000)

5.2 Environmental Organizations

5.2.1 National instrument

We showed in the theoretical analysis that environmental organizations should prefer emission ceilings or grandfathered tradable permits at the national level. The main advantage of these instruments for environmental organizations is that they have a high certainty of realizing the policy objective.

Environmental organizations do not, however, give a clear preference for a national instrument in their statements on the Internet. Only the Environmental Defense Fund (EDF) states a preference for a single instrument. According to the EDF, 'Mandatory, permanent emissions caps are imperative, but they will be effective only if they are practical, enforceable, and equitable. To achieve this, EDF has suggested a system based on tradeable emissions allowances' (Environmental Defense Fund 1993).

Other organizations emphasize that more than one instrument is needed. For example, the Natural Resources Defense Council (NRDC) states that 'tax incentives must be created in order to promote mass transit and encourage industries that develop efficient technologies and renewable energy sources' and 'the US must institute mandatory limits on global warming pollution, using standards that optimize environmental performance, such as limiting the pounds of carbon emissions per unit of electricity output' (Lynch 1998). The Sierra Club Canada and the Worldwide Fund for Nature also have detailed plans containing a wide array of instruments (Comeau 1998 and WWF 1997a, 1997b, 1997c). The case for a diversity of instruments as opposed to only using tradable permits is most eloquently stated by the NRDC: 'Advocates of emissions trading think that you sit down at the piano and you play one emissions-trading key, and the sonata will play itself. We need to press keys for energy efficiency, and we need to play renewable energy keys. We need to press this series of keys to make houses, buildings, industry, and vehicles more efficient' (Lynch 1998).

Another feature of the statements by environmental organizations is their concentration on technical solutions to the problem of global warming. This discussion is in many cases far more important than their discussion of the choice of instruments.

So we find no clear preference for national instrument by environmental organizations. The most likely explanation for this is that they are geared to showing that emissions can be reduced with existing techniques. By doing this they put pressure on both the government and industry, which now have to explain why they do not take action to curb emissions. Because of their concentration on abatement techniques, they have neglected the issue of instrument choice. Whether they further their interests best in this way remains to be seen. It does show, however, that environmental organizations are more interested in reducing emissions than in how this is done.

5.2.2 International trading scheme

The theoretical analysis showed that environmental organizations should prefer credit trading at the international level. Credit trading will make trade in hot air impossible and will thereby lead to a lower emission level. However, credit trading can be combined with government trading. In this way, trade in hot air is possible anyway. To remedy this, environmental organizations will demand quantitative restrictions on international emissions trading.

As with the instrument choice at the national level, we do not find a clear preference for an international emissions trading scheme. The EDF supports the flexibility mechanisms of the Kyoto Protocol and gives a preference for permit trading, although this is not stated very strongly (Environmental Defense Fund 1993, 1998). The Sierra Club is the only environmental organization that clearly prefers credit trading (Corbett et al. 1997 and Rolfe 1998). The reason for this is that only credit trading will prevent trade in hot air. Other environmental organizations do discuss international emissions trading but give no preference for any scheme. Some organizations can even see some merit in emissions trading, but they also see 'many ways in which a global emissions trading regime could go badly wrong' (Greenpeace 1998).

Many environmental organizations view international emissions trading as a loophole that enables industrialized countries to 'avoid taking domestic action ... and continue on a path of dangerous emissions. This is not only iniquitous but it is also ecologically ineffective' (Climate Action Network 1999). The WWF had already stated before the negotiations that the Kyoto Protocol should 'not include an emissions trading system unless much stronger reduction targets than those currently proposed by industrialized countries are adopted' (WWF 1997d).

International emissions trading is even rejected in principle because 'emissions trading is unfair because it rewards large industrialized polluters without compensating poorer nations which will suffer the worst effects of climate change' (WWF 1998).

In general, environmental organizations prefer a cap on emissions trading. One reason for this is that it reduces the possibility of trade in hot air. Hence, restrictions on international emissions trading will result in lower aggregate emission levels. However, another reason also seems to be very important. According to Friends of the Earth (FOE), 'the majority of emissions reductions must be achieved through domestic, verifiable emission reductions' (FOE 1998). The reason for this is that 'it is essential to provide a clear signal to begin with redirecting investments to environmentally sustainable technology' (FOE 1998). Another reason is that 'placing a limit, or "cap", on the proportion of Parties' Kyoto targets that can be achieved abroad will promote new technologies for domestic reductions and minimize trading in hot air' (WWF 1999).

Only the EDF rejects restrictions on emissions trading (Environmental Defense Fund 1998). Several reasons are given for this. Caps on trading will increase compliance costs for industry without giving any additional benefit to the environment. Furthermore, contrary to the other environmental organizations, the EDF argues that caps will lead to less innovation. The EDF also sees caps on trading as superfluous because a large part of emission reductions will be realized domestically anyway.

Table 6.4 Preferences of environmental organizations

Organization	Location	National instrument	International trading scheme	Caps on trading
Greenpeace	Global	-	-	Yes
CAN	Global	-	-	Yes
WWF	Global	-	-	Yes
FOE	Global	-	-	Yes
EDF	USA	Permits	Permits	No
NRDC	USA	Standards	-	-
Sierra Club	USA/CAN	-	Credits	Yes

Notes: A dash indicates that preferences on this issue were not found.

Source: Boom and Svendsen (2000)

This section shows again that the main interest of environmental organizations lies in the reduction of emissions. Most organizations do not discuss the advantages and disadvantages of the different international emissions trading schemes, but only call for a cap on trading. One reason for this is to limit the trade in hot air. This would then lead to lower emission levels. Besides this reason for limiting trade, it is also argued that such a limit will spur technological innovation. Only the EDF is against limits on trading. According to them, limits lead to higher costs and to less innovation. The overall results on environmental organizations are summarized in Table 6.4.

6.   CONCLUSIONS

The most cost-efficient way of organizing international emissions trading is by implementing a permit trading scheme. Hence, from a welfare point of view, this is the optimal instrument. However, as so often, the optimal instrument is not the one that gets most support from interest groups. Therefore, it is not likely that permit trading will be implemented on a large scale.

At the national level, there is some support for tradable permits. However, many organizations prefer some form of direct regulation. This implies that if these organizations prefer some form of private international emissions trading, they can only choose credit trading. This is also what the analysis shows. Almost all organizations support credit trading. Often, they want it to be combined with government trading.

Although there is a great degree of agreement on which instrument should be implemented, the reasons for supporting the instruments are very diverse. Industry wants credit trading because it prefers private trading. However, since it prefers relative standards at the national level, its choice is limited to credit trading. To make trade in hot air possible, and to give more opportunities for rent seeking, industry would like to combine credit trading with government trading. Furthermore, caps on trading are rejected because they give higher costs of compliance. For labor unions, the same reasoning holds.

Environmental organizations, on the other hand, prefer credit trading because it excludes hot air trading. They do realize, though, that private trading can be combined with government trading, which would make hot air trading possible again. Therefore, they want to implement caps on trading.

The environmental bureaucracy supports a combination of credit and government trading. These both need a large amount of bureaucratic labor input. They also give bureaucrats a large level of control over trading. For the same reasons, the bureaucrats will prefer caps on trading.

The empirical evidence presented largely supports the theoretical analysis. It shows that industry prefers relative standards set through voluntary agreements at the national level and credit trading at the international level.

Government trading is not mentioned very often, but this may be caused by strategic considerations. Caps on trading are rejected very catagorically.

Environmental organizations show no clear preference for a national instrument or an international emissions trading scheme. They mostly concentrate on technical solutions to reduce emissions, showing that abatement is possible at reasonable cost. This indicates that environmental organizations are only interested in reducing emissions and not so much in the regulatory framework within which this should be done. Their support for a cap on trading also fits within this line of reasoning; it will reduce hot air trading and force countries to take domestic action.

Our analysis shows that most interest groups prefer a combination of credit trading and government trading. Since their influence will be large, it is likely that international emissions trading will be organized along these lines. Governments will probably trade at the beginning of the implementation phase of the Kyoto Protocol. In this way, the major differences in marginal abatement costs can be reduced. By allowing credit trading between individual emission sources after this, further improvements in efficiency are possible.

REFERENCES

Baumol, William J. (1966), *Business Behavior, Value and Growth*, (rev. edn), Harcourt, Brace & World.

Bohm, Peter (1999), *International Greenhouse Gas Emissions Trading – with Special Reference to the Kyoto Protocol*, TemaNord 1999:506, Copenhagen: Nordic Council of Ministers.

Boom, Jan Tjeerd (2001), 'International Emissions Trading under the Kyoto Protocol: Credit Trading', *Energy Policy*, **29** (8), 605–613.

Boom, Jan Tjeerd and Nentjes, Andries (2000), *Level of International Emissions Trading: Should Governments Trade, or Should Firms?*, Economic Discussion Papers 4/2000, Odense: Department of Economics, University of Southern Denmark.

Boom, Jan Tjeerd and Svendsen, Gert Tinggaard (2000), *The Political Economy of International Emissions Trading Scheme Choice: Empirical Evidence*, Discussion Paper 00-19, Institute of Economics, University of Copenhagen.

BRT (Business Roundtable) (1997), *Rush to Judgement: A Primer on Global Climate Change*, http://www.brtable.org.

BRT (Business Roundtable) (1999), *Principles for the Design of an Emissions-Credit Trading System for Greenhouse Gases: Issues and Implications for Public Policy*, White Paper, Washington, DC: BRT.

CEA (Canadian Electricity Association) (1999), *Climate Change*, http://www.canelect.ca.

Climate Action Network (1999), *COP5 CAN Position Paper*, http://www.climatenetwork.org/finalrecs.html.

Comeau, Louise (1998), *Rational Energy Plan: Update and Summary of Key Measures to the Year 2010*, http://www.sierraclub.ca.

Confederation of British Industry (1999a), *Emissions Trading Offers a Way Forward to Reduce Greenhouse Gases and Global Warming*, http://www.cbi.org.uk.

Confederation of British Industry (1999b), *UK Emissions Trading Could Start from April 2001*, http://www.cbi.org.uk.

Corbett, Lois, Hornung, Robert and Rolfe, Chris (1997), *Delegation Report, Sierra Club of Canada*, Third Meeting of the Parties to the United Nations Framework Convention on Climate Change.

Cribb, Bridson (1998), *Australia's Response to the Kyoto Protocol*, Pulp and Paper Manufacturers Federation of Australia (PPMFA), http://www.ppmfa.com.au.

Dewees, D. N. (1983), 'Instrument Choice in Environmental Policy', *Economic Inquiry*, **21**, 53–71.

Dijkstra, Bouwe R. (1999), *The Political Economy of Environmental Policy: A Public Choice Approach to Market Instruments*, Cheltenham: Edward Elgar.

Duijse, P. van, Nentjes, A., Krozer, J., Blok, K. and Brummelen, M. van (1998), *Verhandelbare CO_2-emissierechten*, Achtergrondstudies 002, The Hague: VROM-raad.

EEI (Edison Electric Institute) (1998), *Global Climate*, http://www.eei.org.

EEI, FECP and UNIPEDE (1999), *Joint Statement for COP-5*, Ref: 1999-420-0020.

Electric Power Supply Association (EPSA) (1998), *EPSA Supports Policies that Are Pro-Competitive and Pro Environmental*, http://www.epsa.org.

Ellerman, A. Denny (1998), *Obstacles to Global CO_2 Trading: A Familiar Problem*, Report 42, MIT Joint Program on the Science and Policy of Global Change.

Environmental Defense Fund (1993), *Emissions Trading: A Good Deal on Global Warming*, New York: EDF.

Environmental Defense Fund (1998), *Cooperative Mechanisms under the Kyoto Protocol: The Path Forward*, New York: EDF.

European Chemical Industry Council (1997), *The European Chemical Industry Firmly Opposes New Energy Taxes*, Position Paper, http://www.cefic.be.

European Chemical Industry Council (1998a), *Long-Term Agreements on Energy Efficiency: The Preferred Policy Response to Climate Change Concerns*, News Release, http://www.cefic.be.

European Chemical Industry Council (1998b), *Post-Kyoto Views on Climate Policies*, Position Paper, http://www.cefic.be.

Fay, Kevin J. (1999), *Statement before the House Committee on Government Reform*, National Economic Growth, Natural Resources and Regulatory Affairs Subcommittee, ICCP Press Release, http://www.iccp.

FOE (Friends of the Earth) (1998), *Emissions Trading and Joint Implementation*, http://www.foei.org.

GCC (Global Climate Coalition) (1999), *GCC Agrees with Clinton Administration*, http://www.globalclimate.org.

Greenpeace (1998), *Guide to the Kyoto Protocol*, Amsterdam: Greenpeace International.

Hahn, Robert W. and Stavins, Robert N. (1999), *What has Kyoto Wrought? The Real Architecture of International Tradable Permit Markets*, Discussion Paper 99-30, Washington, DC: Resources for the Future (RFF).

IFIEC (International Federation of Industrial Energy Consumers) (1998), *Negotiated Agreements: The Industrial Response to Kyoto*, http://www.ifiec-europe.be.

Industriforbundet (1999), *Restriktioner för Kvothandeln Äventyrar Kyoto-protokollet och Skadar den Globala Miljön: Gemensamt Uttalanda av den Nordiska Industrin*, http://www.industriforbundet.se.

Keidanren (1997), *Opinion Relating to COP3 and to Measures on Global Warming*, http://www.keidanren.or.jp.

Kinsman, John D., McGrath, Michael, McMahon, Richard, Rucker, Michael, Shiflet, Ronald and Tempchin, Richard (1996), *A Status Report on Climate Challenge Program's Voluntary Initiatives to Manage U.S. Electric Utility Greenhouse Gases*, Paper Presented at the 89th Annual Meeting and Exhibition of the Air and Waste Management Association, Nashville, Tennessee.

Leidy, Michael and Hoekman, Bernard M. (1994), '"Cleaning Up" While Cleaning Up? Pollution Abatement, Interest Groups, and Contingent Trade Policies', *Public Choice*, **78**, 241–258.

Lynch, Colum (1998), 'Stormy Weather', *e-Amicus*, Winter, http://www.nrdc.org.

Meller, Eberhard and Hildebrand, Manfred (1998), 'Kohlendioxid-Minderung der öffentlichen Elektrizitätswirtschaft in Deutschland – Erklärung der VDEW zum Stand und den Perspektiven', *Elektrizitätswirtschaft* (EW), **23**, 9–14.

Metz, Paul E. (1998), *The Fruits of Kyoto for the Sustainable Energy Business*, European Business Council for a Sustainable Energy Future (e^5), http://www.e5.org.

Næringslivets Hovedorganisasjon (1998), *Dette Mener NHO om Energiutvalgets Innstilling*, NHO Posisjonspapir, NHO, http://www.nho.no.

Næringslivets Hovedorganisasjon (1999), *Energipolitikk 2000: Bidrag fra NHO til et Utvidet Energipolitisk Perspektiv*, http://www.nho.no.

NAM (National Association of Manufacturers) (1999), *Issue Brief: Global Climate Change*, http://www.nam.org.

Nentjes, Andries and Dijkstra, Bouwe R. (1994), 'The Political Economy of Instrument Choice in Environmental Policy', in M. Faure, J. Vervaele and A. Weale, (eds), *Environmental Standards in the European Union in an Interdisciplinary Framework*, Antwerp: Maklu, 197–216.

NZBR (New Zealand Business Roundtable) (1996), *Submission on the Working Group on CO$_2$ Policy's Discussion Document*, http://www.nzbr.org.nz.

NZBR (New Zealand Business Roundtable) (1999), *Submission on the Ministry for the Environment's Climate Change: 'Domestic Policy Options Statement'*, http://www.nzbr.org.nz

Rolfe, C. (1998), *Kyoto Protocol to the United Nations Framework Convention on Climate Change: A Guide to the Protocol and Analysis of its Effectiveness*, Sierra Club Canada.

Stavins, Robert N. (2000), *Experience with Market-Based Environmental Policy Instruments*, KSG Working Paper 00-004, Cambridge, MA: Harvard University.

Svendsen, Gert Tinggaard (1998a), 'A General Model of CO$_2$ Regulation: The Case of Denmark', *Energy Policy*, **26**, 33–44.

Svendsen, Gert Tinggaard (1998b), *Tradable Permit Systems in the United States and CO$_2$ Taxation in Europe*, Cheltenham: Edward Elgar.

Toyoda, Shoichiro, Maucher, Helmut and Stigson, Björn (1997), *Joint Statement of the ICC, Keidanren and WBCSD to the 3rd Conference of the Parties to the United Nations Framework Convention on Climate Change*, http://www.keidanren.or.jp.

UNCTAD (1998), *Greenhouse Gas Emissions Trading: Defining the Principles, Modalities, Rules and Guidelines for Verification, Reporting and Accountability*, Geneva: UNCTAD.

Union of Industrial and Employers' Confederation of Europe (UNICE) (1998), *EU Strategy Responding to Climate Change*, UNICE Input to CoP 4, http://www.unice.be.

UNIPEDE and EURELECTRIC (1999a), *Greenhouse Gas and Electricity Trading Simulation*, Ref. 1999-420-0013.

UNIPEDE and EURELECTRIC (1999b), *Preparing the Global Assessment: Response to the Questions Raised at the Commission's Workshop on the Fifth Environmental Action Programme (5EAP)*, Ref. 1999-410-0019.

VBO-FEB (Verbond van Belgische Ondernemingen/Fédération des Entreprises de Belgique) (1998), 'Protocol van Kyoto: Unaniem Standpunt van VBO, VEV, UWE en VOB', *Infor VBO*, **33**.

VNO-NCW (1999), *Convenant Verplicht Industrie tot Toppositie Efficiënt Energieverbruik*, http://www.vno-ncw.nl.

Weyerhaeuser Jr., George H. (1996), 'Climate Change: A Global Challenge', *On Paper*, October.

WBCSD (World Business Council for Sustainable Development) (1998), *COP4: A Business Perspective*, http://www.wbcsd.ch.

WWF (Worldwide Fund for Nature) (1997a), *Key Technology Policies to Reduce CO₂ Emissions in Japan: An Indicative Survey for 2005 and 2010*, Geneva: Worldwide Fund for Nature.

WWF (Worldwide Fund for Nature) (1997b), *Policies and Measures to Reduce CO₂ Emissions in the EU*, Geneva: Worldwide Fund for Nature

WWF (Worldwide Fund for Nature) (1997c), *Policies and Measures to Reduce CO₂ Emissions in the US*, Geneva: Worldwide Fund for Nature.

WWF (Worldwide Fund for Nature) (1997d), *WWF Position Statement for COP3 Kyoto, Japan 1–10 December 1997*, http://www.panda.org/climate.

WWF (Worldwide Fund for Nature) (1998), *Glimmer of Hope for Closing Loopholes in Kyoto Climate Change Agreement*, http://www.panda.org/climate.

WWF (Worldwide Fund for Nature) (1999), *Summary of WWF's Concerns and Proposals for COP5*, http://www.panda.org/climate.

Zhang, Zhong Xiang and Nentjes, Andries (1999), 'International Tradable Carbon Permits as a Strong Form of Joint Implementation', in Steve Sorell and Jim Skea (eds), *Pollution for Sale: Emissions Trading and Joint Implementation*, Cheltenham: Edward Elgar, 322–342.

7. Conclusion

Christoph Böhringer and Carsten Vogt

Climate change due to anthropogenic greenhouse gases is one of the most challenging and complex environmental issues facing the world over the next century. Despite the uncertainty about the concrete impacts on the ecosystem, there is a broad consensus about the necessity for reducing greenhouse gas (GHG) emissions in order to stabilize the climate system. However, the world community has been struggling for nearly a decade to agree on an effective international climate policy strategy. In this book, we have tried to shed some light from different perspectives of economic research on the problems involved in establishing an international agreement for controlling climate change.

Chapter 2 adopted a game-theoretic approach to discuss incentive problems for sovereign states that prevent them from joining and complying with international environmental agreements (IEAs). Due to the pure public good nature of limiting GHG emissions, countries face two major free-rider incentives that are closely linked to each other.

Firstly, countries may want to free ride by not signing any IEA at all or by joining a coalition that carries a lower abatement burden than other countries. Within the framework of reduced stage game (RSG) models, it was shown that, whenever cooperation would be most beneficial, the effective equilibrium coalition achieves only little in terms of abatement and overall welfare gains.

Secondly, countries may want to free ride by not complying with the obligations of agreements. Building on the concept of renegotiation proofness within repeated games, the way the design of an agreement affects its stability was analyzed. It was shown that the success of any IEA depends crucially on the incentive-compatible specification of credible enforcement rules (sanctions), which include the magnitude and duration time of punishment, the frequency of compliance monitoring, and the discounting of time by governments. Moreover, there is a policy-relevant trade-off between the credibility of threats to deter the violation of an IEA and the enforcement of cooperation.

The role of transfers, issue linkage and monitoring for enhancing the level and stability of international cooperation was discussed in detail. Monetary transfers are an efficient and flexible instrument to balance asymmetries in welfare distribution across countries. Transfers may also be used to increase participation in an agreement by providing non-signatories with an incentive to cooperate. As a prerequisite, however, the transfer system between donors and recipients as well as within the coalition of donors must be stable. Like transfers, issue linkage can be used to balance slack enforcement and lack of enforcement power. Whereas issue linkage aims at balancing enforcement power between issues, transfers aim at balancing enforcement power between countries. It was demonstrated that linking environmental treaties to trade agreements or R&D treaties may lead to more environmental cooperation, since trade and R&D treaties provide club goods which are exclusive to their members. However, if the club members prefer a small club, issue linkage may have a negative effect on the stability of an IEA. From a practical point of view, issue linkage bears some serious restrictions because it can be very difficult to design compensation deals at a multilateral level. In comparison to monetary transfers issue, linkage is less efficient because it only indirectly targets the balancing of asymmetries. The crucial role of an independent monitoring authority was stressed. Monitoring will be incomplete, since the costs of monitoring have to be traded off against the welfare gains from increased enforcement.

Chapter 2 also provided some reasoning why fixed uniform quota regimes have been so popular in past IEAs. Although it is an inefficient policy instrument compared to emission charges or tradable emission permits, it may have advantages with respect to enforcement: little information is required in the negotiation process, and the distribution of welfare as well as the free-rider incentives are relatively symmetric across countries.

Application of game-theoretic considerations to the Kyoto Protocol revealed the lack of any enforcement measure as a major drawback, given the high free-rider incentives for most Annex B countries. Even if sanction measures were established, any non-complying party could withdraw from the treaty within one year, which does not leave much leeway to design renegotiation-proof sanction procedures.

Altogether, Chapter 2 illustrated that game theory is a useful tool for investigating the fundamental incentive problems that are faced by countries when deciding whether to enter an IEA and whether to stick to its obligations.

Several open questions, however, still remain. The analysis of how many and which countries join an IEA mainly focused on the formation of a single coalition. However, there is no clear reason why the analysis should be restricted in this way. Particularly when dealing with non-identical, heterogeneous countries, it may be helpful to allow for the simultaneous formation of multiple coalitions. In this case, the choice of a burden-sharing rule becomes a central issue. Research on the implications of alternative burden-sharing rules on the success of IEAs has just started and demands additional efforts in the future. Issue linkage in the case of non-separable utility functions of countries provides another line of future analysis. A further extension of previous game-theoretical analysis is the incorporation of politico-economic aspects to model governments' behavior in a more realistic way.

Finally, from a policy maker's point of view, it is necessary to link theoretical research closer to the actual economic, political and institutional environments. For instance, applied cost-benefit or cost-effectiveness analysis can deliver valuable information on the payoff functions of countries and the appropriate design of enforcement measures.

Chapter 3 presented a computable general equilibrium (CGE) model for the comprehensive cost-effectiveness analysis of alternative climate policy strategies to achieve the Kyoto abatement targets. The simulation results revealed why the USA has withdrawn while several other Annex B countries, such as Australia, Canada and Japan, have pushed hard for an implicit relaxation of their Kyoto targets via the accounting of sinks and unlimited Annex B emissions trading. Emission constraints as originally mandated under the Kyoto Protocol induce non-negligible adjustment costs to OECD countries, because emission targets are stated with respect to 1990 and translate into much higher effective carbon reduction requirements with respect to business-as-usual emission levels during the Kyoto budget period 2008–2012. At the domestic level, OECD countries would have to impose high carbon taxes in order to meet their obligations, with significant adjustment costs towards less carbon-intensive production and consumption patterns.

Not surprisingly, international trade in emissions significantly reduces the total costs of compliance with Kyoto through the equalization of marginal abatement costs across regions. It was shown that the cost reduction associated with a shift from Annex B trading to global emissions trading is much smaller than that generated by the move from the no-trade scenario to Annex B trading. The reason is that hot air from Eastern Europe and Russia accounts for a larger share of welfare gains achievable through permit trading. Among Annex B countries, only the OECD regions benefit from global emissions trading as compared to restricted Annex B trading. Global trading increases the supply of emission abatement developing countries, which further relieves the emission constraints on OECD countries. Russia and Eastern Europe, in this case, suffer from a decline in the permit price, which implies a substantial loss in their income from permit sales and makes them worse off as compared to Annex B trading. Avoided leakage through global emission trading will more or less offset hot air from Eastern Europe and Russia – global emissions, therefore, will be roughly the same for the no-trading case and the global-trading case.

Abatement in Annex B countries produces significant spillovers to non-abating regions through induced changes in international prices, i.e., changes in the terms of trade. Most important are adjustments in international markets for crude oil and coal. The cut-back in global demand for these fossil fuels implies a significant drop in prices, providing economic gains to fossil fuel importers and losses to fossil fuel exporters. These effects explain most of the welfare impacts on developing countries.

Sub-global action on behalf of Annex B countries has important implications for comparative advantage and the pattern of trade for energy-intensive goods. The unilateral energy cost increase in OECD countries diminishes competitiveness of their energy-intensive production sufficiently to induce larger changes in trade flows of energy-intensive goods, with adverse impacts on carbon leakage.

Chapter 3 also explored the robustness of results with respect to changes in the values of key elasticities as well as other major assumptions, such as the baseline growth path, transaction costs of emissions trading, revenue recycling or the scope of the abatement coalition (Kyoto with and without the USA). The sensitivity analysis helped to provide insights as to why empirical estimates in the literature on the magnitude and distribution of costs from GHG abatement strategies can vary substantially.

The static CGE framework underlying the simulations omitted various factors that are potentially important for the assessment of GHG abatement strategies. Among the factors that rank high with respect to policy-relevant extensions of the basic model are the explicit incorporation of non-CO_2 gases and sinks, the representation of endogenous investment responses in a dynamic setting with rational expectations, as well as the implementation of induced endogenous technological change.

As indicated above, one shortcoming of game-theoretic research is the little attention it has paid so far to the public choice perspective of the decision-making processes within countries. In the tradition of welfare economics, mainstream game-theoretic reasoning is typically based on the idea that governments involved in international environmental negotiations try solely to maximize national net benefits. Governments are thus supposed to act as national welfare maximizers. However, in reality, any government is, at least to some extent, also motivated by the objective of maximizing its political support. In this vein, the standard public choice approach assumes that governments try to maximize their chance of being re-elected. They have, therefore, to obey the preferences of their voters which imposes a restriction on what would be acceptable to a government in international environmental negotiations. In this vein, governments should only enter into agreements that are acceptable to their voters.

Particularly, it should be expected that 'green preferences' of national pivotal voters would lead to more ambitious contributions to global public goods than would be predicted by standard game-theoretic models.

However, Chapter 4 showed that the incorporation of a public-choice perspective in which governments obey the median voters' environmental preferences may lead to an even worse outcome compared to the standard public good game in which governments act as national welfare maximizers. Only when voter preferences are 'sufficiently' green will the non-cooperative Cournot-Nash outcome be improved. It was noted that for the case of 'overly' green preferences, the public environmental good may be supplied beyond the globally optimal level. In the empirical section of Chapter 4, some evidence on the low willingness to pay for combating climate change in industrialized countries was provided. As a consequence, any observable climate treaty should be more symbolic than substantial. This prediction is supported by the climate negotiating history, which shows how the Kyoto Protocol is being pushed more and more towards a symbolic low-cost agreement.

Chapter 5 went a step further in the public choice analysis by assuming that some environmental targets such as the Kyoto GHG reduction objectives have already been agreed upon, but there remains the problem of choosing a suitable method of implementation. In practical policy making, a predominance of command and control instruments can be observed, although economists favor market-based instruments such as emission taxes or tradable permits for reasons of efficiency. What are the reasons for the divergence between policy recommendations and actual implementation? The main objective of Chapter 5 was to understand why certain policy instruments are implemented and others not, thus providing some idea of their political feasibility.

The starting point of the analysis was the different economic and environmental impacts caused by the use of the alternative policy instruments, ranging from relative standards and emission ceilings to emission taxes and tradable emission rights (both auctioned and grandfathered). Linking the different impacts of instruments to the different objectives of interest groups (industry stakeholders, workers, environmental groups, government, environmental bureaucracy) has provided some rationale for group-specific preferences.

Based on partial equilibrium studies, it was argued that even the theoretical evidence on the preference of interest groups is mixed, due to different assumptions about the arguments in the agents' objectives. Likewise, the empirical evidence is mixed. It was asserted that most of the public choice literature on environmental policy instruments does not account for the important role of managers in organization. Their objectives can be rather different from those of stakeholders, revealing a severe principal–agent problem: Managers may have a preference for firm size, i.e. a high level of production, and, therefore, favor relative standards. Stakeholders are profit-maximizing and, thus, prefer grandfathered permits that typically create higher profits (rents). This aspect of interest, the heterogeneity and principal–agent relations *within* the various interest groups, has also been illustrated with respect to environmental groups and environmental bureaucracy, where a distinction is made between command minimalists (preferring market-based instruments) and command expansionists (sticking to command and control policies).

The analysis in Chapter 5 warrants some qualification with respect to the generalization of the results. The theoretical results have been derived within a partial equilibrium framework under competitive market assumptions, and crucially depend on the assumptions about agents' objectives. The restrictive analytical framework as well as the ambiguity in the concrete objectives of larger, heterogeneous groups may explain why it is rather difficult to find unequivocal empirical evidence on theoretical propositions.

Future research demands an empirical analysis of the arguments in the interest groups' objectives as well as an elaboration of a more stringent and concise theoretical framework.

Chapter 6 narrowed the public choice discussion on alternative policy instruments to three different international emission trading schemes that could take place under the Kyoto Protocol: government trading, permit trading, or credit trading. The objective of Chapter 6 was to predict which trading system is most likely to be chosen, given the preferences of several interest groups. In order to perform a consistent analysis, the preferences for national instruments across interest groups were first laid out, since the choice of the international emission trading scheme is dependent on the choice of national instruments. The theoretical analysis concluded that while industry would prefer emission trading between private entities at the international level, this is in sharp contrast with its choice of performance standards at the national level. Consequently, the consistent international scheme from the perspective of industries is credit trading. In addition, the industries in OECD countries opt for complementary government trading because this allows them to access 'abundant' emission rights (in terms of hot air) from Russia, which received much more emission rights under the Kyoto Protocol than its projected emissions under a business-as-usual scenario. Moreover, government trading is supposed to increase rent-seeking options for industry. Caps on trading are rejected as they create higher costs of compliance. For labor unions, the same reasoning holds.

Chapter 6 also argued that environmental organizations, whose concern is to reduce emissions as much as possible, prefer credit trading because this makes trade in hot air impossible. If credit trading were to be combined with government trading, environmental organizations would call for restrictive ceilings on international trading in order to minimize hot air. The environmental bureaucracy supports a combination of credit and government trading. These both need a large amount of bureaucratic labor input; they also give bureaucrats a large amount of control over trading. For the same reasons, the bureaucrats prefer caps on trading. Empirical evidence based on information from the Internet largely supports the theoretical analysis.

Chapter 6 concludes that a combination of credit trading and government trading is politically most feasible because most interest groups prefer such a system. Although this policy is not first-best, it allows for substantial efficiency gains as compared to purely domestic action, because differences in marginal abatement costs across countries can be reduced to a larger extent.

The phenomenon of climate change not only provides a major challenge for natural science but also for economic research. There are several methods within the economic discipline of identifying key problems involved in the design response strategy, that are economically meaningful and politically feasible. Throughout this book, we have presented three established approaches for the economic assessment of global pollution problems: game theory (Chapter 2), cost-effectiveness analysis (Chapter 3) and public choice (Chapters 4, 5, and 6). These approaches focused on different aspects of supranational environmental problems. Game theory provided important insights as to why countries face incentive problems entering international agreements or sticking to obligations. It also outlined important measures on how to overcome free-rider incentives and establish or enforce cooperation.

Public choice provided an important framework for a better understanding of the process of environmental policy making, although it seems difficult to derive unambiguous theoretical results that are backed by empirical evidence.

Applied cost-effectiveness analysis delivered estimates on the magnitude and distribution of emission abatement strategies that give policy-relevant insights into the potential efficiency and equity trade-offs for alternative policy options. However, strategic interactions of agents are typically omitted, which might affect quantitative results and qualitative conclusions.

It is our belief that future economic research on the field of climate should aim at combining the three approaches presented in this book. By doing so, it will be possible to keep the specific strengths of the various approaches while improving in their areas of specific weaknesses. Chapter 4 illustrated a simple combination of standard game theory with public choice to represent government behavior with respect to global pollution problems in a more realistic way. Trade-offs between opposing objectives (e.g. costs of monitoring *vis-à-vis* benefits from increased compliance) or asymmetries in payoff functions can be evaluated using quantitative estimates from cost-effectiveness analysis. Likewise, the impacts of alternative policy instruments on various interest groups could be quantified by means of cost-effectiveness analysis to obtain insights into their political acceptance. In turn, aspects of strategic behavior that are at the core of game theory or public choice may be embedded in cost-effectiveness analysis. This integration should accommodate the assessment of economic incentives for countries to join or stay with international environmental agreements. With respect to policy relevance, such extensions should aim at the quantitative analysis of concrete proposals. Applied research, then, would be able to assess the prospects of success for alternative climate change control strategies.

Whether one should pursue a direct integration of the various approaches (hard linkage) or undertake a rather loose connection (soft linkage) will depend on the concrete policy issue under investigation as well as on the existing methodological tools. While the former offers advantages with respect to overall consistency, the latter might be the more pragmatic approach. In both cases, bringing together the three different research lines promises to be a powerful tool for the comprehensive economic analysis of global pollution problems.

Index